On Spiritual Unity

A SLAVOPHILE READER

ESALEN-LINDISFARNE LIBRARY
OF RUSSIAN PHILOSOPHY

On Spiritual Unity

A SLAVOPHILE READER

Aleksei Khomiakov
Ivan Kireevsky

---

with essays by Yury Samarin,
Nikolai Berdiaev, and Pavel Florensky

TRANSLATED AND EDITED BY

Boris Jakim and Robert Bird

 LINDISFARNE BOOKS

The texts for this book were translated from Russian
by Boris Jakim and Robert Bird.

© Copyright Lindisfarne Books, 1998

Published by Lindisfarne Books
3390 Route 9, Hudson, NY 12534

Library of Congress Cataloging-in-Publication Data

Khomiakov, A.S. (Aleksei Stepanovich), 1804–1860.
    On spiritual unity : A Slavophile reader / Aleksei Khomiakov,
    Ivan Kireevsky, with essays by Nikolai Berdiaev, Pavel Florensky, and
    Yury Samarin ; translated and edited by Boris Jakim and Robert Bird.
        p. cm. — (Esalen-Lindisfarne library of Russian philosophy)
    Includes bibliographical references and index.
    ISBN 0-940262-91-6 (pbk.)
    1. Philosophy, Russian—Religious aspects. 2. Religion—Philosophy.
    3. Nationalism—Russia. 4. Slavophilism. I. Kireevskii, Ivan Vasil 'evich,
    1806–1856. II. Jakim, Boris. III. Bird, Robert. IV. Title. V. Series: Library of
    Russian philosophy.
    B4231.K45 1998
    197--dc21   98-38587
                                                                                    CIP

10 9 8 7 6 5 4 3 2 1

Printed in the United States of America

CONTENTS

PART TWO: PHILOSOPHY
Ivan Kireevsky

PART THREE: TWENTIETH-CENTURY
RESPONSES TO KHOMIAKOV
Pavel Florensky & Nikolai Berdiaev

GENERAL INTRODUCTION

The term *Slavophilism*, originally one of several somewhat deroga-
tory names for a casual association of Russian thinkers, refers to an
original core group of six young landowners: Konstantin Aksakov,
Aleksei Khomiakov, Ivan Kireevsky, his brother Peter Kireevsky,
Aleksander Koshelev, and Yury Samarin. Koshelev, Khomiakov, and
the Kireevsky brothers met in the early 1820s, but a coherent group of
Slavophiles formed only in the "marvelous decade" of the forties,
which saw the rise of many great Russian thinkers and movements.
Even then, however, the Slavophiles were as likely to disagree as
agree with each other; in particular, each major article by Kireevsky
was followed by a critical retort by the ever-polemical Khomiakov. In
any case, as the Slavophiles themselves stressed repeatedly, if they
were united in a single movement, it was not by any partiality for the
Slavic race, but rather by a shared commitment to the religious and
universal calling of Russia; they appear to have preferred calling their
movement the "Orthodox-Russian orientation." The superficial similarity of their views with the ideological program of the government,
and their more profound kinship with Pan-Slav nationalists such as
the poet Fedor Tiutchev, always cast a fierce pallor over the movement; by the 1860s, after the deaths of Aksakov, Khomiakov, and the
Kireevsky brothers, the name *Slavophile* became loosely applied to an
even more varied group of religious nationalists and statist conserva-
tives, further confusing the identity of Slavophilism. Yet the name
Slavophile has stuck most firmly to Khomiakov, Ivan Kireevsky, and
their closest allies, as the proper name of the first Russian religious-
philosophical movement.

As we shall see, *Slavophilism* is just one of several terms that have
somewhat mysteriously, yet stubbornly and irrevocably, attached
themselves to the "Orthodox-Russian orientation in thought." Indeed,
Khomiakov's and Kireevsky's major contributions to Russian and
world thought are inextricably linked to two other terms that neither

of them ever used: *sobornost* and integral knowledge (*tsel'noe znanie*).[1] In a curious way, even as its representatives forsook literature for philosophy, theology, and politics, Slavophilism remained a process of word creation, culminating in these two terms of universal significance. Like two immortal poems, they express entire worlds in their compact energy and unfathomable depth, demanding an almost equally intuitive comprehension, and rewarding one generously for such efforts. All the particulars of Slavophile thought must be unfolded from this living center, like the growth of life from a life-bearing seed. On the other hand, keeping in mind their absence in the Slavophiles' own works, one must not mummify or fetishize them as "key words" or slogans, severing them from their particular context. These terms retain a certain fragility characteristic of attempts to express the inexpressible. Russian thought remains profoundly philological, both in the sense that it reasons through living words (instead of using words to avoid or cloud reasoning), and requires a full appreciation of the sanctity of words, as expressions of the absolute.

The Slavophiles' thought is all about sobornost and integral knowledge; these concepts stand, both at the beginning and at the end of their writings, at the source and at the delta of their intellectual journey. For the reader, they stand as both the invitation to read and the expected reward. In order for these concepts to come to life, however, the reader must first retrace the Slavophiles' journey, with a readiness to experience together with them both the vagaries of the terrain and the joy of unexpected vistas they reveal on religion and culture.

* * *

By 1830, after a century and a half of intense westernization, Russian culture had begun to develop a distinctive new identity. For the moment, the emerging Russian identity was manifest largely in the realm of poetry. In the words of a later Slavophile, Ivan Aksakov, Russian poetry:

---

1. On Khomiakov's non-usage of *sobornost* see Hildegard Schaeder, "'Sobornost'—in der Schriften von A. Chomjakov," *Kyrios* Bd. VII Heft 3/4 (1967). Kireevsky uses the phrases "living and integral cognition" (*zhivoe i tsel'noe poznavanie*) and "integral thinking" (*tsel'noe myshlenie*).

was called to accomplish in Russian society … a spiritual upsurge that was beyond the powers of our scholastic, dependent learning, and to accelerate the process of our national self-consciousness. It … received the historical task of manifesting, in the given poetic form, all the variety, all the power and beauty of the Russian language, to cultivate in it flexibility and transparency, capable of expressing the subtlest shades of thought and feeling.[2]

At the time, Russians turned especially to German thinkers for help in conceptualizing the thoughts and feelings that had begun to find expression in their poetry; the thinkers who were destined to become known to the world as the Slavophiles were no exceptions to this general trend. Yet, as one reads through the Slavophiles' discussions of Hegel, Schelling, and other Western thinkers, it becomes clear that they have another source of inspiration and another final destination, allowing them to articulate an original metaphysical vision quite apart from any definable influences. The distinctive basis of Slavophile thought, what one historian has called their "third heart," is their sensitivity to intuitive, nonrational knowledge, such as is revealed in poetry and religion.[3]

Both of the major Slavophile thinkers, Aleksei Khomiakov and Ivan Kireevsky, began their intellectual careers in the realm of the artistic word. Khomiakov was for many years best known as a poet of the Pushkin school, the author of a long dramatic poem *The False Dmitrii*. Kireevsky, for his part, made his debut in 1827 with a story, "Tsaritsyn Night," and he first attracted widespread attention soon after as an original literary critic. Romanticism and German Idealism were in the air; however, they attracted these young thinkers mainly by the theoretical help they offered with the very real and urgent task of assessing the significance of a homegrown literary culture.

Kireevsky's first articles already display an original application of principles culled from the German Idealists. In an article of 1830, the young critic traced the progression of Russian poetry through periods

---

2. Ivan Aksakov, "Fedor Ivanovich Tiutchev," *Russkii arkhiv* 1874, no. 10, pp. 97–8.
3. See Peter K. Christoff, *An Introduction to Nineteenth-Century Russian Slavophilism. A Study in Ideas. Volume II: I. V. Kireevskij* (The Hague, Paris: Mouton, 1972) 35.

of French and German influence, marked respectively by technical refinement and idealistic reverie; now, he averred, poetry was accomplishing a turn toward the reality of Russian life, an achievement personified by a poet who was just beginning to be recognized as the greatest Russia had known, Alexander Pushkin. Kireevsky's three-step process is, of course, reminiscent of similar historical schemes in Schelling and Hegel, with Russian realism representing the superior synthesis of the previous, one-sided principles. Still, like Pushkin's poetry in Kireevsky's interpretation, this scheme achieves its power not through its theoretical fullness, but rather through its own engagement with the positive content of Russian life; Western philosophical schemes were not simply to be attached to a new context, but reshaped by it. The striking distinctiveness of the Russian language and Russian life, and not some formal-logical prowess, is what ultimately would lend originality to Kireevsky's thoughts.[4]

As the rise of an original literary school evoked a more general awakening of the Russian mind, Kireevsky noted, "We need philosophy: the entire development of our mindset requires it. By it alone does our poetry live and breathe, it alone can grant soul and wholeness to our fledgling learning, and our very life, perhaps, will borrow the elegance of harmony from it. But where shall it come from? Where shall we seek it?"[5] Although Kireevsky initially saw the West as the only source of culture and learning, he soon began to apply to philosophy the lesson he had drawn from poetry. If Russia is capable of uttering a new word in poetry, may it not be able to do so in other realms of human endeavor, or must it resign itself merely to retreading paths taken by the West? The question "Whither Russia?" was obviously contingent on its corollary, "Whence Russia?": does Russia owe its fledgling culture wholly to European influence, or has it arisen in interaction with, or even opposition to, the latter? The Slavophile movement, which began to coalesce precisely at the beginning of the 1830s, was the primary effort to answer these questions in a way that would affirm Russia's unique status while recognizing her intricate relationship to Europe.

---

4. On Kireevsky's literary criticism see the fascinating article by Yury Mann: "Ivan Kireevskii," *Voprosy literatury* 11/1965, 130–154.

5. I. V.Kireevskii, *Polnoe Sobranie Sochinenii* (Moscow: Put', 1911) I 27.

While Slavophile philosophical thought largely took German Idealism as its point of departure, the demand for realism and historicism provoked a search for the roots of Russian distinctiveness. One negative symptom of this search was the publication in 1836 of Peter Chaadaev's "First Philosophical Letter," in which the author wholly denied that Russia had any history at all. Khomiakov countered this claim by pointing precisely to the verbal achievements of Russian culture:

> Does any nation in Europe, apart from the Scots, have legends and songs such as ours? Who has such an abundant, native soul? Whence hover those rich voices of the round-dances, incomprehensibly full of feeling?—Read Kirill Danilov's collection of ancient Russian poems and legends. What Christian nation can boast a Nestor [an early Russian chronicler]? Which of the nations has such wise proverbs? And aren't proverbs the fruit of a magnificent, past, national life?[6]

Khomiakov hints that the Russian skill with words stems from the inheritance it received from Greece: belief in the Word.[7] For the Slavophiles in general, what began as a historical quest for distinctive Russian culture resulted in a rediscovery and recognition of Eastern Orthodoxy. The question of Russia and Europe became a transcription of the question of Orthodoxy and Western Christianity, and vice versa. It is often disputed whether Russia or Orthodoxy enjoyed primacy in the thought of each Slavophile thinker, whether the Russian mind is the product or agent of Orthodox culture. Yet, however damaging the "Slavophile controversy"—the allegation of nationalism—has been to them, the ease with which the Slavophiles recognized the religious, and therefore universal, roots of Russian culture testifies to the integrity of their attempt to understand the Russian present. This authenticity or wholeness originates in the very genesis of the movement under the wing of poetry.

---

6. A. S. Khomiakov, "Pis'mo K g-zhe N.," ed. Richard Tempest, *Simvol* 16 (1986) 132. Khomiakov owed much of his knowledge of Old Russian folk songs to the studies of Petr Kireevsky, Ivan's brother, Russia's first great folklorist and "the inspirer of Moscow Slavophilism"; Peter K. Christoff, *Kireevskij*, 71.
7. Ibid., 130.

While the progression from a naive idealism to Orthodoxy comprises the major content of Slavophile thought, its style is best characterized by the intellectual freedom it inherited from the intellectual and spiritual ferment of the 1820s. The heyday of the Slavophile movement, from the late 1830s to the late 1850s, was not a fortuitous time for the development of a new worldview. The repressive regime of Nicholas I (1825–1856) had consolidated its ideological program in the tripartite slogan: "Orthodoxy, Autocracy, and Nationality," the greatest effect of which was to make those three concepts quite odious to most thinking people. Slavophilism reached an affirmation of these three concepts by way of free analysis and speculation, and was therefore ideologically suspect both to other intellectuals and to the state, which mistrusted any free thought. Each Slavophile experienced a certain degree of intellectual isolation from the main currents of Russian thought in those years. On the other hand, government prohibitions and repressive censorship made it well-nigh impossible for them to conduct their own forum and publish regularly. That we can nonetheless refer to a considerable body of original work is a testimony to their intellectual and moral courage; that many questions concerning their views and lives remain unanswered is a lamentable consequence of a repressive time.

* * *

ALEKSEI STEPANOVICH KHOMIAKOV was born 1 May 1804, into a wealthy family of the Russian landed nobility. Like many young Russians of the day who reached maturity at the peak of Russia's European power and at the beginning of its cultural revival, Khomiakov was a precocious youth. He received a degree in mathematics from Moscow University, studied painting, and learned English and French well enough that later in life he composed elegant theological works in those languages. In agriculture he may have been a dilettante, but he was certainly an enlightened and innovative one; in 1851 he traveled to London in order to receive a patent for a steam engine he invented for agricultural use. In the late 1850s, together with some of his fellow Slavophiles, Khomiakov played a significant role in formulating the impending emancipation of the serfs, which was accomplished in 1861. However, he did not live to see this momentous event; an amateur homeopathic physician, he contracted cholera while treating peasants on his estate. The disease made quick progression, and he passed away on 23 September 1860.

In 1823 Khomiakov became a founding member of the Society of Wisdom-Lovers, where he met many of the most promising minds of his age in an atmosphere permeated by pantheistic idealism and poetic romanticism. Soon he began to compose poetry, and it was in this field that he first made his name. One of the themes of his early poems is the special calling of the poet:

> He raised his tranquil gaze to heaven,
> A hymn to God rose in his soul;
> He gave the earth a subtle voice,
> And gave a tongue to dead creation.
>
> ("The Poet," 1827)

In 1828–29, Khomiakov fought with the Russian cavalry against the Turks in Bulgaria, adding military honors to his growing list of accolades. By the early thirties, Khomiakov was a major cultural figure at the center of Europeanized Russian life, attending numerous salons and intellectual circles.

In contrast, however, to most of his contemporaries and all of the other future Slavophiles, from his earliest youth Khomiakov was distinguished by a profound Christian faith and constant piety. Discussions with close friends such as Chaadaev and Vladimir Odoevsky made Khomiakov known as an advocate of traditional Orthodoxy and old Russian culture; early on, Khomiakov took to wearing a beard, quite a provocative gesture in the regimented Russia of Nicholas I. In 1846 Khomiakov recalled that he had been "either supposed a sycophant or considered as a disguised Romanist [i.e., Roman Catholic]; for nobody supposed the possibility of civilization and Orthodoxy being united."[8] But the natural and confident nature of Khomiakov's beliefs allowed him to combine his national pride with a deep respect and even love for Western civilization. Consistently throughout his writings, Khomiakov expressed the need for Russia to turn to the West in order to develop the means of achieving its own

---

8. See page 153 below.

spiritual potential; at the same time, he did not foresee a bright future
for Western civilization without spiritual guidance from the East. As
he wrote in perhaps his most famous poem, "A Dream" (1935):

> Oh, grief afflicts me! There descends thick gloom
> In the distant West, the land of holy wonders:
> The former lights are fading, burning out,
> And the brightest stars are tumbling from the heavens …
> Oh! Since creation earth has never seen
> Above itself such fiery lights of heaven!
> But grief! Their age has passed, a deathly veil descends
> And covers up the West. There shall be gloom so deep …
> So hear the voice of fate, arise in a new glow,
>   Awake, O sleep-bound East!

It can, in fact, be argued that it was precisely the universal and enlightened character of Khomiakov's national and religious patriotism
that first compelled him to formulate his theological views. Russia's
distinctive role in the world is tied to its being an integral part of universal Christianity; the instinctive feeling that Russian culture has
something to say to the West led him to seek this "something" in the
religion they shared, but which now divided them. Culturally, Khomiakov found in traditional Russian culture a sense of community (ob-
shchinnost'), buttressed not by a sense of common profit or security,
but by love. Seeking the religious roots of this feeling, he came upon
the Orthodox understanding of the Church as the free unity of Christians in the Holy Spirit.

The Church for Khomiakov shares many characteristics with his
ideal of Russia. Both are in a sense utopias, since their radically universal nature tends to dissolve their spatial borders; but the Church,
and Russia to a certain extent, represented for him examples of an
accomplished utopia, free and open eucharistic communities, permeated by the mutual trust that comes from a shared faith. Christ and
the Holy Spirit illuminate the believing community with love, reason, and freedom, which are otherwise only partially attainable for
humanity. Individual believers achieve positive freedom and true
knowledge through faith, which establishes a direct connection to the
Truth. The vertical relationship between each individual and God,

and the horizontal connection between all believing individuals of all nations and ages, are thus mutually dependent, each being unattainable outside of the other. Scripture, God's word to humanity, is inseparable from Tradition, the human history of God's word. The Church is thus a whole; indeed she is "unity par excellence." Dogmatically Khomiakov supports this interpretation with the Creed, which describes the Church as "catholic"—"in accordance with everything" or "in accordance with the unity of all."[9] The Slavic translation of *catholic*, "*sobornyi*," one of the earliest examples of Slavic word-creation, supports his view; it comes from the word *sobor*, which can mean gathering, council, or cathedral, implying that the Church is based in the gathering of all her members. It was Khomiakov's insistent citation of this definition of the Church that identified his teaching with the abstract noun sobornost, the quality of being in accordance with the unity of all, of the unity of humanity in God. Khomiakov himself never discusses this abstract concept except as a descriptive modifier of the living and historical Church.

Like all of Khomiakov's ideas, his interpretation of the word "catholic" bears a sharply polemical edge. It implies radical disagreement with the Roman Church's understanding of "catholic" as merely "universal," embracing all nations under a unified head. For Khomiakov, this is an external or geographical unity that is foreign to the Church, which abides in the essential unity of her members, based on a unanimity of soul and mind, under the sole authority of God. By reinterpreting the free unity of Christians as a formal union, the Western Church removed itself from the living unity of the Church. Western doctrinal innovations merely confirmed the arbitrary ambition of the Pope to speak for the entire Church. The true Church remains the Eastern Orthodox Church, not due to any proud claims to exclusivity, but precisely because she has remained *sobornyi*. The *sobornyi* character of the Eastern Church is what has in turn assured its faithful preservation of dogma and doctrine without parochial additions or adaptations.

Khomiakov's concept of the Church involves a complex dialectic between her transcendent and immanent aspects. Transcendently, the Church is one, untouched by human conflict and discord; the historical

9. A. S. Khomiakov, *Polnoe sobranie sochinenii*, 4th ed. (Moscow, 1900) II 312.

Church, however, does not fully manifest this transcendent unity, and to humanity she can often seem divided. Still, Khomiakov affirms that the community of believers, as long as it remains truly *sobornyi*, is essentially identical to the transcendent Church.

Stressing the immanent aspect of the Church can lend Khomiakov's expressions the appearance of national or cultural exclusivity. This is true of Khomiakov's voluminous *Notes on World History*, which anticipated the later historiosophical studies of Nikolai Danilevsky, Oswald Spengler, and Arnold Toynbee by dividing the world into two types of civilization, Kushite and Iranian; true Christianity is presented as contingent on the virtues of Russian national identity, as the highest expression of the Iranian principle. Traces of this can be found in Khomiakov's polemical works, where his proud defense of Orthodoxy can alternate with hymns to the pious and meek Russian character. Vasily Rozanov gave a facetious summary of Khomiakov's theological thought on the hundredth anniversary of his birth in 1904: "How did they dare in the West to think, suffer, and reason, while we in the East snoozed and, in particular, dreamed golden dreams about the 'glory of my Kiev.' This is the astonishingly parochial, carping, egotistical and haughty question through the prism of which all of Khomiakov's theological criticism passes."[10]

In actuality, the Orthodox Church was and is less than a model of universal concord, even on important matters of faith. Disagreements between her Greek and Russian branches led Khomiakov's English correspondent, William Palmer, to conclude that the relationship between the various communities of the Eastern Church and the transcendent Church of unity was much more distant than Khomiakov claimed. While these criticisms may cast some doubt on the descriptive value of Khomiakov's portrayal of Orthodoxy, his ecclesiological writings played an important role in restoring the Church to the believing community, as its heritage and its responsibility, its freedom and its obligation.

Khomiakov gradually extended his considerations of theological questions into the realm of philosophy; his three major philosophical essays can be seen as descriptions of human consciousness and

10. V. V. Rozanov, "Pamiati A. S. Khomiakova (1 maia 1804–1 maia 1904 g.)," *Okolo tserkovnykh sten* (Moscow: Respublikag, 1995) 422.

cognition within the Church. Accepting Kireevsky's major distinctions, Khomiakov proceeds to elaborate on the role of the will in overcoming the subject/object dichotomy inherited from German Idealism. Among the formal capacities of human cognition, the will appears as the bearer of life, directing the reason toward this or that goal. The cognitive significance of the will means that all knowledge is faith, since reason must assume the existence of an as-yet-unknown object before it can actually know it. On the other hand, the act of knowledge is not merely a formal operation of a passive rational capacity, but the communication of will to the object. Khomiakov ends up with a vision of people and things joined by a kind of energy field, exchanging parcels of being through the will and gaining knowledge through faith. It is difficult to say how consistent this is with Kireevsky's understanding of cognition, but it does go a long way toward explaining how integral knowledge is possible: energies communicate not only the palpable representation of the object, but a full image of its being.

The extension of one's sphere of knowledge also augments one's being, bringing one into spiritual community with the objects of knowledge. Some similarity has been noted between Khomiakov's philosophy and Schopenhauer's metaphysics of the will, in which individual representations are called to enter a state of sympathy or mutual compassion. However, relations among people in the Church are not ruled by pity, but by an active love, which gives of itself in order to receive. Khomiakov's philosophical ideas are bound to undergo a reevaluation because of their similarity to the energetism of Orthodox Hesychasts, the ancient, mystical tradition that found theoretical expression in the theology of St. Gregory Palamas (1296–1359). Whereas sobornost has long been accepted as an essential foundation of Orthodox ecclesiology, the philosophical complement of synergy, or syzygy, has only recently begun to receive the attention it deserves. Khomiakov's powerful intuition remains an inexhaustible stimulus and inspiration within Orthodoxy. In time, it may help to forge a unified theological and philosophical vision that will justify his belief in Russia's special spiritual mission.

* * *

IVAN KIREEVSKY was born on 3 April 1806, into a cultivated, but ancient and traditional family of landowners. His father, Vasily, died when Ivan was six, but his mother Avdotya Petrovna (née Elagina) would remain a powerful presence throughout his life. She was related to the prominent poet Vasily Zhukovsky, who aided in Ivan's education and would later become his literary patron. In 1824, Ivan passed his university exams and began working in Moscow at the Archives of the Ministry of Foreign Affairs.

The Archives brought Ivan into the circle of philosophically minded young men that formed the Society of Wisdom-Lovers. The circle was broken up due to the transfer of some members to Petersburg, and also due to the inauspicious political climate after the attempted coup in December 1825 by another unofficial group, subsequently known as the Decembrists. Ivan exhibited his independent mind by refusing to follow a civil service career and remaining in the more traditional Moscow. Soon he made up his mind to become a writer, answering the protestations of his friend Aleksander Koshelev by asking, "Is not contributing to the culture [*prosveshchenie*] of the nation the greatest benefit that one can bring it?"[11] Unfortunately, Kireevsky's noble intention was mitigated by his natural inclination to indecision and inaction, and over the next thirty years, until his death from cholera on 23 June 23 1856, he would produce only a dozen or so full-length articles. Kireevsky's life was so poor in outer events, and his personality so perfectly embodied the "superfluous man" of nineteenth-century Russia, that the central mystery of his life and works is how he managed to become one of Russia's most significant cultural figures and the father of an entire tradition in religious philosophy.

Kireevsky's first works displayed an original view of Western philosophy and Russian culture; as shown above, he sought to elucidate Russia's particular role in the general progression of universal civilization. In 1834, under the influence of his bride Natalya Arbeneva, Kireevsky underwent some kind of conversion. First of all, his wife brought him into contact with a monastic elder [*starets*], Father Philaret. Their relationship was a precursor to Kireevsky's celebrated spiritual friendship and literary collaboration in the late 1840s

---

11. Kireevskii, *Polnoe sobranie sochinenii*: I 10.

and 1850s with Makary, the most famous starets of Optina pustyn', a center of Russian spirituality. Second, Kireevsky's wife exerted a strong intellectual influence upon her husband by acquainting him with the works of the great Fathers of the Church. It is told that when, at Kireevsky's request, his wife read works by Victor Cousin and F. W. I. Schelling, she claimed that they added nothing to what she had already learned from the Fathers of the Church. Gradually, Kireevsky began to read the Fathers, especially Isaac the Syrian and Maximus the Confessor.

By the 1840s, Kireevsky had set it his goal to restore the Eastern Fathers to the center of Russian culture, both by assisting in the publication of their texts at Optina pustyn', and by undertaking a reinterpretation of their thought for modern civilization. Due to the sparsity of his writings and even sparser biographical information, Kireevsky's personal religious life is little understood. He remained much closer personally to Westernizing intellectuals (such as Chaadaev) than Khomiakov, and his Orthodoxy was sometimes regarded the product more of conscious commitment than inner belief. Some have seen Kireevsky as the initiator of a tradition of "stylized Orthodoxy," continued by Konstantin Leontiev and Pavel Florensky, whose advocacy of disciplined monastic culture allegedly concealed an almost decadent, and profoundly modern, aestheticism. Although his indefatigably individualistic streak may have seemed incompatible with sincere Orthodoxy, the respect Kireevsky won from one of Russia's greatest monastics, and surviving records of his personal humility and piety, indicate that, at least by the final decade of his life, Kireevsky was unquestionably speaking from within the Church. The ultimate goal of his philosophy was to find expression for this experience, in the hope that Russia might develop "a faithful philosophical language, in accordance with the spiritual language of Slavic and Greek spiritual writers."[12]

In the first issue of his journal *The European* [*Evropeets*], in 1832, Kireevsky had noted a new trend in Western European culture that appeared to him capable of resolving Europe's own philosophical crisis and, at the same time, integrating Russia into the world cultural

---

12. Sergii Chetverikov, *Optina pustyn': istoricheskii ocherk i lichnye vospominaniia* (Paris: YMCA-Press, 1926) p. 116.

process.[13] There, Kireevsky identified Schelling's *Philosophy of Revelation* as the culmination of Western philosophy, integrating the formal refinements of Kantian and post-Kantian thought with objective reality, and turning the negative, potential capacities of the mind into positive means of knowledge and morality. For Kireevsky, Schelling inaugurated a process that would introduce a natural equilibrium between society, culture, and religion. Russia, lacking the heritage of classical culture, had always remained outside of European culture, and this had prevented its particular virtues from translating into universal achievements; "the culture of each nation is measured ... only by its participation in the culture of all humanity, by the place it occupies in the general process of human development."[14] The new quality of European culture provided a providential opportunity for Russia to join itself to the universal process and achieve an independent culture. On the face of it, Kireevsky here is not so far from the impassioned critique of Russian culture by his lifelong friend Chaadaev.

By the late 1830s, after his conversion, Kireevsky had reinterpreted this picture in an attempt to determine the positive significance of Russia's cultural purity and isolation. He discovered that the element of unity so dear to the German Romantics had been fully realized in traditional Russian institutions, which had developed under the exclusive influence of Christian doctrine without pagan remnants. At first, Kireevsky found it necessary to deny any connection at all between the Russian culture of unity and Western civilization. In his 1838 essay "In Answer to A. S. Khomiakov," Kireevsky wrote that Russia's lack of a pagan heritage had allowed it to accept Christianity in a pure form and build its social relations on Christian truth without compromise. Within a few years, Kireevsky appears to introduce a distinction between European culture (*prosveshchenie*) and Western civilization (*obrazovannost'*); he now argues that Russia had actually received the former in its pure form as an inherent part of Byzantine Christianity, but that it was free from the rationalistic development that European culture had undergone in the West.

---

13. Nicholas I understood Kireevsky to be advocating revolution, and had the journal banned; this was the first in a series of prohibitions that removed the external motivation for Kireevsky to write.

14. Kireevskii, *Polnoe sobranie sochinenii* I 104.

In 1845, Kireevsky wrote that, instead of universities, spreading doubt and rationalistic scholasticism, Russia had developed a living system of monasteries that spread enlightenment and culture in its original, spiritual wholeness. Thus, Russia had best preserved Christian culture, not having sullied it by any anti-Christian survivals, and it was now poised to develop a new, preeminently Christian civilization. Kireevsky thus progressed from a European-centered universalism to one based on Orthodox Christianity, but the ideal of a unified civilization remained largely intact. In a way, this confirms the story of Kireevsky's conversion: his conversion to Russian Orthodoxy was simply a recognition that it was more likely than Schelling's Idealism to achieve his original ideal of unity in culture and civilization.

Kireevsky attempted to give a philosophical account of the unity he found manifest in Russian-Christian culture. Due to the inauspicious external circumstances, he never managed to complete this account, but what he did write is perhaps best characterized as a philosophy of integral being or integral spirit, similar in several crucial respects to Vladimir Solovyov's subsequent metaphysics of all-unity. This philosophy of integral being or spirit can also be referred to as the doctrine of integral knowledge, a term that Kireevsky probably never used, but which became a cornerstone of later Russian philosophy (cf. Solovyov's *Principles of Integral Knowledge* [1877]). Kireevsky bases himself on the intuition—never fully explained, to be sure—that humanity must strive to develop all of its inherent capacities in a harmonious and balanced way, in order that a proper correlation and hierarchical subordination of powers might be attained. Harmonious being results from "the concentration, gathering, and wholeness of inner powers."[15] The point of concentration is the heart, where one becomes conscious of God and achieves a light that illumines all the lower spheres. Reason uses this light to see and know the world, while the rationalistic understanding orders the world and makes sense of it. Severed from the heart, Western philosophy has restricted itself to these lower, subordinate powers, resulting in the ascendancy of blind understanding and distorted reason.

---

15. See page 214 below.

This anthropology means that true knowledge can originate only in integral being—that is, where reason is subordinated not to the logical understanding, but to the heart: "Only essentiality can touch the essential."[16] Here we must mention a key distinction introduced by Kireevsky: that is, the distinction between *razum* and *rassudok*. *Razum* (cf. the German *Vernunft*) is integral reason, uniting all the faculties of heart and mind. It is rendered here as "reason," and the adjective formed from it, *razumnyi*, is rendered as "reasonable" or "rational." By contrast, *rassudok* (cf. the German *Verstand*) is the analytic, rationalistic understanding—the "fallen" reason. *Rassudok* is rendered here as "rationalistic understanding," and its adjectival form (*rassudochnyi*) is rendered as "rationalistic." It is the logical, conceptualizing faculty of the mind abstracted from the other faculties of the human soul. Since integral being is attainable only in an organic, integral society, knowledge becomes inherently social, or interpersonal. In his "Fragments," Kireevsky extends this view to include Khomiakov's understanding of the Church, and knowledge becomes inherently ecclesiastical. Kireevsky's epistemology therefore dissolves in a general vision of unity on all levels: in the Church, in society, and in each individual. History has shown that Kireevsky's epistemological ideal can be detached from particular levels of unity, from Russia, from the peasant commune, but it cannot be severed from his basic intuition that unity is the basis of all.

How is it that the heart is able to gather and order the various human capacities, introducing unity into the world? Kireevsky affirms the primacy of moral knowledge, which is in turn the preeminent domain of religion. Unity is above all a moral imperative, causing humanity to struggle against the apparent dividedness and divisiveness of the world.

Each moral victory hidden in a single Christian soul is already a spiritual victory for the entire Christian world.... For as in the physical world the celestial bodies gravitate to each other without any material mediation, so in the spiritual world each spiritual personality, even without visible action, by the mere fact that it abides on a moral height, lifts and attracts to itself all that is

---

16. See page 284 below.

similar in human hearts. But in the physical world each being lives and is supported only by the destruction of others; in the spiritual world the creation of each personality creates all, and each breathes the life of all.[17]

Kireevsky's privileging of feeling and will in the individual psyche can be traced to the moral character of these faculties; they are able to reinvigorate reason with the immediacy of the spiritual sphere. At the same time, this nonrationalistic view of the mind has certain consequences for philosophy itself. "As long as a thought is clear to one's reason," Kireevsky wrote to Khomiakov in 1840, "or is able to be expressed, it cannot affect the soul and will. It reaches maturity only when it develops to an inexpressible state."[18] Accordingly, "the ultimate meaning of any philosophy lies not in individual logical or metaphysical truths, but in the relationship in which it places humanity with respect to the ultimate truth that is sought—in the inner imperative that dominates the mind imbued with the philosophy."[19] One can understand Kireevsky's central intuition of spiritual unity in a similar vein, rising from the status of moral imperative to the pillar and ground of the truth, and seeking expression in a new philosophical language.

Still, it is legitimate to inquire whether Kireevsky was ultimately concerned with the realization of unity or a theoretical justification of Russia. What he ultimately fails to prove, in the eyes of many critics, is that the wholeness of Russian society was formed by Christianity, and not vice versa. His critique of the Roman Church, for example, issues wholly from his understanding of the Western mentality and has little to do with theology; St. Augustine is wrong not because of his opinions, but because of his rationalistic method of argumentation, incompatible with spiritual truth. Kireevsky's apparent privileging of ethnic style over spiritual substance is exacerbated by the utterly idealized picture he paints of Russian history and social relations; this

---

17. See p. 288 below; on the moral sphere in Kireevsky see especially V. V. Zenkovsky, *History of Russian Philosophy*, trans. George L. Kline (New York: Columbia University Press, 1953) I, 214–219.
18. Kireevskii, *Polnoe sobranie sochinenii*, I 67.
19. See page 246 below.

has led some scholars to classify Kireevsky primarily as an ideologist, privileging the national idea over factual evidence.[20] Kireevsky's ideological fervor reached its peak during the Crimean War, which pitted Orthodox Slavs against a coalition of Western Christian and Islamic nations. In his diary for 1854 we read: "the spectacle of great events has been prepared for the entire world: Europe's war with Russia, which, if it takes place and continues, will most probably lead to conflict and the rival development of the most fundamental principles of Western-Roman and Eastern-Orthodox civilizations."[21] The conflict is based not on religion, but on a mutual hatred for each other's moral character. This side of Kireevsky's thought is represented here by his 1852 essay "On the Nature of European Culture and on Its Relation to Russian Culture," in which Kireevsky gives an entire litany of distinctions between Russian and Western history, each one of which is based on obvious simplifications and subject to serious dispute.

Despite the uneven nature of Kireevsky's historical argumentation, his biting critique of Western culture and civilization ultimately reveals a positive ideal of lasting and universal significance. The historical culture of the West reveals manifold contradictions and compromises between Christian ideals and practical life, which ultimately call into question both the seriousness of Europe's original commitment to Christianity, and its ability to serve as a bearer of Christian truth. In opposition to this negative example, and on the basis of his personal experience of Russian culture, Kireevsky is able to describe a truly Christian culture and civilization, in which everything, from art to economic relations, is governed by the activity of the Holy Spirit. Kireevsky's stern nationalism is much less obligatory in his philosophy than is Khomiakov's more religious patriotism. Russian life (*byt*) may have inspired Kireevsky's philosophy, but it did so by illustrating a universal example of the wholeness of being (*bytie*). Indeed, time and the process of history do not find any formal place in Kireevsky's metaphysics, yielding to timeless spiritual truth and the timelessness of traditional Russian culture.

---

20. See Abbot Gleason, *European and Muscovite: Ivan Kireevsky and the Origins of Slavophilism* (Cambridge: Harvard University Press, 1972) 162.
21. Eberhard Müller, "Das Tagebuch Ivan Vasil'evic Kireevskijs, 1852–1854," *Jahrbücher für Geschichte Osteuropas* Neue Folge Bd. 14 (1966) Heft 2, 185.

* * *

The Slavophiles labored in many different realms of intellectual endeavor, sometimes leading to the appearance of universal dilettantism; Sergei Aksakov, the father of the Slavophiles Ivan and Konstantin Aksakov, once said that, "It is possible to cut ten people out of Khomiakov and each one would be better than he is."[22] Yet this casual group of Russian squires, ridiculed in their own time for parochialism and indolence, has established itself as one of the most significant intellectual movements of its age.

The selection of essays presented in this volume is by no means exhaustive, although it includes practically all of the Slavophiles' most important writings on philosophy and religion. Inasmuch as Khomiakov and Kireevsky are the major theological and philosophical writers among the Slavophiles, they (with the exception of Samarin's essay on Khomiakov) are the only Slavophile thinkers represented here. This anthology also includes two important twentieth-century responses to Slavophile ideas: essays by the prominent Russian philosophers Pavel Florensky and Nikolai Berdiaev. Some of the texts are presented here for the first time in English; all previous translations have been edited anew. In sum they introduce the reader to the Slavophiles' experience of sobornost and integral knowledge.[23]

Robert Bird

---

22. Quoted from Peter K. Christoff, *An Introduction to Nineteenth-Century Russian Slavophilism. A Study in Ideas. Volume I: A. S. Xomjakov* (The Hague, Paris: Mouton, 1961) 84.
23. The author of the General Introduction would like to thank Boris Jakim for his important comments and suggestions.

PART ONE

Theology

Aleksei Khomiakov

I

THE CHURCH IS ONE
Aleksei Khomiakov

EDITOR'S INTRODUCTION

It is not known exactly when Khomiakov wrote the essay that has
come to be known as "The Church Is One." In 1846–1848, Khomiakov undertook several attempts to publish it in Greek and French
translations, without success. It was published for the first time—
posthumously and with the title "On the Church"—in the journal *Orthodox Review* (*Pravoslavnoe obozrenie*) in 1864 (bk. 3); and in the
same year an English translation was published in Brussels, which
has remained beyond our reach. In Khomiakov's *Collected Works*, it
was called "A catachetical exposition of the doctrine of the Church,"
but the title "The Church Is One" is the title chosen by the most recent
edition.[1] The English translation by John Birkbeck, first published together with the Khomiakov-Palmer correspondence, has been reprinted at least twice during the twentieth century. For this volume,
"The Church Is One" has been translated anew from the Russian by
Robert Bird.

"The Church Is One," Khomiakov's first essay in theology, radically changed Orthodox ecclesiology and has even been credited with
influencing the Second Vatican Council of the Roman Catholic
Church. The originality of Khomiakov's conception has been widely
disputed; some point to the German theologian Moehler as the source
of the concept of the Church as the community of faith. Needless to
say, Orthodox thinkers have also found it important to demonstrate

---

1. A. S. Khomiakov, *Sochineniia v dvukh tomakh. Tom 2: Raboty po bogosloviiu*,
ed. V. A. Koshelev (Moscow, 1994). Koshelev's textual introductions and V. M.
Lur'e's notes to "The Church Is One" in this edition have been used in preparing
the translation and preface.

Khomiakov's lack of originality, that is, the extent to which he was faithful to the Fathers of the Church.[2]

According to Khomiakov, the transcendent Body of Christ and the immanent community of believers are two names, two aspects, of a single reality, the Church. This concept of the Church has been criticized for overemphasizing her immanent aspect, subordinating the Body of Christ to a group of people or a nation (see, for example, the essay by Florensky in this volume). More constructive criticism has sought to augment the formal role of the transcendent aspect within Khomiakov's general scheme. In any case, Khomiakov succeeded in restoring freedom and community to their rightful place in Orthodox theology.

---

2. See V.V. Zenkovsky, *A History of Russian Philosophy*, trans. George L. Kline (New York: Columbia University Press, 1953) II 184.

1.

The Church Is One

1. The unity of the Church follows necessarily from the unity of God, for the Church is not a multiplicity of persons in their personal separateness, but the unity of God's grace, living in the multitude of rational creatures who submit themselves to grace. Grace is granted also to the unsubmissive and to those who do not take advantage of it (those who bury their talents [Matt. 25:25]), but these are not in the Church. The unity of the Church, however, is not illusory: it is not metaphorical but true and essential, like the unity of the numerous members of a living body.

The Church is one despite her seeming division for people who still yet live on the earth. Only with respect to humanity is it possible to accept the division of the Church into visible and invisible; her unity, in contrast, is true and absolute. Those who live on earth, those who have completed their earthly paths, those who are not created for earthly paths (such as angels), those who have not yet begun their earthly paths (the future generations), all are united in the one Church—in the one grace of God. For God's as yet unmanifested creation is manifest to Him, and God hears the prayers and knows the faith of those who have not yet been summoned by Him from non-being into being. The Church herself, the Body of Christ, is made manifest and is perfected in time without changing her own essential unity and her own inner life of grace. Therefore, when it is said: "The Church visible and invisible"—this is said only with respect to humanity.

2. The visible or earthly Church lives in complete communion and unity with the entire church body, the head of which is Christ [Col. 1:18]. She has abiding within her Christ and the grace of the Holy Spirit in all of their vital fullness, but not in the fullness of their manifestations, for she creates and obtains knowledge not in full measure but only insofar as it is pleasing to God.

Since the earthly or visible Church is not yet the fullness and perfection of the entire Church, which the Lord appointed to be made manifest at the Last Judgment of the entire creation, she creates and has knowledge only within her bounds without judging the rest of humankind (according to the words of the Apostle Paul to the Corinthians [1 Cor. 5:12–13]). For the Church, only those who have removed themselves from her are seen as being excluded—i.e., not belonging to her. The rest of humankind, whether alien to the Church or tied to her with bonds that God has not desired to reveal to her, she leaves for the judgment of the great day. The earthly Church judges only herself by the grace of the Spirit and by the freedom granted to her through Christ, summoning the rest of humankind to unity and to adoption by God in Christ, but she does not pronounce sentence over those who do not heed her call, knowing the command of her Savior and Head "not to judge another's servant" [Rom. 14:4].

3. From the creation of the world the earthly Church has abided on the earth uninterruptedly and she shall abide until the completion of all of God's works, according to the promise given to her by God Himself. Her distinguishing features are: an inner holiness that does not allow the slightest admixture of falseness, for within her there lives the spirit of truth; and external unchangeability, for unchangeable is her Preserver and Head, Christ.

All of the distinguishing features of the Church, both inner and external, are perceived only by the Church herself and by those whom grace calls to be her members. For those who are alien to her and remain uncalled the distinguishing features are incomprehensible, for an external change of ritual seems to the uncalled to be a change of the very Spirit made manifest in the ritual, as, for example, with the transition from the Church of the Old Testament to that of the New Testament, or with the changing of church rituals and tenets from apostolic times. The Church and her members know with the inner knowledge of faith the unity and unchangeability of her Spirit, which is the Spirit of God. Those who are outside and not called, however, see and know the changing of external ritual by an external knowledge incapable of grasping the inner, just as the very unchangeability of God seems to them changeable in the changes of His creation.

Thus the Church was not and could not have been changed, obscured, or fallen away, for then she would have been deprived of the spirit of truth. There could not be any time in which she would have accepted falsity into her bosom, in which laypeople, presbyters, and bishops would have submitted to instructions and a teaching inconsistent with the teaching and spirit of Christ. Anyone who says that there could be such an impoverishment of Christ's Spirit within the Church does not know her and is alien to her. The Church does not and could not revolt against one false teaching while preserving or accepting other false teachings, for in her, by her essence, there should always be preachers, teachers, and martyrs, confessing not a partial truth with admixture of falsity, but the full truth without admixture. The Church knows not part-truth and part-falsity, but rather the full and pure truth. One who lives in the Church does not submit to a false teaching, does not accept a sacrament from a false teacher whom one knows to be false, and does not follow false rituals. And the Church herself does not err, for she is truth; she displays neither artifice nor cowardice, for she is holy.

In precisely the same way the Church, by her unchangeability, does not recognize as falsity what she once recognized as truth; and having declared by general council and common agreement the possibility of error in the teaching of some private individual or some bishop or patriarch,[3] she cannot acknowledge that any particular private individual or bishop or patriarch or their successors are immune from succumbing to error in doctrine and that they are protected from error by some special grace. What would hallow the earth if the Church lost her own holiness? And where would truth be if her verdict of today contradicted that of yesterday?

In the Church—that is, in her members—false teachings do arise, but then the infected members fall away, constituting a heresy or schism and not desecrating the holiness of the Church.

4. The Church is called *one*, *holy*, *sobornyi* (catholic and universal), and *apostolic* because she is one and holy; because she belongs to the whole world and not any locality; because she hallows all humanity and all the earth and not one particular nation or one country; because her essence consists in the harmony and unity of the spirit and life of all her members who recognize her over the entire earth; and because,

---

3. As, for example, with the teaching of Pope Honorius at the Chalcedon Council. [Khomiakov is mistaken; the council in question is the Sixth Ecumenical Council, held in Constantinople in 680. — TRANS.]

finally, all the fullness of her faith, her hopes, and her love are contained in Scripture and apostolic teaching.

From this it follows that when some Christian society is called a local Church, for instance, the Greek, Russian, or Syrian, this name denotes only the gathering of those members of the Church who live in a certain country: Greece, Russia, Syria, and so on, and does not entail the claim that one community of Christians could ever express the Church doctrine or give dogmatic interpretation to Church doctrine without the agreement of the other communities. It is still less supposed that any community or its pastor might prescribe its interpretation for others. The grace of faith is inseparable from the holiness of life, and no one community and no one pastor may be recognized as the preserver of the entire faith, just as no one pastor and no one community may be considered representatives of the entire holiness of the Church.

Nevertheless, every Christian community, without claiming for itself the right of dogmatic interpretation or teaching, has a full right to change its rituals, to introduce new rituals, as long as it does not lead other communities into temptation. Rather than do this, it ought to abandon its own opinion and submit it to that of the others, lest what might seem harmless or even praiseworthy to one should seem blamable to another; or lest that brothers and sisters should lead one another into the sin of doubt and division. Each Christian should set a high value upon the unity of Church rituals, for it is here that the unity of spirit and doctrine is made visibly manifest, even for the unenlightened; for the enlightened, on the other hand, it is the source of living and Christian joy. Love is the crown and glory of the Church.

5. The Spirit of God, alive in the Church, guiding her and making her wise, is manifested in her in multiple forms: in Scripture, in Tradition, and in works; for the Church, performing the works of God, is the Church that preserves Tradition and wrote the Scripture. It is neither individuals nor a multitude of individuals in the Church that preserves Tradition and wrote the Scripture, but the Spirit of God, alive in the sum of the Church. Therefore it is impossible and improper to search for the foundations of Tradition in the Scripture, or for proofs of the Scripture in Tradition, or for justification of the Scripture and Tradition in works. To one who lives outside of the Church neither the

Scripture, nor Tradition, nor works are comprehensible. To one, however, who remains within the Church and who is in communion with the Spirit of the Church, their unity is made evident by the grace that lives in her.

Do works not precede the Scripture and Tradition? Does Tradition not precede the Scripture? Did Tradition not exist for our forefathers, beginning with the first progenitor, Adam? Were not the works of Noah, Abraham, and the forefathers and representatives of the Old Testament Church pleasing to God? Did Christ not give freedom to humanity and verbal teaching before the apostles bore witness to the work of redemption and the law of freedom with their own writings? For this reason, there is no contradiction, but perfect agreement between Tradition, works, and the Scripture. You understand the Scripture to the extent that you preserve Tradition and perform works pleasing to the wisdom living in you. But the wisdom living in you is not given to you personally, but rather is granted to you as a member of the Church, and it is given to you only partially without completely destroying your personal falsity. In contrast, wisdom is given to the Church in the fullness of truth and without admixture of falsity. For this reason do not judge the Church but obey her so that wisdom might not be taken from you.

Anyone seeking proofs of Church truth thus displays his doubt and excludes himself from the Church, or gives himself the appearance of a doubter, while retaining the hope of proving truth and reaching it by his own strength of reason. But the strength of reason does not reach God's truth, and human weakness is made manifest in the weakness of proofs. He who accepts only Tradition and bases the Church on it alone actually rejects the Church and hopes to create her again by his own efforts; he who accepts only Tradition and works and belittles the importance of the Scripture actually rejects also the Church and becomes a judge of the Spirit of God, Who spoke by the Scripture.

Christian knowledge, on the contrary, is not a matter of a questioning reason but of graceful and living faith. Scripture is external, and Tradition is external, and works are external; in them only the Spirit of God is inner. From Tradition alone, or from Scripture or works, people can receive only external and incomplete knowledge, which can contain truth for it issues from truth, but is at the same time necessarily false, because it is not complete. A believer knows the truth, while a nonbeliever does not know it or knows it only with external and incomplete knowledge.[4] The Church does not prove herself as Scripture or Tradition, nor as works, but she bears witness to herself just as the Spirit of God, Who lives in her, bears witness to Himself in Scripture. The Church does not ask: Which Scripture is true, which Tradition is true, which council is true, and which work is pleasing to God? For Christ knows His own inheritance, and the Church in which He lives knows with inner knowledge and cannot help but know her own manifestations. Holy Scripture is the name for the collection of Old and New Testament books that the Church recognizes as her own. But there are no limits to Scripture, for any Scripture that the Church recognizes as her own is Holy Scripture. Such, preeminently, are the confessions of the Councils, especially the confession of Nicaea-Constantinople. Thus Holy Scripture has been up till our time and, if it please God, thus shall Holy Scripture remain. But there never has been and never will be in the Church any contradiction either in Scripture, Tradition, or works, for in all three is the one and unchanging Christ.

6. Every action of the Church, guided by the Holy Spirit, the spirit of life and truth, represents the sum of all His gifts—faith, hope, and love. For in Scripture is made manifest not only faith, but also the hope of the Church and God's love. In work that is pleasing to God there is made manifest not only love, but also faith, and hope, and grace. And in the living Tradition of the Church, which awaits its crown and perfection from God in Christ, there is made manifest not only hope, but also faith and love. The gifts of the Holy Spirit are indissolubly joined in one holy and living unity; but even as a God-pleasing work most belongs to hope, so a God-pleasing confession most belongs to love; and even as a God-pleasing prayer most belongs to hope, so a God-pleasing confession most belongs to faith; and it is not false to call the confession of the Church the confession of faith, or the Creed.

---

4. Therefore, one who is not made holy with the spirit of grace can know truth, as we would also hope that we know it, but this knowledge is itself nothing but a more or less certain supposition, an opinion, a logical conviction or external knowledge, which has nothing in common with inner and true knowledge, with faith that sees the invisible. Only God knows whether we have faith.

For this reason it is proper to understand that a confession, a prayer, and works are nothing by themselves, but are only an external manifestation of inner spirit. Thus, neither one who prays, nor one who performs works, nor one who confesses the confession of the Church is pleasing to God, but rather one who performs works, confesses, and prays according to the Spirit of Christ living within. Not everyone has the same faith or the same hope, nor the same love, for you may love the flesh, hope for the world, and confess falsity; you can also love, hope, and believe only partially and not in full measure; and the Church calls your hope "hope," your love "love," and your faith "faith," for thus do you call them, and she will not argue with you over words; but she herself calls love, faith, and hope gifts of the Holy Spirit, and she knows that they are true and perfect.

7. The Holy Church confesses her faith by her entire life: by her doctrine, which is inspired by the Holy Spirit; by her sacraments, in which the Holy Spirit acts; and by her rituals, which He administers. The confession of faith is preeminently the Creed of Nicaea-Constantinople.

The confession of Church doctrine is contained in the Creed of Nicaea-Constantinople, but in order that it be known that the hope of the Church is inseparable from her doctrine, her hope is also used; for it is said "we look for [await]," and not only that "we believe," that it shall be.

The Creed of Nicaea-Constantinople, the full and complete confession of the Church, from which she does not allow anything to be excluded, and to which she allows nothing to be added, is the following:

I believe in one God, the Father, the Almighty, the Maker of heaven and earth, and of all things visible and invisible. And in one Lord Jesus Christ, the Son of God, the Only Begotten, begotten of the Father before all ages. Light of Light; true God of true God; begotten not made; of one essence with the Father, by Whom all things were made; Who for our sake and for our salvation came down from heaven; and was incarnate of the Holy Spirit and the Virgin Mary and became man; and He was crucified for us under Pontius Pilate; He suffered, and was buried; on the third day He rose again, according to the Scriptures, and ascended into heaven, and sits at the right hand of the Father; He shall come again in glory to judge the living and the dead; Whose kingdom will have no end. And in the Holy Spirit, the Lord, the Giver of Life, Who proceeds from the Father; Who with the Father and the Son together is worshiped and glorified; Who spoke by the prophets. I believe in one holy, catholic [*sobornyi*] and apostolic Church. I confess one baptism for the remission of sins. I look for [await] the resurrection of the dead, and the life of the world to come. Amen.

This confession is comprehensible, just as is all life of the Spirit, only to a believer and member of the Church. It contains within itself mysteries 'inaccessible to questioning reason and revealed only to God Himself and those to whom God reveals them for inner and living (and not dead and external) knowledge. It contains within itself the mystery of God's being, not only with respect to His external action upon creation, but also to His inner, eternal existence. Therefore the pride of reason and unlawful power that appropriates for itself, in opposition to the verdict of the entire Church (expressed at the Council of Ephesus), the right to add its personal explanations and human conjectures to the Creed of Nicaea-Constantinople, is in itself a violation of the holiness and inviolability of the Church.

Just as the very pride of various Churches, who dared to change the Creed of the entire Church without the agreement of their brothers and sisters, was inspired not by the spirit of love and was a crime before God and the Holy Church, so it was that their blind wisdom, which had not grasped God's mystery, was a distortion of the faith; for faith will not be preserved where love has become impoverished.

For this reason the addition of the word *filioque* contains some illusory dogma unknown to any of the God-pleasing writers, bishops, or apostolic successors in the first centuries of the Church; nor was it spoken by Christ the Savior. As Christ spoke clearly [John 15:26], so did and does the Church clearly confess that the Holy Spirit proceeds from the Father, for not only external but also inner mysteries of God were revealed by Christ and by the spirit of faith to the holy apostles and Holy Church. When Theodoret called those who confessed the procession of the Holy Spirit from the Father and the Son blasphemers, the Church, which had exposed many of his errors, in this case approved the verdict with an eloquent silence.[5] The Church does not deny that the Holy Spirit is sent not only by the Father but also by the Son; the Church does not deny that the Holy Spirit is communicated to all reasoning creatures not only from the Father but also through the Son; but the Church denies that the Holy Spirit had His origin of procession in the very Godhead Itself not only from the Father, but from the Son also.

Those who have disavowed the spirit of love and deprived themselves of the gifts of grace are thus made unable to obtain inner knowledge, or faith, and limit themselves to external knowledge: thus they can also know only what is external but cannot know the inner mysteries of God. Christian communities estranged from the Holy Church could not confess (since they could not even grasp it with the spirit) the procession of the Holy Spirit from the Father alone, within the Godhead, but were obliged to confess only the external sending of the Spirit into all creatures—a sending fulfilled not only from the Father, but also through the Son. They preserved what was external in the law, but lost the inner meaning and God's grace both in confession and in life.

8. Confessing her faith in the Tri-Hypostatic Godhead, the Church confesses her faith in herself, because she considers herself the instrument and vessel of divine grace and considers her works to be the works of God, and not the works of the individuals who comprise her visibly. In this confession she shows that knowledge of her existence is also a gift of grace that is granted from above and is accessible only to faith, but not to reason.

For what need would I have to say, "I believe," if I already knew? Is not faith the evidence of things unseen [Heb. 11:1]? The visible Church is not the visible society of Christians but the Spirit of God and the grace of the sacraments living in the society. For this reason the visible Church is visible only to the believer, since for the nonbeliever a sacrament is only a ritual and the Church only a society.

---

5. The silence of the Church in not refuting a writer is very meaningful; but this silence becomes a decisive verdict when the Church does not reject a verdict pronounced against any teaching, for, in not rejecting the verdict, she confirms it with all her power.

Although with the eyes of the body and of reason the believer sees the Church only in her external manifestations, the believer's spirit recognizes her in the sacraments, and in prayer, and in God-pleasing works. For this reason the believer does not confuse her with a society that calls itself Christian, for not all who say "Lord, Lord" actually belong to the elect and the seed of Abraham [Matt. 7:21]. It is by faith that the true Christian knows that the one, holy, *sobornyi*, apostolic Church will never disappear from the face of the earth until the Last Judgment of all creation, that she abides on the earth invisible to the eyes of flesh and to minds that are wise in the way of the flesh within the visible community of Christians, just as she remains visible to eyes of faith in the Church beyond the grave, which is invisible to bodily eyes. It is through faith again that the Christian knows that the earthly Church— though she be invisible—is always robed in a visible image; that there has never been, could never be, and will never be such a time when the sacraments would be distorted, holiness exhausted, and the doctrine spoiled; and that one is no Christian who cannot say where, from apostolic times, the Holy Sacraments have been performed and are performed, where the doctrine has been preserved and is preserved, where prayers have been sent up and are sent up to the throne of grace. The Holy Church confesses and believes that the flock has never been deprived of its Divine Pastor and that the Church could never fall into error through misunderstanding, for in her there lives the reason of God; nor could the Church ever submit to false doctrines out of cowardice, for in her there lives the strength of the Spirit of God.

9. Believing in the word of God's promise, by which all followers of Christ's teaching are called Christ's friends, His brothers and sisters, and in Him the adopted children of God, the Holy Church confesses the paths by which it pleased God to lead fallen and dead humanity to reunite in the spirit of grace and life. For this reason, after commemorating the prophets, representatives of the Old Testament epoch, she confesses the sacraments by which God sends down upon people His grace in the Church of the New Testament. Preeminently, she confesses the sacrament of Baptism, for the cleansing of sins, since it contains within itself the principle of all the others, for only through Baptism does humankind enter the unity of the Church, which preserves all the other sacraments.

Confessing one Baptism for the remission of sins as a sacrament prescribed by Christ Himself for entrance into the Church of the New Testament, the Church does not judge those who have not entered into communion with her through Baptism, for she knows and judges only herself. God alone knows the hardness of hearts, and it is He also Who judges the weakness of reason according to truth and mercy. Many have been saved and have received their inheritance without accepting the sacrament of Baptism by water, for it was instituted only for the Church of the New Testament. Whoever rejects it rejects the entire Church and the Spirit of God Who lives in her, but it was not granted to humanity from the beginning nor prescribed for the Church of the Old Testament.

Anyone who would say, "Circumcision was the Baptism of the Old Testament," also rejects Baptism for women, for there was no circumcision for them. And what would such people say about the forefathers from Adam to Abraham who did not receive the seal of circumcision? And, in any case, will they not admit that, outside of the Church of the New Testament, the sacrament of Baptism was not obligatory? If they say that Christ received Baptism for the Church of the Old Testament, who will place a bound on the mercy of God, Who took upon Himself the sins of the world? Baptism thus is obligatory, for it alone is the door into the Church of the New Testament, and only in Baptism does a person express agreement to accept the redeeming action of grace. Thus, it is only in Baptism that one is saved.

Indeed we know that, confessing one Baptism as the origin of all sacraments, we do not reject the others, for believing in the Church we together with her confess seven sacraments—Baptism, Eucharist, Laying on of Hands, Chrismation, Marriage, Repentance, and Extreme Unction. There are also many other sacraments, for any work performed in faith, love, and hope is inspired in humankind by God's Spirit and summons the invisible grace of God. But the seven sacraments are performed actually not by any one person worthy of God's mercy, but by the entire Church in one person, even if he be unworthy.

Concerning the sacrament of the Eucharist, the Holy Church teaches that in it is accomplished in truth the transformation of bread and wine into the body and blood of Christ. She does not reject also the word "transubstantiation," but does not ascribe to it the material sense attributed to it by the teachers of the churches that have fallen away. The transformation of bread and wine into the body and blood of Christ is completed in the Church and for the Church. If you receive the sanctified gifts, or venerate them, or think of them with faith, you truly receive, venerate, or think of the body and blood of Christ. If you receive them unworthily, you actually reject the body and blood of Christ; in any case, whether in faith or in unbelief, you are sanctified or condemned by the body and blood of Christ. But this sacrament is in the Church and for the Church and not for the world outside, not for the flame, not for corruption, and not for those who have not heard Christ's law.

Within the Church herself (we mean the visible Church), for both the chosen and the reprobate, the Holy Eucharist is not a simple remembrance of the mystery of redemption, not the presence of spiritual gifts in bread and wine, not merely a spiritual reception of the body and blood of Christ, but the true body and blood. Not in spirit alone did it please Christ to unite with believers, but both in body and in blood, in order that the union be complete and not only spiritual, but also bodily. Equally displeasing to the Church are the meaningless interpretations concerning the relationship of the Holy Sacrament to the elements and unreasoning creatures (for the sacrament is instituted only for the Church), and the spiritual pride that despises the body and blood and rejects bodily union with Christ. It is not without the body that we shall be resurrected, and no spirit except God can be called fully bodiless. One who despises the body sins with a pride of spirit.

Concerning the sacrament of the Laying on of Hands, the Church teaches that, through it, the grace that accomplishes sacraments is transmitted by succession from the apostles and Christ Himself. This is not to be understood in such a way that no sacrament could be accomplished in any way other than by the Laying on of Hands (for any Christian can through Baptism open the door of the Church to an infant, a Jew, or a pagan), but in such a way that the Laying on of Hands contains in itself all the fullness of grace granted by Christ to His Church. The Church herself, communicating to her members the fullness of spiritual gifts, has appointed differences of degrees in the Laying on of Hands, on the strength of her God-given freedom. There is one gift for a presbyter, who accomplishes all sacraments except the Laying on of Hands, another gift for bishops, who accomplish the Laying on of Hands, while above the episcopal gift there is nothing. The sacrament gives the recipient of the Laying on of Hands the great significance that, even though unworthy, in performing this mysterious service, he acts not on his own behalf, but on behalf of the entire Church—that is, on behalf of Christ, who lives in her. If the Laying on of Hands were to cease, all sacraments except for Baptism would cease, and humanity would be cut off from grace: for the Church herself would then bear witness that Christ has departed from her.

Concerning the sacrament of Chrismation, the Church teaches that in it are communicated to the Christian the gifts of the Holy Spirit, Who confirms the recipient's faith and inner holiness; this sacrament can be performed, according to the will of the Holy Church, not only by bishops, but also by presbyters, although the chrism [oil] itself can be blessed only by a bishop.

Concerning the sacrament of Marriage, the Holy Church teaches that God's grace, which blesses the succession of generations in the temporal existence of the human race and the holy union of husband and wife for the formation of a family, is a mysterious gift, which places upon its recipients the lofty obligation of mutual love and spiritual holiness, through which the sinful and material is clothed in righteousness and purity. Wherefore the great teachers of the Church—the apostles—recognize the sacrament of Marriage even among pagans, for, in forbidding concubinage, they uphold marriage between pagans and Christians, saying that a husband is hallowed by a faithful wife, and a wife by a faithful husband [1 Cor. 7:14]. The words of the Apostle do not mean that a nonbeliever is saved by union with a believer, but that marriage is sanctified; for it is not the human being, but husband and wife that are hallowed. One person is not saved through another person, but husband and wife are hallowed in respect to their very marriage. So, marriage is not profane even among idolaters; but they themselves do not know of the mercy of God that is granted them. The Holy Church, however, through its ordained ministers, recognizes and blesses the union of husband and wife, which is blessed by God. For this reason marriage is not a ritual, but a true sacrament. For it is perfected only within the Holy Church, for only in her is anything holy accomplished in full.

Concerning the sacrament of Repentance, the Holy Church teaches that without it the human spirit cannot be purified from the slavery of sin and sinful pride, that it itself cannot absolve its own sins (for we are able only to condemn, and not justify ourselves), and that the Holy Church alone has the power of justification, for in her lives the fullness of Christ's spirit. We know that the firstborn of the Heavenly Kingdom, after the Savior, entered God's holy place by his self-condemnation—that is, by the sacrament of Repentance—saying: "For we receive the due reward of our deeds" [Luke 23:41], and receiving absolution from Him Who alone can absolve and does absolve through the mouth of His Church.

Concerning the sacrament of Extreme Unction, the Holy Church teaches that in it is accomplished the blessing of the entire effort completed by a human being on earth and of the entire path he has traveled in faith and humility, and that in Extreme Unction is expressed the divine judgment over the human being's earthly composition, restoring it to health, when healing resources are ineffectual, or allowing death to destroy the corruptible body, which is now unnecessary for the earthly Church and for the hidden ways of God.

10. Even on earth, the Church lives not by an earthly or human life, but by a life that is divine and endowed with grace. For this reason not only each of her members but all of the Church solemnly calls herself holy. Her visible manifestation is contained within the sacraments; her inner life, in contrast, is contained in the gifts of the Holy Spirit, in faith, hope, and love. Oppressed and persecuted by external enemies, oftentimes unsettled and divided by the evil passions of her children, she has been preserved and is preserved as unshakable and unchangeable wherever the sacraments and spiritual holiness are preserved unchangeably; she never suffers distortion and never has need of correction. She lives not under the law of slavery, but under the law of freedom, she does not recognize any power over her except her own, nor anyone's judgment apart from the judgment of faith (for reason cannot comprehend her), and she expresses her love, her faith, and her hope in prayers and rituals inspired in her by the spirit of truth and Christ's grace. For this reason her very rituals, although they are not unchangeable (for they are created by the spirit of freedom and can change according to the judgment of the Church), can

never, under any circumstance, contain in themselves any, even the smallest, admixture of falsity or false teaching. The rituals themselves, still unchanged, are obligatory for the members of the Church, for their observance grants the joy of holy unity.

External unity is unity made manifest in sacramental communion; inner unity is the unity of spirit. Many have been saved (for example, some martyrs) without having participated in any of the sacraments of the Church (even Baptism), but no one is saved without having participated in the inner holiness of the Church, her faith, hope, and love, for it is not works that save, but faith. Faith itself is not divided, but there is one faith, true and living. For this reason those who say that faith alone does not save, but works are also necessary, and those who say that faith saves apart from works, are unwise: for if there are no works, faith becomes dead; if faith is dead, then it is not true either, for in true faith is Christ, the truth and the life, and if it is not true, then it is false, or external knowledge. And can falsity save? If it is true, then it is living, or accomplishes works; and if it does works then what other works are needed?

The divinely inspired apostle says: "Show me in your works the faith of which you boast, just as I show my faith by my works" [James 2:18]. Does he recognize two faiths? No, but he exposes unwise boasting. "You believe in God, but the demons also believe" [James 2:19]. Does he recognize faith in the demons? No, but he condemns the falsity that boasts of a quality shared by demons. "As a body is dead without a soul, so is faith without works" [James 2:26]. Is he comparing faith to a body and a body to spirit? No, for such comparison would be incorrect; but the sense of his words is clear. As a soulless body is no longer a human being and cannot be called a human being, but is rather a corpse, so also faith that does not do works cannot be called true faith, but rather false, or external knowledge, fruitless and accessible even to the demons. What is written plainly must likewise be read plainly. For this reason those who base themselves on the Apostle James for proof that there is dead faith and living faith, as if faith were divided, do not grasp the meaning of the apostle's words, for the apostle bears witness not in their favor, but rather against them.

Likewise, when the great apostle of the gentiles says: "What profit is faith without love, even such a faith as would move mountains?" [1 Cor. 13:2–3], he does not affirm the possibility of such faith without love; but supposing such a faith he declares it to be useless. It is not in the spirit of worldly wisdom, which argues over words, that Holy Scripture should be read, but rather in the spirit of God's Wisdom and spiritual simplicity. Defining faith, the apostle says: "It is the evidence of things unseen and the affirmation of things hoped for" [Heb. 11:1] (not only things expected or due to come); for if we hope, we desire, and if we desire, we love: for you cannot desire what you do not love. Or do demons also have hope? For this reason there is one faith, and when we ask "Can true faith save without works?"— then we ask an unwise question, or, it is better to say, we do not ask anything, for true faith is a living faith and does works: it is faith in Christ and Christ in faith.

Those who take dead faith—that is, false faith or external knowledge—for true faith, have gone so far in their delusion that, without themselves knowing it, they have made an eighth sacrament out of this dead faith. The Church has faith, but a living faith, for she also has holiness. When, on the other hand, one individual or one bishop definitely has faith, what should we say? Does that individual have holiness? No, for idolaters would want such a person as their servant.[6] But faith abides in that person, though a sinner. So, the faith within him or her is an eighth sacrament, inasmuch as every sacrament is the activity of the Church in an individual, even though he or she be unworthy. What kind of faith abides in individuals through this sacrament? Living faith? No, for they are transgressors; it is dead faith, or external knowledge, accessible even to demons. And is this to be an eighth sacrament? Thus, deviation from truth is its own punishment.[7]

One should understand that it is neither faith, nor hope, nor love that saves (for does faith in reason save, or hope for the world, or love for the flesh?), but it is the object of faith that saves. If you believe in Christ you are saved by Christ in faith; if you believe in the Church you are saved by the Church; if you believe in Christ's sacraments you are saved by them, for Christ our God is in the Church and

---

6. Some manuscripts have here: "No, for he is blinded by transgression and debauchery." — TRANS.

7. Just as infallibility in dead faith is by itself falsity, so its lifelessness is also expressed by the fact that this infallibility is tied to objects of lifeless nature, to place of residence, or to dead walls, or to episcopal succession, or to a throne. But we know who sat on Moses' throne during Christ's passion [Matt. 23:2].

in the sacraments. The Church of the Old Testament was saved by faith in the future Savior. Abraham was saved by the same Christ as we. He had Christ in hope, whereas we have Him in joy. For this reason, one who desires Baptism has Baptism in desire, whereas one who received Baptism has Baptism in joy. Both are saved by an identical faith in Baptism; but you will say: "If faith in Baptism saves, then why get baptized?" If you do not receive Baptism, what is it you desire?

It is evident that a faith that desires Baptism is fulfilled in the reception of Baptism itself, which is its joy. For this reason the house of Cornelius also received the Holy Spirit without having received Baptism [Acts 10], and the leper was filled with the same Spirit following Baptism [Acts 8:26–39]. For God can glorify the sacrament of Baptism before it is accomplished, just as after it. Thus the difference between *opus operans* and *opus operatum* disappears.[8]

We know that many have not baptized infants and many have not allowed them to Communion of the holy mysteries, and many have not chrismated them, but the Holy Church, which baptizes and chrismates and allows infants to Communion, has a different understanding. She did not decide thus because she condemned unbaptized infants, whose divine image is always seen by the angels, but she decided this according to the spirit of love that lives in her, so that even the first thought of an infant attaining to reason would already be not only a desire but joy for sacraments already received. And do you know the joy of an infant that seems not to have attained to reason? Did the yet unborn prophet not rejoice at Christ? But Baptism, Chrismation, and Communion of the holy gifts have been taken away from infants by those who, inheriting the blind wisdom of blind paganism, have not grasped the greatness of God's sacraments and have demanded that everything yield reason and utility and, subordinating the teaching of the Church to scholastic interpretations, do not desire even to pray if they do not see in the prayer a direct goal and profit. But our law is not a law of slaves or mercenaries laboring for wages, but a law of adoption and love that is free.

---

8. In Roman Catholic theology, the force of grace (*opus operans*, or "active force") becomes effective only in the context of ecclesiastical ritual (*opus operatum*, or "acted force"). — TRANS.

We know that those among us who fall, fall by themselves, but that no one is saved by oneself. Those who are saved are saved in the Church as her member and in unity with all her other members. When someone believes, that person is in a community of faith; when someone loves, that person is in a community of love; when someone prays, such a person is in a community of prayer. For this reason no one can rely on one's own prayer, and each in prayer asks the entire Church for intercession—not as though doubting the intercession of Christ, the one intercessor, but in confidence that the entire Church always prays for all her members. There pray for us all the angels, apostles, martyrs, patriarchs and the most-high Mother of our Lord, and this holy union is the true life of the Church.

But if the visible and invisible Church ceaselessly prays, why ask her for prayers? Are we not asking for mercy from God and Christ although His mercy anticipates our prayer? We ask the Church for prayers precisely because we know that she gives the help of her intercession even to one who does not ask for it, and that she gives to one who does ask incomparably more than he asks, for in her is the fullness of the Spirit of God. Thus also we glorify all whom the Lord has glorified and whom He glorifies, for how shall we say that Christ lives within us if we do not become like unto Christ? For this reason we glorify the saints and angels and prophets, but most of all the most-pure Mother of Lord Jesus, without considering her to be either sinless by birth or perfect (for Christ alone is sinless and perfect), but remembering that her incomprehensible superiority over all of God's creation is borne witness to by the angel and by Elizabeth [Luke 1:30, 42] and most of all by the Savior Himself, Who called His great apostle and seer John to filial obedience and service before her [John 19:26–7].

Just as each of us demands prayer from all, so we are obliged to give our prayer to all, both the living and those who have fallen asleep, and even to those yet unborn; for, in asking that the world enter the reason of God (as we ask with all the Church), we ask not only for current generations, but also for those that God will yet summon to life. We pray for the living so that the grace of our Lord might be upon them, and for those who have fallen asleep, that they might be found worthy of beholding God. We know not of the middle condition of souls not accepted into the Kingdom of God, yet not condemned to torment, for we have not received teaching concerning such a condition from the apostles or from Christ. We do not accept purgatory—that is, the cleansing of souls by sufferings, from which one may be redeemed by one's own or another's works; for the Church knows of salvation neither by any external means whatsoever, such as suffering (except for Christ's), nor of the bargaining with God that redeems from suffering by good works.

All of this paganism remains among the heirs of pagan wisdom, among people proud of place and name and region, among those who institute the eighth sacrament of dead faith. We, in contrast, pray in the spirit of love, knowing that no one is saved in any way other than by the prayer of the entire Church in which Christ lives, knowing and hoping that, until the fulfillment of the ages, all the members of the Church, both the living and those who have fallen asleep, ceaselessly attain perfection by mutual prayer. The saints, glorified by God, are much higher than we, but higher than all is the Holy Church, which is able to contain in herself all the saints and prays for all, as is evident in the divinely inspired liturgy. In her prayer is also heard our prayer, no matter how unworthy we are to be called children of the Church.

If, in venerating and glorifying the saints, we ask that God glorify them, we do not fall liable to accusations of pride, for we, having received leave to call God our Father, are also granted leave to pray: "Hallowed be His name, His Kingdom come, His will be done." And if we are allowed to ask God to glorify His own Name and fulfill His will, who will forbid us to ask Him to glorify His saints and grant rest to His chosen ones? We do not pray for those who have not been chosen, just as Christ did not pray for the entire world, but for those whom the Lord gave to Him [John 7:9].

Do not say: "What prayer can I spare for one living or fallen asleep when my prayer is insufficient even for myself?" For, being unable to pray, why would you even pray for yourself? In fact, it is the spirit of love that prays in you. Thus, also do not say: "What is my prayer to others, since they themselves pray and Christ Himself intercedes for them?" When you pray, the spirit of love prays in you. Do not say: "It is too late to change the judgment of God," for your prayer is numbered among the ways of God, and God has foreseen it. If you are a member of the Church, your prayer is needed by all her members. If a hand says that it has no need of the blood of the rest of the body, and that it will not give it its own blood, the hand will wither. Thus also are you needed by the Church, since you are in her, and if you refuse to participate in its community, you yourself perish and are no longer a member of the Church. The Church prays for all, and we all together pray for all, but our prayer should be true and a true expression of love, and not a verbal ritual. Being unable to love everyone, we pray for those we do love, and our prayer is not hypocritical, and we ask God that we might also be able to love and pray for everyone without hypocrisy. The blood of the Church is mutual prayer, and her breath is the praise of God. We pray in a spirit of love and not utility, in the spirit of filial freedom, and not of mercenary law that asks for payment. Those who ask: "What use is prayer?" acknowledge themselves to be slaves. True prayer is true love.

Love and unity are above all else; love is expressed in many forms: by works, prayer, and spiritual song. The Church blesses all these expressions of love. If you cannot express your love of God with words, but rather express it with a visible depiction—with an icon—will the Church condemn you? No, but she will condemn anyone who condemns you, for he is condemning your love. We know that one may be saved, and that people have been saved without icons, and if your love does not demand an icon, you will be saved without an icon. But if the love of your brother or sister requires an icon, your condemnation of that person's love will be a self-condemnation. And if you, as a Christian, do not dare to listen to prayer or spiritual song composed by your brother or sister without reverence, how do you dare to look without reverence at an icon created by that person's love and not by artifice? The Lord Himself, knowing the secret of hearts, has willed to glorify prayers and psalms on many occasions: will you forbid Him to glorify an icon or the tombs of saints? You will say: "The Old Testament forbade the depiction of God," but you who understand the words of the Holy Church (that is, Scripture) more than she herself, do you not understand that it is not the depiction of God that the Old Testament forbade, for it allowed cherubim [Ex. 25:18–20], and the serpent of brass [Num. 21:9], and the writing of the name of God, but forbade human beings to create for themselves a God according to the likeness of any earthly or heavenly object, visible or even imaginable.

If you paint an icon for remembrance of the invisible and unimaginable God, you do not make an idol for yourself. If you imagine God to yourself and think that He is similar to your imagination, you erect an idol for yourself: this is the sense of the Old Testament prohibition. In contrast, an icon (the name of God painted in colors) or the depiction of His saints, created by love, is not forbidden by the spirit of truth. Do not say: "Christians will go over to idolatry," for the spirit of Christ, which preserves the Church, is wiser than your calculating wisdom. For this reason you can be saved without icons, but you should not reject icons.

The Church accepts any ritual that expresses spiritual striving toward God, just as she accepts any prayer and icon, but above all rituals she recognizes the holy liturgy in which all the fullness of church teaching and spirit is expressed, and expressed not by some kind of conventional signs and symbols, but by the word of life and truth inspired from on high. Only one who understands the liturgy can understand the Church. Above all else is unity of holiness and love.

11. The Holy Church, confessing that she awaits the resurrection of the dead and final judgment upon all humanity, recognizes that the perfection of all her members will be accomplished with her own perfection, and that future life belongs not to the spirit only, but to the spiritual body also [1 Cor. 15:44], for God alone is completely incorporeal spirit. For this reason she rejects the pride of those who preach the doctrine of incorporeality beyond the grave and, as a consequence, despise the body in which Christ rose from the dead. This body will not be a body of flesh, but will be similar to the corporeality of angels, as also Christ Himself said, that we shall be as angels [Luke 20:36].

At the final judgment our justification in Christ will be made manifest in all its fullness, not only our sanctification, but also our justification, for no one has been sanctified in full, so justification is still necessary. Christ works all that is good in us, whether in faith, hope, or love. We, on the other hand, only submit to His action, but no one, not even from the ranks of the saints, as Christ said, submits in full measure. For this reason we need also justification by Christ's suffering and blood. For who can also speak of the merit of his own works or of a store of meritorious deeds and prayers? Only those who still live under the law of slavery. Christ works all that is good in us, while we can never fully submit, none of us, even from the ranks of the saints, as the Savior Himself said [1 John 1:8–10]. Grace works everything, and grace is given freely and is given to all so that none might complain, but it is not given to all in equal measure, nor by predestination, but rather by foreknowledge, as the apostle says [Rom. 3:24, 8:28–30]. The smallest talent is given to one in whom the Lord foresaw negligence, so that the rejection of a greater gift might not cause greater condemnation. And we ourselves do not cultivate the talents granted to us, but they are given over to merchants so that here also we might not have any merit, but only a lack of resistance to the grace that is growing. Thus the difference between "sufficient and efficient" grace disappears.[9] Grace works all. If you submit to it, then the Lord is perfected in you and perfects you, but do not be proud of your obedience, for your obedience is also from grace. We never submit in full measure; for this reason, apart from sanctification, we also ask for justification.

All is accomplished in the fulfillment of the common judgment, and God's Spirit—the Spirit of faith, hope, and love—will be made manifest in all its fullness, and any gift will achieve its full perfection: love will be above all. It is not to be thought, however, that the gifts of God, faith and hope, will perish, for they are inseparable from love, but only love preserves its name, while faith, reaching fulfillment, will be rather a full inner knowledge and vision; hope in its turn will be joy, for even on earth we know that the stronger it is the more joyful it is.

12. By the will of God, after the falling away of many schisms and of the Roman patriarchate, the Holy Church was preserved in the Greek eparchies and patriarchates, and only those communities can recognize themselves as fully Christian that preserve or come into unity with the Eastern patriarchates. For God is One, and the Church is one, and there is neither division nor disagreement within her.

---

9. According to Roman Catholic theology, "sufficient grace" is given to all individuals, but it is up to each to achieve redemption by activating this reserve, making it "efficient grace." — TRANS.

For this reason the Church is called Orthodox or Eastern, or Greco-Russian, but all of these names are but temporary names. It is improper to accuse the Church of pride in calling herself Orthodox, for she also calls herself holy. When the false doctrines disappear, the name of Orthodoxy will not be needed, for there will be no false Christianity. When the Church extends her domain or when the fullness of nations enters into her, all local nomenclatures will disappear, for the Church is not tied to any locality nor does she retain an inheritance of pagan pride, but calls herself one, holy, *sobornyi*, and apostolic, knowing that all the world belongs to her, and that no locality has any special meaning but can only serve, and does serve provisionally, for the glorification of the name of God according to His unknowable will.

II

FRENCH WRITINGS
Aleksei Khomiakov

EDITOR'S INTRODUCTION

Taken in their entirety, Khomiakov's French writings can be seen as a polemic against what he calls the "Western communions," both Protestantism and especially "Romanism" (Khomiakov's term for the Roman Catholic communion, to which he denies universality, or "catholicity"). These works contain many harsh critiques of what Khomiakov perceives to be the limitations of these two communions, but this harshness is often provoked by the equal (if not greater) harshness, joined to misunderstanding, of the writers Khomiakov polemicizes against. Beyond the polemical aspects, Khomiakov's aim is to reveal the central meaning of Eastern Orthodoxy to the Western communions. In so doing, he provides the clearest modern (since the patristic times) definition of Orthodoxy's essence, and revisits, in a fresh, original way, the Orthodox doctrines of the sacraments, communion, prayer, and so on.

Permeating Khomiakov's discussion of Orthodox doctrine and practice is the spirit of sobornost, the free union of all believers in mutual love in the Church. It is Khomiakov's argument that Romanism and then Protestantism have lost sobornost (in a sense, have stopped being the Church) because of the Great Schism of 1054. And only Eastern Orthodoxy remains the repository of sobornost and thus the true Church.

* * *

The publication history and occasion for writing each individual French work are explained in translator's notes accompanying each work. The six French writings were collected in a volume entitled *L'Eglise Latine et le Protestantisme au point de vue de l'Eglise d'Orient. Recueil d'articles sur des questions religieuses, écrits a differentes époques et à diverse occasions* [The Latin Church and Protestantism from the point of view of the Eastern Church. Collection of articles on religious questions, written at different times and on different occasions] (Lausanne and Vevey, 1872). The three brochures with the similar title ("Some Remarks by an Orthodox Christian Concerning the Western Communions ..."), all signed Ignotus, are the most important. Forming a unity, they are possibly Khomiakov's most important religious writings, representing the most advanced development of his theological ideas.

In editing the French writings, I have decided to emphasize the purely theological ideas, and to tone down somewhat the polemics. The world has changed much since the 1850s, and Eastern Orthodoxy does not have the same need to defend itself against "Romanism" and Protestantism. The enemies are different now, as Samarin perspicaciously points out in his essay on Khomiakov (see below).

The brochure "Some Remarks by an Orthodox Christian Concerning the Western Communions, on the Occasion of a Letter Published by the Archbishop of Paris" (1855) is translated in its entirety (with the exception of Khomiakov's footnotes; some of these have been eliminated or abridged). The "Letter to the Editor of *L'Union Chrétienne* on the Occasion of a Discourse of Father Gagarin, Jesuit" (1860) is translated with only a few minor omissions. (This latter article consists of a crucial discussion of the meaning of the terms *sobornost, sobornyi* as compared to the terms *catholicism, catholic*.) Extracts are given from two other articles: "Some Remarks by an Orthodox Christian Concerning the Western Communions, on the Occasion of a Brochure by Mr. Laurentie" (1853) and "Some More Remarks by an Orthodox Christian Concerning the Western Communions, on the Occasion of Several Latin and Protestant Religious Publications" (1858). Two of the French articles are not included: "Letter to Mr. Bunsen, Preceded by a Letter to the Editor of the Journal *l'Union Chrétienne*" (1860) and "Letter to Monseigneur Loos, (Jansenist) Bishop of Utrecht" (1860).

The following works, translated and edited by Boris Jakim, appear here in English for the first time.

1.

Some Remarks by an Orthodox Christian Concerning the Western Communions, on the Occasion of a Brochure by Mr. Laurentie[1]

[excerpts]

From the time of its foundation by the apostles, the Church was one. This unity, which embraced the whole known world, uniting the British Isles to Spain, to Egypt, and to Syria, was never shaken. When a heresy arose, the Christian world sent its representatives, its high functionaries, to those august assemblies that we call councils and that (despite all the disorders and sometimes even violence that tarnished their purity) offered, in their pacific character and in the loftiness of the questions they attempted to resolve, one of the most noble spectacles of human history. The Church as a whole accepted or rejected the decisions of these assemblies according to whether it considered them to conform to or contradict its faith and tradition. The Church called "ecumenical" those councils that it recognized to be an expression of its intimate thought. Having temporary authority in questions of discipline, these councils had unalterable and irrefutable authority in questions of faith. They were the voice of the Church. Heresies did not destroy this divine unity. Heresies were personal errors, not provincial or diocesan schisms. That was the character of the ecclesiastical life whose intimate meaning has for many centuries been totally misunderstood by the West.

---

1. *Quelques mots par un chrétien orthodoxe sur les communions occidentales, à l'occasion d'une brochure de M. Laurentie*. This work was first published as a separate brochure in Paris in 1853 and is intended as a response to P.-S. Laurentie's work *La Papauté, réponce a M. de Tutcheff, conseiller de S. M. l'Empereur de Russie* [The Papacy. A Response to Mr. Tyutchev, Diplomat in the Service of His Majesty, the Emperor of Russia] (Paris, 1852). In this work Laurentie summarizes his two-year polemic with Tyutchev's work "The Papacy and the Roman Question from the Point of View of St. Petersburg" (1849). Khomiakov's response is directed against Laurentie's thesis that, in the Orthodox lands, especially Russia, the spiritual authority is subordinate to the secular authority. — TRANS.

* * *

Neither God, nor Christ, nor the Church is an authority: An authority is something external. They are the truth: They are the life of the Christian—the inner life. They are more alive in the Christian than the heart that beats in one's chest and the blood that flows in one's veins. But they are one's life only to the extent Christians themselves live the universal life of love and unity, which is the life of the Church. Such is the blindness of all the Western sects that not one of them has yet noticed that the ground on which they find themselves is completely different from that upon which the original Church stood and will always stand.

* * *

The Spirit of God who speaks in the Holy Scriptures, who teaches and enlightens in the holy tradition of the universal Church, cannot be understood by reason. This Spirit is accessible only to the whole fullness of the human spirit under the inspiration of grace. To approach faith and its mysteries solely with the light of reason is, in the eyes of the Christian, an act of audacity as extravagant as it is condemnable. The light that comes from heaven and penetrates the whole soul of a human being is the sole light that can serve that person as guide, and the power bestowed by the Dvine Spirit is the sole power that can carry one to these unapproachable regions where divinity manifests itself.

"One must be a prophet to understand a prophet," says St. Gregory Thaumaturgus. Divinity alone can understand God and the infinity of His wisdom. If one does not have Christ living within, one cannot approach His throne without being annihilated by the greatness before which the purest spirits prostrate themselves with joy and trembling. The holy and immortal Church, living tabernacle of the Divine Spirit, bearing Christ within herself, her Savior and Head, united to Him by an intimacy that human words cannot express and the human mind cannot conceive—the Church alone has the right and the power to contemplate the heavenly majesty and to penetrate its mysteries.

I am speaking here of the *entire* Church, of which the earthly Church forms an inseparable *part*; for what we call the visible Church and the invisible Church do not make up two Churches, but a single Church in two different forms. The fullness of the Church's spirit is neither a collective entity nor an abstract entity. Rather, it is the Spirit of God who knows Himself and cannot fail to know Himself. It is the Church in its entirety that has written the Holy Scriptures. It is the Church in its entirety that makes them live in tradition; or rather, the two manifestations of the same Spirit are a single manifestation. For Scripture is written tradition, while tradition is living Scripture. Such is the mystery of this magnificent unity, where the purest holiness is united with the loftiest intelligence to render intelligence intelligent where, without holiness, it would be as blind as matter itself.

Is it upon this ground that Protestantism will arise? Will this ground support people who set themselves up as judges of the Church, thereby claiming both perfect holiness and perfect reason for themselves? I doubt if such people would be welcomed by a Church whose first principle is that ignorance is just as much the property of every person as sin, and that intelligence, like perfect holiness, belongs only to the unity of all the members of the Church. Such is the doctrine of the universal and orthodox Church, and I boldly affirm that it is not possible to find a principle of rationalism in it.

* * *

The Eastern Patriarchs, meeting in council with their bishops, solemnly declared in their response to an encyclical of Pius IX that "infallibility resides solely in the universality of the Church united by mutual love; and that the protection of both the constancy of dogma and the purity of rite was entrusted not to any hierarchy but to the people of the Church as a whole, which is the body of Christ." This formal declaration of the entire Eastern clergy, received with a respect full of fraternal gratitude by the local church of Russia, acquired all the moral authority of an ecumenical witness; and this is certainly the most remarkable fact of ecclesiastical history in recent centuries. There is no teaching Church in the true Church.[2]

Is it the case then that there is no more teaching [in the true Church]? There is, and much more than anywhere else, for this teaching is no longer confined within narrow limits. Every word inspired

---

2. In a previous section of this brochure, not given here, Khomiakov asserts that, in both the Roman and Protestant communions, there is a separation between the "teaching Church" (the hierarchy) and the "Church of disciples." — TRANS.

by a sense of authentically Christian love, of living faith or hope, is a teaching. Every act stamped with the Spirit of God is a lesson. Every Christian life is a model and an example. A martyr dying for the truth, a judge rendering justice not for people but for God, a laborer whose humble toil is accompanied by a constant elevation of thought toward the Creator—live or die to bestow a lofty teaching upon their fellow human beings. And when it is necessary, the Divine Spirit will place on their lips words of wisdom that the savant or theologian will not find. "The bishop is both the teacher and the disciple of his flock," said Bishop Innocent, the contemporary apostle of the Aleutian Islands. All individuals—however high the place they occupy in the hierarchic scale or however hidden they are in the obscurity of the humblest situation—both teach and are taught. For God distributes the gifts of His wisdom to whom He wishes, without regard to titles or persons. It is not the word alone that teaches, but life as a whole. Not to admit any other teaching but that of the logical word is the essence of rationalism. And in this case, rationalism is more apparent in papism than in Protestantism. That is what the patriarchs declared; that is what the Church confirmed.

The question of teaching brings us to that of examination, for teaching presupposes examination, and without examination it is not possible. I trust I have shown that intelligent faith, which is a gift of grace and, at the same time, an act of freedom, is always accompanied and preceded by examination in one form or another; and that Romanism, which appears to condemn examination, actually admits it as much as Protestantism does, which declares its legitimacy.[3]

At the same time, however, I must observe that if, holding to generally accepted definitions, I have admitted the right to examine the data upon which faith and its mysteries are based, I have not had the least intention of justifying the sense that the Western confessions give to the word "examination." Faith is the consequence of a revelation accepted as revelation; faith is belief in an invisible fact manifested by a visible fact. Faith is not a purely logical and rational belief. It is much more than that. It is not an act of reason alone, but an act of all the

---

3. Khomiakov does not consider the Roman Catholic communion "catholic" (i.e., universal), so he refers to it by the somewhat pejorative names *Romanism*, *Romans*, *Latins*, *Latinizers*, etc. — TRANS.

powers of the mind, grasped and subjugated in their most intimate depths by the living truth of the revealed fact. Faith is not only thought or felt; it is thought and felt at the same time. In short, faith is not knowledge alone, but knowledge and life at the same time.

It is evident that, in questions that relate to faith, examination takes on the character of faith and differs totally from what we usually mean by examination. In the first place, the world subject to examination here is not a world external to humanity, but a world of which humanity as a whole, in the totality of its reason and will, is an integral part. Such examination presupposes fundamental data, moral or rational, that the soul cannot doubt; and it is, so to speak, only the intelligent elucidation of these data; for pyrrhonism (if it could seriously exist) would exclude any idea of serious examination just as it excludes any possibility of faith.[4] Once admitted by a soul *completely* pure, the least of these data would give to this soul all the other data by an invincible deduction, though one that may be imperceptible.

For the Orthodox Church, the totality of these data embraces the whole universe, including the phenomenon of human life, and the whole divine Word, whether written or expressed by the *universal and dogmatic tradition*. And any attempt to take any of these data away from a Christian is an absurdity (as in the case of Protestants, who live in an illegitimate tradition, for they have rejected the legitimate tradition) or a blasphemy (as in the case of the Romans, who have withdrawn both the written Word and the Savior's blood from the laity). Examination, because of the multiplicity of data it must examine and because of its goal (not only the logical but the living truth), requires, therefore, the use of all the powers of the mind both in will and in reason, as well as the intimate examination of these powers.

Examination should, so to speak, consider not only the visible universe but also the power and purity of the visual organ. Its point of departure is therefore the most humble acknowledgment of its weakness; for not only a satanical pride but even an unprecedented dementia would characterize all those who would attribute to themselves both moral perfection and the perfection of reason. But that is what they would have to do if they would attribute individual independence to themselves, considering that in this system a mere

---

4. *Pyrrhonism*: radical, or total, skepticism. — TRANS.

shadow of sin already implies the possibility of error, or rather its necessity in the case where people permit themselves excessive confidence in their own powers or in the gifts of grace that have been
personally given to them. Therefore, Truth can exist only where there
is immaculate holiness, that is, in the totality of the universal Church,
which is the manifestation of the Divine Spirit in humanity.

Just as the character of faith defines that of examination, so the character of examination defines that of teaching. All the powers of the
soul are illuminated by faith. All people acquire faith by examination;
all receive it by teaching. Thus, teaching does not address itself to reason alone and does not act by reason; rather, it addresses itself to the
whole mind and acts by the multiplicity of the latter's powers, which
constitute a living unity. Teaching comes not from Scripture alone (as
it does for the Protestants, whom we thank from the bottom of our
hearts for the multiplication of copies of the Bible); nor from oral or
symbolic commentary (the necessity of which we do not deny); nor
from preaching; nor from theological study; nor from acts of charity.
Rather, it comes from all these manifestations combined. One to
whom God has given the gift of the word teaches by the word; one to
whom God has not given the gift of the word teaches through life.

Martyrs, who died proclaiming that they joyously accepted suffering and death for Christ's truth, were truly great teachers. One who
says to another, "I do not know how to convince you, but let us pray
together!" and converts that person by the ardor of prayer is a powerful instrument of teaching. One who by the power of faith and love
cures a sick person and thereby leads back to God souls that have
strayed is the master of these new disciples.

Certainly, Christianity has a logical expression contained in the Creed;
but this is not separate from other manifestations. It also has a logical
teaching, which we call *theology*. But this is only a branch of general
teaching. To isolate it is a great error; to give it exclusive preference is
madness; to see in it a heavenly gift tied to certain functions is a heresy.
That would be to establish a sacrament of rationalism.

The Church does not recognize a teaching Church other than herself in her totality.

2.

Some Remarks by an Orthodox Christian Concerning the Western Communions, on the Occasion of a Letter Published by the Archbishop of Paris[5]

Foreword

Despite often being attacked by publications that serve as the organs of various Christian communions in Europe, Orthodoxy has long kept silent. Last year I felt it my duty to respond to a new attack that a writer of the Roman confession had directed against the Church to which I belong. And so I addressed myself to the Protestant press of Paris, asking it to publish my work entitled "Some Remarks by an Orthodox Christian Concerning the Western Communions, on the Occasion of a Brochure by Mr. Laurentie."

A Parisian bookseller, Mr. Meyrueis, accepted this delicate commission and published my work, prefacing it with a justifying foreword, full of the most noble sentiments. I then wrote another brochure, which was to serve as the continuation of that first work. And one would think that the deep gratitude I feel toward this highly esteemed publisher should have led me to turn to him once again. But my readers will see from the very first pages of the present brochure that I could not follow a path that would have placed Mr. Meyrueis in a false position: between a refusal to publish this brochure that probably would have been painful to him and a consent that could have had dire consequences for him under the present circumstances.

And so I turned to Germany. Traditionally hospitable, Germany even today justly takes pride in the hospitality it accords to human thought regardless of its land of origin. I dared to count on this noble hospitality.

---

5. *Quelques mots par un chrétien orthodoxe sur les communions occidentales, à l'occasion d'un Mandement de Msgr. l'Archevêque de Paris.* This work was first published in Leipzig in 1855. It is a response to a letter of the Archbishop of Paris, Marie-Dominique-Auguste Sibour, in which, at the beginning of the Crimean War, he calls for a "crusade against the Photians" (i.e., the Orthodox). — TRANS.

I speak for what I consider the truth against what I consider error. I speak to human beings, to my brothers and sisters from one Father. And the rude sincerity of my language will not prevent you, my German brothers and sisters, from according it the advantages of publicity. A great man of our blood, the Bohemian Hus, gave his life in Germany for freedom of thought and of religious preaching. Your Luther was more fortunate than his predecessor, and gained this freedom. I know you will not refuse me a right for which our fathers as well as yours fought and suffered.

Ignotus [The Unknown One]

* * *

Guided by God's invincible hand, each epoch in the history of humanity brings with it a grave teaching. It is good and useful to understand the meaning of what is taught. And it is just and reasonable for individuals to communicate to their brothers and sisters what they believe they have understood of this teaching—in order that the knowledge of all be completed by the faint lights of every individual. To our century, just as to previous centuries, Providence does not fail to give its lofty instructions. And the understanding of these instructions is facilitated by the fact that, thanks to more frequent international relations and a more unconstrained distribution of information, the human word keeps close company with historical deeds and immediately discloses—by revelations that are sometimes reflected upon and sometimes involuntary—the motives behind such deeds.

We have just seen a memorable example of this. Whatever the pretexts or political reasons for the struggle shaking Europe at the present time [the Crimean War], even the most superficial observer cannot fail to remark that one of the two enemy camps solely comprises nations belonging to Orthodoxy, while the opposing camp comprises Romans and Protestants grouped around Islam. This division can certainly be attributed to more or less accidental causes, to racial hatreds, to contradictory interests, to calculations of politics, or to some sort of opposition between social principles. And there is no doubt that all these causes have a very great influence on contemporary events, but a religious hatred has certainly poisoned the quarrel.

If the Russians or Greeks had attributed such a motive to the Latinizing nations, this motive would probably have been indignantly denied and the accusation declared slanderous—but, fortunately, denial is impossible in this case.

It is writers of the Roman confession who acknowledge, proclaim, and boast such a motive. They declare it a sufficient reason to call down upon Western arms the blessings of the God of justice and love. Marie-Dominique-Auguste Sibour, the Archbishop of Paris by the grace of the Holy Apostolic Throne, announces to France that "the war France is going to wage against Russia is not a political war at all but a holy war; that this is not a war between state and state, between nation and nation, but solely a war of religion; that all the other reasons put forward by the cabinets are merely pretexts; that the true cause of this war, the sacred cause, the cause agreeable to God, is the necessity of expunging the error of Photius, of repressing, suppressing this error;[6] that this is the acknowledged goal of this crusade, and that this had been the hidden but unacknowledged goal of all the other crusades."

The Archbishop of Paris was not nearly the first to make such an acknowledgment; many writers of the Roman confession have made it before and after him. But Marie-Dominique-Auguste Sibour is bolder, more candid, more explicit than the others. He apparently pities the Greeks, but what can he do for them? They are sectarians of Photius, and so they must suffer since they prevent the triumph of unity. He is a little embarrassed to be a defender of the Turks, but, at bottom, the Turks are only a pretext. Photius's heresy must be expunged. It is necessary to let the Protestants swell the ranks of the Roman army. A hard necessity—but the Photians must be suppressed. Banners blessed by an imam of Algeria for the French troops must be allowed to march to the crusade side by side with banners blessed by the Archbishop himself. It is all very sad, but it is necessary to exterminate the Photians, who are the true, the sole enemies. And the prelate's gentle, charitable soul submits to this cruel duty.

---

6. Photius (c. 810 – c. 895), Patriarch of Constantinople, was the key figure of the so-called Photian schism (one of the crucial events leading to the Great Schism of 1054) and the first theologian to accuse Rome of innovating in the matter of the Filioque. — TRANS.

Such are the words of the Archbishop of Paris or such is their indisputable meaning. This pontifical voice merely enunciated more clearly what others had already hinted at, and this voice encountered many sympathetic echoes. Were there many voices that were raised against his voice in the lands of Roman obedience? If there were, these voices were so rare and so timid that they were lost in the silence and in the general approbation. What this prelate has said is apparently only the expression of a sentiment more or less commonly held in the Roman world and in the Western world in general.

I have no judgment to pronounce on the moral dignity of the Archbishop of Paris: my duty is only to show the important lesson resulting from his letter.

Among the laws that govern the world of the mind, there is one whose severe, divine justice does not admit exceptions. Every undeserved insult, every injustice strikes the perpetrator more painfully than it does the victim. The victim suffers; the perpetrator becomes corrupt. The victim can forgive and often does forgive, but the perpetrator never forgives. The crime implants in the perpetrator's own heart a seed of hate that constantly grows until an inner renewal occurs to purify that person's whole moral being. This law is of great historical importance.

In a previous brochure, I characterized the Western schism, or rather the Western heresy against the dogma of Church unity.[7] I said that, in deciding a question of dogma without consulting with its Eastern brothers and sisters, the West had implicitly declared the inferiority of the East and its helotism in faith and grace. The West thereby cast its Eastern brothers and sisters out of the Church and, in a word, committed a "moral fratricide." By an inevitable consequence the heirs of this crime had to arrive at the desire for *material fratricide*. That is the instruction we find in the letter of the Archbishop of Paris.

I am far from attributing such a powerful animosity to all the members of the Roman confession. I am even farther from attributing such an animosity to the Protestants, whose hate has been replaced by disdain, a less bloodthirsty sentiment, though one that is always hostile

---

7. "Some Remarks by an Orthodox Christian Concerning the Western Communions, on the Occasion of a Brochure by Mr. Laurentie."

and ready to explode into ferocity in the slightest struggle or rivalry with the disdained party. However, I will say that, in the Western confessions, there is at the bottom of every soul a profound hostility against the Eastern Church.

Such is the witness of history; such is the meaning of contemporary writings published by priests of the Latin confession; such is the reason for the silence of Europe, which reads these writings without rebelling against their barbarity; such, finally, is the indisputable result of the general law about which I spoke above. That is why every friend of the truth must examine his heart and extirpate this seed of hatred. Otherwise, the truth will not be given to him. Let him be instructed and frightened by the sight of the monstrous development of this ruinous sentiment in the soul of Marie-Dominique-Auguste Sibour, Archbishop of Paris by the grace of the Holy Apostolic Throne.

Such reflections, if seriously entertained, can undoubtedly have a salutary influence on the political events. But I have no desire to concern myself with political events: such events, however important we may think them to be, have only a relative and temporary significance. The question with which I concern myself is of a far greater importance, for it has to do with the manifestation of absolute truth on Earth and embraces the totality of humanity's spiritual interests. My goal is to explain to people of the West the real character of the Church by revealing to them our view of the errors of the two communions that constitute the Western schism. And so I had to begin by indicating the moral obstacle that hampers the voice of truth from being heard by impartial souls. As long as people have not cast the gall of a hidden hostility out of their hearts, the spiritual eye cannot see, the ear cannot hear, and the mind cannot judge with rightness. It is always worth undertaking a moral effort when its goal is to uproot an unjust sentiment of animosity. And how much more worthy such an effort is when its recompense can be knowledge of divine truth.

However, before approaching the essence of the religious question, I feel obligated to say that, besides the obstacle about which I have just spoken, that is, a hostile disposition of the heart, there is another, equally serious, obstacle that makes it impossible for both Romans and Protestants to understand the Church.

I have said that, from the early times of Christianity until the great Western schism, knowledge of the divine truths had been considered to belong to the totality of the Church united by the spirit of charity and love. This doctrine, preserved to the present, has recently been publicly proclaimed by a unanimous agreement of the patriarchs and all the Christians of the East.[8]

In the ninth century the West, unfaithful to the tradition of the Church, appropriated the right to alter the ecumenical creed without consulting with its Eastern brothers and sisters, and this at the very moment when the latter showed a fraternal deference to the West by submitting to it for its approval the decisions of the Council of Nicaea. What was the inevitable logical consequence of this usurpation? When the logical principle of knowledge expressed in the exposition of the creed was separated from the moral principle of love expressed by the unanimity of the Church, a protestant anarchy was established in practice. Every diocese could appropriate vis-à-vis the Western patriarchate the right that the latter appropriated vis-à-vis the totality of the Church; every parish could appropriate this right vis-à-vis the diocese; every individual could appropriate it vis-à-vis all other individuals.

No sophistry can allow one to avoid this consequence. Either the truth of faith is given to the union of all and to their mutual love in Jesus Christ, or it can be given to every individual without regard to all other individuals. In order to avoid this consequence and the resulting anarchy, it was necessary to replace the moral law that was found to be constraining for the young pride of the Germano-Roman nations by some new law, whether inner or external, which could give an indisputable authority to the decisions of the ecclesiastical society in the West, or which could at least appear to give such authority. This need gradually led to the idea of the infallibility of the pope. In fact, his administrative and judicial supremacy (which, in itself, does not withstand serious criticism) could not, even if it were admitted in its broadest sense, serve to justify a schismatic doctrine or act.

Neither could it be justified by a conditional infallibility (that is, one that requires that a papal decision be in agreement with the totality of the Church), since a new dogmatic decision was introduced

---

8. See the "Synodal Letter of the Eastern Patriarchs," 6 May 1848, published in response to an Encyclical of Pope Pius IX.

in the ecumenical creed without consultation with the Eastern patriarchates, none of which was even informed. So as not to remain schismatic in the eyes of the Church or to justify by its example all the license of Protestantism, Romanism felt it necessary to attribute an absolute infallibility to the Bishop of Rome. That is the inevitable consequence that was, in the end, accepted by a very large number of Latinizers and that should have been accepted by all of them.

This absolute infallibility, however, has never been recognized as an indisputable dogma and is still not recognized as such at the present time.[9] This is a question that the curia of Rome does not yet dare approach. On the other hand, this papal infallibility had been completely ignored in the early Church (even the Latinizers themselves acknowledge this). Papal infallibility was publicly denied by the fathers in the early years of the Church (witness the work of St. Hippolytus and the condemnation pronounced by an ecumenical council against the memory of Honorius for error in dogma). Papal infallibility was not even referred to in the first discussions of the Latins against the Greeks; nor was it mentioned in the later conferences. In the end, papal infallibility is apparently only a conditional principle accepted retrospectively and by necessity—in order to justify an illegal act prior to it.

The Romans therefore have no other support for their schism than a principle whose conditionality they themselves are aware of. On the other hand, taking as its point of departure the opinion that the West used a legitimate right in altering the creed and having lost all memory of the moral interdependence in which the dioceses of the early Church found themselves, but not being able to feel itself subject to the conditional principle, Protestantism arrived at the inevitable conclusion that every country, every diocese, and, finally, every individual has a right equal to that of the Western patriarchate to separate from the totality of the Church and to create a creed or belief of their own liking.

Thus, deprived of the support of tradition and of the moral tutelage of the Church, which for it is no more than an abstraction, Protestantism finds itself reduced to having no other guide than the Bible. The Bible

---

9. The present work was published in 1855. — TRANS.

itself, however, as a very distinguished Protestant writer says, does not have well-defined limits, unlike the objects of God's direct creation in nature.[10] Whatever may be the role of the Divine Spirit in the book of the Holy Scriptures, this is, at least in appearance, a human work. Without the canon, the Bible does not exist. And outside the Church there is no canon. Perhaps a book considered canonical is actually apocryphal, or vice versa. Should a certain work have been admitted? Or would it not have been better to admit another work, contemporaneous to the first? If, by her nature, the Church does not have infallible knowledge of the truth, then every part of the Bible is just as subject to doubt as the Epistles attacked by Luther. And the totality of the Bible then is only a compilation without well-defined boundaries and one whose authority is accepted only because one does not know how to do without it.

On the other hand, the entire belief of the Protestant is based on something purely conditional. But a conditional belief is only a disguised unbelief. Such a belief impresses its character on the human soul, imposes its habits on the soul, and makes the latter incapable of arriving at an understanding of the real faith. Eastern Christians therefore waste their energy when they attack the beliefs of the West as an absolute faith; all their blows miss their mark, directed as they are by an erroneous assumption.

The West, on the one hand, cannot understand the strange severity of the Church; nor can it believe in the sincerity of the Church's representatives who do not wish to content themselves with a conditional belief but require absolute faith, which the West has forgotten, so to speak. Eastern Christians commit the error of assuming that their Western brothers and sisters are truly conscientious in their faith, though the latter never pretend to such conscientiousness. And Western Christians, in turn, see in their Eastern brothers and sisters a lack of conscientiousness of which they are by no means guilty. And it cannot be otherwise. This constitutes the second obstacle of which I've had to speak, an obstacle that makes it almost impossible for both Latins and Protestants to understand the Church. It is not that they fail to understand this or that article of the faith. No! It is the possibility of absolute faith itself that they fail to admit after having been content

---

10. Probably C. K. Bunsen. — TRANS.

for centuries with a conditional belief and having considered this belief as the only really possible one.[11]

In all things the truth's struggle against error is full of difficulties even if its triumph is ultimately assured. But how much more difficult is the struggle when the obstacles to the reception of the truth are found not only in the mind but also in the will and the passions. This is especially true when the Church has to deal with communities that have separated themselves from it. Whatever the hatred and mistrust between the Western confessions, the nations that belong to these faiths are more or less on an equal footing. They form a single family, so to speak. It is their common life that has created the history of Europe; it is their common efforts that have created contemporary civilization.

Finally, with the exception of Italy and Spain, all European nations count among their citizens members of almost all the Western confessions. The passage from one belief to another does not represent anything extraordinary, anything that insults perhaps the two most invincible forms of human pride: race and civilization. Things are completely different as regards the relations of these same nations to the Church. They must receive the truths of faith from a society that their disdain once rejected and that since then has remained alien to their inner life and their development. They must listen as disciples to the voice of a race that is alien to them by blood, and the progress of whose civilization has indisputably been retarded by a historical life full of suffering and unwinnable battles. They must condemn those they consider the glory of their past and much of what forms the pride of their present. For nations this is a very painful sacrifice; for individuals this is an intellectual expatriation. The clearer and more imperious is the voice of the truth, the more stubbornly the rebelling heart will resist the truth's power and the more diligently will the mind, accomplice of the bad passions of the heart, invent subterfuges, sophistries, and even obvious lies in order to avoid the inevitable conviction.

---

11. For a long time, France has been speaking with admiration about what has been called the faith of the coal miner. Why the coal miner, and not the scholar, sage, or apostle? It is because, in the eyes of the Latinizers, only ignorant persons can have indubitable faith—and this is solely because they do not suspect they are living in a conventional belief. This word contains a complete acknowledgment of unbelief.

This is what should be expected by anyone who has studied humanity and the history of the human mind. And this is in fact what we see happening at the present time. Not daring to attack directly any of the dogmatic teachings proclaimed by the Church, not daring to launch a frontal assault against any of the positions advanced by the Church's organs, one invents schisms, about which the Church has no conception, in order to negate her unity. One invents temporal heads, of which the Church is ignorant, in order to negate the Church's spiritual freedom. And this is being done at the very moment when the power of the Church's living communion is being vividly manifested, when the Church is protesting with great energy against the very suspicion of Erastianism.[12]

But however great they may be, the obstacles should not stop the defenders of the truth. The more openly the evil passions that energize the error are manifested, the greater is the duty to expose them, to combat them, and to call people to the unity of love and faith in Jesus Christ. In a previous work, I showed how Romanism was essentially protestant and rationalist in nature, and that Protestantism was illegitimately traditional whenever it wished to pose as a positive doctrine.[13] I tried to give my Western brothers and sisters an understanding of the character of the Church, while explaining to them in what light their doctrines appear to us. I have not yet been refuted, and I am now continuing a task I consider a duty, hoping that a word said sincerely and with love will not remain completely useless.

I have said that, in the Church, infallibility in dogma—that is, knowledge of the truth—is based on the holiness of the mutual love of Christians in Jesus Christ. I have said that such a doctrine makes rationalism impossible, since the light of understanding is made to depend on a moral law. By breaking this connection, the Western schism enthroned rationalism and protestant anarchy. In order to avoid the logical consequences of this error, Romanism had, much later, to invent papal infallibility and hide the anarchy of the principle under the governmental despotism of the fact.

---

12. *Erastianism*: the ascendancy of the State over the Church in ecclesiastical matters, from the Swiss theologian Thomas Erastus (1524–1583). — TRANS.
13. See the brochure against Mr. Laurentie.

From the point of view of the Church, this new phase of error presents the following aspect: Knowledge of the divine truths attributed to the Bishop of Rome does not depend on his moral perfection (witness Borgia and many others). Nor does it depend on a moral law of the Church (for the point of departure of the infallibility attributed to the pope is an act that can only be characterized as *moral fratricide*). Nor does it depend on intellectual superiority: such a superiority has never been claimed for popes. This knowledge therefore has a completely oracular character. And it is said that this knowledge has its origin in the chief of the apostles.

No fact in the Church can be understood except by analogy with similar facts certified by Scripture. In the New Testament, professions of faith present themselves in two forms. First, there are professions of faith that, being voluntary and triumphant, so to speak, are revelations accorded to holiness and love; such are the professions of Simeon, Nathaniel, St. Peter, and, finally, the most complete of all, that of St. Thomas.

Then there are the involuntary professions of faith, a result of fear and hate: these are the professions of the possessed. We do not know any professions of faith that issue from indifference. Apparently, the supposed privilege of the Bishop of Rome does not raise him to the first category (since it is independent of his moral perfection); rather it casts him into the second category. That is, this privilege makes him closer to the possessed than to the apostles. A sad degeneration of humanity this would be if it were true! I am not speaking of the superstitious respect demanded by the Latinizers for the locality or rather for the name of Rome (for outside of this superstition, which has the character of a local fetish, it is impossible to deny that the bishops of Antioch are just as much the successors of St. Peter as those of the imperial city). Rather, I am saying that, in the eyes of the Church, the privilege of being the involuntary instrument of the truth that is attributed to some individual who at the same time is not a successor of the holiness of the apostles, is analogous only to possession by demons.

Protestantism, a more logical development of the very same principle that had occasioned the schism, arrives at different consequences. Broken into an infinite number of divergent communions, which are, themselves, only nominal unities (for each individual often professes a belief that is opposed to those of all the other individuals), Protestantism recognizes its own general unity only in the fact that it admits the Bible and, so to speak, in a certain cult of the Bible. But this unity is based not on the unity of the meaning of the Scriptures (for the explications are contradictory) but on the unity of the very object, the written word, or, in the end, the book, independently of its meaning and of the thought contained therein. The divergence and anarchy are obvious and real; the apparent unity has all the features of fetishism.

Our Western brothers and sisters should not take offense at the harshness of my expressions. They are harsh not by my own choice. I can give an understanding of the character of the spiritual and organic life that belongs only to the Church only by vividly and clearly showing that stamp of death that we see on both forms of the Western schism. That is why I have found it necessary to show the character of the degradation of human beings when forced to be the organ of an infallible faith against their own will, and to indicate the fetishism of a communion whose only unifying principle is respect for a dead letter of indeterminate meaning. In place of a human machine who renders involuntary oracles, put the whole Church, which professes the divine truth, because she is animated by the divine spirit of mutual love. In the place of a fetishized book, put the whole Church, of which the Bible is only the written word, a word that is therefore always understood—and you will have life instead of death, and the loftiest reason instead of the most obvious insanity. In both cases you will again see before you a living organism, for you have recalled the very principle of life: love.

"But are you asserting," the objection will be raised, "that, for so many centuries in the most civilized countries in the world, Christianity has forgotten the love that is its basis and essence? How can this be? Has not any one of the many illustrious individuals who have preached the faith of the Savior, any one of the many lofty and noble minds, of the many ardent and tender souls who have proclaimed to the peoples of the West the word of religion, have not any of these spoken of the mutual love that is the testament of the dying Christ to the brothers and sisters for whom He died? What you are saying is improbable, impossible."

Yes, it is improbable, impossible, but it is true. Orators and sages, inquirers into the Lord's law, and preachers of His doctrine have often spoken of the law of love, but not a single one has spoken of the power of love. The peoples have heard the preaching of love as duty. They have forgotten about love as a divine privilege that guarantees to human beings knowledge of the absolute truth. What the wisdom of the West is ignorant of, the ignorance of the East teaches.

When the conqueror of death, the Savior of humanity, withdrew from humanity His visible presence, He did not leave it sorrows and tears for a legacy, but rather the consoling promise that He will be with it until the end of the world. This promise was fulfilled. The spirit of God descended upon the heads of the disciples united in the unanimity of prayer and returned to them the presence of their Lord—no longer as a presence graspable by the senses but as an invisible presence, no longer as an external presence but as an inner one. From that time their joy was complete despite the trials for which they were destined.

And we, too, have this perfect joy, for we know that the Church no longer seeks Christ as the Protestants do, but possesses Him; and that the Church possesses and receives Him constantly by the inner action of love without demanding an external phantom of Christ, as the Romans do. The invisible head of the Church did not find it necessary to leave the Church His image for the pronouncement of oracles; rather, He animated the whole Church with His love so that she could have in herself the eternal truth.

That is our faith. The Church, even the earthly one, is a thing of heaven. But both the Romans and the Protestants judge the things of heaven in the same way they judge the things of earth. "There will be disunion," the Roman says, "if there is no authority to decide the questions of dogma." "There will be intellectual slavery," says the Protestant, "if every individual must agree with all the others." Are they speaking according to the principles of heaven or according to the principles of earth? This earthly character that is impressed on heavenly things has, from time to time, caused confusion in the souls of certain elect, who have sought (and who can blame them?) to hide from their own eyes the indelible blemish on the communions to which they belonged.

Perhaps no one experienced this feeling as profoundly (if involuntarily) as a man about whom one cannot speak without veneration, one of the most noble celebrities of our century, the eloquent Pastor Vinet. In an article intended to characterize both Catholicism (that is what he calls Romanism) and Protestantism, he derives them from two tendencies of the human spirit. According to Vinet, the first owes its origin to humankind's involuntary and innate desire to obtain ready-made truth, truth that requires nothing further than acknowledgment; and to the pleasure that the human heart finds in feeling itself united to others in feeling and thought.

The second tendency, Protestantism, owes its origin to humankind's equally innate desire to find the truth by the proper powers of its intelligence, and to the perfectly true conviction that a belief consented to is not yet a belief acquired.[14] Here we see a purely terrestrial employment of humanity's rational powers, and we can only admit the justice of this analysis of Roman and Protestant tendencies. Vinet, however, is struck by the idea that the truth is necessarily one, and the inevitable conclusion that Christianity can only be universal, or catholic, presents itself to his thought.

He adds: "The two tendencies are equally true and equally imperfect. Catholics erroneously consider themselves Catholic, for they are Catholic by anticipation before having the right to be so. The Protestant erroneously believes that Protestantism is destined to remain Protestant, but it is only a pathway to the future Catholicism." The goal of Vinet's desires, of his hopes, is evidently the free, intelligent unity of the Church, which he sees being attained in the remoteness of future centuries.

Poor soul led astray by the false system in which he lived! Lofty and elegant mind, prematurely exhausted by the contradictions between its aspirations and its beliefs! This mind's inner suffering is manifested in the discordance of its positions. The future alone consoles Vinet. The past has given him nothing; the present is barren. Catholicism—that is, the accord of people in the truth—will arrive. But does that mean it never existed? Were not the disciples of Christ, who were illuminated by the gifts of the Holy Spirit, a catholic Church? If not, where is the authority of their word and writings? If they *were* a catholic Church, and if the catholicism of this Church has perished, how will humanity find again the light it has lost, the light that it received from the hands of the Lord Himself? How will it keep that light after having found it again? Does science have stronger and

---

14. These are not Vinet's exact expressions, but that is their sense.

more certain guarantees than those that the Divine Spirit can find? No! Either catholicism is not possible in the future, or it could not have perished in the past. But neither Vinet nor any Protestant can admit that. And the most anti-logical conclusion appears to them to be preferable to a logical conclusion that would make them despair of the truth. Their ideas belong wholly to the earth.

The same inner suffering appears among the best of the Latinizers, but in another form. This suffering is manifested among them in a constant struggle between the desire for analysis and the fear that this power will only raze the edifice they are taking such pains to defend against it. The fact is that, among them as well, everything is the result of an earthly calculation. However, Vinet is partly right. If one returns his intended meaning to the words he uses, then one will have the complete truth. Catholicism, or the universality of the known truth, and Protestantism, or the search for the truth—these are, in fact, the elements that always coexist in the Church. The first element belongs to the totality of the Church, the second to its members. We call the Church universal, but we do not call ourselves catholics;[15] this word implies a perfection to which we are far from pretending.

When the Divine Spirit permitted the holy Apostle of the Jews to receive the deserved censure of the Apostle of the Gentiles [Gal. 2:7–15], the Spirit taught us the lofty truth that the loftiest mind, the most heaven-illuminated soul must humble itself before the catholicity of the Church, which is the word of God Himself.[16] Each of us constantly searches for what the Church constantly possesses. Ignorant, we seek to understand; evil, we seek to unite ourselves to the holiness of the Church's inner life. Always imperfect in all things, we tend to this perfection that manifests itself in all the manifestations of the Church, in her writings, which are the Holy Scripture, in her dogmatic

---

15. When this word or the word *Orthodox* is used in speaking of an individual, this is only for economy of expression.

16. In this is manifested the folly of the Irvingites [i.e., the "Catholic Apostolic Church" whose origin is associated with the Scottish minister Edward Irving (1792–1834) — TRANS.]. They await apostles because they do not understand that the Church of the apostles is much higher than each of the apostles. Particular gifts are only a reflection of the general gift. Moreover, it is clear that Irvingism is nothing more than doubt thirsting for miracles.

tradition, in her sacraments, in her prayers, and finally in her decisions, which make themselves heard when there is a falsehood to refute, a doubt to resolve, a truth to proclaim in her bosom, in order to support the stumbling steps of her children. Each of us is of the earth. Only the Church is of heaven.

But people do not find in the Church something that is alien to them. They find *themselves* there, no longer in the frailty of spiritual isolation but in the power of intimate, spiritual union with their brothers and sisters and their Savior. People find themselves there in their perfection, or rather they find what is perfect in them—divine inspiration, which is constantly lost in the gross impurity of each individual existence. This purification operates by the invincible power of the mutual love of Christians in Jesus Christ, for this love is the spirit of God.

"But how," we will be asked, "can the union of Christians give to each of them what none of them has individually?" A grain of sand does not receive a new existence from the pile into which chance has blown it. Such is a person in Protestantism. The brick of a wall does not experience any alteration and does not receive any perfecting from the place to which the mason's trowel has assigned it. Such is a person in Romanism. But a material particle that has been assimilated by a living body receives a new meaning and a new life from the organism of which it has become an integral part. Such is a person in the Church that is the body of Christ, whose organic principle is love. It is clear that people of the West can neither understand love nor participate in it without renouncing the schism that is its negation; for the Latinizer pretends to a unity of the Church where traces of the Christian's freedom no longer remain, and the Protestant holds to a freedom in the case of which the unity of the Church disappears completely.[17]

But we proclaim the Church to be one and free—one without need for an official representative of its unity and free without this freedom being manifested in the disunion of its members. This Church—if I may speak the language of St. Paul—is a scandal for the Judaism of the Latins and madness for the Hellenism of the Protestants [see 1

---

17. One is the Church minus the Christian, whereas the other is the Christian minus the Church.

Cor. 1:23–24]. But for us it is the manifestation of God's infinite wisdom and mercy on Earth.

Clearly, there is an essential difference between the idea of the Church that *considers herself* an organic unity, whose life principle is divine grace and mutual love—and the idea of the Western communions, whose totally conditional unity is, among the Protestants, only the numerical sum of a certain number of individuals with similar tendencies and beliefs, and among the Latins only the collective action of the subjects of a semi-spiritual state. This difference of ideas must necessarily make itself felt in the character of all the manifestations of these unities, whose principles are so completely opposed. As I said in my first brochure, living faith is the characteristic feature of the Church's manifestations. Rationalism, whether dogmatic or utilitarian, will put its stamp on all the doctrines and collective acts of the opposed communions. A study of the facts confirms the logical conclusions that derive from the principles just expounded.

Let us consider prayer, the earth's purest aspiration toward heaven!

Enter a Protestant temple: Is not an individual completely isolated there? Does the individual feel linked to the congregation in any other manner than through music and a conventional rite? Do individuals address themselves to the congregation as to something of which their own personal lives are only a part? Does the limited congregation feel something more vast beyond the walls of the temple, something from which it draws its spiritual life? Does it feel a real communion with a world of loftier and purer intelligences? Does this congregation address itself to this invisible world to ask for its help or at least to ask this world to participate in its prayers. No! Protestants and the Protestant congregation are at pains to avoid this. Does the Savior's intercession not suffice for them? And why should they make an unprofitable expenditure of their prayers? They are evidently right in the utilitarian sense.

When death terminates the days of a Protestant, the afflicted congregation throws the final handfuls of earth on the remains of a person who had been dear to them. But no prayer is heard over the new tomb; no prayer accompanies the farewells of the living to the sister or brother who has just been taken away from them. After all, is it for people to change God's decrees touching upon the eternal destiny of the one whose earthly career has been terminated? Is it for people, through their prayers, to cover the sins that the Savior's blood did not cover? Once again, this is correct in the utilitarian sense. However, Protestants, too, ask their living brothers and sisters to pray for them. But what can these prayers do for those who already have Christ as an intercessor before God? Protestants ask God to forgive the sins of their sisters and brothers and to purify them spiritually. But how can Protestants believe that the prayer that does not have the right or the power to influence the eternal happiness of those whose earthly career has been terminated, has the right or the power to influence the character of the career, and therefore the future destiny, of those who are living? Is not the one clearly as unjust and impossible as the other? But Protestantism has not dared break with all the traditions of the Church; it is caught in a kind of illogical no-man's land—it has made a kind of deal, but this deal deceives no one, for everyone knows that Protestants ask their sisters and brothers to pray for them without having a sincere need of this prayer, while praying for them, in turn, without sincere hope. Protestants are alone in the world and feel alone.

Enter a Roman temple. Do the prayers of each of the Christians present merge into a common prayer? Is the voice of the choir an expression of the thought of all present? No! Individuals are isolated in relation to a prayer they do not understand and to which their minds cannot respond. This entire cult is external to them: they are not integral parts of it. They are only present at it; they do not constitute it. The ecclesiastical government prays in its governmental language. What need is there for its subjects to mix their accents and their thoughts into the government's conversation with the supreme authority? What takes place in Roman temples would have the appearance of a mockery of prayer if it were not part of a system. Since the link of love has been broken and the holiness of love's power has been misunderstood, individuals find themselves in practice, as I have already indicated, outside the Church, though they remain enclosed within its walls by the laws of a wholly earthly organization.

Romanism, however, could not, or has not dared to, reject the constant tradition of the Church from which it was separated. The fact of the communion of the visible and invisible world, or of the communion of the saints, was too important in the tradition to be rejected. This fact was based on faith in the principle of love, which unites earthly life and heavenly life, just as it unites individuals in earthly life. When this principle was misunderstood, it was necessary to find a new explanation. Communion in prayer was manifested in two forms: a prayer of intercession addressed to an invisible world and a prayer for the invisible world addressed to God. Romanism has placed itself as the intermediary power between paradise and purgatory, that is, between two societies, one above it and one below it; it asks for the good offices of the one and renders them to the other. This essentially meant to add a third form of the Church, the waiting Church, to the two acknowledged forms—that is, the militant Church and the triumphant Church. But I leave aside this fact, in itself quite clear and significant, for its importance is not so great that it cannot yield to higher considerations demanding inquiry.

Latinizers—both in the prayers that they address to the saints and in those they say for the dead—nonetheless remain isolated in the eyes of the Church. Simple citizens of a three-level society, Latinizers are not members of a living organism. From those who are more powerful, they ask lofty protection; and they bestow their small protection upon those who are more insignificant, but their poor individuality is not lost in a superior life of which they are a part.

A mean theory of earthly diplomacy extended to the invisible world has thus replaced faith in the organic unity of the Church; and this theory—arbitrary invention of a disguised rationalism—is as contrary to human logic as it is odious to Christian feeling. Why do we need the intercession of the saints when we have a mediator sufficient for the salvation of all the world? Do we really expect to find among inferior beings a more favorable ear and a more loving heart than our Savior's? Can the soul that has received grace despite its sins offer for us something that belongs to it and that would be agreeable to God? No Christian would dare assert such a thing, for even the saintliest persons have nothing of their own except their sins and rebellions. All that we call the virtues of such individuals are nothing but God's grace and the Savior's spirit, and we should address them directly.

All is absurdity in the prayer addressed to the saints in the Latin theory; all is even more evidently absurd in the doctrine of purgatory. Does the soul separated from the body still have prayer, hope, charity? Does this soul love its brothers and sisters? Does it adore its God and its Savior? If this soul has all these gifts, how dare we believe it to be more unhappy than we, when it has all that is truly precious on earth and when it is emancipated from all that constitutes the unhappiness of the earthly humankind, from the activity of sin? That would be the grossest materialism. To say that its punishment consists in feeling its sins would be ignorance; for, illuminated by the Church, we know that repentance is called the triumph or the joy of penitence that is superior to all the joys of earth. Or will we say that the soul, separated from its mortal envelope, has no charity, no prayer, no love for its brothers and sisters and for its God? By that we would say that this soul enters heavenly joy through an external act at the very moment when it is less worthy of entering therein than when it departed life. Having departed from the Church and its wisdom, the schism has lost itself in absurdity. And, to be sure, one has to praise here the Protestant rationalism for exposing a masked rationalism, so illogical in its utilitarian tendency.

Poor Romans! They would not dare to pray for their sisters and brothers if they were sure that those souls had already gotten out of purgatory. The early Church did not know what it was doing when it prayed for the martyrs!

Clearly, despite the good services that an individual supposedly can receive from some and render to others, this individual is just as isolated among the Latinizers as among the Protestants. Whether debtor or patron, the Latinizer is not linked to the invisible Church by organic ties. The transfer of good works or of meritorious acts, a spiritual banking operation added to the intercession of prayer, not only does not change but even accentuates the juridical character of the latter. Despite the supposed external relationships, the inner isolation of Latinizers with respect to the invisible world remains totally evident, and their isolation with respect to their sisters and brothers in the earthly world is even more pronounced than among the Protestants. This is because the use of an unknown language (the diplomatic language necessitated by the constitution of the Church-State) does not allow the individual's thought to merge with the concert of general thought. Individuals are thrown into a desert by Protestantism, whereas they are walled in by Romanism. The individual is solitary in both. Nevertheless, justice compels me to say that the blame in this case, as in all the other cases, lies with the Roman schism: the primitive rationalism of this schism, fruit of a crime committed against the mutual love of Christians, has produced an entire system whose conclusions the Protestants could deny but whose givens they could never reject.

In order to give a better idea of the poverty of prayer in the Western communions, it is necessary to expound the idea of prayer as it is offered by the Church. But in order to make this idea understood, it is necessary to touch upon some loftier considerations.

From the beginning of creation, God has revealed Himself to created beings by a world of manifestations graspable by the mind or the senses. But this partial and external (so to speak) revelation of His goodness, wisdom, and power was incomplete. Inaccessible to change, unapproachable by evil and temptation, God's moral being remained veiled in the radiant depths of His infinity, which the finite mind can neither fathom nor understand. Some of these minds, created free, rebelled against Divinity by a spontaneous act of their freedom, whereas others, placed in an inferior condition, removed themselves from their creator by an act of freedom, but only after being provoked by an external temptation. These latter, less guilty than the former, received a promise of redemption and forgiveness.

In the course of the ages, at a time determined by His wisdom, God revealed Himself anew to His creature in the Son of Man, and this revelation was much more complete than the first one. What the immensity of creation could not reveal, what remained veiled in the splendors of the firmament, was revealed within the narrow limits of human nature. The divine word revealed itself as a moral being, as the moral being par excellence, as the unique moral being. Evil tried to attack Him but found Him inaccessible. An attempt was made to tempt Him but it failed. The only righteous and pure one, He took upon Himself, because of His love for the sinner, the burden, the shame, and the punishment of the sin that He detested. Tested by pain, humiliation, and death, He accepted pain, humiliation, and death for the sake of the guilty ones who misunderstood Him, for the sake of the men of blood who killed Him, for the sake of the cowardly ones who rejected Him. Master of all creation and worthy of divine glory, He submitted to everything, to the point of feeling Himself abandoned by God Himself—rather than abandon humankind, His brothers and sisters, to the misfortune that they deserved [see Matt. 27:46].

Eternal compassion of God for His creature, expiatory victim, sacrificed once in time but constantly offered in eternity for the sins of the world—He extinguished by his blood the flames of divine justice (making it unjust, so to speak) so that the divine mercy could be all-powerful. Thus, it is in Him and in Him alone that the bliss of fallen intelligences is acquired; and it is in Him that the bliss of unfallen intelligences is justified and completed, for they did not experience temptation. And we know that He is the beloved of His Father because of His ineffable love and His voluntary sacrifice, and all holiness, all perfection, and all glory belong to Him for ages of ages [see John 10:17–18].

In His justice and mercy God permitted that, just as Christ the unique moral being took upon Himself, by virtue of His limitless love, the sins of human beings and their just punishment, so, by virtue of their faith and love for their Savior, human beings could renounce their own individuality—a guilty and evil individuality—and clothe themselves in the holiness and perfection of their Savior. Human beings thus united with Christ are no longer what they were—isolated individuals. They have become members of the Church, which is the body of Christ, and their lives have become integral parts of the superior life and freely submit to this superior life.

The Savior lives in His Church; He lives in us. He intercedes and we pray. He entrusts us to the divine favor, while we mutually entrust one another to our creator. He offers Himself in eternal sacrifice, while we present to the Father this sacrifice of glorification, gratitude, and propitiation for ourselves and for all our sisters and brothers, whether they are still engaged in the dangers of the earthly struggle, or whether death has made them pass into the calm, ascensional movement of heavenly beatitude, whatever be the degree of glory that has been granted them.[18] No question, no doubt accompanies our

---

18. There is ignorance and revelation and therefore an ascensional movement even in the heavenly glory: This was related to us by the Savior Himself (in the speech on the end of the world) [see Matt. 24:36; Mark 13:32] and by the Spirit of truth (in the Epistle of St. Paul to the Ephesians) [see Eph. 3:10]. And according to the testimony of Mark of Ephesus before the assembly of Florence, the Church never doubted this. [The site of Mark of Ephesus' polemic against purgatory, to which Khomiakov refers, was actually Ferrara. The Council of Florence met successively at Ferrara (1438–1439), Florence 1439–1443), and Rome (1443–1445). — TRANS.]

prayer, for as the Russian catechism says: "We pray not in a spirit of fear like slaves, not in a spirit of greed like mercenaries, but in a spirit of filial love, being adoptive children of God by our union with the Son of Man, Jesus the righteous, Son and eternal Word of the Father of mercies." We pray because we cannot fail to pray. And this prayer of all for each and each for all, constantly requested and constantly given, suppliant and triumphant at the same time, always addressed in the name of Christ our Savior to His Father and God—this prayer can be called the blood that circulates in the body of the Church. This prayer is the Church's life and an expression of this life. It is the voice of the Church's love, the eternal breath of the Divine Spirit.

Where is doubt now? Where is isolation? Where is the incredulous timidity of the Protestant? Where is the fable of juridical relationships invented by the Roman? Is it for us to descend from the contemplative heights to which the Church has raised us into the lowlands of rationalism and its utilitarian doctrines fabricated by the schism? Will our Western brothers and sisters dare to summon us there? No! They will not. Perhaps they would even stop us if we fell into such madness. They would feel that if we abandoned the king of the Church, we would disinherit all of humanity of its most glorious hope, and that we would take away from it forever the very possibility of faith.

This holy doctrine, which alone is true, which alone is unassailable by the most severe logic, which, moreover, is far superior to human logic, which alone completely satisfies the most vital feelings of the heart (for it is more vast than the heart's boldest aspirations)—this doctrine has always been the doctrine of the Church. It remains so in our time; and it has been such since the time of the apostles. This doctrine was the legacy of the apostles' disciples in the West as well as in the East, which is clearly demonstrated by the oldest liturgies and especially the Mozarabic liturgy (which was altered later but, of course, not in this sense).[19] At present, however, this doctrine is completely foreign for all the Western faiths, and forms one of the characteristic

---

19. The Mozarabic rite is the conventional name for the liturgical forms that were in use in the Iberian Peninsula from the earliest times until the eleventh century. Its replacement by the Roman rite was a result of the Christian reconquest of Spain. There was resistance to its abolition in Toledo, and here it was allowed to remain in use in six parishes. — TRANS.

features of the Church, which has already been observed by certain Protestant writers.[20]

Why has the West lost this divine tradition? The answer is quite clear. Germanic Protestantism could not reconstruct this tradition, because it could never and can never build anything, because it could only reject and destroy, because it consists entirely of critique in thought and isolation in spiritual life. The older form of Protestantism—that is, Romanism, could not preserve this tradition, because this tradition is the most complete development of unity based on mutual love, whereas Romanism has, from its origin, been the negation of this principle, a heresy against the living unity of the Church. That is why the West has failed to inherit the spiritual communion of prayer. That is why the West had to replace the sublime doctrine of organic unity in Jesus Christ with a meager and absurd system of patronage and clientage, and put utilitarianism in the place of love and association in the place of brotherhood. Human beings were isolated within the narrow bounds of individuality; they turned out to be separated from their sisters and brothers.

Furthermore, they turned out to be separated from God Himself. An eternal process, an eternal discussion of contradictory rights before the spiritual jurisconsults of papal Rome—those are the relations that have replaced the intimate union that Christ's coming had established between the Creator and His creature. Armed with a double-entry accounting book, where the sin is the debit and good works (supported, it is true, by the Savior's sacrifice) are the credit, humankind pleads against God and finds a favorable judge in the Roman casuist. And there is no way this human case can be lost. Provided human beings are citizens of the ecclesiastical state and obedient servants of their chiefs, they will become shareholders in paradise for a relatively moderate contribution of good works and good thoughts. The surplus, if there is any, can be converted for them into a small liquid capital, which they can dispose of as they wish. And the deficit, if there is any, can be covered by borrowing from richer capitalists. As long as there is a balance, God won't mind.

---

20. Here, Khomiakov refers in a footnote, rather imprecisely, to a work from which he drew most of his liturgical information: J. M. Neale, *A History of the Holy Eastern Church*, Part I, *General Introduction*, Vol. I, II, London, 1850. — TRANS.

May I be forgiven the harshness of my irony, for I remain within the limits of the severest truth, and what children of the Church can silence their indignation when they see the apostolic doctrine so completely distorted, so profoundly debased? What, in fact, has Christianity become? Where is the God who gives Himself entirely to humanity? Where are those who can give nothing from themselves except consent to God's bounty. And after this, disbelievers are judged harshly!

Protestantism does not deserve such grave reproaches. Nevertheless, having involuntarily inherited Roman doctrines while rejecting the deductions that result from these doctrines, Protestantism could not escape the juridical character that these doctrines had imposed on religion. Protestantism appears not to admit any human merits, which, for the Romans, constitute humanity's rights before God. In essence, however, Protestantism only tightens the circle and attributes to faith alone what the Latinizer attributes to faith and works. In the eyes of the Protestant, faith is the sole merit, but it is still a merit.

The question of utility is always present in the Protestant's thought: the trial between God and humanity continues. Humanity's advocates are by no means in agreement about what serves as the basis of its justification. The Romans, ignorantly relying on a text where St. James speaks of the works of faith [James 2:14–26], require works of law. The Protestants, relying on St. Paul, whom they do not understand, assert the uselessness of works of faith (although this Apostle is clearly speaking of the works of law). But it is always a question of the utility or uselessness—that is, the juridical merit—of faith and works, and of the justifying documentation that human beings can present in their trial against their Creator.

It is thus that the negation of human fraternity inevitably entails forgetting the divine paternity, and that these words so full of joy and triumph for the Church are no longer preserved in the Western confessions, except as traditional signs whose meaning has been lost. Certainly, the criminal pride that, breaking the unity of the Church, appropriated for itself the monopoly of the Holy Spirit and tried to reduce to the status of serfs all the Churches of the East, could not predict where it would end up itself. But that is the divine law. The perversity of the heart blinds the mind, and the violation of the first of the evangelical commandments could not remain unpunished.

It is sufficient for me to show how the difference of principles that separates the Church from the schismatic confessions manifests itself in prayer, and how this sublime expression of the organic unity of our Savior and His elect has taken on in the West a character of isolation and juridical rationalism. But before I move on, I must comment on the dispute between Romans and Protestants that raged for such a long time and that only now seems to have abated: the dispute concerning salvation by faith alone or by faith and works.

The Church has never been agitated and could never have been agitated by this dispute, whose absurdity is obvious under the illumination of the apostolic tradition. Indeed, faith is not an act of perception alone but an act of the whole mind, that is, of perception and volition in their intimate union. Faith—life and truth at the same time (as I've already pointed out in my first brochure)—is the act by which human beings condemn their own imperfect, evil individualities, and aspire to unite themselves with the moral being par excellence, with Jesus, the righteous one, with the man-God. Faith is an essentially moral principle, but a moral principle that does not tend to manifest itself betrays its own impotence, or rather its nullity. Manifestation of faith is works, for a slight sigh of prayer at the bottom of a contrite heart is as much a work as martyrdom. And these works differ only in the time and circumstances in which God permits a person to profit from the gifts of grace.

What work could the thief have accomplished on his cross? Or was his work, penitence and profession, insufficient? Or is God a God of exceptions? Therefore, to maintain with the Protestants that human beings are saved by faith independently of works is to advance an absurdity; for it is to maintain that they could have been saved by a principle clearly marked by nullity and impotence. To maintain with the Romans that people are saved by faith and works is to advance a meaningless proposition; for it is to maintain that the principle of salvation must not only be strong and powerful but also have the characteristics of power and strength, as if the one does not imply the other.

The absurdity of the Protestant consists in reducing the principle to the state of pure abstraction; the absurdity of the Roman consists in adding together the principle and its symptoms. Both of them, after having isolated human beings from one another and separated them from their God, have also found a means to sunder human beings themselves into two parts in their integral life, and to detach intelligence from the action that is its expression—that is, from its word in the broadest sense. Their philosophical error depends on the false direction (more or less obvious) of their religious thought.

The highly litigious question: By what means can human beings merit salvation? is always hidden at the bottom of their souls and replaces the Christian question, How does God effect human salvation? For us this error is impossible, as I've just said. We know that faith is alive—that is, effective—and that, if it is not manifested in works (a manifestation that is not always perceivable by human eyes), it will no longer be faith but a mere belief, logical knowledge, or, as St. James says [James 2:26], a cadaver.

Having thus made known the error of the schism in its two forms, we feel that it is fair to remark that this error is much more intense among the Romans than among their adversaries. Protestants, though generally being carried away to the point where they equate faith with intellectual understanding, often see the falsity of this doctrine and return to the idea of living faith. Romans, incorrigible legalists, can never refrain from attributing to works a power and action more or less independent of faith and (if I may be permitted to say so) from seeing in works a quantity that can be added to that of faith in the accounts between God and His creature.

The facts thus demonstrate that, in destroying the organic unity of the earthly Church and the moral law of mutual love, which is the sole basis of this unity, the Western schism also destroyed the organic unity of the invisible Church, isolated people from one another, from their Savior, and from their God, and nullified the true communion of common prayer. The moral crime that (as I've shown in my first brochure) deprived the Church of its sole rational basis also distorted the entire spiritual essence of Christianity. In fact, what we saw when we considered prayer, the loftiest aspiration of earth toward heaven, we see once again when we consider the sacraments, the most palpable form of divine grace granted by heaven to earth.

In the first place, one cannot fail to remark that Germanic Protestantism, while wishing to admit only two sacraments [Baptism and Eucharist], constantly attempts in its various sects to reintroduce—in a more or less disguised form—the sacraments that it has rejected. Thus, it sometimes retains confirmation, sometimes requires or advises confession, sometimes seeks to give a sacramental character to its ordination. In order to explain this fact it is necessary to understand the Church sacraments and Protestantism's attitude toward apostolic Christianity.

The sacraments can be divided into two categories. One is directly and immediately related to the Church in its totality; the other relates to the economy of the Church in its earthly appearance. It is evident that, in denying the traditional or earthly Church, the Protestant could not fail to reject the sacraments that directly belonged to the traditional Church; for the laws of logic are rigorous, and individuals, without wishing it or suspecting it, submit to all the consequences of the givens that they have admitted. On the other hand, however, the desire to give some consistency to the new Church they wish to establish, and the importunate remembrance of the apostolic traditions, compel Protestants to make impotent attempts to reestablish what they have destroyed. One is as involuntary and inevitable as the other.

The Church receiving and uniting to Christ those who consent to their own salvation by the Savior's voluntary sacrifice—that is the meaning of baptism.[21]

This apostolic doctrine has been preserved with more or less clarity even amid the errors of the schism, which does not, however, understand all the significance of this doctrine. Protestantism—which denies and rejects the Church herself and does not believe itself united to the Savior except by means of the written word—is greatly embarrassed by a material, palpable fact that, in itself alone, constitutes an entire living tradition; and it is compelled to attribute solely a talismanic power to the sacramental act.[22] On the other hand, considering baptism to be an act of naturalization in a semi-spiritual society, Romanism places virtually no value on individual freedom and is often not far from imposing by coercion an act that, in itself, is the most complete triumph of human freedom. However, these divergences are not great enough for me to give them detailed consideration. I offer

---

21. One cannot baptize oneself. One must be received and introduced into the sphere of the elect by someone else—in order that one know and acknowledge one's own powerlessness. The pride of the Quaker is condemned by the humility of the Christian. Baptism contains the whole Church, the whole of tradition.

22. All religions that, in their doctrine, lose themselves in abstraction, lose themselves, in their material aspect, in fetishism and magic. All error ends in suicide. Buddhism is an example.

these observations only in passing, though their truth appears incontestable to me.

The Church uniting all its members in a bodily communion with its Savior—that is the meaning of the Eucharist. And here the character of the schism appears to be exposed completely. Protestantism reduces the Eucharist to a mere commemoration accompanied by a dramatic act. And this commemoration, which evidently does not differ from any other commemoration, must, according to the Protestants, bestow upon those who participate in it gifts of grace that are totally indeterminate. The whole fogginess of Germanic Protestantism is clearly exemplified in this doctrine, which appears to have a meaning, but which actually does not have any.[23] Romanism, on the other hand, by insisting on the foundation of the sacrament, that is, on the conversion of earthly elements into a heavenly body, understands the spiritual act in a purely material sense, according to its usual habit, and debases the sacrament to nothing more than an atomistic miracle.[24]

The blind vanity of scholastic ignorance was never more nakedly exposed than in the polemic between the Romans and the Protestants concerning the sacrament of the Eucharist. Never were the laws of the material world—or rather our meager knowledge of these laws or of their manifestations—applied so blasphemously as a measure of the action of God's power. The Romans reason about the physical substance of the sacrament, distinguishing it from its accidents, as if (thanks to the explanations of Peter Lombard or Thomas Aquinas) they understood the difference between the two. Protestants deny the possibility of the presence of the body of our Savior in the sacrament, for, according to the testimony of the holy apostles, this body is present in heavenly glory at the right hand of the Father, as if they understood what heaven, glory, and the right hand of the Father mean. Never has the word of faith been heard on either side. Never has the

---

23. In fact, why does the paschal lamb have to be replaced by another symbol whose meaning is basically the same? Is there not an equation between the two symbols?

24. This tendency is so pronounced that when a very pious though not very learned priest once heard me translate the arguments of several Roman theologians in their polemic against the Protestants, he cried with a holy horror: "In the name of Heaven, what are they saying? They seem to be taking the body of Christ to mean the meat of Christ?"

living light of tradition cast a ray into the sad obscurity of these scholastic discussions.

O mad pride of human ignorance and just punishment of the injury done to the unity of the Church! This dispute has abated in our century, as have all the other theological disputes, for the reason I've already mentioned. But the question has not been resolved, and the two branches of the schism remain as before, in the rut into which they have been pushed by their general tendencies: the one materializes the divine act to the point of removing all living principle from it, whereas the other spiritualizes or, rather, vaporizes the sacramental act to the point of removing all real content from it. One affirms while the other denies the miraculous alteration of certain earthly elements, without ever understanding that the principal element of all sacraments is the Church, and that it is for the Church alone that sacrament operates, without any relation to the laws of earthly matter. The realities of faith have been forgotten by those who have become oblivious to the power of love, who have neglected the duty of love.

The traditional Church doctrine of the Eucharist has never changed. This doctrine has retained great simplicity and admirable depth.

It was time: The Son of Man entered Jerusalem for His death on the cross. But before dying, He ardently desired to eat the Passover meal one last time with His disciples, for He loved them with an infinite love. Moses had instituted the Passover meal for wandering humanity, which was to be eaten standing, shoes on feet, staff in hand [Ex. 12:11]. But now humanity's pilgrimage is over; the disciples put down their staffs; the hospitable Master who presides at the feast washes their feet, fatigued and dirtied by the road. Let them recline at the table! Let them rest! The meal begins. The Master speaks to them of His imminent agony. Not wishing to believe it, but full of an indefinite sadness, they feel, as people do, more vividly than ever how dear is the One they are about to lose. At this moment their human love responds to His divine love. And when the meal ends, the Righteous One wishes to crown their love and his own last meal by the institution of the real Passover. After having shared the last farewell cup, He broke the bread and gave them wine, saying unto them that this was His body and His blood. And accepting with a humble joy the new Passover, the testament of its Savior, the Church has never doubted the reality of this bodily communion that He instituted.

Also, the Church never inquired into the relationship between the body of our Lord and the earthly elements of the Eucharist; for the Church knows that the divine action in the sacraments does not stop with the elements but makes them the intermediaries between Christ and His Church, whose faith (I am speaking of the whole Church and not of individuals) actualizes the sacrament. Evidently, neither the Romans nor the Protestants can understand this, for they have lost the idea of the totality of the Church and see in the Church only individuals, who do not become less isolated for being scattered or agglomerated. From this come their error and their doubts, as well as the scholastic requirements of their catechisms. From this also comes their rejection of the prayer by which the Church has, from early times, consecrated the earthly elements, making them the Savior's body and blood.

But do people know what the body is in relation to the mind? Ignorant and blind, but proud in their ignorance and blindness, as if they have the power of knowing and seeing, do they think that, because they are slaves of their flesh, Christ is also a slave of material elements? He to Whom His Father gave all, He Who is master of all, is He not master of His body? And can He not make anything, without any change of physical substance, become this body, the body that suffered and bled for us on the cross (although He could have freed Himself from the laws of matter, as He showed on Tabor)? Finally, is the body for the triumphant Christ anything but His manifestation? Also, the joyous and grateful Church knows that her Savior has given her not only the communion of the Spirit but also the communion of manifestation. And through a material act, a flesh-enslaved person assimilates matter, in which Christ clothes Himself by virtue of a spiritual act.[25] O profundity of divine love and of infinite mercy! O heavenly glory that is granted to us even in enslavement to the earth! Such is the doctrine of the Church since her origin.

Those who see in the Eucharist only a commemoration, and those who insist on the word *transubstantiation*, or replace it with *consubstantiation*—that is, those who vaporize the sacrament and those who make of it an entirely material miracle—dishonor the Last Supper by

---

25. See in the Orthodox ritual the Easter chant that the priests repeat after communion: "O sublime and holy Pascha ..." etc.

approaching it with questions of atomistic chemistry.[26] Meanwhile, they also dishonor Christ Himself by a tacit supposition that matter is in some way independent of our Savior's will. Both misunderstand the relationship between Christ and the Church.

The same error, the same tendencies to materialization or abstraction, the same absence of real life, can be found in other forms in the Western communions' doctrine of the sacraments that have a direct relation to the economy of the visible Church, whether they admit or reject their sacramental character. Protestantism, as I have already said, being more frank and more consistent, had to refuse them this character; whereas Romanism (Protestantism disguised and marked by a utilitarian rationalism) distorted the sacraments, while thinking it was preserving them.

From apostolic times we see the laying on of hands following baptism. The Church has faithfully preserved the apostolic tradition in the form of chrismation.[27] Romanism has given it the name *confirmation*. Several Protestant sects have preserved it without calling it a sacrament. These sects have reduced it to a mere examination, a school ceremony accompanied with white robes, flowers, and music. Such is Protestant confirmation. It has no real meaning, for it is not possible to see in it an act by which the baptism conferred upon the child is accepted by the young reason of the adult. Any other religious act prior to confirmation would have the same significance. Good sense can see here only a sort of examination taken by a young person before the Protestant community, and thus cannot attach to it any religious meaning.

The Protestant error, however, was involuntary and only a logical conclusion drawn from Roman antecedents. Indeed, what does the word *confirmation* mean? Does it mean the confirmation of baptism? Isn't baptism strong enough? Is it incomplete? To admit such a blasphemous supposition would be to expel confirmation from the number of sacraments, but that is the conclusion that flows most naturally from the Roman practice.

---

26. The Church does not reject, it is true, the word *transubstantiation*, but it places it in the rank of several other indeterminate expressions that do nothing more than indicate a general change, without any scholastic definitions. The liturgy does not know this term.

27. Anointment with chrism (consecrated oil), signifying confirmation in the Eastern Church. — TRANS.

Apostolic history shows that the laying on of hands followed baptism and was often accompanied by visible gifts of the Holy Spirit. But was that always the case? No! I am speaking of visible gifts, and I cite as my witness the great Apostle of the Gentiles, who evidently does not consider that the visible gifts of grace necessarily belong to all Christians [1 Cor. 12:4–14, 40]. On the other hand, have there been examples of the bestowal of the visible gifts of the Holy Spirit at baptism before the laying on of hands? There *have* been, as witnessed by the eunuch baptized by St. Philip.

Thus, the laying on of hands did not have as its purpose the sanctification of the faithful by the visible or invisible gifts of the Holy Spirit. It has a different significance. A comparison of cases where the laying on of hands is mentioned in the Holy Scriptures shows that it is always accompanied by a transmission of powers, a new commission imposed on a member of the Church, or the elevation to a superior grade in the ecclesiastical hierarchy. The right of laying on of hands in the sacramental sense did not belong to the faithful in general. It did not even belong to the preachers of the faith, regardless of their personal saintliness (see the Acts of the Apostles). In the early Church it belonged only to the apostles, whereas later on it belongs only to bishops. The meaning of this right is thus clear. Those admitted into the Church by baptism, but still isolated on earth, were admitted into the community of the earthly Church and received their ecclesiastical grade by the laying on of hands. Once the meaning of the sacrament is understood, it is easy to understand that the power to bestow this sacrament should be strictly reserved to the heads of the earthly community, apostles or bishops, and that the visible gifts of the Holy Spirit accompanied the laying on of hands in order to glorify not those who received it, but the holy community into which they had just been admitted.

By introducing us into the bosom of the community, or of the earthly Church, confirmation makes us participants in the benediction of Pentecost; for this benediction was bestowed not upon the individuals present at the miracle but upon their assembly.[28] Therefore, we see that

---

28. In fact, the disciples received neither the gift of miracles (they already had that gift) nor the gift of prophecy. Nor did they receive any other individual gift. What they received was the gift of tongues, a preeminently social and symbolic gift for a community destined to embrace the universe. By no means do I claim that the other gifts were excluded. What I am saying is that this is the only gift that was manifested.

the apostolic laying on of hands (the holy chrismation of the Church) testifies against the Protestant by showing us the importance of the earthly Church in God's plans and the concentration of the ecclesiastical community in individuals of episcopal rank.[29] And it testifies against the Roman by tearing down the wall of separation that Rome has raised between clerics and laity, for we are all priests of the Most High, though to different degrees [priests but not pastors]. But we also see why neither the Roman, who sunders the Church, nor the Protestant, who denies it, can understand this sacrament, why one replaces it with an empty ceremony and the other with an absurdity.

"You have not chosen me, but I have chosen you" (John 15:16), our Savior told His disciples. And the spirit of God said with the lips of the Apostle: "The less is blessed of the better" (Heb. 7:7). Such has always been the doctrine of the Church as regards her organization. The Church does not ascend from imperfection to perfection. No! Her point of departure is perfection and omnipotence, which raise imperfection and weakness to themselves. The opposite course could never be allowed; such a course would have been condemned by the word of God. That is why the fullness of ecclesiastical rights bestowed by Christ upon His apostles has always been found on the summit of the hierarchy, which blesses the lower grades and faithfully observes the law revealed at the establishment of the Church. Such is the meaning of the episcopal order; such is its immense importance.

Germanic Protestantism must necessarily have misunderstood this order at the very moment when it rebelled against tradition, and in our own century we see the savants of Protestantism exhaust themselves in fruitless efforts to find in the organization of the early Church something that could justify the disorganization of their communities. From time to time these savants believe that they have made a marvelous conquest, as when they discovered that local churches without bishops existed after the age of the apostles. But what do they gain from this? Nothing but the poor advantage of knowing that the word *bishop* was perhaps not generally used. In philology this is a meager discovery; in ecclesiastical history, it is nothing.

---

29. The holy chrism is always consecrated by bishops.

Even if the name *bishop* was unknown in certain communities, is it less true that these communities were headed by men (whether elders or presbyters) empowered with a fullness of ecclesiastical rights that the rest of the faithful did not have? Is it less true that these men were invested with their functions by other, equally empowered men and not by the community, which had a voice in the election, but not the decisive one? Is it less true that the superior functions were neither conferred nor confirmed solely by men empowered with inferior functions, although the fraternal concourse of the prayers of all was required at the moment of ordination?

There could temporarily have existed communities where the medium grade (that of priests) was missing, but there could not have existed a community where the superior grade (that of bishops) was missing, even if it existed under a different name. It is impossible to abolish the episcopate, for it represents the fullness of ecclesiastical rights united in an individual. The only thing that can be done is to transpose the episcopate, either by bestowing it upon all priests or, which is more logical, by bestowing it upon all the faithful, both male and female. To reestablish the episcopate by a consecration from below—from individuals without the fullness of ecclesiastical rights— is to violate directly the clearest precepts of the New Testament and to invert completely the order established by Christ and His Apostles; for the bishop and priest are not functionaries of a local community. Rather, they are functionaries of Christ in the general community, and it is through them that the earthly Church attaches herself to her divine founder over the course of the centuries. It is through them that the Church is constantly raised to the One who laid His hands on the apostles.

Election, or presentation, can belong to the community; confirmation and benediction (for that is the meaning of ordination) belong only to those who themselves have received this benediction, which crowns all the others, in order that the Church not find herself unfaithful to the apostolic precept, and in order that all the inferior functions draw their source and their sanctification from the superior function. Such is the doctrine of the Church in relation to the episcopal order, of which the other clerical orders are only a consequence. That is why the Church accepts the decisions of the bishops in matters of discipline, bestows upon them the right and honor to declare its dogmatic decisions, while reserving for herself the right to judge whether they have been faithful organs of her faith and tradition.[30] And, more particularly, she imposes upon them the service of the divine Word and the duty of teaching it.[31] She does not, however, deprive any of her members of this sublime privilege, which has been bestowed by the spirit of God to all Christians. Clearly, all these rights relate to hierarchical functions and have no connection with the inner life of the individuals who are empowered with them. The Church that considers the perfection of faith a duty of all Christians (who are deprived of it only by sin) can see only an unparalleled absurdity in a bishop's claim to be infallible in faith. That would be the same as a bishop's claiming, in virtue of his functions, to be perfect in Christian love. What is a moral duty for all cannot be the privilege of anyone.[32]

Protestantism has been unfaithful to the order established by the Divine Spirit. It has bestowed upon the inferior the right to bless its superior. But, in this case as in all the others, the principle and example have been provided for it by Romanism. All bishops are equal despite any differences in the size or importance of their dioceses. Their jurisdictions and their honorific distinctions vary (as indicated by the titles Metropolitan or Patriarch), but their ecclesiastical rights are always the same. That is not the case as regards relations between bishops and the pope. The supposed privilege of infallibility is not an honorific distinction; it is not an extension of jurisdiction; in short, it is not a conditional thing. It constitutes a difference that is essential and sacramental.

The name *bishop* is just as inapplicable to the pope as the name *priest* is inapplicable to a bishop. And when bishops consecrate a pope, their action is as illegitimate as would be the action of priests who would attempt to consecrate a bishop, or that of lay people who would attempt to consecrate a priest. Inferiors bless a superior. The order of the Church is inverted, and the Protestants are completely

---

30. That is the meaning of the whole history of the ecumenical councils, and that is the doctrine clearly expressed by the Eastern patriarchs.

31. See the discussion of teaching in my first brochure, against Mr. Laurentie.

32. If instead of faith we suppose that this bishop pretended only to perfection of logical knowledge of things of the visible world, we would admit the sacrament of rationalism; in other words, the absurd supposition of a sacrament that would confer upon an individual a power that is not alien to demons. (See the Epistle of James.)

justified. Such is the nature of all error: it bears within itself the seed of suicide. Life and logical consistency belong only to the truth.

"But from the beginning of the creation God made them male and female" (Mark 10:6), says our Savior. These divine words reveal all the holiness of marriage, whose mysterious meaning was later indicated by the spirit of God in the writings of the Apostle of the Gentiles [see Eph. 5:24–32]. Holy and perfect laws were given to the earthly life of humanity, whose prototype was given in the first human couple. "Male and female." The type of this earthly path of all of humanity, of this holy and perfect law, is renewed by every Christian couple in the sacrament of marriage. For the male, his companion is not *a* female, but *the* female. For the female, her husband is not *a* male, but *the* male. For both of them, the rest of the human race has no sex. Attached by noble ties of spiritual community to all beings similar to them, the Christian wife and husband, Eve and Adam of all epochs, are alone united by the sweet, blessed tie of the physical and moral law that was given as the basis of the earthly life of the human race. That was why the first manifestation of the divine Christ was the blessing of the conjugal union at Cana, just as God's first act for the human race was the creation of the first couple.

Thus, marriage is not a contract; it is not a legal obligation, not legal servitude. Rather, it is a renewal of a type established by divine law; it is an organic and therefore mutual union. That has always been the meaning of marriage in the eyes of the Church, which has recognized it as a sacrament and mystery. This meaning has been certified by the apostolic rules and all the rules of the first centuries of Christianity, which forbade new converts from dissolving a union contracted before baptism. Into what have Protestants transformed marriage by allowing divorce? A legal fornication. Into what have Romans transformed marriage by proclaiming its indissolubility even in the case of adultery? A civil servitude. The idea of an organic, mutual union—the inner holiness of the conjugal state—has disappeared for both Protestants and Romans. For adultery is the death of marriage in the Christian sense, just as divorce is legalized adultery.

The holy union instituted by the Creator could not be sinlessly dissolved by human will. But the sin of adultery dissolves it, for this sin is the direct negation of marriage. The male who has become just *a* male for his wife, and the female who has become just *a* female for her husband, are no longer and can no longer be wife and husband in the eyes of the Church. We see that the Church alone is the repository of the truth in this case as in all cases. We also see that the schism, ignorant of spiritual things, has also misunderstood the earthly forms of human existence. All is held together, interlinked, in the divine law: the magnificent holiness of voluntary virginity, the joyous holiness of the conjugal relation, the austere holiness of widowhood. But the error of the schism has demolished all this with a single blow. Human life has lost its crown of beauty.

To show in detail the errors and inconsistencies of the schism, or Western protestantism in its two forms, Germanic and Roman, would be to impose upon oneself a sad and boring task. But I found it necessary to corroborate by an analysis of the facts the consequences of the principles I have advanced. And one sees that this analysis confirms these principles with a striking testimony. For both the Roman and the Protestant, prayer has lost its sublime meaning and people have been isolated from one another and from God by a utilitarian rationalism. For both the Roman and the Protestant, the sacraments have lost their profound and mysterious meaning. Sadly vaporized by the one, as it were, and desiccated and materialized by the other, the Eucharist, this divine joy of the Church, this bodily communion of Christians and their Savior, is now nothing more than a scholastic discussion concerning physical atoms. Rejected by the Protestant and misunderstood by the Roman, the laying on of hands—this sanctification of the earthly Church, admission of the believer to the Pentecost of disciples, and ordination to the first ecclesiastical grade—is now nothing more than a useless complement of baptism. Hierarchical ordination, based on the clearest precepts of the apostles, on the most indisputable traditions of the first centuries of the Church, disappeared among the Protestants and became an absurdity among the Romans, though they think they have definitively consolidated it. Finally, marriage, converted into temporary concubinage by the Protestants and into a completely external obligation by the Romans, dishonored by both, no longer bears traces of its original holiness.

That is a summary of the facts. Let our Western sisters and brothers consider them with an impartial eye. Let them understand the Church and her living character by its opposition to the stamp of death that lies on their communions, and especially let them ask themselves if unbelief is not justified and if it does not have all the chances of success vis-à-vis beliefs that are so illogical and so removed from the Christian truth. The human soul has an instinctive sense for all that is beautiful, true, and holy. And the nations respond with an unreflecting skepticism to the pretensions of a doctrine without depth, without real faith, and without organic principle. One certainly cannot blame them, for, in the face of religious error, a sorrowful unbelief becomes a virtue.

The final triumph of religious skepticism has not yet arrived. But even at the present time one can consider that Western Europe as a whole does not have any religion, although it does not dare to admit this. Individuals are tormented by the desire to have a religion and, when they don't find one, they usually content themselves with what the Germans have admirably called *religiosity* (a wonderfully ironic word, which corresponds to Neander's subjective *religion* and is the reverse of the coal miner's *faith*).

States, or governments, knowing full well the social advantages of a religion of any sort, especially for the lower classes of the people, pretend to have one so as not to be faced with open unbelief.[33] All—both governers and the governed—are guided by the Machiavellian precept: "If God did not exist, it would be necessary to invent Him." Both the governers and the governed, however, content themselves with a phantom or with an approximation of a religion.

Perhaps the clearest expression of the present state of affairs would be to say that the Latin idea of religion has triumphed over the Christian idea of faith and that the world has not yet noticed this. The world without faith wishes to have some sort of religion—religion in general. Only unbelief is sincere, and it is most often attacked not because it is unbelieving and thus bad, but because it is sincere and thus good and noble. Public indignation persecutes the French peer who, from the rostrum, proclaims his own unbelief and that of his listeners. Public indignation persecutes the poet whose works are a hymn to atheism.[34] It persecutes scholars who, by laborious research,

---

33. This certainly does not prevent governments from sometimes having, like individuals, a more or less strong dose of religiosity.

34. Poor and admirable Shelley! The accents of his unbelief are often full of a Christianity that he never understood, and should inspire only a profound compassion for this noble mind that strayed so fatally.

undermine the foundation of a religion they do not believe in. But public indignation has nothing to say about religious hypocrisy, which is, so to speak, the sole religion of the West.

One should not be surprised by this. I have already said in a previous brochure that the struggle between Romanism and Protestantism—a struggle that is only a series of defeats for the two parties without alternation of victories—has been a permanent triumph for skepticism. The alliance with social interests, the alliance with governments, the alliance with nations, the alliance with the arts, truces (fruits of lassitude), calls for agreement and common action (the acknowledgment of despair); all this tends to accelerate the definitive fall of the Western communions. For both the religious Machiavellianism of states and the vacillating religiosity of individuals, the threatening figure of triumphant disbelief looms in the imminent future. This is why the trembling society is so angered by the sincerity of contemporary atheism. "The future is yours": that is what, at the bottom of their hearts, governments and individuals tell atheism. "But at least leave us the tranquillity of the present moment. Veil your thought; cover your doctrines with some shred of hypocrisy! We will not ask anything more of you, but at least grant us the little we ask of you, and do not do injury to our weakness with a display of your powers."

Generally speaking, unbelief is still complaisant enough to lend itself to such deals, which do it no harm. But with every day unbelief becomes more open and its message more clear. Unbelief feels that it is powerful and victorious enough even to be indulgent and civil toward Christianity, and sometimes to give Christianity the alms of a word of praise thrown with a noble pride and always received with a joyous gratitude. The anger that unbelief excites becomes less intense as the weakness of the means of resisting it becomes more evident. And sensing that it is dying of exhaustion, the Christianity of the West stops fearing a violent death.

This is because the Christianity of the West has committed suicide, because it stopped being Christianity when it stopped being the Church; because it received death itself into its bosom when it decided to imprison itself within a dead letter; because it condemned itself to death when it decided to be a religious monarchy without organic principle; because in order to live and to resist the effects of the centuries and of human thoughts, it is necessary to be truly alive—to have within oneself a principle of indestructible life.

Also, the religious polemic in the West entirely lacks (as I said in my first brochure) conviction, conscientiousness, and dignity.[35] Neither the indeterminate belief of the Protestant nor the commanded belief of the Roman, both rationalistic, can struggle with any success against the bold, open rationalism of unbelief. Nothing living, nothing organic, can be felt in the one or the other. The words of Christian apologists are just as poor, just as barren, just as devoid of teaching as those of their adversaries, and this for a very simple reason: the apologists themselves do not understand the spiritual life of Christianity; nor can they understand its historical life on earth. Therefore, they have nothing to teach those against whom they are defending the residue of their belief.

God gave to the first ages of the world the tradition of monotheism, and complete freedom of understanding and adoration. But this freedom was powerless to preserve this imperfect revelation. This tradition had disappeared or faded among all the human tribes, all the nations. A man was called.[36] He and His tribe, alone in the entire human race, knew God, and they knew Him not as an idea, not as a philosopheme, but as a living fact, indubitable, traditional. The unity of God, the fall of humanity, the future coming of the Messiah—these are the three beliefs that Israel was charged to preserve for the rest of the world. All three of these beliefs had belonged to other peoples, as we know from their myths,[37] but these beliefs had disappeared almost completely in the deluge of all kinds of idolatries.

Israel had preserved these beliefs. But it had preserved them not in the grandeur of freedom (of which humankind without Christ is

---

35. To the examples already cited, let me add that of a preacher in vogue in Paris, who at the foundation of the necessity of believing placed the impossibility of knowing anything with certitude. Such a defense, absurd in the eyes of all serious people and almost blasphemous in the eyes of all true Christians, makes attack unnecessary.

36. Abraham. See Genesis 12. — TRANS.

37. The Golden Age, the first couple of the Persians, the first ages of the Hindus, Sesiosch, the future Avatar of Vishnu, Hercules the liberator, Mete, and many others. If messianism were absent in Scripture, a responsible critique would have supposed a lacuna in it.

incapable), but in the slavery of the law. The individual freedom of Melchisedek blesses the glorious servitude of the race of Abraham. This race will be cast into chains, into the sufferings of the desert, into the dangers of a war of extermination, into various seductions of the most fanatical, the most voluptuous, the most demoralizing idolatry, into the corruption of power and riches, into all the temptations of its own ardent, uncontrolled passions, which will constantly draw it onto the path already followed by all the other nations. This race could not keep its pledge, but it *did* keep it thanks to the law, severe mentor, and protector. It kept this pledge intact for us until the time determined by the divine wisdom, so that the heirs of Israel could say with the Apostle: "All our fathers were under the cloud, and all passed through the sea; and were all baptized unto Moses in the cloud and in the sea" (1 Cor. 10:1–2); for Israel had for centuries found itself in the slavery of the law so that we could forever be in the freedom of grace.

Let it be the case that some verse or other is an interpolation, that the Pentateuch contains chaldeisms.[38] These indicate a modification or redaction subsequent to the time of Moses,[39] that some fact or other had been clothed in forms of myth, that the Semitic character had sometimes imparted a mysterious color to common things. But can all these critiques, all these analyses, these immense agglomerations of words (which, however, I consider useful and instructive), nullify the living and organic fact? Can they nullify the fact that the Jewish people were the only people in the world to preserve the doctrine of the unity of God and of the destiny of the world? Can they nullify the fact that this doctrine bears in each of its traits the character of tradition? Can they nullify the fact that the warriors, sages, and seers of Israel had, by virtue of deed and word, preserved this doctrine at the center of the most unrestrained idolatry, through the most frightening misfortunes, in the midst of all the temptations, finally, in

---

38. By *chaldeisms* Khomiakov means arameisms in the Hebrew. — TRANS.

39. It would perhaps not be impossible to show that certain passages of Genesis are probably, even as written tradition, prior to Moses. Such, among other passages, is the first version of the story of the creation of humankind. The ancient tradition of the Hebrews knows sages prior to Moses in the race of Israel. See Chronicles. There are also implied traditions, such as the coincidence of the Tower of Babel with the birth of Peleg [see Genesis 11:16–19]; but this is of little importance.

the midst of circumstances under which the keeping of the sacred pledge had become impossible? Can they nullify the fact that all these sages and seers had the character not of innovators or philosopher-ideologues but of simple instruments of tradition? Finally, can they nullify the fact that we feel in the depths of our hearts and in the marrow of our bones that it is only thanks to the preserving power of the law that we, a wild olive branch, could have been grafted to the good olive tree of God and allowed to participate in its roots and its nourishing sap, that is, in the knowledge and adoration of the Eternal, our creator? But one must be alive to understand life.

At a time determined by His wisdom, God revealed Himself through His beloved Son, the divine Word become human. He revealed Himself in all the perfection of His moral being, in all the infinity of His love. And humanity regained freedom so that people could worthily receive this perfect revelation.[40] The slavery of the law was abolished. The nation that had been put under the protection of the law lost its exceptional significance among all other nations. Even the language that had been the instrument of the law of servitude was cast down to a lower rank. Its was not the glory of transmitting to future ages the words of the law of freedom. The grace come down from heaven to sanctify all human language chose for its first interpreter the ancient idiom of intellectual freedom par excellence.

In withdrawing His visible presence from the world, the Lord gave the pledge of faith and the tradition of His doctrine not to individuals, His disciples, but to the Church of disciples freely united by the holy power of mutual love. It was this earthly Church as a whole, not the individuals who temporarily composed it, that was glorified by the visible gifts of the Spirit of God in the Pentecost. It is from this Church alone that all tradition of doctrine draws its authority, or rather its witness.

If the character of this living fact had been understood, many useless efforts could have been avoided by the unbelievers who savage the

---

40. It may not be inappropriate to cite here an observation of the eloquent Metropolitan of Moscow, Filaret. Human freedom is so important in God's eyes that the angel of the Annunciation did not leave until he heard from Mary's lips the words: "be it unto me according to thy word" [Luke 1:38]. Thus, God does not execute the greatest of His designs concerning humankind without having first obtained the consent of human freedom. [Khomiakov paraphrases Filaret's words. — TRANS.]

holy word with frank hatred and open doubt and the apologists who defend it with all the feebleness of a faith unsure of itself. What does it matter if memory has sometimes erred, if the tradition concerning some fact or other has been represented in contradictory forms? Our Lord did not wish to leave a reproduction of His likeness or a stenographic transcription of His words. How tall was He? What were His features, His appearance, His bearing, the color of His eyes and hair? What was His accent like, or the sound of His voice? Have the apostles told us? Those who recognized their triumphant Savior only according to His acts and the meaning of His words, but never recognized Him according to His appearance or the sound of His voice, knew that the image of Christ, even the material image, could be perceived only by an intellectual and moral act of the human soul. They remained silent. At least let someone repeat to me the words that Christ spoke on earth! The apostles did not think it necessary to preserve them for us in their original form, with the exception of the two or three words that had accompanied some miracle or the four words with which our Savior had exhaled the most bitter, the most inexpressible of His sorrows. The rest is a translation and therefore an alteration.

But is the fact concerning His material form more important for us than the material form of the word? In both the fact (I am not speaking of the unique fact of the incarnation, of the sacrifice, and of the triumph) and the word, there is nothing permanent but the meaning. I repeat: Our Savior did not wish to leave a likeness of Himself or a stenographic transcription of His words. His features will remain unknown to us. His words will not reach our ears in their original form. His acts will remain poorly defined, unfocused, sometimes uncertain in their details. Let us bless the Savior for this and the wisdom with which He inspired His Church, for the letter kills but the spirit alone quickens.

At the present time, unbelief is attacking not only the accuracy of the Gospel narratives but also the relation of the Gospels and Epistles to the persons to whom their redaction is attributed. Unbelief is maintaining that the Gospels are not by St. Mark, or by St. Luke, or by St. John, and that the Epistles are not by St. James, or by St. Jude, or by St. Paul. Be that as it may. But they *are* of the Church, and that is all the Church needs. Is it the name *Mark* that gives authority to the Gospel that is attributed to him? Is it the name *Paul* that gives authority to the Epistles? Not at all. Rather, St. Mark and St. Paul are glorified because they have been judged worthy of attaching their names to writings that the Spirit of God—by the common agreement of the Church—has recognized as its own.

And what does it matter if one redactor appears to attribute to Enoch a book of indisputably later origin, or if another appears to accept—concerning a rock touched by Moses [see Exodus 17:6]—a tradition not accepted by the Church? Even if something like this is truly the case, it happens solely because the redactor, who (like all people) is of the earth, has put the personal stamp of earthly nature upon the material form of the writing, but that the Church, which (being sanctified by mutual love) is of heaven, has recognized as her own the meaning of this writing. Once again, the name of the redactor is much less important than the form of the redaction.

That is what unbelief has to learn. But that is also what Protestantism can never teach it, for in order to understand the Church's relation to the Holy Scripture it is necessary to understand the inner life of the Church. Isolate the individual, break the bond that unites Christians in a single living individuality (as Germanic Protestantism has done), and you will have broken the bond that unites Christians to the Holy Scripture. You will have turned the Book into a dead letter, an object completely external to people, a story, a doctrine, a word that witnesses nothing. You will have turned it into black markings on white paper, a mere sound in the air, something that finds its authority neither within itself nor outside itself, something, finally, that must be killed by doubt and swallowed by oblivion. One who has denied the Church has condemned the Bible.

For the Roman, the Holy Scripture, which has become an official state document, is more strongly attached to the organism of the Church, although (as with all things in Romanism) the connection here is more external than inner. But, on the other hand, the Latinizer does not understand the sublime significance of the Church in its historical development and therefore cannot explain this significance to others. Slave of a new law invented by the juridical rationalism of the Roman world, the Latinizer cannot tell unbelievers how our Savior delivered us from the chains of legal slavery so that the fullness of human freedom could worthily preserve the fullness of the divine revelation. Pentecost has no meaning for the Roman.

By contrast, we [the Orthodox] recognize in Scripture not a dead letter, not an external object nor a document of an ecclesiastical state, but a witness and word of the whole Church—that is, our own word to the extent we are of the Church. Scripture is therefore from us and cannot be taken away from us. The story of the New Testament is our story: It is us that the waves of the Jordan made—in the baptism—participants in the Lord's death. It is us that the Last Supper united—in the Eucharist—with Him through bodily communion. It is upon our feet, broken by the pilgrimage of the ages, that the divine Christ poured the water of hospitality. It is upon our heads that the Holy Spirit descended on Pentecost in the sacrament of the holy chrism, so that the grandeur of our freedom sanctified by love could serve God more perfectly than the slavery of ancient Israel.

Three centuries passed. During these three centuries the Church was attacked by the hostile pride and deceiving sophistries of a false philosophy, by a fanaticism of lying inspirations, by the sanguinary hatred of peoples who trembled before the vengeance of gods rejected by Christianity, by the implacable hatred of the Caesars, who saw the most dangerous of rebellions in the rejection of the state religion. At the end of these three centuries, the Roman Empire found itself conquered by the alluring power of the Christian word and by the triumphant courage of the Christian martyr.

The human mind, ennobled by Christianity, demanded precision of logical expression from faith. Ignorance, pride, and human passions produced heresies. Arius and Dioscorus denied the Trinity—the inner definition of divinity.[41] They denied the tradition while pretending to remain faithful to it. To stop this false doctrine, Christians did not address themselves to any particular authority, to any religious or political power. Rather, they addressed themselves to the totality of the Church, united in harmony and in mutual love; for love does not usurp, does not monopolize grace, and it does not reduce one's brothers to spiritual helotism.

The Church answered the appeal of her members. She gave (as was fair) the right to formulate her faith to her elders of the episcopal

---

41. The heresiarch Arius (c. 250–c. 336) was the champion of the subordinationist teaching about the Person of Christ. Dioscorus (d. 454), Patriarch of Alexandria from 444, supported the heresiarch Eutyches (see *infra*). — TRANS.

order, while reserving for herself the right to check the formula that they had adopted. The Council of Nicaea laid the foundation of the Christian confession. It defined divinity itself, and by this definition implicitly declared that moral perfection, like all perfection, can belong only to the Eternal.[42] Later, meeting in a council, the emperors, the patriarchs (including the Patriarch of Rome), and the majority of the bishops betrayed the truth and signed a heretical confession. The Church, illuminated by her divine Savior, remained faithful and condemned the ignorance, perversity, or weakness of her functionaries and, with her witness, established forever the Christian doctrine of divinity.

The relation between God and His rational creature served as a theme for new errors. The schools of Nestorius and Eutyches sought to distort the apostolic tradition. The one rejected the true divinity of the divine Christ, whereas the other rejected His true humanity. Both heresies (which, essentially, were the same heresy) placed an impassable abyss between God and humankind. Both heresies denied God the power to manifest Himself as a moral being with elective freedom, and therefore took away from humankind the happiness of being able to penetrate by love into the intimate depths of divine love. The Church gathered her elders together and bore witness: the rational creature is the *image* of its creator to such an extent that God was able to be and was human. The abyss is overcome: humanity receives the glorious privilege of plumbing the perfection of the eternal being. Human beings receive the happy obligation of aspiring toward moral perfection, for they are like God. That is the sense of the councils' decision.

Subsequently, the error of the Monothelites led the Church to bear witness to the identity of spiritual nature and will, and to the moral perfection manifested by the divine Word within the bounds of human nature. And the Christian doctrine was revealed for all ages to come in all its grandeur and divine beauty.

A new question then arose. The reverent use of icons was accepted by the Church, but popular superstition often transformed reverence into adoration. Passionate, irrational zeal desired that the Church, not satisfied with condemning the abuse, would also condemn the use. That is the meaning of the heresy of the iconoclasts. They themselves

---

42. As an inevitable logical deduction Arianism attributed moral perfection to the Logos-Savior without admitting His divinity.

did not understand the import of their demands. They did not understand that the question of icons encompassed that of rite as a whole. But the Church understood. In condemning the iconoclasts, the Church bore witness to the fullness of its freedom. The second Council of Nicaea declared that the Church, a living individual and animated by the spirit of God, has the right to celebrate the divine majesty by word, sound, and image. Finally, it declared the freedom of adoration under all the symbols with which love inspires the unanimity of Christians. That is the meaning—so rarely understood—of this council. *The preceding councils had saved the Christian doctrine; this one saved the freedom of Christian feeling.*

Such is the history of the Church. It is the history of a living and indestructible organism withstanding centuries of struggle against oppression and error. It is a history of intellectual freedom sanctified by mutual love, bearing to the fullness of divine revelation a sublime witness that should be the heritage of all ages to come.

Will the Protestants be the ones to tell us this history? But for them it is only a chaos of meaningless events, of idle discussions, of personal or popular passions, of oppressive majorities, of factious minorities, of unimportant individual opinions, and of decrees without any authority. It is perhaps a treasure for libraries but nothing for humanity.

Will the Romans be the ones to tell us this history? But they see in it only a great comic spectacle without serious meaning, only the verbiage of several centuries, only the prolonged ignorance of a society that, in the course of five hundred years, usurped the right to discuss questions of dogma without suspecting that in its midst there was a legitimate power to which alone this right was given by Divinity itself.

No! The history of the Church, the intellectual and moral leaven to which the West owes what it has of greatness and glory, is no longer intelligible to the schism, which has rejected its principle. It is for us and for us alone to tell this history, as severe as science in its logical development, as poetical as the hymns of the first centuries of Christianity, so completely different from all the rest of human annals and so infinitely superior to all the material and political agitations of humanity.[43] "But

---

43. I cannot refrain from remarking that the order of the councils coincides with the order of the most ancient hymns of the Church (e.g., the Gloria, the quiet Light, etc.): the Trinity (the first epoch), the Incarnation (the second epoch), Glorification, and prayer (the second Council of Nicaea).

the East is dead," say the men of the West, "and we, we live." I am speaking not of social, material, or political life, but of intellectual life, insofar as it bears the character of religious life, that is, insofar as it is a manifestation of the Church.

For centuries the West has been free, rich, powerful, and enlightened, while the East has been poor, benighted, largely reduced to slavery, and entirely sunk in ignorance. Be that as it may. But compare the manifestations of Christianity in these two regions with such different political destinies.

Let us look for some manifestation of the Church in Protestantism, some movement of life in its doctrine! The multiplication of new sects; the dissolution of the oldest communions; the absence of any fixed doctrine; constant efforts to form either a system of doctrines or a community with a permanent creed, efforts constantly resulting in failure; individual labors that prove sterile and are lost in the universal chaos; years that pass without gathering the heritage of previous years and without leaving any legacy to the following years; everywhere uncertainty and doubt—such is the Protestant world from the religious point of view. Instead of life, we find nothingness or death.

Let us look for some manifestation of the Church in Romanism! A multitude of political agitations, popular movements, disputes or alliances with cabinets, some administrative measures, a multitude of noise and flash, but not a word or act that bears the stamp of spiritual life, which is the life of the Church. Again, is that not nothingness? However, one has recently seen the appearance of an obligatory decree come down from the pontifical throne on a dogmatic question.

---

43. *(continued)* Not understanding this order of Christian hymns, the scholar Bunsen (whose works are otherwise quite admirable) has fallen into the singular error of taking a truncated example of the Gloria for the original, and of considering as an interpolation the name of the Holy Spirit placed between the Word considered as God and the Word in His incarnation. The same work that contains this error also contains such philosophical errors as the idea that the Church is the incarnation of the Holy Spirit in the same way that Christ is the incarnation of the Word. The celebrated scholar thus does not understand that, according to his own definition, the incarnation, like all objectivity, enters into the domain of the Word, which he considers as the *divine object* (God-object). The philosopher thinks he knows more than the Church, but the Church has the admirable quality of always being more rational than human rationalism.

This is therefore a completely ecclesiastical act in the highest sense of the word, and it deserves special attention, since it is the first such act to be promulgated in many years. This decree announces to all of Christianity and to ages to come that the blessed Mother of the Savior was, from Her conception, exempt from all sin, even original sin. But did not the Holy Virgin undergo death like the rest of the human race? She did undergo it. And, as the Spirit of God says through the Apostle, is death not the punishment for sin?[44] But suddenly we find out that death is no longer such punishment. By papal decree, it has become independent of sin. It has become a mere accident of nature, and Christianity as a whole is caught in a lie. Or has the Holy Virgin undergone death like Christ, taking sin upon Herself for others? But we would then have two Saviors, and Christianity would again be caught in a lie. That is how the divine mysteries are manifested to the Roman communion. That is the legacy it leaves for the future. What do we thus find in Romanism? Silence or falsehood. Nothingness or symptoms of spiritual death appearing as soon as it attempts to give itself an appearance of ecclesiastical life.

The Church does not speak unless there is a grave necessity. But in our own time, Rome, with its pontiff at the head, has attacked the Church, and the Church has answered.[45] Out of the depths of ignorance and humiliation, out of the prison in which Islam confines the Christians of the East, a voice sounded and told the world that *"knowledge of the divine truths was given to the mutual love of Christians and had no other guardian but this love."* These words were recognized as the Church's words. These words constitute the general formula of the Church's history and have become a magnificent legacy for future ages. For us, children of the Church, this is a hymn of triumph in the midst of suffering. It is the voice of the One who is the Father's beloved by virtue of His love and His voluntary sacrifice. But I am not afraid to say that—for every noble and serious soul, whatever its belief or unbelief—these words will be among the most beautiful ever uttered by human lips. Where then is the legacy of past ages? Where is the continuation of the history of the Church? Where

---

44. Literally: "the wages of sin."
45. Khomiakov is referring to the "Synodal Letter of the Eastern Patriarchs," 1848. — TRANS.

is true life in the presence of apparent death? Where is true death in the presence of apparent life?

In my first response to an unjust attack against the Church, I showed that the two sections of the Western schism are nothing more than two forms of protestantism, and that both, denying the moral basis of religious knowledge, are eminently rationalistic and therefore have no right to complain about the rationalism that is attacking them. I also showed that both sections of the Western schism, caught in a logical antinomy, had always seen Christianity only from a single point of view, understanding it as a unity without freedom or as freedom without unity. I showed that both of them, incapable of a serious defense against one another or against unbelief, now find themselves in an age of exhaustion and decadence and can only hasten their own fall by the methods they use to resist unbelief—that is, by their inevitable struggles and alliances.

Now I've shown the real and intimate life of these two branches of the schism. Their common basis is rationalism. The whole superstructure is conditional; it lacks greatness, harmony, and inner connectedness. An impoverished prayer, deprived of all meaning; misunderstood and distorted sacraments; a nullified history or one that is reduced to nothing more than a prolonged absurdity—that is what the two protestantisms, Germanic and Roman, oppose to the analytical work of human thought. They are also wrong to think that unbelief will kill them. To be killed it is necessary to be alive. But, despite their agitations and apparent struggles, they bear death within their bosoms, and unbelief has only to remove the corpses and sweep out the arena.

That is the just punishment for the crime committed by the West against the holy law of Christian community.

The religious thought of the world is now our task. Whoever our enemies are and however ferocious they may be, nothing—not the vague reveries of individual religiosity, not the Machiavellian craftiness of state religions, not the subtlety of sophistries, not the ardent efforts of a preaching ignorant in its benevolence, not the implacable hatred that transforms the old attempts at *moral fratricide* into a desire for *material fratricide*—in short, neither seductive words nor powerful arms—can wrest humanity away from the One who died for it and who left it no other faith but love. To be sure, in all ages there will be those who are perverse and *do not want to believe*. But there will no longer be pure and honest souls who *cannot believe*. The future is the Church.

Perhaps I will be reproached for the crudeness of my language. But let one reflect deeply upon what I am saying. If I have not gone beyond the truth, if I have not put forward anything I have not proved, it is the *fact* that is rude, not *my words*.

* * *

Much blood has already been shed in the East, and blood exacerbates all hatreds. But I have so lofty an idea of the human soul and of its nobility that, even at present, I hope to find among you, readers and brothers, people capable of lending me an impartial ear.

Despite its great political agitations, its social troubles, which are far from over, despite its bloody wars and the apparent dominance of material interests, our century is a century of thought, and that is why it must have a very great influence on the future of the human race. To be sure, social passions can agitate thought and brutal force can paralyze it for a moment. But passions become exhausted and subside; brutal force is broken or becomes tired; and thought survives and continues its immortal work, for thought is truly from God.

In the course of centuries of intellectual development, the West did great and glorious things. But the moral leaven of all the truly great things that it produced was—Christianity. This salutary leaven acted as powerfully upon the unbelievers who denied it as it did upon those who were religious and gloried in their faith, for to love justice and protect the weak against the attacks of the powerful; to abolish venality, torture, and slavery, was already to be a Christian (at least in part). To preach charity and to work to improve the conditions of labor and ameliorate the life of the poor (whose lot we still do not know how to make completely happy)—was already to be a Christian (at least in part). Also, despite its social sores and the shakiness of its faith, England (like many other contemporary European states) is much more Christian than the kingdoms of the Middle Ages, with their blind and lying, though so vaunted, piety. But don't be deceived: Christian morality cannot survive the doctrine upon which it is based. Deprived of its source, it dries up. Morality without doctrine soon becomes an inconsistency and an arbitrary principle, which only habit can preserve—for a period of time. But soon it is rejected by interest and passion.

But the greatest danger at this moment lurks in the fact that thought in the West has overtaken the religion whose rationalism and inconsistency it has exposed, and an overtaken religion is a condemned religion.

It is a question then of saving all the good and beautiful, all the great and glorious things you have. It is a question of saving your intellectual and moral future; for at this moment your heart is more Christian than your belief, but this cannot continue long.

This is not a new dogma that we are teaching you; rather, it is the dogma of original Christianity. This is not a new tradition that we are seeking to impose upon you; rather, it is the tradition your fathers had preserved until they wished to cast our fathers into spiritual serfdom. The edifice of your faith is crumbling and sinking. We do not bring you new materials to reinforce this edifice. No! We do no more than return to you the cornerstone[46] rejected by your ancestors, the mutual love of Christians and the divine graces attached to it. Put back the cornerstone of the building, and—henceforth indestructible, defying or rather inviting the mind's critical work—this building will rise in all the grandeur of its sublime proportions to be the salvation, happiness, and glory of all future generations.

I know that my words will be greeted by much prejudice, but I do not dare call this prejudice unjust. I know that, whatever your errors, you have innumerable reproaches to address to us. I know that you have the right to demand of us a rigorous accounting of the fruits by which truth should make itself known among the nations that are guardians of this truth, fruits that mere gratitude requires of us and that our ingratitude does not bring forth. We will not try to justify ourselves; we will not speak of the struggles or sufferings of our history, nor of the falsity of our civilization that, for more than a century, we have been drawing from corrupted sources.[47]

None of this excuses us. Whatever your accusations, we will consider them just. Whatever vices you reproach us with, we will acknowledge them humbly, sorrowfully, bitterly. But in order to be

---

46. Literally: keystone of the vault (*la clef de voute*). — TRANS.
47. From the time of the Petrine reforms, in the early eighteenth century. — TRANS.

fair to yourselves and to Christianity, be indulgent toward us! Do not ask if it is likely that God, to summon you, should use instruments so rebellious against His will. Say rather that God's ways are inscrutable for human reason! Do not ask if we are worthy of bringing you words of truth, but think rather that the truth is beautiful and worthy of being received by you whoever the messengers might be! It does not please God that the sins and hardness of heart that are our shame should cause you unhappiness, and that their inevitable punishment should be doubly severe for us because of the evil they would have caused you by inspiring in you an invincible prejudice against the divine law itself. "How beautiful and sweet is the harmony of brothers! It is the sweet-smelling ointment that flows down upon Aaron's locks and his garment. It is the beneficent dew that the night spreads upon the summits of Hermon and upon the blessed hills of Zion."[48] If your heart has ever responded to this hymn of ancient Israel, the moral effort you will have to make upon yourselves will not appear painful to you. To condemn a crime committed by the error of your fathers against innocent brothers—that is the sole condition under which you can regain the divine truth and save your spiritual life from an inevitable dissolution. Accept this condition and you will receive the right, given by the Church to its children, to say: "let us love one another so that with one accord we may confess the Father, the Son, and the Holy Spirit."[49]

When we say this, we have our own interest in mind, of course; for to acquire brothers and sisters is the greatest happiness given to people on Earth. But is not our interest also yours? Is an act of justice so difficult? The obligation to say to one's brothers and sisters toward whom one is guilty, "we have sinned against you, but accept us anew as your beloved brothers"—is this obligation so hard and so impossible to fulfill? Readers and brothers, test, I implore you, your hearts and your thoughts!

---

48. Paraphrase of verses from Psalm 133. — TRANS.
49. The priest's words before the recital of the Nicaean Creed in the Orthodox liturgy.

3.

Some More Remarks by an Orthodox Christian Concerning the Western Communions, on the Occasion of Several Latin and Protestant Religious Publications[50]

[excerpts]

Let us try to elevate ourselves to the calm, serene heights from which the Church contemplates the Truth in its divine harmony. On these heights there will be no more internal contradictions in doctrine, no more errors that condemn themselves by their own development. On these heights we will no longer feel a moving ground trembling beneath our feet, and we will no longer see the *ignes fatui* of individual thought casting their deceptive lights in the midst of the general darkness. On these heights we will stand on an unshakable rock, and our eyes will be illuminated by the light of a cloudless day, for this is the Kingdom of the Lord!

God, eternal principle of all that exists, was first revealed to His intelligent creatures as a limitless, infinitely wise power. In the course of the ages, God revealed Himself to these same creatures as the sole moral Being in the Son of Man, Jesus the righteous, our Savior. And the beings whose moral sense recognized His infinite love glorified Jesus and, in Him, the Father of mercies in the ages of ages.

As yet, this was only a historical revelation. The Spirit who is of God and who is God has not refused His faithful a complete revelation. He called the Son "the Lamb offered in sacrifice from the foundation of the world" [See Rev. 13:8]; and the divine mystery was revealed in its infinite profundity. Humankind lives constantly in the present (for it is our very life that we call the "present"); but this present is, for us, only a passage from what was the future to what has

---

50. *Encore quelques mots par un chrétien orthodoxe sur les communions occidentales, à l'occasion de plusieurs publications religieuses, latines et protestantes.* First published in French in Leipzig, 1858. The first part of this work continues the polemic begun in the brochure against Laurentie; the second part further develops the doctrine expounded in the brochure against the Archbishop of Paris.

become the past. The present does not have real existence in time; the present one wishes to name has already ceased to exist before one has named it. It is otherwise for God. All that we understand by the past or by the future is united for God in the present, in the unchangeable unity of His eternity. The revelation of the Son of Man, a revelation surging forth on the moving face of the ages, is still God's eternal thought; and we recognize that God is not only a stranger to evil but also *the conqueror of evil from all eternity by Christ's thought.*

Moral freedom is the essence of the finite intelligence. This freedom is the freedom of choice between the love for God and egoism, or between justice and sin. And it is this choice that determines the relation of the finite intelligence to its eternal source. But the whole world of finite intelligences, all of creation, lies in sin, either in fact, as having sinned, or virtually, as not having been preserved from sin except by the absence of temptation and by divine grace. No entity is pure in the eyes of God; none is without sin; none has righteousness in itself by virtue of its own freedom. Every creature carries its sentence within itself; every creature is separated from God; every creature is irreconcilable. That is the law; the severe, inflexible, inexorable law; the law of which the Old Testament was only the symbol, as is explained to us by the Holy Spirit through the Apostle's words (for he is not speaking solely of the ceremonial law) [see Heb. 10:1].

The creature cannot be reconciled with the Creator, just as sin cannot be joined to perfection. The creature is thus destined to be unhappy: *That is the law of justice*, but the justice of the law has not yet been manifested. Indeed, God, the infinite Entity, cannot serve as the measure for the limited entity. And, on the other hand, since the finite intelligence lies entirely in sin, sin becomes a real necessity, and justice is now nothing more than an abstract possibility without a real basis. But the infinite Entity, in whom nothing is abstraction but all is reality, becomes the limited entity in Christ. And Christ, come in time but being the Father's eternal thought, Christ, a human being like us, enchained by weakness, ignorance, suffering, and temptation, returns in all the perfection of divine justice solely by virtue of His human will. Thus, from all eternity, Christ is the sole just condemnation of sin. Christ alone is the measure of all creation; and He is therefore the supreme judge, as the Spirit of God has told us.

But Christ is not only the justice of the Eternal Father. He is also the Father's infinite love. He is not only the condemnation of sin but also the only possible salvation of the sinner. God's nature cannot accept sin because sin is inherently the voluntary separation from God; it is the egoism of the creature who prefers himself to God. But Christ's love does not abandon the creature; He does not wish to separate Himself from the creature. He unites Himself with the creature in a perfect, intimate union. He accepts the burden of sin of which He is the condemnation. With and for the creature, He really becomes a sinner, for, as a limited being, He *can* be a sinner. What eye can measure this abyss of humiliation and suffering? Who can understand the horror of the struggle, the tears, and the bloody sweat? Who can find in himself a feeling of love capable of responding to this infinite love?

Christ is no longer the preeminently pure and perfect being. He has united Himself with every creature that does not reject Him. He has taken upon Himself every sin. He finds Himself under the weight of divine anger and under the weight of condemnation of which He Himself is the manifested justice. Upon Him is executed the sentence that has been imposed upon Him. This sentence is death. But this death consummates the victory. Sin (which is the egoism of the creature), accepted freely by love, is quickly transfigured: it becomes the perfection of sacrifice and the crown of divine perfection, so to speak. On the other hand, the same act that, in uniting Christ with the imperfect or guilty creature, makes Him responsible for sin—has allowed the sinner to participate in the perfection of His Savior. That is why every entity that does not reject Christ is reconciled with God; every sin is converted into righteousness; every sinner becomes a child of God; for by His not abstract but real union with the creature, Christ is the justification of the virtual imperfection of some, that is, of the absence of immanent justice, while being the redemption of the manifested sin of others. This Christ come in time but eternally present before God—shines in eternity, in the very essence of the Father of whom He is the thought and the revelation.

Christ is therefore God's eternal victory over evil. He is the sole condemnation of sin from all eternity and the eternal salvation of all sinners who do not reject Him. All moral relations between God and the creature are distorted, fictive, impossible without Christ, Jesus the righteous, the One who is eternally the beloved Son of the Father of mercies.

Where, then, are the juridical merits invented by Rome when all is sin outside of Christ and all is righteousness in Christ? Where is the fatalism of the Calvinist when human freedom in Christ is the sole condemnation of sin and the sole salvation of the sinner? Where, finally, is the blind philosophy of the Unitarians, who believe they can have a God without Christ? (Alas! If they can, how can they desire this?) The eyes of the Church's children, illuminated by the rays of the apostolic tradition, embrace limitless horizons from the height of the holy mountain and can only cast looks of sorrowing pity upon the region of error and darkness where heresy wanders at random.[51]

Such are the marvelous mysteries that the Spirit of God has condescended to reveal to us. The Spirit of God has revealed to us that the Father's justice is manifested in the free perfection of His beloved Son, Jesus the righteous, incarnation of the eternal word, and that the Father's infinite love is manifested in the divine Lamb's free love, the Lamb who is sacrificed for His brothers and sisters. All is the work of freedom, whether Christ's justice that condemns us or Christ's love that saves us by the real, ineffable unity into which He admits us. All is just, for (judicial) justice is merely the manifested logical law; in fact, nothing has disappeared without a trace. Sin has not been pardoned, absolved, or abolished; that would be contrary to the laws of reason. But it has been transfigured into perfection by the complete union of human individuals with their Savior. Such is the divine mystery. But what is the form of its earthly revelation? It is the obscure life of a poor Hebrew, which ends in an infamous execution on the cross. Whose eye will thus pierce this thick veil of humiliation and misery? To whom will it be given to understand what the heavenly intelligences cannot divine?

The mystery of moral freedom in Christ and of the union of the Savior with the intelligent creature can be worthily revealed only to the freedom of human intelligence and to the mutual love that the Spirit of God came to consummate and crown on the great day of

---

51. If my memory does not betray me, the celebrated Möhler once wrote that "a time will come when humanity will understand that it is impossible to imagine a world without God or a God without Christ." This sublime thought, which in the West could come only obscurely to an eminent man at a moment of special inspiration, is manifested in all the clarity of its logic to every child of the Church.

Pentecost, when tongues of fire came down upon the heads of the disciples, gathered in hope, prayer, and adoration. In fact, the faith that fathoms the divine mysteries is not belief but knowledge. But it is not knowledge of the kind we have of the external world. It is inner knowledge similar to the knowledge we have of the facts of our own intellectual life. It is thus a gift of divine grace: it is the presence of the Spirit of truth within us. But the union of earthly human beings and their Savior is always imperfect: it becomes perfect only in the region where they deposit their imperfection in the perfection of mutual love that unites Christians. In this region, people no longer rely on their own powers, which are only weakness. They no longer count on their own individuality; they count only the holiness of the bond of love that unites them with their sisters and brothers; and their hope cannot deceive them, for this bond is Christ Himself, who makes the greatness of all from the humility of each.

Thus, in Antioch, the first head of the holy phalanx of disciples fell into an error that compromised the whole future of Christian freedom, and did not rise except by humble deference to the voice of a new convert [see Gal. 2:11–14]. (Alas! Those who pretend to be his successors scarcely understand his greatness.) In this example, we come to know the relation of each apostle to the Church of the apostles, that is, the relation of each believer to the Church of all the ages to come; we recognize the very mystery of the Church and we dare, without fear of blaspheming, to consider it as the body of Christ Himself, of the man-God, our Savior (which does not mean that we should insanely consider ourselves, in our individuality, as incarnations of divinity). Indeed, it is not the members of the Church taken numerically nor their visible assembly that makes up the Church, but the bond that unites them.

The Church is the revelation of the Holy Spirit to the mutual love of Christians, and it is this love that leads them to the Father by His incarnate Word, Jesus, our Lord. The Church's divine mission is not only to save souls or to perfect individual beings but also to keep the truth of the revealed mysteries pure, intact, and complete through all the generations as a light, a measure, a judgment. The secret bonds that unite the earthly Church to the rest of humanity have not been revealed to us. Therefore, we have neither the right nor the desire to presume a severe condemnation of those outside the visible Church, especially since such a presumption is contradicted by divine mercy. The words about the Spirit of God in St. Paul's Epistle to the Romans and in the narrative of the centurion's conversion [Rom. 8:14–16; Acts 10] permit us, on the contrary, to nourish sweet hopes for all our brothers and sisters, whatever the errors of their doctrines are. We know well that, without Christ and without love for Christ, people cannot be saved.

But, in this case, it is not, as the Lord told us, a question of His historical revelation.[52] Christ is not only a fact; He is a law. He is a realized idea. And there are those who, by the decrees of Providence, have never heard of the Saint who suffered in Judaea, but nevertheless adore the very essence of our Savior, whose divine name they do not have the happiness to bless. Those who love justice, do they not love Christ? Those whose hearts are open to compassion and charity—are they not disciples without knowing it? Those who are prepared to sacrifice their happiness and life for their sisters and brothers, do they not imitate the only Master, Who is the perfection of love and sacrifice? Those who acknowledge the holiness of the moral law and who, in the humility of their hearts, also acknowledge its extreme inferiority to the ideal, have they not erected in their souls an altar for the righteous, before which the army of heavenly intelligences prostrates itself? They do not have knowledge, but they love One they do not know, just as the Samaritans adored God without knowing Him. Or rather, do they not love Him under other names: for justice, compassion, charity, love, sacrifice, finally, all that is truly human, great, and beautiful, all that is worthy of respect, imitation, or adoration—all this represents only different forms of the name of our Savior. Others heard His law preached, but this preaching presented it in a false light. And they have not been able to separate the truth from the mixture of errors under which it was presented, while being attached to this truth by all their desires and aspirations.

In the end, do not all Christian sects, in their bosoms, contain individuals who, despite the error of their doctrines, usually hereditary, pay homage by their thoughts, words, actions, by their whole life, to the One who died for His guilty brothers and sisters! All, from the idolater to the sectarian, are more or less submerged in shadows. But,

---

52. The sin against the Son of Man as opposed to the sin against the Spirit.

in the midst of the darkness, all see a few rays of the eternal light, revealed by diverse means. These rays are faint and insufficient; they are always prone to be eclipsed in the night of doubt. But they emanate from God and from Christ, and are all concentrated in the sun of truth that shines for the Church.

It is from the inexhaustible treasure of intimate knowledge or of faith entrusted to the Church that the sects that are separated from the Church have received the residues of revelations that they still possess. It is the Church's glorious battle against Arius's error that taught these sects that, in the world of intelligences, nothing can be like God in moral perfection (for such is the moral principle contained in the dogmatic confession). It is the battle against Nestorius and Eutyches that, by affirming the principle that God and humankind are so alike that God could make Himself human, at the same time imposed on individuals the obligation of never being satisfied with an approximate perfectedness, but of striving, ceaselessly and with all their strength, toward absolute perfection. It is the battle against monothelitism that manifested God's justice and gave validity, in Christ, to the rights of human freedom. Here I consider only the moral aspect of the dogma, for it is this aspect that has constituted the whole intellectual and social life of peoples who have called themselves Christians. It is the Church that, in the second Nicene council, established the freedom of the forms of adoration and of rite. It is the Church that, in our century, has undermined the foundations of all rationalistic heresies, by revealing the mystery of the moral law that governs it and by declaring, through the patriarchs, that the Truth has been given only to mutual love....

If at this time I have been permitted to explain the eternal shining of the incarnate Word, if I have succeeded in showing that, without this incarnation, without the God-man, all the moral relations between the Creator and the creature, both condemnation and salvation, are fictitious and impossible; if I have been able to expose in a logical chain what the sages of the West have never been able to say and never dared contradict—I owe this right, power, and authority to the happiness of being a son of the Church, and not to any personal quality of my own. I say this boldly and proudly, for it does not befit me to be humble in things I receive from the Church.

Such being the greatness of the Church, all Christians, reflecting on this greatness and on their own lowliness, cannot fail to feel how unworthy they are of the lofty mission and of the glory in which they are called to share. This sense of profound unworthiness, this justly severe judgment with which they judge themselves—forces them to exclude themselves by thought from the divine world, of which they desire to be, but do not dare think themselves, a part. It is to their sisters and brothers that they expose their unworthiness and the condemnation that they have directed against themselves. It is a charitable and indulgent hand that will reopen for them the doors that they themselves do not dare to reopen; for being able to condemn themselves, they do not have the right to absolve themselves.

Such is the sacrament of penitence that has often and justly been called a renewal of baptism—not because baptism is in fact repeated, but because, just as in baptism one does not dare associate oneself arbitrarily with the communion of the elect and of Christ, so, in the sacrament of penitence, excluding oneself from the Church by thought, one does not believe oneself to have the right to reenter her except by the judgment of one's brothers and sisters. It is the sincerity of the condemnation one has directed against oneself that gives to the judgment to which one submits its true character of absolution. One is not condemned by an external accuser, by an external power. One accuses and condemns oneself, but one is justified, delivered of the weight of the condemnation that one has pronounced, and received again into her bosom by the Church.

This sacrament, poorly understood by the Latins, has naturally been rejected by the Protestants, for whom the earthly or historical Church has become completely devoid of mystery. This sacrament has been confused with ordinances or disciplinary rules that can be associated with it but are not an integral part of it. It has been considered as a privilege of the hierarchy, whereas it is only a natural consequence of relations of unity between all the members of the Church, a unity of which the pastors are the visible expression.

If penitence manifested in its sacramental form (that is, by the intermediary of the community of the faithful) is a necessary expression of the humility of Christians and of their organic union with their sisters and brothers, and if this penitence is eminently natural in the course of the life of every child of the Church, no matter how highly placed (for priest and bishop are just as subject to it as all others), then how much more natural it is that penitence should precede the most important act of a Christian's life, the act whereby the spiritual unity of the Church receives on earth its heavenly crowning. I am speaking of the Eucharist. If Christians ever feel their own extreme abjectness, the moral majesty of their divine Savior, and all the glory of the privileges that Christ has bestowed upon His Church; if, full of a holy terror, they ever feel the justice of the condemnation that they can evade only by uniting with the Son of Man, whose body is the Church; if, at the same time, they feel the need to exclude themselves from this Church by a verdict they themselves pronounce, and to re-enter the Church by the charitable love of their brothers and sisters and their community—all these sentiments should be manifested in them with an irresistible force at the terrifying moment when they are called by divine grace to unite themselves with Christ, not only intellectually but also materially, not only in thought but also in body, which is destined to become the manifestation of thought. For, as I have said, the Eucharist is a real union of soul with soul, and of body with body. And the whole world of the elect can only be the body of Christ by His intimate union with them, as St. John of Damascus said in the inspired hymn that the priest repeats after communion.[53]

But for the union to be crowned, it must exist in reality, in the principle of the common life and in its manifestation, in the doctrine confessed by all, in the sacraments accepted and received by all, finally, in the rites, which are nothing else but the expression of the relation of the community to the dogma it professes. In its earthly mission, the Church is visible and invisible at the same time. The Church is, in fact, the society of God's elect, a body and a soul. In this sense, it is the invisible Church. But the Church is also the society of people who, whatever their inner and individual life, recognize the principle of Christian life and submit to it, at least in appearance.

Christians do not judge their sisters and brothers. The community judges them with indulgence, sometimes perhaps with excessive indulgence (such is human weakness). The community does not test hearts; it does not refuse its communion to those who are repentant, even if the repentance is only external in character. But the community's attitude is different toward brothers and sisters who deny the

---

53. O Christ, holy and sublime Pascha! O Word, wisdom and power of God! Give us an even more perfect communion in the unfading day of your eternal kingdom.

very principle upon which the unity is based. Even then the community does not judge them; but it distances itself from them. The human bond continues to exist between individuals. But the mysterious bond of the Church has visibly ceased to exist by the explicit will of the apostates. The special grace attached to this bond is withdrawn from them.

Such is the principle of the visible Church, which exists, therefore, only to the extent that it is subject to the invisible Church and consents to be its manifestation. And, on the other hand, by her very nature, the invisible Church cannot accept as her manifestation a religious society that does not submit to the very principle of Christian communion. This principle, as I have said, is that of mutual love in Jesus Christ and bears the fruits of sanctification and the knowledge of divine mysteries, that is, faith. As long as this principle exists and is accepted by all, the visible Church subsists even in the case of a general ignorance of external things, even in the case of individual corruption or the crudeness of the civil and political relations produced by the historical destiny of nations (for all these things are not subject to the judgment of the invisible Church). From the time the principle ceased to be accepted, however, what constituted the visible Church ceased to exist in this sense, and the invisible Church finds herself obliged to manifest herself and to become visible through protest.

Thus, there is nothing more absurd than to suppose that an invisible Church (that is, a Church without manifestation) has been lost in the course of centuries in the midst of a religious society that professes erroneous doctrines and dogmas and celebrates rites unworthy of Christianity. What could it have been, this invisible Church whose members could have had communion among themselves only through corrupted sacraments? What could it have been, this invisible Church whose members could have had neither knowledge of the truth nor the courage to proclaim it? If they did not know it, where was the grace of faith? If they possessed it, where was the obligatory courage of confession? How could these individuals who did not know the truth be the Church of the Apostles? Or why did these cowardly ones not die rather than profess error?...

* * *

No one avoids sin and no one ... is exempt from error; the accord of all is the truth in the bosom of the Church, which is the body of our Lord by the law of love that is her principle.

All of Church history is the exposition of this law. All give their intellectual work to all; all receive from all the result of the common work. Therefore, when an error passes itself off as the truth of the Church, the refutation can sometimes be expressed by a single person; but the decision belongs to all. Arius appears; he desires to pass off his individual folly as the expression of the common faith. The most powerful voice raised against him came from a man who was completely unimportant in the community, a mere deacon. But this voice was a call to the faith of all. It said: "Christians, return to yourselves. Test your hearts and consciences! What is the Faith that you have received from the Apostles? What is the Faith that you bear within yourselves?" The council meets and bears witness. The Church judges and recognizes the council as the true expression of the thought of each of the faithful. And the ages honor the name of Athanasius, to whom God gave the word of the Truth so that he would be the voice of his brothers. The ecclesiastical form belonged as much to Arianism as to Orthodoxy, but Arianism lacked the Spirit that is the inner life of the Church.

* * *

An external unity, which rejects freedom and is therefore not a real unity—that is Romanism. An external freedom, which does not bestow unity and which is therefore not real freedom—that is Protestantism. The mystery of the unity of Christ and His elect, a unity actualized by His human freedom, was revealed in the Church to the real unity and real freedom of the faithful. Knowledge of the powers that actualized our salvation was necessarily bestowed upon similar powers. Knowledge of unity could not be bestowed upon discord, nor knowledge of freedom upon slavery. Rather, both were bestowed upon the Church, whose full unity is the harmony of individual freedoms.

It is not uncommon to hear Protestants deny the freedom of the Church because the Church depends on its past, on its decisions, on its councils, and on the meaning, if not form, of its rites. This objection is completely puerile; for, in pursuing it to its logical end, one would have to say that the Church cannot be free, because it cannot at the same time be true and disagree with the Holy Scripture and with the whole world of divine revelations. The freedom of the human mind does not consist in creating the universe. Rather, it consists in understanding the universe by the free employment of its intellectual powers independently of all external authority.

The Holy Scripture is divine revelation that is freely understood by the mind of the Church; the decisions of the councils, the meaning of the ritual ceremonies, in short, the whole dogmatic tradition, are all an expression of this selfsame revelation, but freely understood under other forms. Inconsistency and disagreement may be a proof of error but not of freedom; for what is true today was also true in past ages. The contemporary thought of the Church, that is, the mind of its members united by the moral law of mutual love and illuminated by grace, is the same thought that wrote the Holy Scriptures, the same thought that, later, recognized them and declared their holiness, the same thought that, still later, formulated their meaning in the councils and symbolized this meaning in rite. The contemporary thought of the Church, like that of past ages, is a continuing revelation. It is inspiration from the Spirit of God.

To understand this intellectual movement, it is necessary to understand the history of the dogma of the Church. All the mysteries of faith were revealed to the Church of Christ from the very foundation of this Church. The whole inner science of divine things (to the extent such a science is possible for earthly humanity) was given to the Church of Christ from the beginning. And all these mysteries and this science were expressed by Christ's first disciples. But they were expressed only by the Church and could be understood only by the Church. God and divine things are, in fact, inexpressible; the human word can neither define nor describe them. All it can do is to awaken in the mind (that is, in the human world) a thought or an order of thoughts corresponding to the reality of the divine world.

Even in human things, we know that the words that express not simple abstractions but ideas belonging to living reality (be it material or intellectual) are intelligible only for the individual who possesses physical organs or spiritual capacities necessary to understand them. In other words, they are intelligible to this individual only insofar as they are a part of this individual's life. A blind person does not really understand the words *light* and *color*. A person deprived of the sense of beauty does not understand the words that express it, and the soul made crude by gross or sensual egoism hears words of love, admiration, or respect without ever being able to penetrate their meaning. And, with even more justification, we can say that the words that express the ideas of the divine world can be intelligible only to those whose very life is in harmony with the reality of this world. Just as these ideas are inaccessible to human thought in the isolation of its weakness and individual perversity, and can be understood only by means of the Spirit of God who reveals them to the moral unity of Christian society, so the words that express these ideas manifest a real meaning only to those whose life is part of this unity that is the Church.

The intellectual freedom of a member of the faithful is not subject to any external authority. But the justification of this freedom consists in the fact that it accords with the Church, and the measure of this justification consists in the consent of all the faithful.

All of God's mysteries were revealed to us from the beginning. What then is the significance of the later work, of the work that continues even now, which will continue in all the ages, and which the historians of our century improperly call "development"?

As I have said, God and divine things do not have definitive or descriptive names that embrace their essence. The human word itself is only a more or less conventional sign whose meaning varies not only according to language, not only according to epoch, but also according to the development of science and of the intellectual life of individuals in relation to purely human things. And the Church received from the blessed Apostles not a heritage of words, but a heritage of inner life. It received a heritage of inexpressible thought, but of thought that always strives to express itself. The Church's word changes in order to bear witness to the infinity of the idea: otherwise, this word would be a mere material echo, sounding from age to age but manifesting only sterility and feebleness of intellectual activity, or even the complete absence of such activity.

We see this from the very beginning: If the mysterious and eternally adorable name of the Son of God had embraced the whole Christian idea of the One who became incarnate for our salvation, why would He also have received the divine name "the eternal Word"? Or if the name "the Word" had been necessary to express this idea, why would it not have been pronounced from the very beginning of the evangelical preaching? The savants of our century devote their attention to development. The Germans, in characterizing this development, even call it the doctrine of the Word (*die Logos-lehre*); but all these words are devoid of meaning. Many times while reading the works of the Apostles prior to that of St. John, one experiences an involuntary dissatisfaction caused by the failure to find the so characteristic word that shines from the first line of St. John's Gospel. "The image of the Father," "the splendor of glory," and similar expressions reveal to us the same thought that is contained in the term *Word* (or *Logos*), but they indicate this thought less clearly.

Does this term therefore signify the Church's progress? Not at all. The fullness of ecclesiastical thought can already be felt in expressions of St. Paul; but the listener has changed. The Jew, the Roman, the Greek artisan would have understood nothing if St. Paul had spoken of Logos. This word would have awakened no idea in their minds; it would have been devoid of meaning for them. But a new personal element, a new historical life, namely students of Greek philosophy, entered Christ's Church. An expression more concise and clearer than hitherto became possible. St. John utters it, and the Church joyfully repeats it on the day of its most triumphal solemnity. Does this mean that the Church has found a word to express its thought? What? *Logos*, the *Word*—this fugitive sound in the air, or this sign mute or engraved, this variable and conditional thing, this thing that has nothing in it, that has no proper or personal life—could this expression embrace and define the essence of God, our Savior, the essence of the One who is absolute life and truth? Such a supposition is inadmissible. No! The Church rejoices not in having expressed its thought but in having clearly indicated to its children a thought that no human language can express.

Our words, if I dare say so, are not the light of Christ, but His shadow on earth. Blessed were those who, contemplating this shadow on the fields of Judaea, could divine the heavenly light of Tabor. This light shines constantly for the Church. But it is revealed only through the shadows of matter, for our language is wholly material, not only in form but also in almost all its origins, whatever it may be in its principle. If the Apostle had addressed himself to other listeners, if he had found in them a different intellectual education, he might have used different expressions. In the face of philosophical systems resembling those of present-day Germany, he might have used the word *Object* to render the thought he expresses by *Logos,* and this form, although less perfect, would also have been fully legitimate. By no means do I think that these two expressions are comparable. I know very well that the word *Logos* is much more clearly marked by the relationship of generation that exists between thought and its manifestation. But I also know that the word *Object* can be used to convey the concept of manifested and self-recognized thought. The goal set by the Church would therefore be attained, that is, the goal of indicating divine things by an induction drawn either from the visible world or from operations of the human mind. Therefore, the most magnificent example of this intellectual work, never, by God's mercy, ceasing in the Church, can be found in the one who can be called, par excellence, the Apostle of the Church, the apostle *ad intra*, just as the two other great luminaries of the Christian world were called the Apostle of the Hebrews and the Apostle of the Gentiles—that is, the Apostles *ad extra*.[54] St. John was truly the confirming Apostle, confirmer of revelation, and this mission was assigned to him from the height of the cross, just as the words addressed to him after the Resurrection, had, evidently, besides their direct sense, a symbolic sense.[55]

The Lord said: "I ascend unto my Father, and your Father; and to my God, and your God" (John 20:17). St. Thomas, inspired by the Spirit of truth, said to Him: "My Lord and my God" (John 20:28). The whole mystery of the Incarnation was clearly revealed to us from that moment. But centuries passed before the Church, rejecting all the erroneous formulas proposed by Nestorianism and Eutychianism, enclosed its faith within a strict, concise formula.

The blessed Apostles teach us that the Spirit who is God proceeds from the Father and knows all His mysteries. These words contain the whole truth. But a century and a half later, Irenaeus, a disciple (through Polycarp) of the beloved Apostle, said it even more clearly:

---

54. *Ad intra*: "on the inside"; *ad extra*: "on the outside." — TRANS.
55. It may perhaps be relevant to mention that, on another occasion, St. Peter casts himself into the sea in order to rejoin his resurrected teacher as quickly as possible; but it is John who recognizes Him and says: "It is the Lord" [John 21:7]. The clarity of knowledge is a gift that appears to have been bestowed upon him specially.

"The Spirit crowns Divinity by giving the name Father to the Father and the name Son to the Son." Through Irenaeus's words the Church manifested the profound knowledge of God's mysteries that had been given to it by Christ.

The same movement makes itself felt in the expression of all the dogmas: The terms *eternal birth*, *eternal procession*, *Trinity*, *Persons*, and so on appear and gain currency only gradually. But the whole movement remains enclosed within the terminology and can by no means be considered a development of doctrine. On the contrary, it is fixed and unchangeable. Generally speaking, heresies or false definitions provided to the children of the Church the occasion to enunciate the truth in the strictest and most definitive formulas. But the scientific (so to speak) movement of ecclesiastical terminology did not really need these errors to manifest itself. It quite naturally flowed from the need to show that the Christian doctrine is not an assemblage of terms learned by heart and retained by memory, but an approximate expression of a divine truth constantly contemplated and understood by the inner sense of the Church's children. This truth remains the same in all ages. Knowledge of this truth does not change, but the expression of this truth, an always insufficient expression, necessarily changes according to the development of the analytical language and according to the character of the intellectual habits of each epoch. Individuals freely contribute their more or less successful efforts to the common work. The Church accepts or rejects these contributions without condemning the individuals, even when they are in error, provided their efforts are conscientious and their contribution is offered humbly and is not imposed dictatorially on their brothers or sisters.

The illustrious Gregory of Nyssa could (according to Barsonophius) give the most erroneous explanation of the reasons that justify human misery on earth. The saintly bishop of Hippo, in wishing to explicate the mystery of the nature of God in the Trinity of His hypostases, could write things that bring an involuntary smile to the lips of an intelligent reader. But the Church never considered condemning Gregory for his error or Augustine for the puerility of his definitions. Both contributed to the edification of the Church. And if the imperfection of their nature led them to mix straw and wood shavings with the more solid materials that they offered, the fire of grace that is in the Church purified the offering, and only the useful materials were placed in the wall.

* * *

Individuals reflect and seek to express their reflections with words. The Church judges these words: it approves them when they are true and condemns them when they are erroneous and lead the minds of the faithful onto false paths. It also condemns them when they are arrogant and claim to embrace truths they can only indicate. All individuals, therefore—always blind and protestant as a result of moral imperfection—always find themselves in the presence of the Church, which is seeing and universal, because the Church is holy by the gift of the Holy Spirit and the grace of mutual love in Jesus Christ. Thus, the freedom of the individual mind is not subjugated. But the work of the mind is subject to the review of the Church, which decides. And this decision is based not on logical argumentation but on an inner sense that comes from God and that (as is witnessed by history) is refused neither to ignoramuses nor to savants, neither to the shepherds of actual flocks nor to the shepherds of souls.

I have already shown that the whole history of the Church has been that of human freedom illuminated by grace and bearing witness to Divine Truth. In this work of freedom it is necessary to distinguish two forms of the same power. In the Church in its totality, there is complete freedom in Jesus Christ, which is infallible both in the present and in the past, and which is always sure of itself and of the gifts of the Spirit of God. In individuals, there is the humble freedom of Christians, who, strong in the conviction that error is impossible for the Church, make their contribution to the general work, believe themselves always to be beneath their sisters and brothers, and ask of God only the happiness of being instruments of the common faith. This is the freedom that never lacks divine blessing.

In Protestantism, freedom for the community is a freedom of constant vacillation, which is always ready to revoke the sentences that it has pronounced in the past and that is never sure of the decisions that it pronounces in the present. For individuals, who do not believe in the community any more than the community believes in itself, freedom is either the freedom of doubt (if the individuals, knowing themselves, see their own weakness) or the freedom of an absurd faith in oneself (if the individuals make an idol of their pride). This is freedom minus divine blessing. It is freedom in the political sense, not in the Christian sense.

True inner unity, product and manifestation of freedom, unity based not on a rationalistic science nor on an arbitrary convention, but on the moral law of mutual love and prayer; unity where, with all the hierarchical gradations of sacramental functions, no one is subjugated but all are equally called to participate and cooperate in the common work; finally, unity by the grace of God and not by a human institution—that is the unity of the Church.

In Romanism, if it is properly understood, unity for Christians is solely the unity of obedience to a central power. It is the subjugation of Christians to a doctrine in which they do not cooperate, and it remains permanently external to them (for it resides in a sole hierarchical head). Finally, it is a legal indifference to faith, which entirely consists in submission to the faith of another. This is clearly unity in the conditional sense, not in the Christian sense.

Freedom and unity—these are the two forces upon which was worthily bestowed the mystery of human freedom in Christ, saving and justifying the creature by His perfect union with it. The result of these forces is, by the grace of God, neither belief nor analytical knowledge but inner perfection and divine wisdom: it is faith that, in both its character and its principle, is unassailable by disbelief.

* * *

The West has rejected the fundamental doctrine of mutual love that alone constitutes the life of the Church. As a consequence of this error, the very principle of Christianity is subjected to judgment, as once was the man-God from whom Christianity originated....

In the East, the Church, which is faithful to the whole apostolic doctrine, which embraces in an inner communion all the faithful of the present time and the elect of past ages, and which extends the beneficence of her prayers to future generations who will, in turn, pray for their predecessors—the Church summons into her bosom all the nations and awaits with hope the coming of her Savior. The Church sees with a tranquil eye the wave of the ages, the storm of historical agitations, and the currents of human passions and thoughts that strike and swirl around the rock on which she stands and knows to be unshakable. This rock is Christ.

4.

Letter to the Editor of L'Union Chrétienne, *on the Occasion of a Discourse by Father Gagarin, Jesuit*[56]

Sir,

Whatever opinion I may have of the program of your publication, the questions that you treat in your journal touch me so closely that I cannot remain indifferent to the polemic they engender and to the attacks they attract against the Church. I dare hope you will not refuse to publish a few remarks in response to a brochure of Father Gagarin ("A Russian's Response to a Russian").

In a recent discourse, the respected father wrote:

> Would you believe, my brothers, that in the Slavonic translation of the Creed the word *catholic* has been replaced by an *obscure and vague* expression that does not give the idea of universality. In chanting the Creed, millions of Christians, instead of saying, "I believe in the catholic Church," say: "I believe in the synodal Church.[57] And, after this, *we* are accused of distorting the Creed!

To this absurd accusation you responded that the word *sobornyi* means "catholic," that this is the meaning it has in the ecclesiastical dictionary, that this is the meaning it has in the title of the Epistle of St. James, and so on. The purpose of Father Gagarin's brochure is to justify his initial attack, but, pushed to the wall, convicted of ignorance, what does he find to say in his justification? Here are his words: "However the matter may stand, one sees that it is permissible to regret that the Creed, as it is chanted in Russian churches, does not

---

56. *Lettre au rédacteur de l'Union Chrétienne, à l'occasion d'un discours du Père Gagarine, jésuite.* First published in French in *l'Union Chrétienne* in 1860, No. 45. In this work, Khomiakov takes issue with the interpretation of the meaning of the word *sobornyi* in two brochures by Father I. Gagarin: *De la Réunion de l'Eglise orientale avec l'Eglise romaine*, Paris, 1860; and *Réponse d'un Russe à un Russe*, Paris, 1860. — TRANS.

57. *Synodale* (English, *synodal*) is the French equivalent of *sobornyi*. — TRANS.

contain an expression that can make the meaning of the word *catholic* shine with all its brilliance." ...

Let us first look at his criticism that the Russian expression is "obscure and vague." Perhaps. But the word he prefers has *no meaning*. It means nothing in French, German, or Italian; nor in any language except Greek. In order to make it understandable, one must explain it, retranslate it. But the vague expression can also just as easily receive, through explanation, a more definite meaning. Where then is the accusation? But the word *sobornyi*, we are told, is used in other senses too. It can mean synodal, cathedral, and even public. I admit that. But is it the case that the Greek word *catholic* has no other meaning except that assigned to it by the Creed? It seems that the Jesuit father not only lacks all familiarity with Greek but that he doesn't even have a poor little Greek dictionary in his cell in which he could look up different meanings of this word in the only language in which it has any meaning whatever. Where then is the accusation?

This is the ridiculous side of the critique, but here is the serious side of the question. Does the Jesuit father understand the word *catholic*?

"Universal," says the Jesuit father. But "universal" in what sense? I ask. "But that's perfectly clear—in the sense that the Church embraces all the nations." I do not extract from Father Gagarin an explanation other than what he gives himself, for here are his words:

> What the Eastern communion lacks most of all, the thing whose absence is the most striking—is catholicity, universality. One has only to open one's eyes to see that the Churches of the Eastern communion are local, national Churches, that they do not form a universal Church. In this respect, they are in a situation inferior to that of Protestantism: There are Protestants everywhere; one cannot say the same thing about the Eastern communions.

"Catholic" thus means: belonging to all the nations. But what then is the catholic Church? Where is it? In Rome? Show me the Roman Church among the Turkish nation in Turkey, among the Persian nation in Persia, among the blacks in the interior of Africa! I will be told that I am nitpicking, and that the important thing here is "more or less." One must have all the frivolousness of the most frivolous children of our age to believe that the Creed of the Church of Christ can contain such base definitions. "More or less!"

What about when the Church was in its cradle, within the narrow enclosure that was illuminated by Pentecost's tongues of fire—was it the Church or was it paganism that was catholic in your sense? And when victorious Islam extended its hawk's wings from the Pyrenees to the frontiers of China, enclosing within its immense grasp the little world of the Christians—who was catholic in your sense? The Church or Islam? If we do nothing more than count heads, is not Buddhism at present more catholic than Rome? Alas! In your sense, the word *catholic* can be attached only to the ignorance and vice that characterize all nations and all countries.

Or will it be said that the Church is and has always been catholic, not in the sense that she already embraces all the nations, but in the sense that she bears within herself the promise of embracing all the nations, in the sense that she is catholic in virtue of her future? I believe that. But then *how can the absence of a thing that is to come leap out at the eyes* in the present? No! The Jesuit father was not thinking of the future. He was thinking only of the grandeur of the contemporary rule, of the extent of the present domain, and he imperceptibly fell into absurdity under the vague idea that the whole universe was already Roman, or virtually so. For him, numbers are everything. A few more million people and several colonies, and then Protestantism would, in his eyes, have the most important and characteristic trait of Catholicism. That's what his words imply.

That is not how the Church thinks. The Church attributes to herself other traits than a universality to come. Whatever may be the destiny of the world's material forces, the intellectual movements of nations, or even the success of the Apostolate, the character of the Church's catholicity is independent of all this. This character does not change and never will change. That is how St. Athanasius understood it. He did not say, "We are more populous, or more widely distributed in the universe" (that would have been doubtful in relation to the Arians and even more doubtful in relation to the Nestorians, who came later). Instead, he said: "In whatever country you may be, you are everywhere only Arians, Ebionites, or Sabellians. But, as for us, we are everywhere catholics, and recognized as such." (Not having St. Athanasius's works in front of me, I give his meaning, not his exact words.)

It is a question not of numbers, or extent, or of geographical universality, but of something much loftier. "Your names are due to human chance; ours come from the very essence of Christianity." That is how St. Athanasius understands catholicity. How does the Church understand it?

Father Gagarin regrets that the Slavonic Creed does not contain an expression that can make the idea of universality shine with all its brilliance. Be that as it may. But what is the reason for that? Should one suppose that the translators did not find or did not wish to find this so-regretted expression? Was the Slavonic tongue too poor, or were the translators too feeble to master its riches?

Let us begin with the translators. From the very outset, the Apostles of the Slavs wished to give a translation of the Holy Scripture to the people they were summoning to Christ. Is it probable, is it possible that they would not have immediately translated the Creed? True, we do not have copies that date from the time of the translators, but there is no doubt that the translation itself has come down to us from them. And the Apostles Methodius and Cyril, Greeks by origin, but in communication with Rome, are claimed, wrongly, by the Latinizers as their own. Cyril and Methodius must thus have a certain authority even in Father Gagarin's eyes. It is they who chose the word *sobornyi* to render the Greek term *katholikos*; and so it is by the word *sobornyi* that one can judge about the meaning they attributed to *katholikos*. Was there a word in the Slavonic language that could express the concept of universality? One can find several, but it suffices to cite two, *vsemirnyi* and *vselenskii*, to be assured that there was no shortage of expressions to render this idea.

The first of these words occurs in very old homilies. The second is indisputably ancient and is used to render the idea of the universal Church (*vselenskaia tserkov*) or in the ecumenical sense (*vselenskii sobor* = ecumenical council). Thus, the first translators could have used such expressions to render the word *catholic*, if they had understood it in the universal sense. I am certainly not denying that *katholikos* (deriving from *kath'-ola* and implying *ethne*, *klimata,* or some other related expression) can have this sense of universality. But I assert that the Apostles of the Slavs did not understand this term in this way. The geographic or ethnographic definition of the Church did not enter their heads. It appears that such a definition was not part of their theological system. The word they chose was *sobornyi*. *Sobor* implies the idea of an assembly, not necessarily gathered in some place or other, but existing virtually without a formal gathering. It is unity in plurality. It is therefore evident that, in the thought of the two great servants of God sent by Greece to the Slavs, the word *katholikos* came not from *kath'ola* but from *kath'olon*. *Kata* often means "according to" (*kata Loukan, kata Ioannen* = "according to Luke," "according to John"). The catholic Church is the Church *that is according to all*, or *according to the unity of all*, the Church of free unanimity, of perfect unanimity, the Church in which there are no more nationalities, no more Greeks or barbarians; in which there are no more differences in conditions, no more masters and slaves. This is the Church prophesied by the Old Testament and realized by the New. This, finally, is the Church as St. Paul defined her.

Was it a profound knowledge of the character of the Church, a knowledge drawn from the very sources of the truth in Eastern schools that dictated the choice of the word *sobornyi* to translate the "katholikos" of the Creed? Or was it a yet loftier inspiration sent by the One who alone is the truth and the life? This question I do not dare answer. But I do dare to emphasize that the word *sobornyi* contains a profession of faith. Romans, you who claim the Apostles of the Slavs as your own, hasten to deny them! You who have broken the unanimity and unity by altering the Creed without consulting with your Eastern brothers, what can you make of the definition of the Church that has been bequeathed to us by Cyril and Methodius? This definition condemns you. Keep your pretensions to geographic universality. You cannot go beyond them. Let your children, the Protestants, hold to the same explanation of the word *catholic*, for the true sense of the word condemns them as well. The Church of the Apostles in the ninth century is neither the Church *kath'eskaston* (according to each) as with the Protestants, nor the Church *kata ton episcopon tes Romes* (according to the bishop of Rome) as with the Latinizers. It is, rather, the Church *kath'olon* (according to the unity of all) as it was before the Western schism and as it still is with those whom God has preserved from the schism; for this schism, I repeat, is a heresy against the dogma of Church unity. . . .

III

LETTERS TO
WILLIAM PALMER

Aleksei Khomiakov

EDITOR'S INTRODUCTION

William Palmer, fellow of Magdalen College at Oxford, was a Tractarian and leader of the Oxford Movement in Anglicanism. In the early 1840s, Palmer began traveling to the Orthodox East with the intention of fostering relations between Orthodoxy and Anglicanism. Nothing concrete came of these trips, and Palmer's decision to convert to Orthodoxy was met with contradictory and rather indifferent responses from Orthodox prelates. Eventually, Palmer followed John Henry Newman into the Roman Catholic Church, as the only body representing both apostolic succession and manifest unity.

Palmer brought home from one of his trips some of Khomiakov's poetry. He sent Khomiakov his translation of one particularly touching poem, and Khomiakov responded with a warm letter. The ensuing correspondence, of which eighteen letters survive (twelve by Khomiakov), gave Khomiakov his first opportunity to develop his theological views, which had not been finding much of an audience even within Russia. Many of the letters deal with Palmer's frustrated intention to join Orthodoxy. Khomiakov claims that the variety and insularity of the Orthodox churches does not impinge on their fundamental unity, from which the Western confessions have severed themselves.

We have chosen Khomiakov's third and fifth letters here, from 1846 and 1850 respectively. The English text belongs to Khomiakov himself and is given as printed by W. J. Birkbeck, with the addition of scriptural references in square brackets.[1] Two short passages, touching on various personal matters, have been deleted; they are marked by ellipses (…). [2]

---

1. Reprinted from: *Russia and the English Church during the Last Fifty Years*, ed. W. J. Birkbeck (London: Rivington, Percival & Co., 1895). Pp. 54–64, 66–72, 91–8.
2. Since these letters were written in English, except for punctuation and spelling, they remain largely unedited in order to preserve the original character of Khomiakov's words. — ED.

1.

Third Letter to William Palmer

Most Reverend Sir,

Accept my heartiest thanks for your friendly letter, and my excuses for having been rather slow in answering it. I cannot but call your letter a friendly one, though it contains some very severe attacks on us; but a truly friendly disposition lies in my opinion at the bottom of them, and is manifested by the honest frankness of their expression. I think your attacks generally wrong, but they are sincere, and show a serious desire to find out truth, and to come to a satisfactory conclusion in the debated question. Every doubt, every difficulty, and every accusation, let it be ever so hard for the accused party, should be candidly and clearly stated; this is the only way for establishing the difference between right and wrong. Truth must never be evaded; it should not even be veiled in truly serious questions.

Permit me to resume briefly your accusations. First: "If we pretend (as indeed we do) to be the only Orthodox, or Catholic Church, we should be more zealous for the conversion of erring communities, as the Spirit of apostleship, which is the true spirit of Love, can never be extinct in the true Church; and yet we are manifestly deficient in that respect." Secondly: "Our pretensions are evidently contradicted by the admission (proposed by some of our most important divines) of a communion with the Latin Church on very easy conditions." Thirdly: "Slight errors (proved by a change of rites) have been admitted by our own Church, and therefore we cannot logically uphold the principle that the true Church can never have fallen into a dogmatical error (be it ever so slight), or have undergone any change, be it ever so unimportant."

I have fairly admitted our deficiency in Christian zeal, though at the same time I exculpated our Church from that accusation with respect to the Western communities. You explain that same faintness by a latent conviction of our Church, which, you suppose, feels herself to be no more than a part of the whole Church notwithstanding her pretensions to the contrary. This explanation seems to me quite arbitrary, and has no right to admission till it be proved that no other explains the case quite sufficiently. But the question stands differently. The distinction I made between our relations to the heathen and our relations to Europe you consider rather as an evasive than as a direct answer, yet I think it is easily maintained by a very high authority. I had said, "What new tidings can we bring to the Christian West? What new source of information to countries more enlightened than we are? What new and unknown doctrine to men to whom the true Doctrine is known though disregarded?" These expressions imply no fear of a contention which indeed would show weakness and doubt, no distrust of the strength of our arguments and authorities, perhaps even no great want of zeal and love. They simply imply a deep conviction that the reluctance of the West to admit the simple truth of the Church arises neither from ignorance nor from rational objections, but from a *moral obstacle* which no human efforts can conquer, if it is not conquered by the better feelings of the better part of human nature, in those who can know the truth but do not wish to confess it. Such a disposition can exist, though the question is whether it exists in the case I am speaking of. Did not the Father of Light and Source of Love say in the parable by the lips of Abraham: "Have they not Moses and the prophets? If they do not listen to them, they will not listen to Lazarus, even if he was to rise from the dead" [Luke 16:29]. Do not, I pray, consider this quotation as being made with an intention of offense. I would not make injurious accusations; and, having once confessed a want of zeal in our country and people, I would confess it again; but my conviction is, that indeed in the present case the words of Christ may fairly be applied, and that you are separated from us by a moral obstacle, the origin of which I have tried in my former letter to trace to its historical beginning.

But does not this faintness of zeal—which I admit (with regard to the heathen nations)—imply a defect in the Eastern Church herself, and prove her to be no more than a part, perhaps even not so much as a part of the whole true Church? This I cannot admit. It may be considered as a defect of the nations to whom the destiny of the Church is temporarily confided (be they Russians or Greeks), but can nowise be considered as a stain to the Church itself. The ways of God are inscrutable. A few hundreds of disciples in the space of about two centuries brought to the Flock of Christ more millions of individuals than there were hundreds in the beginning. If that burning zeal had continued to warm the hearts of the Christians, in how short a space of time must not all the human race have heard and believed the saving Word? Sixteen centuries have elapsed since that epoch; and we are obliged to confess with all unwilling humility that the greater and by far greater majority of mankind is still in the slavery of darkness and ignorance. Where then is the zeal of the Apostle? Where is the Church? That would prove too much if it proved anything at all. Many centuries, particularly in the Middle Ages, and at the beginning of modern history, have hardly seen some few examples of solitary conversions and not one national, and not one remarkable effort at Proselytism. This seems to inculpate the whole Church. The spirit of missions is now most gloriously awakened in England, and I hope that that merit will not be forgotten by the Almighty in the days of trial and danger which England has perhaps to meet; but this noble tendency is a new one, or at least has become apparent only very lately. Is it a sign that the Church of England is now nearer to truth than it was before? Is it a proof of greater energies or purity? No one can admit the fact. Or let us take the Nestorian community, which you hold out as a parallel to us. I do not consider the parallel as a caricature, though you have added that word, probably with an intention to avoid offence. The Nestorians are generally ignorant, but ignorance (in point of Arts and Sciences) was our own lot not more than a century ago. The Nestorians are generally speaking poor; but that is no great blemish for any man and particularly for a Christian. They are few, but the truth of a doctrine is not to be measured by the number of its votaries. The Nestorians have been richer and more learned and more numerous than they are at present. They have had the spirit of Proselytism. Their missionaries have extended their activity over all the East as far as the inner India and the center of China, and that Proselytism was not ineffectual. Millions and millions had embraced Nestorianism (Marco Polo's testimony is not the only one to prove their success). Was Nestorianism nearer to truth in the time of its triumph than in our time? Mohammedanism and Buddhism would give us the same conclusion. Truth and error have had equally their time of ardent zeal or comparative coldness, and the characters of nations may certainly produce the same effects as the characters of epochs. Therefore I see no reason for accusing the Orthodox Church in herself of a defect or weakness which may, and in my opinion evidently does, belong to the nations that compose her communities.

Having thus distinguished the notes of the Church herself from the national qualities or defects of the Eastern community which alone represents it temporarily, permit me to add that the comparison which you institute between the zeal of the Romanists and the seeming indifference of the Eastern World is not quite fair. I do not deny the fact itself, nor do I express any doubt concerning the apparent superiority of the Latins in that respect; but I cannot admit their spirit of proselytism to be anything like a Christian feeling. I think it should be left quite out of the question as being the necessary result of a particular national or ecclesiastical organization, nearly akin to the proselytising spirit of Mohammedanism in the days of its pride. I will not condemn the zeal of the Romanists; it is in some respects too praiseworthy to be ill or even lightly spoken of; I can neither praise nor envy it. It is in many respects too un-Christian to be admired, as having produced and being always ready to produce more persecutors than martyrs. It is, in short, a mixed feeling not dishonorable for nations which belong to Romanism, but quite unworthy of the Church, and not to be mentioned in questions of ecclesiastical truth. I am, I trust, very far from having the disposition to boast, and yet I cannot but call your attention to a strange and generally unnoticed fact, viz., that notwithstanding the apparent ardor of Romanism and seeming coldness of Orthodoxy as to proselytism, yet that since the time of the Papal Schism (which certainly begins not with the quarrels of Photius and Nicolas, but with the interpolation of the Symbol when the West declared itself *de facto* sole judge of Christian doctrine) it has been the destiny of Orthodoxy to be happier in its conquests than its rival community. No one will doubt the fact if he considers the numerical superiority of Russian Orthodox Christians over the inhabitants of Scandinavia and about a third part of Germany, which were called to the knowledge of Christ after the time of Charles the Great. To this comparison you must add that even of that lesser number more, and by far more, than a half was not converted, but driven into the Latin Communion by cudgel, sword, and fire. I repeat that I am rather ashamed of our having done so little, than proud of our success; but in the unaccountable ways of Providence it is perhaps a particular dispensation of the Eternal Goodness to show that the Treasury of Truth must and shall thrive though confided to seemingly careless hands. No Anscar or Wilfried, no Willbrod or Columban[3]

---

3. Ansgar (ca.801–865), Wilfrid of York (634–709), Willibrod of Utrecht (658–739), and Columban (543–615) were missionaries to Scandinavia, South Saxons, Frisians, and Franks, respectively.

came to instruct Russia. We met them more than halfway, impelled by the grace of God. In aftertimes we have had our martyrs, we have had and still have our missionaries, whose labor has not been quite fruitless. I admit they are few in numbers; but is not the voice of truth which calls upon you, the voice of the whole Church? You have as yet seen no Russian or Greek missionary. But did Cornelius reject the Angel's voice and declare that he would not believe till the Apostle came [Acts 10:1–48]? He believed, and the Apostle came only as a material instrument of Christian confirmation; and shall the message of God, the emanation of the whole Church, the voice of truth, be the less powerful or the less acceptable because no single individual has been found worthy of bringing it to you? The Church may have and has undoubtedly many different forms of preaching.

The second point of accusation concerning the easy conditions on which Communion was proposed to the Latin Community may equally be answered without difficulty. Firstly, I readily admit that Mark of Ephesus went too far by his concessions; but in a fair trial of that great man and eminent divine we should, I think, rather admire his undaunted firmness than condemn his moments of human weakness. His was a terrible task. He felt, and could not but feel, that in rejecting the alliance of the mighty West he was literally condemning his country to death. This was more than martyrdom for a nobler spirit, and yet he stood the trial. Are we not to be indulgent in our judgment over an unwilling error inspired by the wish of saving his country, and are we not to bless the memory of his glorious opposition? Other divines of a later period [may have] consulted to a communion with Latins requiring nothing but a restitution of the Symbol to its ancient form and other less material changes in doctrine. These you consider as too easy conditions. "Would Athanasius [you ask] have admitted Arius to communion and allowed him the liberty of teaching Arianism everywhere excepting [in] the Symbol?" Very certainly he would not; but there is an immense difference between the heresy of Arius and the false doctrine of the Latins. The first rejects the true doctrine; the second admits it, and is only guilty of adding an opinion of its own (certainly a false one) to the holy truth. That opinion in itself has not been condemned by the Church, not being directly contrary to the holy Scriptures, and therefore does not constitute a heresy. The heresy consists in calumniating the Church and in giving out as her tradition a human and arbitrary opinion. Throw the interpolation out of the Symbol, and tradition is vindicated; opinion is separated from Faith; the keystone is torn out of the vault of Romanism, and the whole fabric falls to ruins with all its proud pretensions to infallibility, as if Romanism were the sole judge of Christian truth; the rebel spirit is hewed down and broken. In short, all is obtained that need be obtained. A deeper insight into the question would show (and that observation did not probably escape our divines) that the [human] opinion which is [merely] added to [the true] traditionary doctrine and implied in the *Filioque* has indeed no other support but the decision of ignorant Synods, and the declarations of the Roman See. Being once rejected out of the Symbol, and consequently out of Faith and Tradition, it could not stand by itself, and would be sure to fall and be forgotten like many other partial and local errors, such as, for instance, the error of considering Melchizedek as an apparition (though no incarnation) of Christ. The high majesty of the Church, most reverend sir, has nothing to do with individual opinions, though false, when they do not run directly against her own doctrine. They may, and do, constitute a heresy only when they dare to give themselves out as her doctrine, her tradition, and her faith. This seems to me a sufficient justification of the conditions proposed to the Romans and a proof that they did not imply the slightest doubt of the Eastern Orthodoxy and of her doctrine being the only true one.

Your third accusation is not positively stated; it is rather insinuated by a comparison with the sale of Indulgences than directly expressed; but I cannot leave it without an answer. Your own expressions that "the rebaptizing of Christians was prevalent for many years and even sanctioned by local canons" would be sufficient for our justification; for local errors are not errors of the Church, but errors into which individuals can fall by ignorance of the ecclesiastical rule. The blame falls on the individuals (whether they be Bishops or laymen signifies nothing). But the Church herself stands blameless and pure, reforming the local error, but never in need of a reform. I could add that in my opinion even in this case the Church has never changed her doctrine, and that there has only been a change of rites without any alteration in their meaning. All Sacraments are completed only in the bosom of the true Church, and it matters not whether they be completed in one form or another. Reconciliation renovates the Sacraments or completes them, giving a full and Orthodox meaning to the rite that was before either insufficient or heterodox, and the repetition of the preceding Sacraments is virtually contained in the rite or fact of reconciliation. Therefore the visible repetition of Baptism or Confirmation, though unnecessary, cannot he considered as erroneous, and establishes only a ritual difference without any difference of opinion. You will understand my meaning more clearly still by a comparison with another fact in ecclesiastical history. The Church considers Marriage as a Sacrament, and yet admits married heathens into her community without remarrying them. The conversion itself gives the sacramental quality to the preceding union without any repetition of the rite. This you must admit, unless you admit an impossibility, viz., that the Sacrament of Marriage was by itself complete in the lawful union of a heathen pair. The Church does not remarry heathens or Jews. Now, would it be an error to remarry them? Certainly not, though the rite would seem altered. This is my view of the question. The re-baptizing of Christians did not contain any error, but the admission of the error (if error it be) having been a local one is quite sufficient for the justification of the Eastern Church. The case is quite different with the sale of Indulgences. It was an error of the whole Roman Church, being not only sanctioned by her infallible head, but emanating directly from him. But I will be content to leave that argument aside, decisive though it be for a true Romanist, and will admit that the sale of Indulgences was attacked by some divines who were never condemned as heretics. It matters little whether it be so or not. The error remains the same. The sale of Indulgences cannot be condemned from a Roman point of view. As soon as Salvation is considered as capable of being obtained by external means, it is evident that the Church has a right to choose the means, considering the different circumstances of the community. Charity to the poor may be reasonably changed into charity to the whole body of the visible Church or to her head, the See of Rome. The form is rather comical; but the doctrinal error does not lie in the casual form; it lies in the doctrine itself of Romanism, a doctrine which is fatal to Christian freedom, and changes the adopted sons of God into hirelings and slaves.

I have thought it necessary to answer the accusation hinted at by the comparison you institute between two errors of Romanism and Orthodoxy, yet I do not much insist on accusing Rome in that particular case. The only thing I wanted was to show that we have a right to uphold the doctrine that no error, even the slightest, can ever be detected in the whole Eastern Church (I neither speak of individuals nor of local communities); and permit me to add that without this doctrine the idea itself of a Church becomes an illogical fiction by the evident reason that the possibility of an error being once admitted, human reason stands alone as a lawful judge over the holy work of God, and unbounded rationalism undermines the foundations of faith....

Having thus answered your remarks, I will take the liberty, most reverend sir, to add some observations on the whole tenor of your friendly letter. It is a friendly one, not to me alone, but to all of us children of the Orthodox Church. We could not have asked for larger concessions, nor for a greater agreement in points of doctrine. That yours is not a solitary instance may lie inferred not only from your quotations in your most valuable book about the Russian Catechism, but still more from the letters and professions of the Reverend Bishop of [the Scottish Church at] Paris. Believe me, this assurance is a source of great and heartfelt joy for all who feel an interest in truth and unity; and yet, sad to say, what have we gained? Nothing. We have been tried in our doctrine and found blameless; but now we are again tried in our morals (for zeal and love, which are the impelling motives of the Apostle, are nothing but a part of Christian morality), and we are found defective, as indeed we are, and our doctrine is to be condemned for our vices. The conclusion is not fair. You would not admit it if a Mohammedan was to bring it as an objection against Christianity itself, and yet you urge it against Orthodoxy.

Permit me to search into the latent causes of this fact, and excuse me if you find something harsh or seemingly offensive in my words. A very weak conviction in points of doctrine can bring over a Romanist to Protestantism, or a Protestant to Romanism. A Frenchman, a German, an Englishman, will go over to Presbyterianism, to Lutheranism, to the Independents, to the Cameronians, and indeed to almost every form of belief or misbelief; he will not go over to Orthodoxy. As long as he does not step out of the circles of doctrines which have taken their origin in the Western world, he feels himself at home; notwithstanding his apparent change, he does not feel that dread of apostasy which renders sometimes the passage from error to faith as difficult as from truth to error. He will be condemned by his former brethren, who will call his action a rash one, perhaps a bad one; but it will not be all utter madness, depriving him, as it were, of his rights of citizenship in the civilized world of the West. And that is natural. All the Western doctrine is born out of Romanism; it feels (though unconsciously) its solidarity with the past; it feels its dependence from one science, from one creed, from one line of life; and that creed, that science, that life was the Latin one. This is what I hinted at, and what you understand very rightly, viz., that all Protestants are Crypto-Papists; and indeed it would be a very easy task to show that in their Theology (as well as philosophy) all the definitions of all the objects of creed or understanding are merely taken out of the old Latin System, though often negatived in the application. In short, if it was to be expressed in the concise language of algebra, all the West knows but one datum, a; whether it be preceded by the positive sign +, as with the Romanists, or with the negative –, as with the Protestants, the a remains the same. Now a passage to Orthodoxy seems indeed like an apostasy from the past, from its science, creed, and life. It is rushing into a new and unknown world, a bold step to take, or even to advise.

This, most reverend sir, is the moral obstacle I have been speaking about; this, the pride and disdain which I attribute to all the Western communities. As you see, it is no individual feeling voluntarily bred or consciously held in the heart; it is no vice of the mind, but an involuntary submission to the tendencies and direction of the past. When the Unity of the Church was lawlessly and unlovingly rent by the Western clergy, the more so inasmuch as at the same time the East was continuing its former friendly intercourse and submitting to the opinion of the Western Synods the Canons of the second Council of Nicaea, each half of Christianity began a life apart, becoming from day to day more estranged from the other. There was all evident self-complacent triumph on the side of the Latins; there was sorrow on the side of the East, which had seen the dear ties of Christian brotherhood torn asunder—which had been spurned and rejected, and felt itself innocent. All these feelings have been transmitted by hereditary succession to our time, and more or less, either willingly or unwillingly, we are still under their power. Our time has awakened better feelings; in England, perhaps, more than anywhere else, you are seeking for the past brotherhood, for the past sympathy and communion. It would be a shame for us not to answer your proffered friendship; it would be a crime not to cultivate in our hearts an intense desire to renovate the Unity of the Church; but let us consider the question coolly, even when our sympathies are most awakened.

The Church cannot be a harmony of discords; it cannot be a numerical sum of Orthodox, Latins, and Protestants. It is nothing if it is not perfect inward harmony of creed and outward harmony of expression (notwithstanding local differences in the rite). The question is, not whether Latins and Protestants have erred so fatally as to deprive individuals of salvation, which seems to be often the subject of debate—surely a narrow and unworthy one, inasmuch as it throws a suspicion on the mercy of the Almighty. The question is whether they have the truth, and whether they have retained the ecclesiastical tradition unimpaired. If they have not, where is the possibility of unity?

Now permit me to add some observations not only on your letters, but on your book (which I have received with the greatest gratitude, and perused with unmixed pleasure), and on all the mode of action of those Anglicans who seem, and are indeed, nearest to us. You would show that all our doctrine is yours, and indeed at first sight you seem quite right. Many Bishops and divines of your communion are and have been quite orthodox. But what of that? Their opinion is only *an individual opinion*; it is not the *Faith of the Community*. The Calvinist Usher[4] is an Anglican no less than the bishops (whom you quote) who hold quite orthodox language. We may and do sympathize with the individuals; we cannot and dare not sympathize with a Church which interpolates the Symbol and doubts her right to that interpolation, or which gives Communion to those *who declare* the Bread and Wine of the High Sacrifice to be mere bread and wine, as well as to those who declare it to be the Body and Blood of Christ. This for an example—and I could find hundreds more—but I go further. Suppose an impossibility—suppose all the Anglicans to be quite Orthodox; suppose their Creed and Faith quite concordant with ours; the mode and process by which that creed is or has been attained is a Protestant one; a simple logical act of the understanding, by which the tradition and writings of the Fathers have been distilled to something very near Truth. If we admit this, all is lost, and Rationalism is the supreme judge of every question. Protestantism, most reverend sir, is the admission of an unknown [quantity] to be sought by reason; and that unknown [quantity] changes the whole equation to an unknown quantity, even though every other

---

4. James Usher (1580–1656) was a British prelate and scholar with strong Calvinist leanings.

datum be as clear and as positive as possible. Do not, I pray, nourish the hope of finding Christian truth without stepping out of the former Protestant circle. It is an illogical hope; it is a remnant of that pride which thought itself able and withal to judge and decide by itself without the Spiritual Communion of heavenly grace and Christian love. Were you to find all the truth, you would have found nothing; for we alone can give you that without which all would be vain—the assurance of truth.

Do not doubt the energies of Orthodoxy. Young as I am, I have seen the day when it was publicly either scoffed at or at least treated with manifest contempt by [too many in] our [high] society; when [I] myself, who was bred in a religious family and have never been ashamed of adhering strictly to the rites of the Church, was either supposed a sycophant or considered as a disguised Romanist; for nobody supposed the possibility of civilization and Orthodoxy being united. I have seen the strength of the Eastern Church rise, notwithstanding temporary aggression, which seemed to be fatal, or temporary protection, which seemed to be debasing. And now it rises and grows stronger and stronger. Romanism, though seemingly active, has received the deadly blow from its own lawful child, Protestantism; and indeed I would defy anybody to show me the man with true theological and philosophical learning who is still at heart a *pure* Romanist. Protestantism has heard its knell rung by its most distinguished teachers, by Neander, though unwillingly, in his letters to Mr. Dewar, and consciously Schelling in his preface to the posthumous works of Steffens. The ark of Orthodoxy alone rides safe and unhurt through storms and billows. The world shall flock to it. Let us say with the beloved Apostle: "Even so, come, Lord Jesus" [Rev. 22:20].

Accept my thanks for your book. I consider it as a very valuable acquisition not only for your countrymen, but for all truly and seriously religious readers. The books contained in the parcel sent to me from Cronstadt I have forwarded to their respective addresses except the one for C. Potemkin, whose address I have not yet found out. Pray excuse the length of my letter and the frankness of some expressions which are perhaps too harsh, and believe me, most reverend Sir, your most obedient servant,

Alexis Khamecoff
The 28th of November 1846

2.

Fifth Letter to William Palmer

Most reverend and dear Sir,

More than a year has elapsed since I have received your kind letter, and I should confess myself guilty of a long tardiness in answering it if I had not a sufficient justification in a violent inflammation of the eyes which has confined me for weeks to a dark room and made me for months unable to take a pen, or even a book, in hand. For a long while medical aid was not only of no use, but seemed rather to augment the intensity of the malady, till at length homeopathy was recurred to and achieved the cure in a very short time and only left a slight weakness in the eyes which does not hinder me in my habitual occupations.

The condition I was in during these ten months of involuntary and almost complete idleness was very disagreeable. Among many privations I consider as one of the most painful the impossibility of answering your letter, and of calling your attention to a very important event in the history of the Church. So many political events of high, or seemingly high, importance have troubled the last two years and engrossed the thoughts of all Europe that the one I mean has probably either passed quite unobserved or has been noticed by only a very few persons, and that rather accidentally than otherwise. No opinion is more common than that the abstract questions of religion are less interesting and less important than the practical questions of diplomacy and politics. I think that opinion very natural, and yet I believe there is none more erroneous and false, not only from the philosophical point of view (as religious questions refer to eternal truths, and to the only true welfare of man), but even from the historical point of view. For example, no man that is not altogether blind to the light of historical science can doubt for an instant that the Arian doctrine and its rejection at Nicaea have for centuries given a peculiar course to the destinies of European nations by having united the interests of Catholicism with some of the German tribes and having put them in opposition to other German tribes which were broken down in the conflict; or that the separation of East and West by a religious question has been of the most vital importance to the whole history of Europe by causing the western nations to sacrifice the Eastern Empire and by reducing the East to an isolated, tardy, and insufficient development of its energy. The common answer to such examples is that they are exceptions; but in reality, instead of being exceptions, they are only manifest illustrations of the common rule. Even in our time the greatest part of the European commotions, though seemingly produced by material interests, sometimes of the lowest character, is indeed nothing but a veil to the deep religious questions which, without his being conscious of the fact, direct the actions of man. I am sure this opinion will find your approbation, and I hope that you will likewise admit that I was right in considering the following fact as a very important and remarkable event.

You have probably heard of the inroad the Pope attempted in the East when as yet he had not so much ado with Italy and his own rebellious subjects. This inroad was made in the form of an address directed to the Roman Catholic subjects of the Sultan, but was indeed an evident, though perhaps not quite fair, attack on Eastern Orthodoxy. The Patriarchs and Bishops of the East considered themselves called upon for an answer, and they gave an answer signed by thirty-one Bishops. This fact is important in itself as being the only instance for more than a hundred years of a declaration of Faith coming so near to an ecumenical act, and as giving a splendid example of Unity; but some expressions contained in the answer are still more worthy of notice. I cannot quite approve of its general form and style. The phrases have a strong tendency to Byzantine rhetoric; but then it should be considered that, however strange to us, such a style is natural to men nurtured under the influence of a tasteless school. The polemical part, though not quite without merit, might certainly have been more powerful; but again that seems to be of only secondary importance. The expressions of the Synod, while speaking about their Roman adversaries, might have been milder; but this last circumstance, if not quite excusable, should not be judged too severely. In the last ten years or more the expressions of Roman writers when attacking the Eastern Church have been peculiarly harsh; it has even been very common with them to compare her with Arianism. No great mildness could have been expected in the reply. But a still more weighty excuse is to be found in the danger which seemed to threaten

Orthodoxy in the East. Never had the missionaries of Rome been so active and, in some instances, so successful. The Pope had acquired a great personal celebrity; he seemed to be on the best terms with the Divan, and the energy of his mind and character were supposed to be bent towards attaining a political as well as a spiritual ascendancy. There was much of fear in the harshness of the Grecian bishops. Still I do think that a milder tone would have been more dignified. But polemics belong to individuals, and never can have an ecclesiastical or ecumenical character. The only truly important part of the Patriarchal Encyclical is to be sought in the expressions which the Bishops use in speaking of their own Creed and Dogmas. These are of an immense importance, and have been a cause of joy to many of us, and indeed, I think, for all those who take a serious interest in religious matters. I daresay you have felt long since, as have most of us, that the difference between the Eastern Church and all the Western communities, whether Roman, or sprung out of Rome in the form of Protestations, lies not so much in the difference of separate dogmas or portions of creed as in something else which has not been as yet clearly defined or expressed. This difference consists in the different manner of considering the Church itself. I have tried in some straggling essays, and still more in some as yet unpublished historical disquisitions, to state that difference clearly and explicitly; still all explanations given by a solitary individual and by a layman had no authority whatever, and could not be considered as serious expressions of the Church's own self-notions. Doubts and direct negations were natural, and the more so as I must confess that my explanations were in evident opposition to many definitions of the Church and its essence given by some of our divines educated, I fear, under the influence of Western tendencies and science, which are rather predominant in Russian schools. The expressions used by a Synod of three Patriarchs and twenty-eight Bishops have a very high authority, and may be considered, now that they have been reprinted in Russia with the assent of our Church authorities, as something very near an ecumenical decision of the Eastern Church. These expressions, as worded in §17, are of the following import: "The Pope is greatly mistaken in supposing that we consider the Ecclesiastical Hierarchy to be the guardian of the dogma [of the Church]. The case is quite different. The unvarying constancy and the unerring truth of Christian dogma does not depend upon any

Hierarchical Order: it is guarded by the totality, by the whole *people* of the Church, which is the Body of Christ." Examples follow. The same idea is still more clearly illustrated, I think, in §11 (I have not the Encyclical with me, and can only quote from memory); the meaning of the passage is as follows: "No Hierarchical Order nor Supremacy is to be considered as a guarantee of truth. The knowledge of truth is given to mutual love." It would be difficult to ask for explanations more positive and more clear. The gift of truth is strictly separated from the hierarchical functions (viz., from Sacramental and Disciplinarian power), and the essential distinction from the Roman notion is thus established; the gift of unvarying knowledge (which is nothing but faith) is attributed, not to individuals, but to the totality of the ecclesiastical body, and is considered as a corollary of the moral principle of mutual love. This position is in direct contradiction to the individualism and rationalism which lies at the bottom of every Protestant doctrine. I am happy to say that I consider one of the most important bases of our Catechism to be duly and solidly established forever; and this fact I am inclined to deem almost miraculous when I reflect upon the deep ignorance, and perhaps moral debasement, of the Grecian clergy, and upon the tendency to spiritual despotism which I cannot but suspect in our more learned and enlightened churchmen. The strength of the vital and latent principle, when called upon, bears down before it all the obstacles which to our eyes and reason would seem unconquerable. I hope you will not blame me for my rather triumphant style; the joy we have felt in reading the Encyclical was the more intense inasmuch as it was quite unexpected. I am sure you will sympathize with us in this as you would sympathize in the many and many heavy feelings which we experience daily.

The general aspect of things, at least in matters of religion, is very favorable in our country, and would be still more so if we had not too much of political religion, and if the State was more convinced that Christian truth has no need of constant protection, and is rather weakened than strengthened by an excessive solicitude. A greater share of intellectual liberty would go far to break down the innumerable heresies of the worst description which are constantly either springing up or spreading their deleterious influence in the ranks of the common people. But then all this is nothing but a temporary error of rather timid politicians, and will pass; let the principles themselves be more

clearly expressed and better understood, and all will go well. I hope
such is the case with us. How does it stand with you, or rather with
your country? The hopes that had so unexpectedly rewarded your
constant exertions, are they likely to be fulfilled, at least in part? If
they were, and if I could hear of such a fortunate event, I should consider that day as one of the happiest in my life. Believe me, these are
not mere words. The spiritual welfare of England is one of the objects which are nearest to my heart. I do not say that I sympathize
with your indefatigable exertions; that expression would be too
weak. I can say that they are the theme of constant and anxious
thoughts. I suppose that you were scarcely more rejoiced in seeing
symptoms of a possible return or approximation to Catholicism during your journey to Scotland than I was in hearing of them. The
country to which the world is so much indebted, I will not say for liberal institutions or for progress of sciences, but for the noble efforts
of many of her children who have borne far and wide the name of
Christ and the blessing of adoring Him, this country seems to me
worthy of a clearer insight into the wonders of Christ's Church than
any other. Such are likewise the feelings of our Metropolitan. He was
strongly moved by the perusal of your letter and highly approved all
that you had done and proposed. The last news from Oxford is far
from being satisfactory. It seems that some defections have taken
place to ultra-Protestantism or to flat Rationalism, which is quite on
the verge of infidelity, if, indeed, it is not a total rejection of religion.
I think it could not be otherwise. The equivocal position of Anglicanism between Popery and ultra-Protestantism must manifest itself in
its consequences. The noble genius of Newman has not avoided one
of these deviations; others of less note, but perhaps of sincere tendencies to truth, fall in the opposite extreme. I hope these defections
have not had any influence on your nearest friends or on your own
energy. I feel it would be not only strange, but completely absurd, if I
entertained an idea of giving you any advice, or of forewarning you
against despondency. You know better than anybody the obstacles
that lie in your way, and a struggle of many years has proved your
energy and perseverance; but I could not avoid expressing my opinion on the fact I have heard of (perhaps a false rumor), and some
slight anxiety lest this fact should have damped the hopes of your
friends. No man is above a momentary weakness, and perhaps it will

not be quite useless to you to know that in a country far distant from your own there are hearts which feel all the immense importance of the task you have undertaken, and are alarmed at hearing of things which may render it still more arduous, and pray God as fervently as they call for your ultimate success....

Accept, most reverend and dear Sir, the assurance of the sincere respect and devotion.

Your most obedient servant

Alexis Khamecoff
Oct. the 8th, 1850

IV

ON THE THEOLOGICAL WRITINGS OF ALEKSEI KHOMIAKOV
Yury Samarin[1]

1.

Introduction to the Theological Writings of Aleksei Khomiakov

[excerpts]

Khomiakov *lived in the Church* (to be sure, in the Orthodox Church, for there cannot be two Churches).

But we feel that such a definition will seem too broad and meager for the majority of readers.

The crux lies in what meaning to attach to the words "to live in the Church." In the sense in which we are using them, these words mean, first of all: to have the doubt-free conviction that the Church is not only something useful and even necessary but that she is also really what she claims to be and all she claims to be: that is, a manifestation on earth of unalloyed, indestructible truth. Secondly, they mean: to

---

1. In theology, the important Slavophile thinker Yury Samarin (1819–1876) was a direct disciple of Khomiakov (see a discussion of Samarin in the introduction to the present book). The present work is a substantial extract (about two-thirds of the whole) from Samarin's celebrated introduction to the first Russian edition of Khomiakov's theological writings (Prague, 1867), which Samarin edited. Samarin's essay not only provides an intimate, spiritual biography of Khomiakov but also clearly formulates the Slavophiles' conceptions of sobornost and the Church. According to Samarin, "the Church is not a doctrine, not a system, and not an institution. The Church is a living organism, an organism of truth or love, or more precisely: *truth and love as an organism*" (The italics are Samarin's; see page 171). It is in this essay that Samarin gives his famous characterization of Khomiakov as a "teacher of the Church" (see page 183). This extract has been translated from the Russian by Boris Jakim. — TRANS.

submit's one's will wholly and completely to this law, which governs the Church. Finally, they mean: to feel oneself a living particle of the living whole that calls itself the Church, and to consider one's spiritual communion with this whole loftier than anything else in the world.

If we are asked, Do not all the Orthodox *live* in the Church? we will answer without reflecting: far from all. We live in our family, in our society, even, to some extent, in the humanity that is contemporary to us. We also live, though to a lesser extent, in our nation. But as for the Church, we do not *live* in her but are *registered* in her, as it were. We sometimes go to Church, sometimes consult with her, for that is the usual practice and is sometimes necessary. For example, under the influence of material worries, when, say, we are concerned about keeping our fields from being harmed by cattle or our forests from being damaged by illegal tree-cutting, we will remember that the Church teaches patience to the needy and forbids encroachments on someone else's property. It does in fact teach that, but it teaches not only that, but much else. Or, having learned one fine day that Russia has been overrun with nihilists, we throw everything we can against them: existing laws, political economy, Europe's public opinion, and religion to boot—seeing it is handy. And here it is again indisputable that nihilism is condemned by faith. It is a pity, however, that we remember this too late, when we are frightened, and that we need it only as a stone to throw.

In general, one can say that our relationship to the Church is one of obligation, of duty, akin to our relationship to respected relatives of hoary age whom we drop in to see two or three times a year, or to those good friends with whom we have nothing in common but from whom—in extreme need—we sometimes borrow money. Khomiakov did not have a *relationship* to the Church. This is because he *lived* in her, and he lived in her not from time to time, not in spurts, but always and constantly, from his early childhood until the moment when he obediently, fearlessly, and without shame met the "destroying angel" sent to him.[2]

For him the Church was a living center in which all his thoughts originated and to which they all returned. He stood before the face of the Church and judged himself with an inner judgment according to her law. All that was dear to him he held dear in relation to the

---

2. These words are from a poem by Khomiakov. — TRANS.

Church. He served the Church, defended her, cleared a path to her from errors and prejudices, rejoiced in all her joys, was tormented by all her sufferings inwardly, profoundly, with all his soul. Yes, he *lived* in the Church. There is no better expression for it.

In order to clarify our thought, let us indicate a fact that in itself is insignificant but that can serve as a good example. When we are invited to a wedding or a dinner party, we put on tails and a white tie. Why do we do that? Solely because everyone does it, because that is the accepted practice in the milieu, in the society we call our own. But why do we obey the codes of this society? Because we do not dare and do not wish to offend it. And we do not wish to offend it because we *live* in it and value our participation in it. All his life, in Petersburg, in civil service, in the Guards regiment, during military campaigns, abroad, in Paris, in his own home, while visiting, Khomiakov strictly observed all fasts. Why? For the same reason: because *everyone* did it, that is, *everyone* who was of *his* society. Because it could never enter his head to separate himself from the society called the Church by breaking with its traditions. Finally, because he was gladdened by the thought that, on the same day and at the same hour, *his* whole society, that is, the whole Orthodox world, was fasting or break-fasting with him, commemorating the same event, the common joy or common sorrow.

Of course, the majority had a different view of this and shrugged their shoulders. When he was laughed at, he laughed back. But he would become truly indignant when well-intentioned *non-fasting* people would tell him that it was pleasant to see such an attachment to good old traditions, which, at least in part, support the social order. He was indignant because, truly, there was no arduous feat, no great merit here on his side. He acted thus because he could not act otherwise, and he could not act otherwise because he did not have a *relationship* to the Church but just *lived* in the Church.

This trait of his (let us call it a strange peculiarity) did not of course draw him closer to the society contemporary to him. Rather, it isolated him. Not finding any sympathy around him, or even any attentiveness to what was holy for him, he spent his whole youth and the greater part of his mature years in such inner solitude. Everyone will agree that such a position is a difficult one, and even almost unbearable. When struggle is impossible (for what struggle can there be against indifference?), the sense of constant opposition to the social milieu, from which one cannot and does not wish to tear oneself, will certainly result either in inner embitterment or in a victory of personal consciousness that will harden this consciousness and make it forever unshakable. Indifference can be defeated only by laughter or tears.

Khomiakov laughed in company and cried when he was alone. The public heard this infectious ringing laughter and concluded that he was merry and carefree. This conclusion was not completely correct. During the siege of Sebastopol[3]—at the very moment when the national pride painfully awoke from its intoxication, when, one after another, all the beautiful illusions disintegrated before our eyes, and we witnessed all the grotesqueness and poverty of our activity—one evening, in the company of friends, Khomiakov was particularly merry and carefree. At that moment his mood diverged so radically from the tone of his company that it offended one of his close friends, who addressed an indignant reproach to him: "I don't understand how you can laugh when everyone else is dying of heartache and is choking back tears." Khomiakov bowed his head. His face took on a serious, but also joyous, expression, and, leaning over to the friend who had reproached him, he answered: "For thirty years I have wept to myself while everyone around me was laughing. Try to understand that now I have the right to laugh when I see all these tears leading to salvation."

If this had been said by anyone else, it would have been attributed to the speaker's wishing to pose as an unrecognized prophet. But such a thought would never have entered the head of anyone who even slightly knew Khomiakov. Khomiakov almost never spoke about himself. No one ever heard any pretty phrases from him—not because he avoided them but because he was innately incapable of emitting such phrases. If he were at all capable of playing a role, of doing something that would draw attention to him, then the public's attitude toward him would have been different, and his position in society would not have been as it was. And we would not have to undertake the writing of an explanatory foreword to his works.

To this point we have been speaking about how Khomiakov did not resemble other people and why he was not, and could not be, esteemed at his true value, or even recognized. But one cannot say

---

3. A battle in the Crimean War. — TRANS.

that he passed by without leaving any trace at all. On the contrary, he did leave a trace, and we think it is an indelible one, to which, sooner or later, all will turn. He had influence, and an enormous influence, although one that has not yet been fully noticed, an influence that was greater in its depth than in its breadth—an influence, if not on many, then one that was strong and stable.

In what ways did he converge with his contemporaries and influence them?

Khomiakov represented an original *manifestation of total freedom in religious consciousness*, one nearly unprecedented in our land.

With this he astonished everyone he met, not only those who tended to share his views but also his most fervent opponents. Upon first meeting him, you could not help becoming convinced that he thoroughly knew, had thoroughly reflected upon and felt everything that, in our time, is destabilizing and undermining faith. He was intimately familiar with both pantheism and materialism in all their forms. He knew the results that contemporary science had arrived at, both in the study of natural phenomena and in the critical analysis of Scripture and Church traditions. Finally, he had spent many years studying the history of religions, and so he was deeply familiar with that variable, eternally fluctuating side of human beliefs that seems to bear such convincing witness against any truth that is immutable and not subject to the laws of historical development. Despite this, his convictions were unshakable.

That was the first impression that he made on everyone. Then, when you got to know him better, you could not fail to notice another trait of his: not only did Khomiakov *value* faith, but he was deeply certain that it was *stable, unshakable*. Thus, he did not fear for it, and because he did not fear, he always looked at all things with eyes wide open. He closed his eyes to nothing; he did not try to evade anything; he never tried to deceive himself, to lie to himself. Completely free, that is, completely truthful in his convictions, he demanded the same freedom, the same right to be truthful for others. At a time when our higher authorities proposed that the atheism that had become common in our high schools should be countered by using the Book of Genesis as the textbook for teaching geology, Khomiakov decisively wrote that many of the results at which the natural sciences and the historical critique had arrived in their own legitimate way contradict accepted traditions; that this should not be concealed; and that it would be both imprudent and offensive for faith to constrain the free development of science, since, on the one hand, science itself has by no means said its last word, and, on the other hand, no one can say if we have understood everything that has been told to us, and if we have understood it correctly.

Anyone who has observed the usual type of pious individual encountered here and elsewhere in educated circles, has probably noticed that this individual often values his faith not as an indisputable truth but for the sake of the personal peace that he gains in it. This individual protects and tends his faith like a treasured thing, but one that, at the same time, is fragile and not completely reliable. On the one hand, this attitude toward faith is often permeated with a concealed unbelief, of which the believer is often not conscious but which is quite noticeable for others; and, on the other hand, it is characterized to some degree by a special kind of egoism—the egoism of *self-salvation*. For this reason, by virtue of the fact that there has crept into his soul a suspicion that his faith is not unshakable, the pious individual so often exhibits extreme condescension and cowardly tolerance toward those pathological growths that, always and everywhere, are encountered on the historical husk of the Church. In both manifestations of pseudopiety his inner consciousness sees superstition, straining, deception, or falsehood. But his tongue does not move to call things by name: he sees an abuse, but he cannot raise his hand to remove it—he's frightened.

All this appears to be sanctified by the Church; all is smoked through with incense, sprinkled with holy water. "What if," he thinks, "by removing the growth, one will wound the living body, and will it withstand the operation? All around stand doctors who long ago sentenced it to death. What if they are right?" And forgetting that this body for which he is afraid is the body of Christ and not the body of the clergy, or of Russia, or of Greece, the pious individual pretends that he neither sees nor hears anything, keeps silent when necessary, delivers appropriate answers in writing, plays the hypocrite before himself and before others, justifying in words what he condemns in his soul.

Completely opposite to this type, familiar to all of us, was Khomiakov. He valued faith as the *truth*, and not as satisfaction for himself, apart from and irrespective of its truthfulness. The very thought that some admixture of falsehood or untruth could so firmly attach itself to the truth that it would be necessary, in the interests of truth, to spare this falsehood and untruth—this thought would make him more indignant and offend him more powerfully than anything else. And he persecuted this form of unconscious cowardice or conscious pharisaism in all its manifestations with merciless irony. He had the daring of faith. Because of this it happened that pious people would cross themselves and turn away from him, and say that there was nothing sacred for him, while nihilists would say: "What a pity such a one is mired in Byzantinism." For those indifferent to faith, Khomiakov was strange and ridiculous. For those who deigned to bestow upon faith their lofty protection, he was insufferable; he agitated them. For those who consciously and, in their own way, conscientiously rejected faith, he was a living objection that nonplussed them. Finally, for those who preserved in themselves the acuteness of an undamaged religious sense but who had become entangled in contradictions and divided in their souls, he was a kind of emancipator: he led them out into wide expanses, into God's light, and returned to them the wholeness of religious consciousness.

Above we spoke of the impenetrable cloud of misunderstanding that is spread between the Church and those who believe or who feel the need to believe—this cloud that hides the true face of the Church from the majority.[4] There are many such misunderstandings, so many that there is no possibility of enumerating all of them. But we would hardly be in error if we say that they ultimately reduce to a single misunderstanding: the presumption that it is impossible to harmonize that which the Church teaches and prescribes with the living, legitimate, innate human need for freedom. We have used the most indefinite word—*freedom.* And we do not consider it necessary to define it more precisely, for it does not have a sense in which it is opposed to the Church. Such are our present conceptions.

Take civil freedom, in the sense of the absence of external compulsion in matters of conscience, and you will hear that it is incompatible with the Church. Why does one think this? Because in practice this freedom collides with certain laws and orders of things from which unbelief concludes that faith and fanaticism are the same thing. Fanaticism demands persecutions, and unbelief thinks that the Church

---

4. This passage is not included in the present extract. — TRANS.

would necessarily demand them if secular power, having struggled out from under the Church's tutelage, did not to some extent restrain the Church's innate tendencies.[5]

Take political freedom, in the sense of the manifested and legitimized participation of citizens in government affairs, and here you will encounter a seeming contradiction. For, taking compliments uttered on certain occasions as dogmas, rhetoric for doctrine, and flattery for confession, unbelief has succeeded in convincing many that the Church not only blesses the *idea of the state* (that is, a national union under a generally recognized authority) but supposedly sanctifies just one of the forms of state union with the exclusion of all others; that it supposedly accepts this authority as God's direct gift, as the private property of an individual or a dynasty, and thereby opposes all political progress, condemning it in advance as an attack on a divine commandment.

Finally, take freedom of thought, the most precious, most sacred, most necessary of all the freedoms, and here you will hear not solitary voices but a whole chorus proclaiming that faith and freedom of thought are two mutually exclusive concepts; that it is not by chance that a *believer* (*croyant*) and a *free thinker* (*libre penseur*) are always contrasted to each another; that whoever values his thought must say good-bye to the Church, whereas whoever cannot do without faith must invariably trim the wings of his thought, shut it in a cage, impose a prohibition upon it, and restrain its innate striving for truth, and for truth alone. But why do people think thus? Because all concepts have been distorted and have gone astray. Because, thanks to the narrowness, imprecision, and obsolescence of the scholarly frame in which the doctrine of the Church is offered, the concept of *faith* has been transformed into the concept of *knowledge*, but a knowledge that is unexamined, confused, unjustified in itself, or it has even been transformed into the concept of conditional and coerced, as it were, *acknowledgment*. Because a free relation to the known and assimilated *truth* has become identified in the opinion of the majority with subordination to *authority*, that is, to a power (be it

---

5. For example, do many people know that criminal punishment for lapsing from the true faith is, in essence, more contrary to the spirit of the Church than to so-called humanism or liberalism?

a book or an institution) that we have agreed to accept as truth, although we know full well (and even make peace with our conscience) that it is no more than a fiction, but a fiction that no manner of communal living can dispense with. Because, finally, we have even stopped understanding that the same word—*faith*—serves to designate both the object, that is, the complete and unconditional truth revealed to us, and the subjective capacity or organ for acquiring this truth; and that therefore anyone who conditionally receives what is conditional, receives not what the Church offers but something homegrown, something that is his own, and he receives it not by faith but by opinion or conviction. I *acknowledge, submit, subordinate* myself; hence, I do not *believe*. The Church offers faith alone, evokes faith alone in the human soul, and does not settle for less. In other words, the Church receives only *free* individuals into her bosom. Anyone who brings her a slave's acknowledgment without believing in her is not within the Church, is not of the Church.

We are far from claiming to elucidate, or even to enumerate, all the age-old misunderstandings that darken honest minds and perplex consciences not only here in Russia, but everywhere. We do not wish to enter into a debate with atheism. Rather, we wish only to hint at the nature of these misunderstandings and to refresh in the memories of those readers who personally knew Khomiakov the main themes and characteristics of his polemical conversations. We might describe their effect by saying that nearness to Khomiakov produced in living minds and sensitive souls the conviction, or at least the feeling, that living and life-giving truth is never revealed to plain curiosity but is always given in direct proportion to the inquisitiveness of the conscience that seeks edification, and that in this case the act of intellectual understanding requires a spiritual discipline of the will; that there is no scientific truth that cannot be harmonized with or that cannot ultimately coincide with the truth revealed; that there is no feeling or aspiration irreproachable in the moral respect; that there is no rational need, of whatever kind, that we must reject, despite our consciousness and our conscience, in order to buy peace within the bosom of the Church; in brief, that one can believe honestly, conscientiously, and freely; that other than honestly, conscientiously, and freely it is impossible to believe. That is what Khomiakov clarified, developed, and proved by his powerful, irresistible word, and he himself served his word with his whole being as a living confirmation and witness. That is the sense in which we called him an emancipator of individuals disposed to believe but frightened and confused by the encounter with apparently unresolvable contradictions. Having come to know him, such individuals began to breathe fully and freely; they felt themselves liberated in their religious consciousness and inwardly justified against all duplicitous and unlawful (though sometimes tempting) deals with that admixture of falsehood, untruth, and convention that, in our concepts, clouds the concept of the Church. For many, a close acquaintance with Khomiakov was the beginning of a turning to what was better, and therefore it will always remain in their grateful memory a significant event of their inner lives.

Till now we have spoken of Khomiakov in relation to the social milieu in which he lived and of his personal, direct psychic effect, so to speak, on his immediate environment. We now turn to his significance in the domain of ecclesiastical science....

What Khomiakov served with his whole life is also what he pursued in his science. *He clarified the idea of the Church in its logical determination.* These words require an explanation.

According to our customary conception, the Church is an *institution*—to be sure, an institution of a special kind, even unique, a divine institution, but still an institution. This conception sins in the same way as almost all our usual definitions and representations of objects of faith: this conception does not directly contradict the truth, but it is insufficient. It brings the idea down into a region that is too lowly and habitual, a too-familiar region, as a result of which the idea, willy-nilly, becomes banal through a close comparison with a group of phenomena apparently homogeneous with it but essentially not having anything in common with it. We know what an institution means, and it is very easy, even too easy, to conceive the Church as an institution by analogy with other institutions. There is a book called the Criminal Code and there is a book called the Holy Scripture. There is a judicial doctrine and there are judicial forms; there is also a Church tradition and there is a Church ritual. There is a criminal-law chamber that has its own code and is empowered to execute this code, to apply it, to judge in accordance with it, and so on—and in parallel, there is a Church that, guided by Scripture, proclaims doctrine, applies it, sifts through doubts, judges, and decides. In one case we have conditional truth, the law, and, attached to the law, the magistracy, wielding the law, officers of the law.

In the other case we have the unconditional truth (that's the difference), but a truth that is also contained in book or word; and attached to it, once again, are officers and savants—the clergy.

The Church does in fact have its doctrine, which constitutes one of its inalienable manifestations. The Church does in fact, in its historical manifestation, come into contact, as a kind of institution, with all institutions. Nevertheless, the Church is not a doctrine, not a system, and not an institution. The Church is a living organism, an organism of truth and love, or more precisely: *truth and love as an organism.*

From this definition flows the Church's relation to all falsehood. This relation is the same as the relation of any organism to what is hostile to and incompatible with its nature. The Church casts, removes, separates falsehood away from herself, thereby building a wall between herself and falsehood. In this way the Church determines herself, that is, the truth. But the Church does not argue with falsehood, does not refute, explain, or define it. All this—argument, refutation, explanation, definition of errors—is the business not of the Church but of a school contained in the Church. This is the task of ecclesiastical science, that is, theology.

With regard to the Eastern heresies, the Orthodox school developed the Church's teaching of the essence of God, the Trinity, and the God-man into a harmonious doctrine. The cycle of this grandiose development of human thought, illuminated by grace from above, ended before the falling away of Rome. Then the historical destiny of the East soon changed: scientific enlightenment in the East went into eclipse; at the same time, the intellectual productivity of the Orthodox school went into decline. Meanwhile, the stream of rationalism injected by the Roman schism into the Church herself raised new theological questions in the West, questions of which the Orthodox East was ignorant. In its further flow this stream divided into two currents and finally produced two opposed doctrines: Romanism and Protestantism.[6]

All these new formations came out of local, exclusively Romano-Germanic elements. Universal tradition played in them the role of the

---

6. Like Khomiakov (see the French writings in the present volume), Samarin does not consider the Church of Rome "Catholic," so he avoids using the term *Roman Catholic.* Instead, he generally uses the term *Latinstvo* ("Latinism"), which I render as "Romanism," to make it consistent with Khomiakov's usage. — TRANS.

passive material, which was gradually worked upon, distorted, and adapted to popular notions and needs. The whole intellectual movement from Pope Nicholas I to the Council of Trent, from Luther and Calvin to Schleiermacher and Neander, occurred entirely outside the Church and without any participation of the Church.[7] It could not have been otherwise. The Church remained what she was; the lamp entrusted to her did not go out; its light was not dimmed. But attacks from the West, the threatening pressure of Western propaganda, attempts to overturn the universal tradition by which the East has maintained itself and continues to maintain itself and then to seek a rapprochement with the East, to make a deal with it—all this should have caused the Orthodox school to enter into battle, should have drawn it into a polemic, and should have made it take one position or another vis-à-vis Romanism and Protestantism.

What did the school do? Its role can be expressed in a single word: it *defended* itself. In other words, it took a defensive posture, and therefore one that was subordinate to the opponents' mode of action and to their methods. The school deliberated upon questions posed by Romanism and Protestantism. It accepted them in the form in which they were stated by Western polemics, not suspecting that falsehood lay not only in the solutions but in the very posing of these questions, even more in the posing than in the solutions. Thus, involuntarily and unconsciously, without having a presentiment of the consequences, the school slipped off the solid continent of the Church and slid onto the shifting, pitted, undermined ground to which the Western theologians had lured it. On this ground the school got caught in a cross fire, and, to defend itself against attacks directed against it from the two opposite sides, it was compelled to grasp whatever weapons were available— and these turned out to be the weapons that had been adapted long ago by the Western confessions for their domestic, internecine war. And so, with each step becoming more and more mired in the Latin-Protestant antinomies, the Orthodox Church too was, in the end, sundered apart. Two schools formed in this Church: an exclusively *anti-Latin* school and an exclusively *anti-Protestant* school. It was as if the Orthodox

---

7. Friedrich Schleiermacher (1768–1834) was the great systematic theologian of nineteenth century Protestantism. The *General Church History* of the ecclesiastical historian Johann Neander (1789–1850) exercised great influence. — TRANS.

school stopped existing. Of course, it cannot be said that the war was an unsuccessful one for us: We evinced much ardor, erudition, and fortitude. We even won many particular battles, especially when it came to exposing Latin forgeries, concealments, and stratagems. As for the final result, it goes without saying that Orthodoxy was not shaken. But this should not be credited to the school, and we are forced to acknowledge that it waged the war incorrectly.

The error it made at the very beginning, when it went over onto foreign soil, had three inevitable results: First, the anti-Latin school took on a Protestant cast, and the anti-Protestant school took on a Latin cast. Second, as a consequence, every success of one school in the battle with its foe constantly turned into a defeat for the other school, arming its foe against it. Third and most important, *Western rationalism seeped into the Orthodox school and congealed in it in the form of a scientific frame for the dogmas of faith*, in the form of proofs, interpretations, and conclusions....[8]

Thus, over nearly two centuries, the polemic of the two Orthodox schools against the Western communions continued, accompanied, of course, by the internecine, domestic polemic of these schools one against the other....

Our Orthodox school was capable of defining neither Romanism nor Protestantism, because, having left *its own* soil, it split into two, and each of the halves stood *against*, not *above*, the foe.

Khomiakov was the first to look at Romanism and Protestantism *from inside the Church*, and therefore *from above*. Therefore, he was able to *define* them....

Foreign theologians were perplexed by his brochures.[9] They sensed in them something unprecedented in their polemic with Orthodoxy, something unexpected, completely new. Perhaps they did not clearly recognize what the novelty consisted in, but we comprehend it. They heard, finally, a voice that was neither anti-Latin nor anti-Protestant, but of the Orthodox school. For the first time, having encountered Orthodoxy in the domain of ecclesiastical science, they dimly sensed that, heretofore, their polemic with the

---

8. Samarin presents some specific examples (omitted in this extract) of these developments. — TRANS.
9. See footnote on page 175. — TRANS.

Church had revolved around certain misunderstandings; that their age-old dispute with the Church, which had seemed almost over, was only now beginning, on a completely new ground, and that the very positions of the sides had changed: namely, they, the papists and protestants, had become the accused and were forced to justify themselves. This was the first impression that preceded a clear judgment and that was produced not so much by the content as by the tone of the brochures. The tone was indeed special and unprecedented. Alien to it were both the belligerence into which polemical writers of the last century often fell and the inappropriate timidity noticeable in some of the more recent champions of Orthodoxy. Instead, this tone was distinguished by a rigorous and straightforward statement of the problems, by mercilessness in condemnation, and noble boldness in proclaiming fundamental principles. In no way did this boldness resemble arrogance. It could not be called conceit. No. In Khomiakov's tone one could hear a doubt-free faith in the rightness of his work, a faith that one no longer encounters in the Western religious literature. Even his prejudiced opponents freely admitted this.

Not less distinctive were the author's polemical methods, the system of dispute chosen by him. Before Khomiakov, our learned theological debates would get lost in particularism. Every proposition of the opponents and every single one of their arguments would be analyzed and refuted separately. Before Khomiakov, we had been exposing forged inserts or false excisions, restoring the meaning of distorted quotations, contraposing text against text, evidence against evidence, and exchanging proofs from Scripture, from tradition, and from reason. By arguing successfully, we would disprove our opponents' positions. Sometimes, we would even demonstrate that their positions contradicted Scripture and tradition: this meant that their positions were false and had to be rejected. Of course, this removed the error in the form in which it appeared before us.

But that is not everything. One had yet to clarify how, whence, and from what inner motives the error was born; what precisely was false in these motives; where the root of this falsehood is. These questions were not resolved. They went virtually undiscussed. And it would therefore sometimes happen that, having disposed of an error expressed in one form (as a dogma or decree), we did not recognize it in another form. It would even happen that we would assimilate the error in the very process of refutation, transporting the motive that evoked it into our own point of view. The root of the error remained in the ground, and the sprouts that it gave off often contaminated our soil too. Khomiakov's approach is a completely different one. Proceeding from manifestations to initial motives, he reproduces, if one can phrase it this way, the psychic genealogy of each error and reduces all of the errors to a common origin in which falsehood, by becoming obvious, exposes itself in its inner contradiction. That is what it means to tear error out by the roots.

Looking deeper and going from system to content, we remark yet another distinguishing feature in Khomiakov's theological works. At first sight, they have a predominantly polemical character. But, in fact, polemic occupies only a secondary place in them; or, more precisely, polemic is virtually absent in them in the strict sense of refutations of a purely negative character. One cannot remove the negative side (objections and refutations) of his works without also removing the positive side (clarifications of Orthodox doctrine). This is because the two sides are inseparable in his works; the two constitute an indissoluble whole. In Khomiakov there is not a single argument against the Romans that has been taken from the Protestants, and not a single argument against the Protestants taken from the Roman arsenal. There is no argument in Khomiakov that is not directed against both Romanism and Protestantism. This is because every one of his arguments is, in essence, not a negation but a direct positing, but one that is sharply pointed for polemical purposes.

If we wished to trace this process in detail, we would have to repeat the whole content of at least Khomiakov's three main brochures.[10] It would be better, however, for readers to verify our words by their own impressions. But in order to express more clearly that distinctive trait we have indicated, and which in our opinion constitutes Khomiakov's

---

10. That is to say, the three works (offered in the present anthology, entirely or in part) under the titles: "Some Remarks by an Orthodox Christian Concerning the Western Communions, on the Occasion of a Brochure by Mr. Laurentie," "Some Remarks by an Orthodox Christian Concerning the Western Communions, on the Occasion of a Letter Published by the Archbishop of Paris," and "Some More Remarks by an Orthodox Christian Concerning the Western Communions, on the Occasion of Several Latin and Protestant Religious Publications."— TRANS.

main achievement, we will permit ourselves to use the following comparison.

When people find themselves in a cloud or fog, they are conscious only of the absence, or deficiency, of light. But where the fog has come from, whether it spreads far, and where the sun is—these things they do not know, do not see, and cannot say. But when the sky is clear and the sun shines brightly, every chance cloud is clearly delineated against the sky, as a cloud, as an opposite to light.

Khomiakov clarified the region of light, the atmosphere of the Church. And against the Church, false teaching stood out as the negation of light, as a dark spot on the sky. The boundaries of false teaching became clear; they were defined. We speak of false teaching, not of false teachings, though we mean both Romanism and Protestantism, for both confessions seem to us to be a single error, and this unity can be scrutinized only from the standpoint onto which Khomiakov placed us, that is, from the Church. Prior to Khomiakov, our Orthodox school had always considered Romanism and Protestantism to be two mutually exclusive opposites, two poles. They actually do thus appear in the West, because there the religious consciousness has definitively split into two, and one has lost the very concept of the Church, that is, the medium out of which these two confessions separated, under the influence of Roman and Germanic elements.

The very same idea of these confessions was transmitted to us as well; we assimilated ready-made definitions and looked at Romanism with the eyes of the Protestants, and at Protestantism with the eyes of the Romans. But now, thanks to Khomiakov, everything is shifting. Formerly, we had seen two sharply defined forms of Western Christianity, and, *between them*, Orthodoxy, which had stopped at the crossroads, as it were. But now we see the *Church*, the living organism of the truth, entrusted to mutual love, while outside the Church we see logical knowledge detached from the moral principle, that is, *rationalism* in two stages of its development: (1) Romanism, or rationalistic understanding that grasps at the *phantom* of truth and surrenders freedom to enslavement by external *authority* and (2) Protestantism, or rationalistic understanding that seeks its *own, home-made* truth and sacrifices unity to *subjective* sincerity.

Perhaps it has become easier to understand what we said above— that Khomiakov clarified the idea of the Church to the extent (always incomplete) to which any living phenomenon is subject to logical determination. He expressed this idea precisely, strictly, in a definitive form, to which nothing can be added and from which nothing can be subtracted. That is Khomiakov's achievement in the domain of theology. He opened a new era in the history of the Orthodox school.

With these words we come to a concluding discussion of his further development.

First of all, there arises the question: Was it in this way that Khomiakov's theological works were understood and assessed by specialists in such matters, our learned clergy?

An educated, learned layperson, interceding for Orthodoxy and entering into combat with foreign confessions—such a rare phenomenon could not, of course, fail to excite a pleasant surprise in the circle of specialists.

A sincerity of conviction heard in a voice emanating from a social milieu tending more toward flaccid skepticism than toward anything else; strict, logical consistency in argumentation; the unexpectedness and iron strength of arguments, acknowledged by the opponents themselves—all this, naturally, was greeted with joy.

Without fearing any objections, it seems that one could say that all the specialists rejoiced in the unexpected help and greeted in the person of Khomiakov a first-class polemicist. One could also say that the orientation of his thought and the substance of his view of objects of faith evoked, in *some* specialists, approval and sympathy, which the late author valued more than the flattering judgments of the foreign press.

But far from all the specialists acted this way toward him. The majority applauded him from afar but did not follow him, did not even openly recognize him. In general, in the opinions and judgments that reached us from this circle, we often remarked, in part, a deliberate restraint and, in part, a completely sincere dualism of impressions. On the one hand, we remarked a heartfelt desire to agree, while on the other hand we perceived a fear of assimilating something new, or at least unexpected, something luminous, to be sure, but perhaps too luminous. To this was added a certain regret, as if an anguished longing: there was a sense that, if one took up the weapons forged by Khomiakov, one would probably have to take off a substantial part of the scholastic armor one was used to wearing—a heavy and inconvenient armor, to be

sure, that did not defend one against anything and was even full of
holes, but an armor that had become one with the body. One would
have to sacrifice logical methods and techniques that, true, everyone
was tired of, that had lost all effectiveness, but that had been memorized
long ago and were therefore easy. Finally, from the arsenal of definitions and proofs one would perhaps have to discard some things as
totally useless, things that, true, even now are not absolutely
approved—are even condemned as weak and unreliable, but are condemned, on the whole, in "one's own house," as it were, in one's own
conscience or in a circle of trusted friends, not in public.

Everything in these fears is quite understandable; much, namely
everything that is sincere, even deserves a certain respect. Nevertheless, these fears seem completely groundless to us, and we hope that
they will soon be dissipated. We are even certain of this, for if they
receive confirmation and justification in some strong authority, the
consequences for the future of our Orthodox school will be extremely
unfavorable.

Khomiakov moved the dispute between the Church and the Western confessions to new ground. All specialists seem to agree that he
changed the position. The suitability of the new position for both
defense and attack is acknowledged by many specialists, in fact, by
virtually all. But that is not all. The fact of the matter is that this position is not one of many possible positions, not even the best position,
but the only possible position. Sooner or later, the whole school must
take this position, and the sooner the better, for, given the nature of
the battle that faces us, we have no other position on which we can
stand. These words will probably provoke doubt. We will be asked:
"What battle are you talking about? A battle had really raged, a battle
that seemed truly terrifying, in the sixteenth and seventeenth centuries, when Romanism and Protestantism, then full of strength and
self-confidence, advanced at us from two sides. But we fended them
off. But what now?..."[11]

Our old opponents are leaving the stage. But a new opponent is
rising up in their wake: rationalism, armed with all the conclusions
of the empirical sciences, imposing themselves with all their self-

---

11. In the following section, omitted from this extract, Samarin points to the weakness, even decadence, of the two Western communions. — TRANS.

evidence and with all their methods, seductive in their supposed infallibility. A new battle now faces us: with this opponent. This is not a new opponent. It is the same old opponent, only stronger, grown to full self-awareness. It is the same opponent that our grandfathers battled, not recognizing its face beneath the mask of Romanism and Protestantism. This opponent is now advancing against us again, only from the other side. Formerly, this opponent disputed our dogmas and our doctrine, opposing its own dogmas and its doctrine to them. But now, with the balance, measure, and whetstone of the historical critique, our opponent approaches the actual foundations of our beliefs, sifting through bit after bit of evidence, word after word, hoping to fragment them, to smooth them out, to turn them into nothing, offering nothing in return. In essence, we are facing not a new battle but a continuation of the old battle, only with new forces and new weapons. And this battle has already begun. We have had occasion to test how reliable our battle armor is against the improved weapons directed at us. The results of these tests are before our eyes. Tell me frankly: Are you happy with these results? Do you have enough strength, and are you using it properly? Is everything right with you, and are you protected on all sides? We know very well that, if the means of truth are inexhaustible, then, on the other hand, there are almost no limits to negation. Therefore, we do not ask: have you won the definitive victory? Rather, we ask: do you firmly know upon what ground you must win it? It is a question of a greater or lesser certainty of a fact. Thus, can you clarify (have you fully clarified for yourself?) what precisely the Church values in a *fact*, what meaning is attached, in the domain of the Church, to a *fact*, in its material manifestation, within the limits of space and time (considering also the word in its material aspect as a fact)?

Let us turn to the results. Entire generations taught by you rushed headlong, straight from your schools, into the most extreme atheism, and the most astounding thing here is not the number who have fallen away from you but the ease with which they fell.[12] Your pupils abandoned the Church without inner struggle, without regrets, even without thinking twice. What forces won them from you? A couple of brochures by Büchner, two or three little books by Moleschott and

---

12. Samarin is addressing contemporary Orthodox educators. — TRANS.

Vogt, Renan's (not even Strauss's) *Life of Jesus*, a few dozen articles by Dobroliubov and Herzen,[13] and the deed was done. We are not disputing that the specialists would have been perfectly justified in shifting a significant part of the blame to others by pointing out a multitude of adverse circumstances that they were in a position neither to prevent nor to eliminate. We acknowledge all of this, but once again we address to the specialists the same question as before: Would entire generations have been carried away so easily if they had seen the Church as she really is, if they had truly seen the Church present before them, that is, precisely the Church and not a phantom of the Church? The means used to seduce these generations were negligible. The preaching of atheism was weak, bereft of seriousness, inconsistent, though arrogant, but it was a success, an enormous and early success. What, then, was the resistance like?

Why did this come to pass? Think: Did it not come to pass because we offer the truths of faith, like deductions from syllogisms, in an old cracked vessel, and that listeners, in throwing away the vessel, at the same time throw away what it contains? Did it not come to pass because all our efforts are directed at *leading*, through formally correct argumentation, our listeners to dogma, at compelling recognition from them, at securing their agreement, at imprisoning them? Did it not come to pass because that is where we stop, because we do not go into the depths, do not lead our listeners to the very meaning of dogma? Did it not come to pass, finally, because, in battling rationalism, we allowed it to slip into our ranks and (to use a very apt expression, coined not by us) received it into ourselves? Perhaps, made wise by experience, we shall desire to abandon our

---

13. Ludwig Büchner (1824–1899) was a German physician, philosopher, and popularizer of science. Jacob Moleschott (1822–1893), physiologist and philosopher, is often regarded as the founder of nineteenth century materialism. Karl Vogt (1817–1895), German naturalist, was a proponent of biological evolution. Joseph Renan (1823–1892), French philosopher and theologian, is best known for his *Life of Jesus*, which repudiated the supernatural element in Jesus's life. The best known work of the German theologian David Friedrich Strauss (1808–1874), *The Life of Jesus* (1835–1836), applied the "myth theory" to the life of Jesus and denied the historical foundation of all supernatural elements in the Gospels. Nikolay Dobroliubov (1836–1861), Russian writer, was a leading radical social critic. Alexander Herzen (1812–1870), Russian philosopher, social critic, novelist, and memoirist, is one of the nineteenth century's greatest radical political writers. —TRANS.

proofs from reason and shall attempt to place our teaching under the protection of authority. But that would only prove that we have not yet understood in what we are weak. It would be to trade Protestant rationalism for Roman rationalism, since authority for will and conscience is the same thing as an object for reason—something external, subject to, and evoking analysis.

It would appear that, in the light of what is happening before our very eyes, it is finally time to understand that both Romanism and Protestantism, and the whole system of proof worked out by them, are nothing more than conductors to atheism, and that everything we have taken from them comes back to haunt us, handing rationalism the sole weapon it can successfully use against us. That is what Khomiakov was the first to understand and clarify. He raised his voice not against the Roman and Protestant *confessions* but against rationalism, which he was the first to recognize in its original forms, Roman and Protestant. His business was with rationalism: to do battle with it, he forged the only weapon suitable for such battle. He also indicated the ground upon which the battle was possible and success was certain—certain because this ground was not a platform of boards laid on top of saw-horses but the solid continent of the Church, just as indubitable as the fact that no erroneous system concerning the motion of celestial bodies will change their usual course.

And this is not a new ground, alien to you. It is the same ground on which both you, teachers, and we, pupils, now stand, and have always stood *as members of the Church*, but from which you, regretfully, have allowed yourselves to be lured *in the capacity of scholars*, *in the capacity of a school*. It is time to understand this. When a fortress is preparing for a siege, the garrison begins by razing the fortress's outskirts: Without reflecting and without surrendering to irrational mercy, it razes and burns all wooden huts, all rotting straw dwellings, all that is unreliable and unstable, all that was built as an attachment to the fortress wall and that would be used by the foe during his advance. It is time for us too, with the same voluntary sacrifice, to cleanse and save in the arena of spiritual battle the solid ground entrusted to us.

Thus, Khomiakov is not an isolated phenomenon, not a capricious comet in the sphere of theological lights. He finished off Romanism and Protestantism, and at the same time he inaugurated a new era in the history of the Orthodox school, preparing its future victory over contemporary rationalism.[14]

Now that we have sketched out in general terms the significance of Khomiakov in connection with what was prior to him, what was contemporaneous with him, and what looms ahead, readers have the right to demand that we characterize him with a single, concluding word.

In past times, those who performed for the Orthodox world the kind of service that Khomiakov performed, those who, by a logical clarification of one or another side of Church teaching, could win for the Church a decisive victory over some error or other—were called teachers of the Church. How Khomiakov will be called we do not know.

What? Khomiakov, who lived in Moscow, on Sobachia Square, our common acquaintance, who used to wear traditional Russian clothing; this amusing and witty conversationalist, about whom we joked so much and with whom we argued so much; this free thinker, suspected by the police of atheism and a deficiency of patriotism; this incorrigible Slavophile, ridiculed by journalists for national exclusivity and religious fanaticism; this modest layperson, who, seven years ago, on a gray autumn day, was buried in Danilov monastery by five or six relatives and friends, and two comrades of his youth; behind whose grave one could see neither clergy nor the scholarly caste; about whom three days after his burial the *Moscow Gazette* [*Moskovskie Vedomosti*], under a different editorship then, refused to reprint several lines written in Petersburg by one of his friends; who was recently proclaimed by the very same newspaper, under the current

---

14. Though the corpus of Khomiakov's theological works is small, it represents an extraordinary abundance of content. There is a single, dominant theme: "The Church as a living organism of truth, entrusted to mutual love; that is, as freedom in unity and unity in freedom; that is, as freedom in the harmony of its manifestations." Then the development of the main theme occurs through its disclosure in diverse manifestations of the Church: in teaching, in sacraments, in history, etc., and through the contraposition of phenomena of ecclesiastical life to parallel phenomena in Romanism and Protestantism. Finally, apart from the main theme, a multitude of hints, judgments, definitions, characterizations, and critical comments are scattered throughout these works. In this respect, Khomiakov not only did not spare himself, but, on the contrary, in the diversity and number of themes he touched upon, he incited disputes and objections on all sides. [This note by Samarin has been abridged. — TRANS.]

editorship, to be a heresiarch;[15] this retired army captain, Aleksei Stepanovich Khomiakov—was a teacher of the Church?[16]

Yes, the very same.

Calling him by this name, we know well that some will consider our words a brazen challenge, while others will consider them an expression of the blind devotion of a pupil to his teacher. The former will be indignant; the latter will ridicule us. We know all this in advance, but we also know that future generations will be astonished not by the fact that in 1867 someone decided to say this in print and to sign his name under it, but by the fact that there was once a time when even the slightest bit of resoluteness would be required for this.

Moscow, December 1867

---

15. Heresiarch: one who originates or is the chief proponent of a heresy or heretical movement. — TRANS.

16. Samarin's calling Khomiakov a teacher of the Church has provoked much controversy. It is doubtful that the lofty title had been attributed to anyone since patristic times, and certainly not to an "amateur" theologian like Khomiakov. Many Russian theologians and churchmen have accepted Samarin's characterization of Khomiakov as wholly appropriate, whereas others (especially Florensky) have not been convinced of its suitability. — TRANS.

PART TWO

Philosophy

Ivan Kireevsky

I

ON THE NATURE OF EUROPEAN CULTURE AND ON ITS RELATIONSHIP TO RUSSIAN CULTURE

Ivan Kireevsky

EDITOR'S INTRODUCTION

"On the Nature of European Culture and on Its Relationship to Russian Culture (Letter to Count E. E. Komarovsky)" (1852) was Ivan Kireevsky's third and last major work in the in-between and ill-defined realm of ideology, the culmination of an intellectual evolution from enlightened universalism to a partisan allegiance to Orthodox Russian culture. Still, the very title of the work refers us in a sense to Kireevsky's earlier writings. Kireevsky's word for culture (*prosveshchenie*) literally means "enlightenment," in which sense it is customarily used. His innovative use of the word is somewhat problematic; after reading Kireevsky's first major ideological work (1832), Nicholas I suspected that *prosveshchenie* was supposed to mean "liberty," causing him to order the closure of Kireevsky's journal. In any event, Kireevsky's apparent identification of enlightenment and culture points to the universalist character of his thought: he is attempting to define generally valid conditions for the restoration of wholeness in society. He does not attempt to justify this ideal, nor does he elaborate its inner connection to Christian doctrine. Kireevsky's use of the form of an epistle to a close friend, although supported only by the subtitle and preamble, otherwise ignored throughout the long essay, might explain the informal, unsystematic nature of his argumentation.

Kireevsky's glowing assessment of European cultural development, coming on the heels of a year spent in Germany in 1830, was modified radically by 1838, as shown in his essay "In Answer to A. S. Khomiakov." Here he had already indicated the major thrust of his new argument, that Russia is the living embodiment of the universal ideal of unity due to the purity of its Christian culture. "On the Nature of European Culture" develops this thesis further and at some length. Kireevsky softens the opposition between Orthodoxy and classical culture, laying the blame for the West's deviations squarely on the national character of the Western peoples, on their civilization (*obrazovannost'*). Russia's success is correspondingly attributed to Russian national character, more than to Russia's fortuitous acceptance of pure Christianity.

"On the Nature of European Culture and on Its Relationship to Russian Culture (Letter to Count E. E. Komarovsky)" was published in 1852 in the *Moscow Miscellany* (*Moskovskii sbornik*). In 1897 M. A. Venevitinov published sections of the essay that the Russian censor had not allowed, which have been included in all subsequent editions. The essay was translated by Valentine Snow from the 1911 edition of Kireevsky's works.[1] It has been revised for this volume by Robert Bird. Some of Kireevsky's footnotes, which refer to historical studies and sources of his day, have been omitted.

---

1. *Russian Intellectual History: An Anthology*, ed. Marc Raeff (New York: Harcourt, Brace and World, 1966), 175–208.

On the Nature of European Culture and on Its Relationship to Russian Culture

LETTER TO COUNT E. E. KOMAROVSKY

At our last meeting, you and I had a long discussion about the nature of European culture and the characteristics that distinguish it from the culture that belonged to Russia in ancient times, traces of which to this day not only can be observed in the customs, manners, and mindset of the common people, but also permeate the soul, the turn of mind, the whole inner content, so to speak, of any Russian who has not yet been transformed by a Western upbringing. You demanded that I put down on paper my thoughts on this subject, but I was unable to comply with your request at that time. Now that I am to write an article on the same topic for the *Moscow Miscellany*, I ask your permission to cast it in the form of a letter addressed to you. The thought that I am conversing to you will lend warmth and life to my solitary meditations.

Certainly few questions nowadays are more important than this question—of the relationship of Russian to Western culture. How we resolve it in our minds may determine not only the dominant trend of our literature, but the entire orientation of our intellectual activity, the meaning of our private lives, and the nature of our social relationships. And yet only a short time ago this question could not have been posed or, what amounts to the same thing, would have been resolved so readily that there was no point in posing it. The consensus of opinion was that the difference between European and Russian culture was merely a difference of degree, and not of kind, and still less a difference of the spirit and basic principles of civilization. We (it was then said) previously had only barbarism; our civilization began only when we started to imitate Europe, which had outdistanced us immeasurably in intellectual development. In Europe, learning was in full flower before we had any; there it had come to fruition, while ours was only beginning to bud. Hence the Europeans were teachers, while we were only students; still, it was usually added with complacency, we were clever students, capable of learning so quickly that in all likelihood we would soon outstrip our masters.

In Riga, in 1714, draining his glass on a newly launched ship, Peter [the Great] said:

> Who thirty years ago would have thought, lads, that you, Russians, would be building ships with me here in the Baltic Sea and feasting in German dress? Historians postulate that Greece was the ancient seat of learning; from Greece learning passed to Italy, and spread through all the European lands. But the uncouthness[2] of our forefathers hindered it from penetrating beyond Poland, although before that the Poles, and all other foreigners as well, had been plunged into the darkness in which we still live, and it was only owing to the unremitting efforts of their rulers that they were finally able to open their eyes and assimilate European knowledge, art, and lifestyle. I would liken this movement of learning upon the earth to the circulation of blood in the human body; and it seems to me that one day learning will leave its present seat in England, France, and Germany and pass to us for a few centuries, in order then to return once again to its birthplace, Greece.

These remarks explain the enthusiasm with which Peter acted, and they largely justify the extremes to which he went. Love of culture was his passion. He saw culture as Russia's sole salvation, and Europe as its only source. But this conviction survived him by a whole century among the educated class of the Russian people—or, more accurately, among the class he transformed; and some thirty years ago you would hardly have found a thinking person who could conceive the possibility of any culture other than one borrowed from Western Europe.

Since then, however, a change has taken place both in Western European culture and in European-Russian culture.

In the second half of the nineteenth century, European culture has attained such a fullness of development that its special significance has become obvious to any thoughtful observer. Yet the result of this comprehensive development and clarity of conclusions has been an almost universal feeling of dissatisfaction and frustrated hopes. Western culture has proved unsatisfying not because learning has lost its vitality in

---

2. Peter used the word *die Unart*.

the West; on the contrary, it appears to flourish more richly than ever before. Again, the reason is not that there are some forms of outer life that impede human relationships or prevent them from developing in the prevailing direction; on the contrary, a struggle against external obstacles would only strengthen the bias for the favored orientation, and it would seem that never before has the organization of outer life so heeded and agreed with the intellectual requirements of learning.

But a feeling of dissatisfaction and disconsolate emptiness has descended onto the hearts of those whose thought was not circumscribed by fleeting interests precisely because the very triumph of the European mind has revealed the narrowness of its basic aspirations; because, despite the great wealth and magnitude of particular discoveries and advances in learning, the general conclusion from this entire sum of knowledge has been only of negative value for the inner consciousness of humanity. This is because, despite all the brilliance and the convenience of life's exterior improvements, life itself has been drained of its essential meaning; not being bolstered by a strong, generally held conviction, it could neither be decorated with lofty ideals nor warmed by deep sympathy. Cold analysis over the course of many centuries has destroyed the very foundations on which European culture rested from the very beginning of its development. As a result, the very fundamental principles from which it grew have become irrelevant and alien to it, in conflict with its contemporary conclusions. At the same time, its direct inheritance is now found to be the very analysis that destroyed its roots, this self-propelling scalpel of reason, this abstract syllogism that recognizes nothing but itself and its own personal experience, this autocratic understanding, or more accurately, this logical activity that is detached from all of humanity's other cognitive faculties save the coarsest and most primitive sensual data on which it erects its ethereal dialectical edifices.

It should be remembered, however, that the feeling of dissatisfaction and despondency now experienced by the people of the West was not suddenly discovered at the first obvious triumph of their destructive rationalistic nature. Having overthrown their age-old convictions, the people of the West placed boundless trust in the omnipotence of their abstract reason, precisely because the convictions it had destroyed had been so great, strong, and comprehensive. In the first moments of success, their joy was not only unmixed with regret; on the contrary, intoxicated with self-confidence, they reached a state of poetic exaltation. They believed that, by using their own abstract mind, they could forthwith create a new, rational life for themselves and build a veritable paradise on the earth they had transformed. They were not frightened by their dreadful, bloody experiments; gross failures did not cool their hopes; individual suffering only set a martyr's crown on their bedazzled heads. Perhaps an eternity of unsuccessful attempts might only have exhausted them, but it would have been unable to shatter their self-confidence had not the very abstract reason they had relied upon developed in such a way that it reached a consciousness of its limited one-sidedness.

This latest result of European civilization has not yet, it is true, become universal, but it is apparently beginning to predominate among the leading thinkers of the West. It belongs to the latest, and probably the conclusive, epoch of abstract philosophical thinking. Philosophical views do not, however, remain for long the property of the professorial podium. What is today the product of the meditation of a scholar closeted in his study will tomorrow be the conviction of the masses; the fate of philosophy becomes the fate of the entire intellectual life of people who have no faith save in rational science, and who recognize no other source of truth save the conclusions of their own logic. Philosophy is not only the point of convergence of all branches of learning and all worldly affairs, the point of connection of the shared consciousness; from this node, this shared consciousness, guiding threads issue forth again into all branches of learning and all worldly affairs, giving them meaning, establishing links between them, and shaping them according to their own tendency.

Thus we have often seen that in some remote corner of Europe an unnoticed idea will germinate in the brain of some scholar whose very face is barely noticeable to the crowd around him, and that twenty years later the unnoticed idea of this unnoticed man will rule the minds and desires of that selfsame crowd, making itself manifest in the wake of some dramatic historical event. This happens not because some solitary thinker seated in his dark corner can order history about at will, but because history reaches self-consciousness through the mediation of his system. He merely records and adds up the prevailing results, and any arbitrary element in his thought robs it of all its power over reality; for only that philosophic system attains dominance that follows as an inevitable conclusion from the convictions that have previously enjoyed ascendancy. Thus in the organism of peoples whose convictions are based solely on their own reasoning, the philosopher's brain is a necessary natural organ that conducts the circulation of their vital forces, ascending from external events to inner consciousness and from inner consciousness returning once more to the sphere of overt historical action.

Hence it may be said that it is not that Western thinkers have become convinced of the one-sidedness of logical reason, but that Europe's logical reason itself, having reached the highest degree of its development, has become aware of its limitations. Having clarified the laws of its own activity, it has found that the full capacity of its self-propelling force does not extend beyond the negative aspect of human knowledge; that its speculative concatenation of derivative concepts must be founded on premises taken from other sources of knowledge; that the higher truths of the mind, its living insights and essential convictions, all lie outside the abstract circle of its dialectical process and, although they do not contradict its laws, are nevertheless not derived from them and are in fact beyond the reach of the mind's activity, if the latter has been separated from its original unity with the other faculties of the human spirit.

Thus Western humanity, having through the exclusive development of its abstract reason lost faith in all convictions not derived from this abstract reason, has now, owing to the development of this same reason, lost its last faith in reason's omnipotence. It has been compelled, therefore, either to content itself with a semi-bestial indifference toward anything higher than sensual concerns and commercial calculations (which many have done, but which many are unable to do, being the product of the remnants of Europe's former life) or to return to those rejected convictions that animated the West before abstract reason reached its final development. Thus some have done, but others have been unable to do so because those convictions, as they were shaped in the historical development of Western Europe, were already permeated by the disintegrating effect of abstract reason. Therefore they have passed from their original sphere, from a state of self-sufficient fullness and independence, to the level of a rational system, so that Western humanity sees them not as a higher, life-giving principle, but as having all the one-sidedness of reason itself.

What then remains for thinking Europe to do? To go back still further, to the original purity of those basic convictions before they were influenced by the rationalistic nature of Western Europe? To return to those principles as they had been before Western development began? This is a well-nigh impossible undertaking for minds surrounded and saturated by all the delusions and prejudices of Western civilization. This is perhaps why most European thinkers have sought an escape, being unable to accept either a narrowly egoistic life limited to sensual goals and personal considerations, or a one-sided intellectual life in direct contradiction to the fullness of their intellectual consciousness, and being unwilling to be left without any convictions or to devote themselves to obviously false convictions. Their escape consisted of each beginning to invent in his own head new, common principles of life and truth for the entire world, searching them out in the individual play of their dreamy thoughts, mixing the new with the old, and the impossible with the possible, giving themselves wholly over to unbridled hopes, each contradicting the others and each demanding general recognition by the others. Everyone became Columbus; they all set out to discover new Americas within their own minds, seeking the other hemisphere of the earth in a vast sea of impossible hopes, individual suppositions, and rigorously syllogistic conclusions.

This state of European minds had the opposite effect in Russia from what it eventually had in the West. Only a few Russians, and then only for a moment, were fascinated by the superficial glitter of these foolish systems, were deluded by this artificial comeliness that was rotten to the core. But most of the people who followed the phenomena of Western thought became aware of the inadequacies of Western civilization and turned their attention to those cultural principles, underestimated by the West, which at one time had formed the basis of Russian life and which can still be found in it despite European influence.

The result was active historical research, collation, and publications. In this we owe a great deal to our government, which discovered so many valuable historical documents gathering dust in forgotten archives and remote monasteries and published them for all to read. Perhaps for the first time in 150 years, Russian scholars took an objective, searching look within themselves and their fatherland and, by studying elements of intellectual life that were new to them, they were struck by a strange phenomenon: they saw with amazement that they had heretofore been mistaken about nearly everything having to do with Russia, its history, its people, its faith, the basic roots of its culture, and the clear, still-warm traces left by that culture on Russian life of old and on the mind and character of the people—I mean to say, about nearly everything. They saw that they had been mistaken, not because anyone had intentionally sought to deceive them, but because their strong bias toward Western civilization and their unconscious prejudice against Russian barbarism had made it impossible for them to understand Russia. Perhaps they themselves, under the sway of the same prejudices, had in the past helped to spread the same delusion. The spell was so potent that it concealed from them the most obvious objects that were before their very eyes; but then their awakening occurred so rapidly that its unexpectedness is surprising. Every day we see people who share the Western orientation, many of them people with highly cultivated minds and firm characters, who change all their convictions simply because they have turned their attention within themselves and their fatherland. In the latter they learn those basic principles that comprised the peculiarity of Russian life. Within themselves they discover those essential faculties of the spirit that found no place and no nourishment in the development of the Western mind.

It must be said, however, that it is not as easy as some may think to understand and formulate the basic principles that comprised the peculiarity of Russian life. For the fundamental principles of Russia's culture have not manifested themselves as clearly in its life as have the principles of Western culture in its history. One must seek them in order to discover them; they do not catch the eye, as does European civilization. Europe has had its full say. In the nineteenth century, Europe may be said to have completed the cycle of development it began in the ninth. Although in the early centuries of its history Russia was no less civilized than the West, it was constantly hampered and set back in its cultural growth by external and presumably accidental obstacles, so that it was able to preserve for the present not a complete and perfect culture, but only certain hints, so to speak, of its true meaning, only its first principles and their first impress on the minds and lives of Russians.

What are these principles of Russian culture? In what do they differ from the principles from which Western culture developed, and are they capable of further development? And if they are, what can they do for the intellectual life of Russia, and what promise do they hold for the intellectual life of Europe? For, after the accomplished inter-penetration of Russia and Europe, it is no longer possible to conceive of any development in Russian intellectual life that would not affect Europe, nor of any development in European intellectual life that would not affect Russia.

The principles underlying Russian culture are totally different from the constituent elements of the culture of European peoples. True, each of these peoples has something peculiar in the character of its civiliza-tion; but their individual, ethnic, political, or historical peculiarities do not prevent them from forming a spiritual whole into which they all fit as living members into a single body. Hence, amidst all the accidents of history, they have always developed in close and sympathetic interrela-tion. Russia, having separated from Europe in spirit, lived a life sepa-rate from Europe's. The Englishman, the Frenchman, the Italian, and the German never stopped being Europeans, while always preserving their national traits. Russians, on the other hand, nearly had to destroy their national personality in order to assimilate Western civilization; for both their appearance and their inner cast of mind—which explained and supported each other—were the result of an entirely different type of life, originating from entirely different sources.

Apart from ethnic differences, three historical circumstances gave the entire development of culture in the West its distinct character: the special form through which Christianity reached it; the peculiar aspect in which it inherited the civilization of the ancient world; and, lastly, the particular elements that entered into the formation of state-hood in the West.

Christianity was the soul of the intellectual life of the Western peo-ples, just as it was in Russia. But it was transmitted to Western Europe solely through the Roman Church.

Naturally, each patriarchate, each nationality, each country in the Christian world never ceased to preserve its individual personality, while continuing to participate in the general unity of the entire Church. Each people, owing to local, ethnic, or historical factors, developed some one aspect of intellectual activity; naturally, in its spiritual life as well and in the writings of its theologians, it was to retain this special character, its natural physiognomy, in a manner of speaking, but illuminated by a higher consciousness. Thus the theo-logians of the Syrian lands appear to have paid most attention to the inner, contemplative life of those who have renounced the world. Roman theologians were especially concerned with the aspect of practical activity and the logical concatenation of concepts. The theological writers of enlightened Byzantium seem to have paid more attention than others to the relationship between Christianity and the particular disciplines that flourished around it, which at first warred against Christianity, then later submitted to it. The theologians of Alexandria, waging a double war—against paganism and against Judaism—and surrounded by philosophical, theosophical, and gnostic schools, concentrated above all on the speculative side of Christian doctrine.

These divergent paths led to a single common goal so long as those who followed them did not deviate from that goal. Everywhere, particular heresies sprang up, each closely related to the trend prevailing among the nation within which it arose; but they were all eliminated by the unanimity of the Universal Church, in which all the particular churches were united in one holy concord. There were times when entire patriarchates stood in danger of deviation, when a doctrine that was contrary to that preached by the Universal Church was nevertheless in conformity with the prevailing trend and the intellectual peculiarity of the nations comprising that particular church; but in those times of trial, when the particular church faced the irrevocable choice of either splitting away from the Universal Church or sacrificing its particular views, the Lord saved His Churches through the unanimity of the whole Orthodox world. The specific character of each particular church could have led it into a schism only if it separated from tradition and communion with the other Churches; so long as it remained faithful to the common tradition and the common covenant of love, each particular church, through the special character of its spiritual activity, only added to the common wealth and fullness of the spiritual life of all Christianity. Thus the Roman Church, too, had what we might call its legitimate peculiarity before it broke away from the Universal Church. Once it split off, however, it was naturally bound to transform this peculiar character into an exclusive form through which alone the Christian doctrine could penetrate into the minds of the nations subordinated to it.

The civilization of the ancient pre-Christian world—the second element that entered into the making of European culture—was until the mid-fifteenth century known to the West almost exclusively in that special form that it had assumed in pagan Rome; its other aspect, Greek and Asian civilization, virtually did not reach Europe in its pure form almost until the very fall of Constantinople. Yet, as is known, Rome was far from representative of all pagan culture; it had merely held physical mastery over the world, whereas intellectual supremacy had belonged to the Greek tongue and Greek civilization. Hence, to receive all the experience of the human mind, the entire heritage it had amassed through its efforts over the course of six thousand years, solely in the form given to it by Roman civilization meant to receive it in an utterly one-sided form, with the certain risk of imparting the same one-sidedness to the character of one's own civilization. That is precisely what happened in Europe. And when, during the fifteenth century, Greek exiles flocked to the West carrying their precious manuscripts with them, it was too late. True, European culture became newly animated, but its meaning remained the same: the mind and life of the European had already been given their special cast. Greek learning broadened the scope of knowledge and taste, stimulated thinking, gave minds flight and motion; but it was helpless to change the dominant orientation of the spirit.

Finally, the third element of Western culture—its polity—was characterized by the fact that hardly a single one of the nations of Europe attained statehood through a tranquil development of national life and national consciousness, where dominant religious and social concepts, embodied in social relations, are able to grow naturally, strengthen, and join into a general unanimity that is reflected in the harmonious wholeness of the social organism. On the contrary, owing to some strange historical accident, nearly everywhere in Europe social life arose violently out of a death struggle between two hostile races—out of the oppression of conquerors, out of the resistance of the conquered, and finally out of fortuitous settlements that brought a superficial end to the conflict between the two antagonistic, incommensurate forces.

These three elements peculiar to the West—the Roman Church, Roman civilization, and a statehood arising out of the violence of conquest—were entirely alien to old Russia. Having accepted the Christian religion from Greece, Russia was in constant communion with the Universal Church. The civilization of the pagan world passed to it through Christian doctrine, without provoking a one-sided fascination with it, as the living remnant of some particular nation. It was only later, after it had become firmly grounded in Christian civilization, that Russia began to assimilate the latest fruits of the learning and culture of the ancient world—at which point Providence, it would seem, saw fit to arrest the further progress of its intellectual development, thus possibly saving it from the one-sidedness that would inevitably have been its fate if its rationalistic education had begun before Europe had completed the cycle of its own intellectual development; for, not having yet achieved its final results, Europe could have drawn Russia all the more unconsciously and deeply into the limited sphere of its peculiar development. When Christianity penetrated into Russia, it did not meet with the immense difficulties that it had to overcome in Rome, Greece, and the European countries steeped in Roman civilization. The Slavic world did not present those insurmountable obstacles to the pure influence that Christian doctrine could exert on inner and social life, such as Christianity encountered in the self-contained civilization of the classical world and the one-sided civilization of the Western nations. In many respects, even the ethnic characteristics of Slavic life favored the successful assimilation of Christian principles.

Furthermore, the basic concepts of human rights and duties and concepts of human personal, family, and social relations were not violently composed from the formal conditions of warring tribes and classes, just as, after a war, artificial boundaries are traced between neighboring states in obedience to the dead letter of a treaty obtained by compromise. With no experience of conquest, the Russian nation organized itself in its own way. The enemies who afflicted it always remained outside of it, not interfering in its internal development. The Tatars, the Poles, the Hungarians, the Germans, and the other scourges sent to the Russian nation by Providence, could only halt its formation—and, in fact, did so—but could not change the essential meaning of its inner and social life.

In the meantime, these three elements of early European civilization, alien to Russia—the Roman Church, the ancient Roman world, and statehood achieved through conquest—determined the entire cycle of Europe's further development, just as three points in space determine the circle that passes through them.

The living ruins that had survived the destruction of ancient Roman civilization had an all-embracing influence on the newly emerging civilization of the West. Penetrating into the very structure of social relations, into the language, customs, mores, into the initial development of European learning and art, ancient Rome was bound to inform all aspects of Western humanity with the particular character that had distinguished it from all other peoples; and this particular character, permeating all the relationships that surround humankind, could not help but penetrate to the very composition of human life, shaping and transforming all other influences to a greater or lesser degree in conformity to its dominant trend.

Consequently, the principal feature of Rome's intellectual character was bound to be reflected in the intellectual identity of the West. If we were to describe the dominant feature of the Roman civilization in one general formula, we would not go far wrong if we said that the distinctive cast of the Roman mind consisted in the predominance of superficial rationality over the inner essence of things. This is clearly to be seen in Roman social and family life, which with logic and ruthlessness distorted people's natural and moral relationships, according to the letter of the law's arbitrary composition. We find the same characteristic in Roman poetry, which aspired to perfect artistically the outer forms of foreign inspiration. The same can be said of their language, in which the artificial harmony of grammatical constructions stifled all natural freedom and the living spontaneity of emotional reactions. We see the same thing in the famous Roman laws, where the beauty of outer formality reaches such astonishing logical perfection, despite the equally astonishing absence of inner justice in them. Roman religion—which, for all its external rites, almost forgot their mystical significance—presents the same picture of an external concatenation of ideas achieved at the cost of an inner, living fullness of meaning. Roman religion was a collection of many heterogeneous, and frequently contradictory, deities of the pagan world, externally combined but internally discordant, yet all brought to logical agreement within a single symbolic worship, where the veil of philosophical connection was used to cloak the inner absence of faith.

The same rationalistic tendency was manifest in the mores of ancient Rome, where external activity was so highly esteemed and so little attention was paid to its inner meaning; where pride was held to be a virtue; where all were guided in their actions solely by their own logical convictions; where, consequently, all regarded themselves to be not merely distinct but also different from all other persons, and they could conceive of no attitude toward them except one that was logically deduced from the external circumstances of life. Consequently, Romans knew almost no other bond between people but the bond of mutual interest, and no other unity but partisan unity. The very patriotism of the Romans—the most disinterested emotion of which they were capable—was not what it had been for the Greeks. They did not love the smoke of their fatherland; even the smoke of a Greek hearth had greater attraction for them. What they loved in the fatherland was the interests of their party and, even more, the fact that it flattered their pride in being Roman.

But immediate and spontaneous human feelings were stifled in the Roman soul. With respect to their compatriots, Romans regarded themselves much as great Rome regarded the cities that surrounded it. Equally ready for alliance or war, they risked either on the basis of calculation, ever attentive to the dictates of the passion that generally rules a dryly logical, and selfishly active mind—I mean the passion for dominating others, which occupied the same place in the soul of the Roman that blind love of glory held in the soul of the compassionate Greek. In brief, in all the characteristics of the Romans, in all the nuances of their intellectual and spiritual activity, we find the same common trait: that the superficial harmony of their logical concepts was more essential to them than the very essence of the concepts, and that the internal equilibrium of their being, as it were, consisted for them solely in the balance of rationalistic ideas and of external, formal activity.

Naturally, Christianity—from the moment it sprang into being in the midst of the pagan world—was in direct opposition to this tendency of the selfish personality and arrogantly rationalistic nature of the Roman. By turning the spirit toward the inner wholeness of being, Christianity not only resisted passionate fascinations, even those disguised by noble pretexts, but also, by raising the mind to the living heart of self-knowledge, it prevented that state of spiritual disintegration in which one-sided rationality splits away from all the other faculties of the spirit and fancies itself able to find the truth in the superficial connections of concepts. Whereas to this external, rationalistic wisdom the Christian message seemed utter madness, from the heights of Christian doctrine this arrogant rationality appeared in all the poverty of its unfeeling blindness. Hence during the first centuries of the Church we find even theological writers of the Roman world frequently attacking the fallacies of pagan philosophizing.

At the same time, the predominance of the purely Christian orientation could not erase from their minds the peculiarity of the Roman physiognomy, which, as already noted, when kept within its legitimate limits not only presented no obstacle for the true direction of the spirit, but, on the contrary, was even able to increase its multifarious manifestations, leading into error only whenever its excesses violated the inner equilibrium of the spirit. Thus Tertullian, perhaps the most eloquent of Rome's theological writers, astounds us particularly by his brilliant logic and the outer coherence of his theses; many of his works will always remain an ornament of the Church, although the hypertrophy of his logical faculty or, more accurately, its separation from the other faculties of the reason led him to extremes where his doctrine diverged from purely Christian doctrine. His famous disciple, St. Cyprian, was more fortunate, although no less remarkable for his powerful logical capacity. But of all the Church Fathers, both early and late, surely no one had so marked a predilection for the logical concatenation of truths as St. Augustine, most often called the Teacher of the West. Some of his works are like an iron chain of syllogisms, each link fitting seamlessly into the next. Perhaps for this reason he occasionally allowed himself to become too carried away, and for all the outer harmony he failed to notice the inner one-sidedness of his thought, so that in the last years of his life he found himself obliged to write a refutation of some of his own earlier assertions.

This special fondness of the Roman world for the formal coherence of ideas represented a pitfall for Roman theologians even at a time when the Roman Church was a living part of the Universal Church and when the shared consciousness of the entire Orthodox world maintained a reasonable balance between all special traits. Thus, it is to be expected that after Rome's separation this peculiarity of the Roman mind was bound to attain decisive predominance in the character of Roman theologians' teachings. It may even be that this Roman peculiarity, this isolated rationality, this excessive inclination toward the formal coherence of ideas, had itself been one of the main reasons for Rome's defection. This is hardly the place to analyze either the causes or the circumstances of that defection, and to pose the question whether its main actors were secretly moved by the Roman spirit of domination or by other reasons. Any such hypotheses are subject to argument; but what is not open to doubt is the actual pretext for defection—the new addition of a dogma to the earlier creed, an addition that, contrary to the ancient tradition and shared consciousness of the Church, was justified only by the logical deductions of the Western theologians.

We make special mention of this fact because, better than any other, it helps to explain the character of Western civilization, where, from the ninth century on, the isolated rationality of Rome penetrated into the very teaching of the theologians, destroying with its one-sidedness the harmony and wholeness of their inner speculation.

If we look at the matter from this angle, it becomes clear why Western theologians, for all their rationalistic conscientiousness, could fail to visualize the unity of the Church in any other form than that of the formal unity of the episcopate; why they were able to ascribe essential merit to external human works; why, in the absence of such works, despite the inner readiness of a soul they could see no other means of salvation for it apart from a specified period in Purgatory; why, finally, they were able to credit some persons with an actual excess of good works and use that excess to offset the deficiency of others, again thanks to superficial actions performed for the external benefit of the Church.

In this way, having subordinated faith to the logical conclusions of rationalistic understanding, the Western Church, already in the ninth century, sowed within itself the inescapable seed of the Reformation, which later summoned it before the court of that very abstract reason that it had itself elevated above the shared consciousness of the Universal Church; and at that time a thinking man could already have seen Luther looming behind Pope Nicholas I, just as, according to the Roman Catholics, a thinking man of the sixteenth century could already have discerned Strauss behind Luther.

It is obvious that the same moral cause, the same bias toward one-sided logic, which gave rise to the doctrine of the necessary external unity of the Church, was bound to produce also the doctrine of the infallibility of its visible head. This was a direct consequence of the special type of civilization that was attaining dominance in the Western world. Because of this turn taken by the general state of the European mind, the Frankish Emperor was able to offer, and the Roman hierarch to accept, secular dominion within his diocese. Later, for the same logical reason, the Pope's half-spiritual dominion was bound to extend over all the rulers of the West, giving rise to the organization of the so-called Holy Roman Empire and the entire character of historical development in the Middle Ages, where secular power constantly entered into confusion and conflict with spiritual power, each preparing the other a place in popular opinion for its future downfall, while a similar struggle was taking place in the mind of Western man between faith and reason, tradition and personal presumption. Even as the Church sought to base its spiritual power on secular might, so the spiritual conviction of Western minds attempted to ground itself on rationalistic syllogisms.

Having thus contrived to bring about superficial unity by placing over itself a single head combining both spiritual and secular power, the Western Church caused a split in its spiritual activities, its internal interests, and its external relations with the world at large. The twin towers that usually rise over a Catholic church may serve as a fitting symbol of this dichotomy.

In the meantime, the secular rulers, having accepted the supremacy of the three-crowned ruler of the Church, thereby sealed the feudal organization of the so-called Holy Roman Empire. It may well be that this was the only reasonable solution for the social life of nations whose state organization had arisen out of conquest. The relentless struggle between two warring tribes, the oppressors and the oppressed, had resulted, throughout their historical development, in a lasting antagonism between opposing estates. They continued to face each other without movement, with their conflicting rights, with the exclusive privileges of the one and the profound discontent and endless complaints of the other, with the stubborn envy of the middle estate that arose between them, and the general and eternally painful fluctuation in their relative strength. This engendered formal and coercive terms of reconciliation, terms with which all parties were dissatisfied and which might have been somewhat acceptable in the social consciousness only when based on a principle external to the state.

Meanwhile, the fewer the rights that were granted to the estate descended from the conquered, the less did the estate that descended from the conquerors act with justice. All noble persons strove to become the supreme law regulating their relations with others. The notion of the unified state or nation could not penetrate their independent hearts, shielded as they were on all sides by iron and pride. In outer, formal relationships, only rules that they themselves invented and voluntarily accepted could control their autocratic, arbitrary wills. Codes of honor—though they arose in response to the needs of the times as the only possible substitute for law in the face of utter lawlessness—by their nature reveal such one-sidedness of social life, such extreme emphasis on the external and formal aspect of personal relationships, and such disregard of their essential aspect that, in themselves alone, they could serve as a faithful mirror of the entire development of Western society.

Each noble knight within his castle formed a separate state. For that reason, relations between noble persons could be only external relations, entirely formal in character. That same external, formal character had to mark their relations with other estates. For that reason, civil law in Western states, as it developed, was marked by the same formality, the same disputatious emphasis on the letter of the law, that constituted the very basis of social relations. Roman law, which continued to survive and be applied in a few European cities, still more strengthened this formalistic tendency of European jurisprudence. For Roman law also displays this same formalism that concentrates on the superficial letter of the form while forgetting inner justice—the reason possibly being that the social life of Rome also developed as a result of the unremitting struggle of two hostile nationalities compelled by force to form one state.

Incidentally, this explains why Roman law, although foreign to the European peoples, could be so readily accepted by them, with the exception of the few countries in which society did not arise out of conquest and that, therefore, gave promise of a more integral evolution in the future.

But, having begun with violence, the European states were forced to develop through revolutions, for the development of a state is simply the unfolding of the essential principles on which it is founded. Hence, European societies, founded on violence, cemented by formal personal relationships, permeated with one-sided rationality, were bound to produce not a social spirit, but a spirit of individual separation, and they were held together only by the knots of private interests and parties. Consequently, although the history of European states often presents external signs of a flourishing social life, in fact social forms always served merely to disguise the separate, particular parties, which forgot about the life of the whole state in the pursuit of their private goals and personal systems. Papal parties, imperial parties, city parties, church parties, court, private, governmental, religious, political, and popular parties, parties of the middle estate, and even metaphysical parties were ever contending in the European states, each vying to upset the existing system in accordance with its own particular aims. As a result, European states developed not through peaceful growth but always by means of a more or less palpable revolution. Revolution was the precondition of all progress, until it became not a means to an end, but in itself the distinctive end of popular aspirations.

It is obvious that in these circumstances European civilization was bound in the end to destroy the whole social and intellectual edifice that it had itself erected.

Reason's disintegration into particular faculties, this predominance of rationality over the other activities of the spirit, would ultimately destroy the entire edifice of European medieval civilization; yet in the beginning it had an opposite effect, and the more one-sided it became, the quicker was the development that resulted. For such is the law of the deviation of human reason: the appearance of brilliance is accompanied by inner darkness.

Arab civilization evolved even more rapidly, for it was even more one-sided, though it exhibited the same abstract rationalistic tendency as did medieval Europe. It was easier for Islamic culture to turn its basic convictions into logical formalism than it was for Christian culture, which was essentially living and integral. The systematic linkage of abstract concepts was the highest goal that Muslim intellectual consciousness of self could attain to, and it may be said to have formed the very basis of Muslim faith. It demanded of Muslims only the abstract recognition of certain historical facts and the metaphysical recognition of the oneness of God, but it did not require an integrated wholeness of self-consciousness, thereby calmly allowing a disjointed human nature to persist in its unreconciled duality. It did not indicate to them the supreme purpose of being but, on the contrary, offered them a state of gross sensual pleasures, not only as the greatest reward of life on earth, but even as the highest aim of the afterlife.

Consequently, the scope of Islamic intellectual requirements was limited to the need for abstract logical unity, for bringing thoughts into a superficial order and correctly establishing systematic interrelations among them. The supreme metaphysical problem that the inquiring Islamic mind could set itself—the very poetry of the Muslim's philosophy—consisted in evolving tangible formulas for the intangible activities of the spiritual world, in searching for the talismanic link between the laws of the supercelestial world and those of the sublunar world. Hence their passion for logic; hence their astrology, alchemy, chiromancy, and all their abstract-rationalistic and sensual-spiritual disciplines. This also explains why, although Arabs had borrowed their civilization from Syrian Greeks and maintained close relations with Byzantium, they exerted almost no influence on the evolution of Greek culture.

Their impact on Western Europe, however, was particularly great, because they brought it the brilliance of their flourishing knowledge at the very time Europe lived in almost total ignorance. There can be no doubt that the abstract-logical tendency of their learning helped to strengthen the same tendency in European learning. And, though for only a short while, the varicolored stream of their talismanic speculations mingled with the dominant current of European thought. They were the first to acquaint the Latin theologians with the works of Aristotle, which first became known to them in translation from the Arabic, with Arabic commentaries—so unfamiliar to them was Greek civilization by this time.

Aristotle, who has never been fully understood, but who has been studied ad infinitum in fragments, was, as is known, the soul of Scholasticism, which in its turn represented the entire intellectual development of Europe at that time and was its clearest expression.

Scholasticism was nothing other than an attempt to evolve a systematic theology; for in those days theology was both the supreme goal and the main source of all knowledge. It was the task of Scholasticism not only to combine theological concepts into a rational system, but also to provide them a rationalistic, metaphysical basis. St. Augustine's writings and Aristotle's works on logic were the main tools used. The supreme development of the schools consisted in dialectic debates on articles of faith. The most famous theologians attempted to deduce the dogmas of faith from their logical ratiocinations. From Scotus Erigena to the sixteenth century, there was probably not a single one of them who did not attempt to balance his belief in God's being on the point of an artfully honed syllogism. Their enormous works were filled with abstract subtleties, spun in a logical manner out of nakedly rationalistic concepts. To them, the least essential aspects of thought were objects of learning, causes of partisanship, the purpose of life.

It is not the abstract arguments of the nominalists and realists, nor the strange debates about the Eucharist, grace, the birth of the Most Holy Virgin, and other such topics that can provide a real understanding of the actual spirit of Scholasticism and the condition of minds at the time. No, these are most clearly revealed by what constituted the main object of attention and engaged the most learned philosophers of the day—that is, the posing of arbitrary problems based on improbable assumptions and the analysis of all possible arguments for and against them.

This endless, tiresome juggling of concepts over seven hundred years, this useless kaleidoscope of abstract categories spinning ceaselessly before the mind's eye, was bound in the end to blind it to those living convictions that lie above the sphere of rationalistic understanding and logic—convictions to which people do not attain through syllogisms, but whose truth, on the contrary, people can only distort, if not utterly destroy, through syllogistic deduction.

A spontaneous, integral understanding of inner, spiritual life and a spontaneous, unprejudiced observation of exterior nature were equally excluded from the charmed circle of Western thought. The first was rejected as "mysticism," which by its very nature was hateful to Scholastic rationalism (the term also included the aspects of the doctrine of the Orthodox Church that did not accord with the Western systems); the second was persecuted as "godlessness" (and included the scientific discoveries that contradicted the views of contemporary theologians). For Scholasticism had welded its faith to its narrow understanding of learning into a single, indissoluble fate.

Therefore when, with the conquest of Constantinople, the fresh, uncontaminated air of Greek thought poured in from the East and thinkers in the West began to breathe more easily and freely, the entire edifice of Scholasticism collapsed instantaneously. Nevertheless, traces of Scholastic one-sidedness remained on minds brought up on it. The object and direction of thought were different, but the emphasis on rationality and the blind neglect of living truths were hardly altered.

The great originator of modern philosophy himself provides an instructive example of this fact. He thought that he had completely thrown off the shackles of Scholasticism; nevertheless, without suspecting it, he was still so much a captive that, despite his marvelous comprehension of the formal laws of reason, he was so strangely blind to living truths that he did not regard his inner and immediate consciousness of his own being as sufficient proof until he had deduced it by abstract syllogistic reasoning! This example is all the more remarkable in that it reveals not an individual peculiarity of the philosopher but a general orientation of minds. For Descartes' logical deduction did not remain his exclusive property, but was hailed with delight and became the basis of thought for most modern philosophers until almost the middle of the eighteenth century. Even today, thoughtful people might still be found who base upon it their certainty of their own being, thereby assuaging their civilized need for solid convictions. In any event, the author of these lines still vividly remembers a time in his own life when such artificial thinking processes gave sweet satisfaction to his craving for intellectual tranquillity.

This is not to speak of another of Descartes' peculiarities, which was that, carried away by the rigorous necessity of his deductions, he was able to reach the genial conviction that all animals except human beings are mere external machines, skillfully constructed by the Creator and, having no consciousness, feel neither pain nor pleasure.

It is hardly surprising, therefore, that his disciple and successor as predominant figure in philosophical development, the famous Spinoza, was able to weld together so skillfully and strongly a network of logical deductions concerning the First Cause, the supreme order, and the workings of the entire cosmos that, through continuous and unbroken meshes of theorems and syllogisms, he was unable to discern any traces of the Living Creator in all of creation or notice the inner freedom of humanity. A similar excess of logical rationality concealed from the great Leibniz, behind the intellectual linkage of his abstract concepts, the obvious connection of cause and effect, forcing him to hypothesize his Preestablished Harmony in order to explain this connection, although this theory actually makes up for some of its one-sidedness by the poetry of its basic idea.

I say the poetry of the idea makes up for some of its one-sidedness because it seems to me that when logical merit is reinforced by aesthetic or moral merit, this very combination of qualities enables reason itself to recapture some of its primordial fullness and thus move closer to the truth.

Must we continue to enumerate subsequent representatives of Western philosophy and recall their systems in order to convince ourselves of the general one-sidedness of the Western orientation? Is there any need to recall that Hume—that direct and inevitable result of another branch of Western philosophy, a follower of Bacon, Locke, and other such thinkers—the unprejudiced Hume, using the faculty of unprejudiced reason, proved that no truth of any kind exists in the world and that truth and falsehood are subject to the same degree of doubt? Or that the illustrious Kant, roused by Hume and prepared by the German school, deduced from the very laws of pure reason incontestable proof that for pure reason no proofs of the higher truths can exist?

This may have been but one step from the truth—but the Western world was not yet ripe for it.

One abstract aspect of Kant's system was developed in the system of Fichte, who proved, through a remarkable construct of syllogisms, that the whole external world is but a false phantom of the imagination, and that the only thing that really exists is the self-developing *I*. From this, Schelling developed the opposite aspect of the same hypothesis—that although the outer world really exists, the soul of the world is none other than this human *I*, which develops in the being of the universe only in order to achieve self-consciousness in human beings. Hegel further strengthened and elaborated this system of the independent development of human self-consciousness. At the same time, probing more deeply than anyone before him into the very laws of logical thinking, on the strength of his vast, extraordinary genius, he carried the implications of these laws to their ultimate fullness and clarity, thereby enabling Schelling to prove the one-sidedness of all logical thought. Thus Western philosophy now finds itself in a situation where it can neither continue any further along its abstract-rational path, for it has become conscious of the one-sidedness of abstract rationality, nor can it strike out along a new path, since all its strength has consisted in developing precisely this abstract rationality.

In the meantime, whereas Roman theology developed along the line of Scholastic philosophy, writers of the Eastern Church did not get distracted by the one-sidedness of syllogistic constructs, but retained the fullness and wholeness of speculation that comprise the distinctive feature of Christian philosophy. For we must not forget that at that period all contemporary culture was concentrated in Byzantium. Educated Greeks were well versed in ancient Christian and pagan writers, particularly the philosophical writers, and the manifest traces of a thorough study of these predecessors can be found in most spiritual works until the middle of the fifteenth century. At the same time, the West, unlearned and, one might even say, ignorant in comparison with Byzantium, was restricted in its thinking, until almost the fourteenth century, to the milieu of Latin writers, apart from a very few Greeks. It was not until the middle of the fourteenth century that the first learned academy was founded in Italy by the famous monk Barlaam, Petrarch's teacher—that same miserable betrayer of the Orthodox Church who, having become infected with Western confidence in logical reasoning, had rejected several dogmas of the Christian doctrine he was unable to understand, for which he was condemned by the Council of Constantinople and expelled from Greece in disgrace—which only led to his being welcomed in Italy with even greater honor.

There is no doubt that Aristotle was far better known to the Greeks than to the Latins, although possibly without the additions by which Arab and Latin scholars had enriched him and that, until the fall of scholastic education in Europe, comprised a necessary condition for all intellectual development in the West. Nevertheless, the Greek thinkers did not show any particular predilection for Aristotle. On the contrary, the majority of them clearly preferred Plato—not that the Christian philosophers assimilated the pagan concepts of either, but they probably found that Plato's very manner of thought presents more wholeness in its intellectual reactions and more warmth and harmony in the speculative activity of reason. Hence, very nearly the same relation that obtained between the two philosophers of the ancient world can be found between the philosophy of the Latin theologians, which developed into Scholasticism, and the spiritual philosophy we find in the writers of the Eastern Church, which was expressed with particular clarity by the Holy Fathers who lived and wrote after the defection of Rome.

It is worth noting that the spiritual philosophy of the Eastern Church Fathers who wrote after the tenth century was openly and purely Christian. It was profound, alive, elevating the reason from the status of rationalistic mechanism to higher, morally free speculation, a philosophy that even an unbelieving thinker could well find instructive because of the remarkable wealth, depth, and subtlety of its psychological observations. Despite all its merits (I speak here of speculative merits only, leaving aside its theological significance), the rationalistic tendency of the West had so little capacity to comprehend this philosophy that not only was it never properly appreciated by Western thinkers, but, even more astounding, to this day it has remained almost totally unknown to them. It is, at any rate, not mentioned by a single philosopher or historian of philosophy, although in every history of philosophy there are lengthy disquisitions on the philosophy of India, China, and Persia. The works of Eastern writers were for a long time utterly unknown in Europe; many still are unfamiliar to them; others, while known, have been ignored because they were not understood; still others have been published only recently and remain unappreciated. Although a few Western theological writers have remarked on certain distinctive traits of Eastern writers, they were so little able to understand those characteristics that their comments frequently yield conclusions directly opposite to the truth. Finally, in practically none of the theologians of the West do we note a living trace of the influence that the writings of the Eastern Church would certainly have left on them had they known them even half as well as they knew the ancient pagan writers. Perhaps the only exception to this rule is Thomas à Kempis—or Gerson[3]—if the book ascribed to him was really written by him and is not, as some think, a translation from the Greek, slightly altered to fit Latin views.

---

3. Jean le Charlier de Gerson (1363–1429), French theologian who had a major role in the Great Schism of the Western Church, where his ideas on supremacy of conciliar authority prevailed at the Council of Constance (1415–1418). The attribution to him of *The Imitation of Christ* has generally been abandoned. The probable author of this work is, of course, Thomas Hemerken, or Thomas à Kempis (1380–1471). — ED.

Of course, we will find nothing new with respect to Christian doctrine in those writers of the Eastern Church who lived after the defection of Rome—nothing that may not be found in the writers of the first centuries. But that is precisely their merit; that, I say, is their distinctive trait—that they preserved and maintained the essential Christian doctrine in all its purity and fullness, and that they, keeping always to the heart, so to speak, of true conviction, were able to discern more clearly both the laws of the human mind and the path that can lead it to true knowledge, as well as the external signs and internal causes of its various deviations.

In point of fact, even the early Church Fathers, who lived before Rome's defection and who were consequently recognized by East and West alike, were not always understood identically by West and East. This difference may have arisen because the East was at all times fully familiar with all the writers and teachers of the Universal Church, while Western scholars were acquainted mainly with the Latin writers and with only a few of the Greeks, whom they viewed through ready concepts taken from their Roman teachers. Hence, even in modern times, when they made closer acquaintance with Greek literature, they involuntarily continued to view it through the same narrow window with colored, if not darkened, glass. There is no other explanation for how they could for so long have persisted in the one-sidedness of their rationalistic trend, which otherwise should have crumbled under the combined impact of all the ancient Church Fathers. Having maintained their one-sidedness, they either failed to notice or sometimes had no knowledge of those ancient writers who present an aspect directly opposite to this narrowness, complacently rejecting it as "mysticism."

Hence, apart from their different concepts, East and West also differed in the very method of theological and philosophical thinking. For, in seeking to arrive at the truth of speculation, Eastern thinkers were primarily concerned with the proper inner condition of the thinking spirit, while Western thinkers were more interested in the external coherence of concepts. Eastern thinkers, striving for the fullness of truth, sought the inner wholeness of reason—that heart, so to speak, of intellectual powers, where all the separate activities of the spirit merge into a higher and living unity. In contrast, Western philosophers assumed that the complete truth could be discerned by the separated faculties of the mind, acting independently in isolation. They used one faculty to understand moral matters, and another to grasp aesthetic ones; for practical affairs they had yet another; matters of truth were apprehended by the abstract understanding. And none of these faculties knew what any of the others was doing until its action was completed. They assumed that each path led to a final goal, which had to be attained before all paths could unite in combined motion. They deemed frigid ratiocination and the unrestrained sway of sincere passions to be equally legitimate human states; and when Western scholars in the fourteenth century learned that the Eastern contemplative thinkers sought to preserve the serenity of inner wholeness of the spirit, they ridiculed the idea and invented various mocking appellations for it.

It is true that at times they used the same expressions as those in the East, speaking of the "internal concentration of the spirit," the "gathering of the mind in itself," and so on. But the meaning given to these expressions was generally quite different: not the concentration, gathering, and wholeness of inner powers, but merely their utmost intensity. In general, it may be said that they did not seek the center of spiritual being. Western humanity had no comprehension of that living unity of the highest intellectual powers in which none acts without the sympathy of the others, or of the equilibrium of inner life that marks even the most external actions of those brought up in the traditions of the Orthodox world. For in their actions, even during the most acute crises of their lives, there is a deep calm, a natural rhythm, a dignity coupled with humility, all of which bear testimony to the spiritual equilibrium, profundity, and wholeness of their spiritual being. Europeans, on the other hand—always ready to give way to extreme impulses, forever bustling about (when they are not being theatrical), and eternally restless in their inner and external movements—can impose on these movements an artificial proportionality only through conscious effort.

The teachings of the Fathers of the Orthodox Church reached Russia, so to speak, with the first pealing of Christian church bells. It is under their guidance that the authentic Russian mind, which lies at the foundation of Russian life, was formed.

The vast land of Russia, even when it was divided into petty principalities, remained conscious of itself as a single living organism. It found its center of gravity not so much in its shared language, as in its shared convictions arising from a shared faith in Church resolutions. For covering its vast expanse, like an unbroken net, a countless multitude of isolated monasteries lay scattered, linked by sympathetic bonds of spiritual communion. They radiated a uniform and harmonious light of faith and learning to all the separate tribes and principalities. Not only did the people derive their spiritual notions from them, but all their ethical, social, and legal concepts were subjected to their civilizing influence and returned to the social consciousness, having received a common orientation. The clergy, whose members were drawn without distinction from all classes of society—from the highest to the lowest—in turn transmitted to all social classes and levels the higher civilization that it obtained directly from primary sources, from the very center of contemporary culture, which then meant Constantinople, Syria, and Mount Athos.

This civilization spread in Russia so quickly and to such a degree that, even today, it amazes us to recall that some of the appanaged princes of the twelfth and thirteenth centuries had libraries that even the library of Paris, then the largest in the West, could barely rival in number of volumes; that many of them spoke Greek and Latin as fluently as Russian, while some knew other European languages as well.[4] In some of the compositions that survive from the fifteenth century,[5] we find excerpts from Russian translations of Greek works that not only were unknown in Europe, but had been lost in Greece itself during its decline and have only recently been rediscovered with great effort in the uncataloged treasure troves of Athos. In the distant silence of their monastic cells, often in the depths of the forest, monks studied and copied (in ancient manuscripts that have survived to this day) Slavonic translations of Church Fathers whose profound writings, filled with supreme theological and philosophical speculations, may even today test the wisdom of any German professor of philosophy (though none of them is likely to admit this). Despite the passage of a century and a half since our monasteries ceased to be centers of

---

4. Appanaged princes were those who were supported by the peasants' taxes. — ED.
5. See the writings of Nil Sorskii. [Nikolai Fedorovich Maikov, (1433–1508) took the monastic name Nil (Nilus). He was a leader of the spiritual movement of the Trans-Volga Elders, tied closely to the Hesychast tradition, and a leader of those who opposed monastic possessions (the nonpossessors). — ED.]

culture, despite the fact that the entire thinking segment of the nation, in its upbringing as in its views, has largely deviated from, and in some cases completely abandoned, the former Russian style of life and erased the very memory of it from its mind, this learning was so widespread, so strong, so highly developed, and therefore so deeply rooted in Russian life, that the Russian style of life, fashioned according to and impregnated with the ideas of our former civilization, has survived almost without change among the lower classes of the people. It has survived, although it lives in them almost unconsciously, in the customary tradition, no longer tied to the predominance of formative thought, no longer revivified, as in the olden days, by the concerted efforts of the upper classes of society, nor permeated, as it was before, with inspirational sympathy for the entire sum of the country's intellectual activity.

How great a force it must have been that produced so lasting an effect! And this stability of custom, the result of our earlier civilization, has been manifested by the same people who had so readily shed their pagan civilization when they embraced Christian doctrine.

Hence, these Russian customs and the former life of Russia reflected in them are precious to us, especially since they still show traces of the pure Christian principles that had such an uninhibited effect on the Slavic tribes that submitted to them. It is not any inborn merits of the Slavic race that allow us to place such high hopes in its future prosperity. No! Racial characteristics, like the soil on which an intellectual seed is sown, can only retard or accelerate its early development; racial characteristics can give it healthy or poor nourishment, and they can grant it a free path into God's world or strangle it with alien growths. The actual nature of the fruit, however, depends on the nature of the seed.

Whatever we may think of the coming of the Varangians—whether we hold that the entire Russian land voluntarily asked them to come, or believe one party called them in against another party—their coming did not represent an invasion by a foreign tribe. Neither could it have been a conquest; for if it was so easy to expel them, or a considerable part of them, from Russia one hundred and fifty years later, could they have conquered it so easily before? And how could they have remained undisturbed there against Russia's will? Under the Varangians the formation of social and state relations proceeded calmly and naturally, without any coercive innovations, purely as an outgrowth of the inner composition of Russia's moral notions. With the introduction of Christianity, the moral notions of Russians changed, and with them their attitude toward society; hence all the social organization of Russia, as it developed, was also bound to adopt a Christian orientation.

St. Vladimir's initial and impulsive (but so beautifully impulsive!) desire to forgive all criminals is the best example of the Russians' ready effort from the very beginning to realize in their life the fullness of the new conviction they accepted. The Church herself stopped him from carrying out his purpose, thus drawing the line between personal spiritual obligations and those of secular government. At the same time, the Church established, once and for all, clear boundaries between herself and the state, between the absolute purity of her higher principles and the worldly compromises of the social system, remaining always outside and high above the state and its worldly interests, like an unattainable, radiant ideal that people should strive toward and that transcends their earthly motivations. In guiding the people's private convictions, the Orthodox Church never nurtured any ambition to guide their wills coercively or to acquire any powers of secular government, and even less to seek official dominion over government authorities. The state, it is true, depended on the Church; the more it was permeated by the Church's influence, the stronger its foundations became, the more harmonious its structures, the more integral its internal life. The Church never desired to be the state, however, even as the state, for its part, in humble recognition of its worldly calling, never called itself "holy." If the Russian land was sometimes called "Holy Russia," that was solely due to the sacred relics, monasteries, and churches it contained, not because its structure represented an interpenetration of the ecclesiastical and the secular like that of the "Holy Roman Empire."

Thus, in ruling society as the spirit rules the body, the Church did not endow worldly institutions with an ecclesiastical character, like the monastic orders of knights, the trials of the Inquisition, and other half-secular, half-spiritual institutions of the West. But, by suffusing all of people's intellectual and moral convictions, it invisibly led the state toward a realization of the higher principles of Christianity, while never hindering its natural development. The spiritual influence of the Church on this natural growth of society was all the more complete and pure that there was no historical obstacle preventing people from allowing their inner convictions to be expressed in their external relationships. Unblemished by conquest, the Russian land in its internal structure had not been hindered by the violent forms that were bound to arise from the conflict of two tribes that hate one another yet are compelled to organize their shared life in constant hostility.

In Russia, there were neither conquerors nor conquered. It knew neither an ironclad demarcation of static social estates, nor privileges granted to one estate at the expense of another, nor the resulting political and moral struggle, nor contempt, hatred, or envy between the estates. Consequently, it was also spared the inevitable result of this struggle: artificial formality in social relations and a painful process of social development proceeding through the forcible alteration of the laws and the tempestuous overthrow of institutions. The princes, the boyars, the clergy, the people, and the armed guards of the princes, boyars, towns, and rural communities—all these classes and strata of the population were imbued with the same spirit, the same convictions, homogeneous notions, and an identical need for the general good. There might have been differences of opinion regarding some particular circumstance, but one hardly meets traces of discord in essential matters.

Thus, Russian society developed distinctively and naturally, under the influence of a single inner conviction that was nurtured by the Church and customary tradition. Nevertheless—or, more precisely, *for that very reason*—it was as free from utopian egalitarianism as it was from repressive privilege. It represented not a plane, but a ladder with a great many rungs; but these rungs were not fixed forever, for they were established naturally, as necessary vessels for the social organism, and not violently, owing to the contingencies of war, or deliberately, to correspond to the categories of reason.

Anyone who attempts to imagine Western society in feudal times is bound to compose an image by picturing a profusion of castles, fortified with walls, within which lives a noble knight and his family, and around which the lowborn rabble is settled. The knight was a person; the rabble was part of his domain. The hostile relations obtaining between these individual castles and their relations with the free cities, the king, and the Church, comprise the entire history of the West.

When, on the other hand, we imagine ancient Russian society, we do not see castles, lowborn rabble surrounding them, noble knights, nor a king struggling against them. You see instead a countless multitude of small communes scattered over the face of the Russian land, each under an administrator with a delimited status, each land representing its own consensus, its own small world. These small worlds, or communities, merge into other, larger communities, which in turn form territorial and then tribal communities. Out of these is formed the one shared, vast community of the entire Russian land under the Grand Prince of All the Russias, serving as the support for the entire roof of the social edifice, the foundation for all the ties of its supreme structure.

Given such natural, simple, and concordant relationships, the laws that were meant to express these relations could not be marked by artificial formality. Arising from two sources—popular tradition and inner conviction—they were bound, in spirit, composition, and application, to bear the character of inner rather than exterior truth, preferring the evidence of essential justice to the literal meaning of the form, the sanctity of tradition to logical deductions, and the morality of its prescriptions to utility. Of course, I am not speaking of any one law in particular, but of the general orientation or tendency of ancient Russian law, in which inner equity had the upper hand over superficial formalism.

The jurisprudence of Rome and the West draws abstract logical conclusions from every legal condition, saying, *"The form is the law,"* and endeavors to link all forms into a single, rational system, each part of which should follow logically from the whole, with the whole itself constituting not merely a rational matter but *reason itself in written form.* Customary law, as it was in Russia, on the other hand, arose from life and avoided development through abstract logic. In Russia the law was not prefabricated by some learned legal consultants; it was not ponderously and eloquently discussed at some legislative assembly; and it did not subsequently fall like an avalanche into the midst of an astounded crowd of citizens, wrecking some existing system of relationships. Usually, a law in Russia was not composed, but simply written down after the idea of it had been conceived by the nation, and after it had gradually, by the compulsion of objective necessity, become part of the popular customs and way of life. Logical progress in the law is conceivable only where society itself rests on artificial foundations and, consequently, where any further development of the social order must be governed by the opinion of some or all of the people. On the other hand, the stability of customs, sanctity of tradition, or continuity of customary relationships of a society based on basic consensus cannot be corrupted without destroying the most essential conditions of society's life. In such a society, every coercive change dictated by logical conclusion would be a stab to the heart of the social organism. For here society is based on convictions, and therefore opinions, even when shared by all, would be fatal for it if they governed its development.

Opinion and conviction are two wholly different mainsprings of two entirely different kinds of social order. Opinion differs from conviction not only in that the former is more fleeting while the latter is more stable, and in that the former stems from logical considerations while the latter is the result of a lifetime's experience. From the political viewpoint, we can see yet another distinction: conviction is a spontaneous awareness of the sum total of social relations; opinion is an exaggerated sympathy for that aspect of social interests that happens to coincide with the interests of some one party, thereby concealing its selfish exclusivity with the deceptive appearance of the common good.

Hence, in an artificial society, one founded on a formal linkage of interests, every improvement is introduced as a result of some deliberate plan; a new relationship is instituted because today's opinion gains ascendancy over yesterday's order of things; and each decision forcibly changes the preceding one. Development, as already noted, proceeds according to the law of revolutions, whether from above or from below, depending on where the victorious party concentrated its forces and where the victorious opinion has directed them. On the other hand, in a society that has arisen naturally, through the distinctive development of its basic principles, every upheaval is an illness, fraught with some degree of danger; to such a society, the law of revolutions is not a condition for improvements in life, but rather of disintegration and death; for such societies can develop only in a harmonious and imperceptible way, following the law by which natural growth is conditional upon the retention of the original meaning.

One of the basic differences between the legal systems of Russia and the West consists of their fundamental conceptions of the right to land ownership. All Roman civil laws may be said to be no more than an outgrowth of the unconditional character of this right. Western European social systems also arose out of various combinations of these original rights, which were initially unlimited, and which were subjected to some mutually conditioned limitations only in social relationships. The entire edifice of the Western social order may be said to rest on the development of the personal right of ownership, so that individuality itself—legally speaking—is no more than an expression of this right to ownership of the land.

In the structure of Russian society, the individual is the primary basis of the law, and the right of ownership is merely one of its accidental attributes. The land belonged to the commune because the commune was comprised of families that consisted of persons who were able to cultivate the land. As the number of persons in a family increased, the amount of land at its disposal increased also; as the number decreased, so did the amount of land. The commune's rights over the land were limited by the rights of the landowner or estate-holder; the landowner's rights were determined by his position vis-à-vis the state. The relationship of the landowner to the state did not derive from his estate, but his estate did depend on the personal relationship of the owner [to the state]. This relationship was determined in equal measure by his father's personal relationship and by his own; it was lost if he proved incapable of supporting it, while it grew if his merits proved superior to those of other aggregate personalities. In other words, the unconditional nature of land ownership could arise in Russia only as an exception. Society was made up not of private property to which persons were attached, but of individuals to whom property was attached.

When small principalities were abolished and merged into one administrative structure, any confusion that may have subsequently arisen due to these relationships in the upper strata of society was incidental and would appear to have been the effect of adventitious causes, so that it was not part of the inherent development of the fundamental spirit of Russian statehood. In any event, this very special position, altogether unlike that obtaining in the West (where a person was defined in terms of landed property), was an intrinsic part of the entire sum of social, communal, and moral relationships.

Consequently, interrelationships among Russians were also different from those of the West. I am not speaking of the difference of some particular forms, which may be regarded as negligible national idiosyncrasies. The very nature of popular customs, the very meaning of public relationships and private morals was quite different. Western people fragment their lives into separate aspirations; and though they then unite them into a coherent plan by means of rationalistic understanding, at each moment of life the individual is like a different person. One corner of the heart shelters the Western person's religious feeling, which is called upon on occasions of ritual observance; another, quite separate, harbors the faculties of reason and the capacity for worldly activity; a third corner contains the person's sensual desires; a fourth, a sense of morality and family; a fifth, self-interest; a sixth, the desire for aesthetic pleasure. And each of these separate strivings is subdivided into further aspects, each accompanied by a special state of mind, each manifesting itself separately from the others, all bound together only by an abstract, rationalistic recollection. Western people can easily pray in the morning with fervent, intense, amazing zeal and then rest from that zeal, forgetting prayer and exercising other faculties in their work. They then rest from their work, not just physically but morally, forgetting its dull routine in laughter and the sound of drinking songs. They then forget the rest of the day—indeed, their whole life—in dreamy enjoyment of an artificial spectacle. Next day it will be easy for them to begin again turning the wheel of their outwardly correct lives.

Not so for Russians. When they pray in church, they do not scream in exaltation, beat their breasts, and fall senseless from deep emotion. On the contrary, during the act of prayer they make a supreme effort to preserve mental sobriety and wholeness of spirit. Then, when the fullness of prayerful self-consciousness—rather than the unbalanced intensity of feeling—permeates the soul and the heart is touched by emotion, their tears flow imperceptibly and no passion troubles the deep quiet of the inner state. Thus, they do not sing drinking songs; they partake of their dinner with a prayer. It is with a prayer that they begin and finish every task. It is with a prayer that they enter and leave a house. The lowliest peasant appearing in a palace before the Grand Prince (to defend whose honor he may but yesterday have risked his life in some chance skirmish with the Poles) would not greet his host before bowing to the image of Holiness, which likewise may be found in a place of honor in every hut, large or small. Thus

Russians have always linked all their activities, important or not, directly with the highest concept of the mind and the deepest concentration of the heart.

It must, however, be admitted that this constant striving for the combined wholeness of all moral faculties may have its dangerous aspect. For it is only in a society in which all classes are imbued with the same spirit; where all minds are governed by universally respected and numerous monasteries, those popular schools and institutions of higher learning of a religious state; where, consequently, those who have attained spiritual wisdom may always direct others who have not reached maturity; it is only in such a society that such a disposition must lead people to supreme perfection. But if they lack the care and guidance of a superior mind, not having attained to the distinctive maturity of spiritual life, their lives might present the wrong combination of excess tension and undue exhaustion. Hence we occasionally see Russians who concentrate all their faculties on their work and accomplish more in three days than the prudent German will in thirty. On the other hand, however, then they will for a long time be unable to resume their tasks voluntarily. Because of the Russian's lack of maturity and absence of a sympathetic guide, Germans, for all their limitations of mind, by tabulating and dividing into hours the extent and degree of the Russian's endeavors, can often regulate and order the work of the Russians better than they themselves can.

In ancient Russia, however, this inner wholeness of self-consciousness, which was fostered in Russians by their very customs, was also reflected in their family life, where the law of constant, unceasing self-sacrifice was not a heroic exception but a matter of common and ordinary obligation. The character of peasant life still maintains the integrity of the family. If we decide to look closely at the inner life of the peasant's hut, we shall see that members of the family, constantly at work and at pains to keep the whole household operating successfully, never think of their own selfish interests. They have cut off at the root any thought of personal gain. The integrity of the family is the one common goal and motivation. Any surplus in the household goes to the head of the family, who is accountable to no one; all private earnings are conscientiously handed over to him in full.

The life of the family as a whole usually improves little when the head of the family reaps additional benefits. The various members, however, do not interfere in how they are used, nor do they even seek to learn their total sum, but continue their eternal labors with the same selflessness, as a moral duty, as a mainstay of familial concord. In former times this was even more striking, since families were larger, composed not only of children and grandchildren; they preserved their integrity, however, even when the clan increased considerably. Nevertheless, even today we see everywhere, when there is serious trouble, how readily, how willingly—I would even say how gladly—members of a family will sacrifice themselves voluntarily for one another when they see that their sacrifice will be for the common good of the family.

In the West, family ties were weakened as a result of the general trend of Western civilization. From the higher classes this tendency spread to the lower classes due to both the upper classes' direct influence on the lower and the lower classes' irresistible urge to copy the manners of the ruling class. This passionate bent for imitation is all the more natural the more homogeneous is the civilization of the different classes, and it bears its fruits the more readily the more artificial the nature of civilization is and the more it is subordinated to personal opinions.

In the higher strata of European society, generally speaking, family life very soon became an incidental matter, even for women. From their very birth, the children of noble families were brought up without the mother's involvement. Particularly in those countries where it was fashionable in families of the upper estate to rear daughters outside the family, in convents severed from the family by impenetrable walls, the mother almost lost her family function. Leaving the convent only in order to go to the altar, a young woman immediately entered the charmed circle of social duties before learning her family duties. For that very reason, she was more sensitive to social than to family relations. The selfish and noisy delights of the drawing room replaced for her the alarms and joys of the quiet nursery. The graces of the salon and the ability to live in high society, developing abundantly at the expense of other virtues, became the most essential element of feminine merit. The brilliant salon soon became for both sexes the main source of pleasure and happiness, of wit and culture, and of social influence, and the leading and engrossing goal of their artificial life. Hence, particularly in countries where women of quality were brought up apart from the family, there was a magnificent and enchanting development of social refinements; this development was accompanied by the moral rot of the ruling class, which contained the first germ of what was later to become the notorious doctrine of the comprehensive emancipation of women.

In Russia, in the meantime, the various forms of social life, being a reflection of the wholeness of life, never underwent any separate, independent development, sundered from the life of the entire nation, and therefore could neither stifle the family feeling of people nor hinder the wholeness of their moral growth. The striking peculiarity of the Russian character in this respect was that, in social relationships, no individual person ever sought to display a personal peculiarity of nature as some virtue; all individual striving was limited to a correct expression of the fundamental spirit of society. Even as the salon does not rule a state if all parts of the state are in sympathy with the wholeness of social life; even as a personal opinion does not dominate a society that stands firmly on conviction; even so, such a society is not governed by whims of fashion, for fashion is thwarted by the stability of the general style of life.

Such being the temper of the Russian people, the simplicity of their life and the simplicity of their needs was not the result of a lack of means or of inadequately developed civilization; it was determined by the very character of the dominant culture. In the West, luxury was not a contradiction but the logical consequence of fragmented human and social aspirations; it may be said to have been inherent in artificial civilization. The clergy, going against the general view, may have condemned it, but in the popular mind it was almost a virtue. People did not yield to it as to a weakness, but rather were proud of it, as of an enviable privilege. In the Middle Ages, the people gazed with respect at the superficial glitter that surrounded a person of consequence, and their minds reverently joined this superficial glitter to the concept of human virtue in a single feeling. Russians, on the other hand, venerated the rags of the holy fool more than the gold brocade of the courtier. Luxury did penetrate Russia, but like a pestilence caught from its neighbors. People apologized for it; people succumbed to it as to a vice, always remaining aware that it was wrong, not only from the religious, but also from the moral and social standpoints.

Western humanity sought to relieve the burden of its internal short-comings by developing exterior means. The Russian endeavored to avoid the burden of exterior necessities by inwardly rising above them. Had the science of political economy existed in those days, there can be no doubt that Russians would have found it incomprehensible. They would have been unable to reconcile the existence of a separate science of wealth with the wholeness of their own view of life. They would not have understood why one should intensify people's awareness of outer necessities merely to increase their efforts toward producing material goods. They knew that the development of wealth is a secondary factor in the life of society and should therefore not merely be closely tied to other, higher factors, but be entirely subordinate to them.

Nevertheless, whereas luxury was able to enter Russia as a sort of pestilence—as artificial comfort with its aesthetic pampering—any other deliberate artificiality in life, or dreamy relaxation of the mind, could never have gained a foothold there, being directly and clearly contrary to its dominant spirit.

For the same reason, if there had been time for the fine arts to develop in ancient Russia, they would certainly have taken a very different form from that which they took in the West. In the West their development followed the general trend of thought; consequently, the same fragmentation of the spirit that, in the speculative sphere, resulted in logical abstraction produced fancifulness and disjointed emotions in the fine arts. Hence the pagan worship of abstract beauty. Instead of maintaining an eternal bond between beauty and truth—a bond that, it is true, may impede their progress individually but that safeguards the general wholeness of the human spirit and preserves the truthfulness of its manifestations—the Western world founded its ideal of beauty on a delusion of the imagination. It established its ideal on a fancy it knew to be false, or on an extreme straining of a one-sided emotion, which was born of a deliberate splitting of the mind. The Western world did not realize that a flight of fancy is a lie of the heart, and that an inner wholeness of being is essential not only for the truth of reason, but also for full aesthetic enjoyment.

This trend of the fine arts was not without effect on the life of the Western world. Free art is born of the sum total of human relationships, and having made its entrance into the world, it again returns into the depths of the human spirit, fortifying it or weakening it, gathering its faculties or scattering them. I believe, therefore, that the false orientation of the fine arts distorted European culture even more profoundly than did the same trend in philosophy, which can stimulate development only if it itself results from it. But the voluntary, continuous, and, so to speak, enthusiastic striving for a deliberate split in inner self-consciousness shatters the very root of the soul's powers. Reason is thus transformed into cleverness, sincere emotion into blind passion, beauty into fancy, truth into opinion, learning into a syllogism, essentiality into an excuse for the imagination, and virtue into smugness; all the while, theatricality becomes life's inseparable companion, serving as an external cover of falsehood, even as fancy serves as its internal mask.

By mentioning "smugness" I have touched upon yet another fairly general difference between the Westerner and the Russian. Western people, generally speaking, are nearly always satisfied with their moral state; almost all Europeans are ready at any time, proudly placing their hands upon their hearts, to declare to themselves and to others that they have a clean conscience, that they are innocent before God and humanity, and that they ask from God only that all others should be like they themselves. If their overt acts should happen to come into variance with the generally accepted notions of morality, they will invent their own, original system of ethics, and thus once more pacify the conscience.

Russians, on the other hand, are always keenly aware of their shortcomings, and the higher they rise on the ladder of moral development, the more they demand of themselves, and consequently the less satisfied they are with themselves. When they deviate from the true path, they do not seek to deceive themselves by some ingenious argument, thus lending an appearance of rightness to their inner delusions; on the contrary, even when they are most carried away by passion, they are always ready to recognize its moral unlawfulness.

But let us stop here and summarize all that we have said on the difference between Western European and ancient Russian culture; for surely we have noted enough features to be able to add them up and arrive at a general definition of the two types of civilization.

Christianity was communicated to the minds of Western peoples solely through the teaching of the Roman Church, while in Russia it was kindled by the lanterns of the entire Orthodox Church. In the West, theology became a matter of rationalistic abstraction, whereas in the Orthodox world it retained its inner wholeness of spirit. In the West, the forces of reason were split asunder, while here there was a striving to maintain a living totality. There the mind sought to find the truth by establishing a logical sequence of concepts, while here people aspired to it by elevating their self-consciousness to the wholeness of heart and the concentration of spirit. There we see a search for a superficial, dead unity, while here we find a striving toward inner, living unity. There the Church mingled with the state, uniting spiritual with temporal power and merging the ecclesiastical and the secular in a system of a mixed character, while in Russia the Church remained distinct from worldly goals and structures. There we see Scholasticism and juridical universities, while in ancient Russia we find prayerful monasteries as centers of higher knowledge. There we observe a rationalistic and scholastic study of supreme truths, while here we note an aspiration to a living and integral cognition of them.

In the West, pagan and Christian civilization grew into one another, while here there was a constant effort to keep the truth pure. There statehood arose from violent conquests, while here it arose from the natural development of the nation's life, permeated with the unity of fundamental belief. There we find a hostile demarcation of the estates, while in ancient Russia we see them united in concord while still maintaining their natural variety. There the artificial connection of the nobles' castles with their manors resulted in separate states, whereas here the joint consent of the entire land gives spiritual expression to its indissoluble unity. There land ownership is the primary basis of civil relationships, while here property is merely an accidental expression of personal relationships. There formal-logical law predominates, while here the law is based on life. There the law tends toward outer justice, while here inner justice is preferred. There jurisprudence strives to logical codification, while here, instead of looking for outer connections between forms, it seeks the inner link between legal conviction and the convictions of faith and custom. In the West, laws issue artificially from the prevailing opinion, while in Russia they were born naturally out of the way of life. There improvements have always been effected by means of violent change, here by means of harmonious, natural growth. There we find the turbulence of the partisan spirit, here the firmness of basic conviction.

In the West we find the whim of fashion, here the stability of life. There one finds the precariousness of individual autonomy, here the strength of family and social ties. There we see ostentatious luxury and artificial life, here the simplicity of vital needs and the courage of moral fortitude. In the West is the effeminacy of fancifulness, here the healthy wholeness of reasonable faculties. There we find an inner anxiety of spirit coupled with a rationalistic surety of one's moral perfection, here a profound peace and tranquillity of inner self-consciousness, coupled with constant self-mistrust and an incessant striving for moral improvement.

In other words, in the West we find a dichotomy of the spirit, a dichotomy of thought, a dichotomy of learning, a dichotomy of the state, a dichotomy of estates, a dichotomy of society, a dichotomy of familial rights and duties, a dichotomy of morals and emotions, a dichotomy of the sum total and of all separate aspects of human being, both social and individual. We find in Russia, in contrast, a predominant striving for wholeness of being, both external and inner, social and individual, intellectual and workaday, artificial and moral. Thus, if what we have presented is correct, *dichotomy* and *wholeness*, *rationalistic understanding* and *reason*, are the ultimate expressions of Western European and ancient Russian culture, respectively.

The question naturally arises: Why, then, did Russian civilization not develop more fully than European civilization before Western culture was imported into Russia? Why did Russia not outstrip Europe? Why did it not head the intellectual movement of all humankind, since it has so many prerequisites for the correct and comprehensive development of the spirit?

If, by way of explanation, we were to say that it was due to the supreme will of Providence that the development of the Russian mind was held back for several centuries from what would appear to be its appointed time, that would be true enough, but not an answer to the question. Holy Providence does not lengthen or shorten the appointed path of humankind without moral cause. The people of Israel might have taken forty days to accomplish the journey from Egypt to the Promised Land across the Arabian deserts, but it actually took forty years to traverse. This was simply because their souls strayed from a pure striving toward God, Who was leading them.

We have already mentioned, however, that each patriarchate, each nation, each person of the Universal Church in placing their own individual characteristics at the service of this Church find that the very development of the particular characteristic presents a danger to their inner balance and steadfast harmony with the general spirit of Orthodoxy.

What, then, was the unique characteristic of Russia compared to other nations of the Orthodox world, and what was the danger that threatened it? Did this characteristic develop to excess, so that its mind was deflected from the direct path it should have taken to reach its appointed goal?

The answer to this question can be, of course, only a hypothetical guess. As for my personal opinion, I believe that Russia's distinguishing feature was the very fullness and purity of expression it gave to the Christian doctrine throughout its social and family life. This was the great strength of its civilization; but it also concealed within it the main danger to its development. The purity of expression merged so closely with the spirit it expressed that it was easy for people to confuse the two and to respect the outer form as much as the inner meaning. They were, of course, protected against such confusion by the very nature of Orthodox doctrine, which was primarily concerned with preserving the wholeness of the spirit. Yet the reason of the doctrine one accepts does not liberate one from the weakness common to all humanity. Thus no teaching and no decrees can destroy the moral freedom of will in humankind nor in a nation. Indeed, we see that, during the sixteenth century, esteem for the form in many ways outweighs respect for the spirit.

Perhaps we should look for the origins of this imbalance even earlier, but it had become obvious by the sixteenth century. Certain distortions that had crept into the liturgical books and certain peculiarities in Church ritual persisted stubbornly among the people, despite the fact that constant contact with the East should have convinced them of the differences with the practice of the other [Orthodox] churches. At the same time we see that particular judicial decisions taken by Byzantium were not only studied, but were respected almost as much as Church-wide decisions, and that there appeared a demand that they be applied in Russia as if they were generally obligatory. At the same time in the monasteries, which preserved their outward splendor, one notes a certain decline in the rigor of life. At the same time the relationship between the boyars and the landed gentry, which at first had been sound, deteriorated into the ugly formalism of the complicated *mestnichestvo* system.[6] At the same time the proximity of the Uniate Church, inspiring fear of foreign innovations, augmented the general desire to preserve the entirety of fundamentally Russian Orthodox civilization, even its external and literal aspects.

In this way, respect for tradition—which was Russia's strength—was imperceptibly transformed into respect more for its external manifestations than for its vivifying spirit. This gave rise to the imbalance in Russian civilization, one striking result of which was Ivan the Terrible. A century later, it caused the schisms, and later still, because of its one-sidedness, it caused some thinking people to swing to the opposite extreme: to strive for foreign forms and a foreign spirit.

The essence of Russia's civilization, however, still lives on among the people and, what is most important, in the Holy Orthodox Church. Hence it is on this foundation and on no other that we must erect the sturdy edifice of Russian culture, which heretofore has been constructed out of mixed and, for the most part, foreign materials, and which therefore must be rebuilt with our own pure materials. The construction of this building can be carried out only when that class of our nation that is not wholly occupied with the procurement of material means and whose appointed role in society is therefore to develop the social self-consciousness—when that class, I say, which is still saturated with Western ideas, finally becomes fully convinced of the one-sidedness of European culture; when it grows more keenly aware of the need for new intellectual principles; when, in a reasonable desire for the whole truth, it turns to the pure fountainhead of the ancient Orthodox faith of its nation and, with a responsive heart, hearkens to the distinct echoes of the Holy Faith of the fatherland still clearly to be heard in Russia's former, native life. Then, having thrown off the yoke of the rationalistic systems of European philosophy, the educated

---

6. A system calculating seniority in service according to one's ancestors' service position. — ED.

Russian will find in the depths of the special, living, integral philosophy of the Holy Fathers of the Church—a philosophy inaccessible to Western concepts—complete answers to the very questions of the mind and heart that most perturb a soul deceived by the latest results of Western self-consciousness. In the former life of one's country will be discovered the possibility of understanding how a different culture may be developed.

It will then be possible in Russia for learning to develop on distinctive principles, different from those that European culture offers us. Art, flourishing on native roots, will then be possible in Russia.[7] And social life in Russia will affirm an orientation different from that which it can receive from Western civilization.

In using the word *orientation*, however, it is necessary to add that this word delimits sharply the extent of my desire. For, if ever I were to see in a dream that some long-dead, external feature of our former life had suddenly been resurrected among us and, in its former shape, become part of our present life, I would not rejoice at such a vision. On the contrary, I would be frightened. For such an intrusion of the past into the new, of the dead into the living, would be tantamount to transferring a wheel from one machine into another that requires a different type and size: in such a case, either the wheel or the machine must break. My only wish is that the principles of life that are preserved in the doctrine of the Holy Orthodox Church should permeate the beliefs of all estates and strata of our society; that these lofty principles, in prevailing over European culture, should not force it out but embrace it in their fullness, thus granting it a higher meaning and bringing it to its ultimate development; and that the wholeness of being that we observe in ancient Russia should forever be the destiny of our present and future Orthodox Russia.

---

7. A. S. Khomiakov expressed a number of profound ideas on the present state of the arts and their future development back in 1845, in his article "Pis'mo v Peterburg" ["Letter to St. Petersburg"], published in *Moskvitianin*, No. 2 (1845). But his views seem to have been found premature by his public, for our literature did not respond to those living ideas in the way that might have been expected if a more receptive frame of mind had prevailed.

II

ON THE NECESSITY AND POSSIBILITY OF NEW PRINCIPLES IN PHILOSOPHY

Ivan Kireevsky

EDITOR'S INTRODUCTION

Ivan Kireevsky spent much of his life attempting to articulate an original, "Orthodox-Slavic," "Slavophile" philosophy. The following essay, intended as the first part of a longer study, is the only philosophical work that he published during his lifetime. Indeed, here Kireevsky devotes most space to a summary of his previous writings on Russia and the West, Orthodoxy and the Western confessions, and German philosophy, establishing the urgent need for a new philosophy, but giving precious little detail of the form it might or should take. In any case, Kireevsky foresaw the return of philosophy to life and to the Church, which would restore the wholeness of philosophy in the integral knowledge granted by Christian belief. A continuation of the article, possibly linked to Kireevsky's posthumous "Fragments," was to develop the positive side of the doctrine.

"On the Necessity and Possibility of New Principles in Philosophy" was first published, soon after Kireevsky's death, in the second issue of *Russian Colloquium* (*Russkaia Beseda*) for 1856. The translation here, executed from the 1911 edition of Kireevsky's works, is by Peter K. Christoff.[1] It has been revised for this volume by Robert Bird.

---

1. First published in *Russian Philosophy. Volume I: The Beginnings of Russian Philosophy; The Slavophiles; The Westernizers*, eds. James M. Edie, James P. Scanlan, and Mary-Barbara Zeldin, with the collaboration of George L. Kline (Chicago: Quadrangle Books, 1965) 171–213; also included as an appendix to Christoff's book *An Introduction to Nineteenth-Century Russian Slavophilism. A Study in Ideas. Volume II: I. V. Kireevskij* (The Hague, Paris: Mouton, 1972) 346–375.

On the Necessity and Possibility of New Principles in Philosophy

Not so long ago the predilection for philosophy held sway in Europe. Even political questions were of secondary importance and subordinated to the solutions of philosophical systems, borrowing from them their ultimate meaning and inner significance. But lately the interest in philosophy has diminished perceptibly, and since 1848 the relationship between philosophy and politics has changed completely. Political questions now engage the attention of thinking people. Philosophical works have almost ceased to appear. Few people are concerned with philosophical systems any longer, and justifiably so. There is no room for abstract, systematic thinking within the narrow confines of today's tremendous social developments, developments that are pervaded with universal significance and that follow one after another with the speed of theater sets.

Moreover, the philosophical development of Western Europe has reached such a degree of maturity that the appearance of a new system can no longer agitate people's minds as vigorously and as obviously as before. It no longer confounds people with the contrast between new conclusions and old concepts. The orientation toward autonomous rational thought that began in the West about the time of the Reformation—and whose first representatives in philosophy were Bacon and Descartes—has constantly grown and spread during the course of three and a half centuries. At times it has proliferated into numerous separate systems, while at times it has combined to produce their great summations, passing in this way through all the stages of its possible progress. Thus it has finally attained the last all-inclusive conclusion beyond which the European mind cannot aspire without completely changing its basic orientation. For when people reject every authority except their own abstract thinking, can they advance beyond the view that presents the whole existence of the world as the transparent dialectic of human reason, and human reason as the self-consciousness of universal being? It is obvious that, in this case, the ultimate goal that can be conceived by abstract reason, separated from other cognitive powers, is the goal it has been approaching for centuries, which it has now attained and beyond which there is nothing further for it to seek.

Lacking the opportunity to move forward, philosophy can expand only in breadth, developing details and lending all individual disciplines a common meaning. Consequently, we see that contemporary Western thinkers, however they may differ among themselves, almost all proceed from the same level of basic principles. Hegel's followers speak in a more pedantic language; those who have not read him use a more human language. But almost all—even those who have not heard of him—express the principal conviction that serves as the basis and the final conclusion of Hegel's system. This conviction is in the air, so to speak, of contemporary civilization.

From the fact that few works are published on philosophy, that there is little debate on philosophical questions, and that interest in philosophical systems has waned, we should not conclude that interest in philosophical thought itself has diminished. On the contrary, more than ever it has penetrated all other spheres of reason. Every phenomenon in social life, every discovery of science, transcends in the human mind the boundaries of its apparent sphere and, linking with universal human problems, assumes rational-philosophical significance. The very universal nature of social developments contributes to this turn of mind. Interest in building scholastic systems is dead. All the greater, however, are the efforts by which all educated people seek to draw the guiding strand of their abstract thought through all the labyrinths of social life, through all the marvels of new scientific and scholarly discoveries, and through the infinite variety of their possible consequences. New philosophical systems no longer arise, but the supremacy of rational philosophy continues.

Such rational thought, which achieved its definitive consciousness and expression in modern German philosophy, combines all phenomena of contemporary European culture into a single common meaning and gives them one common character. Life's every movement is permeated by the same spirit, and every intellectual phenomenon prompts the same philosophical convictions. The discrepancies between these rational-philosophical convictions and the doctrines of faith have led some Western Christians to attempt to counter with the former philosophical views based on faith. The most brilliant efforts of Western Christian thinkers, however, have served only further to prove the lasting supremacy of rationalism. For, in their efforts to refute its conclusions, the opponents of philosophy cannot detach themselves from the foundation from which philosophy naturally developed, and from which no other results could be obtained without doing violence to that foundation. For this reason many pious people in the West, staggered by the irresistible tendency of thought toward unbelief and wishing to rescue faith, completely reject all philosophy as incompatible with religion, and they condemn reason in general as contrary to faith. But these pious people in the West fail to note that by such persecution of reason they do even greater harm to religious convictions than the philosophers themselves. For what kind of religion is it that cannot stand in the light of learning and consciousness? What kind of faith is it that is incompatible with reason?

Thus it appears that a believer in the West has almost no means of rescuing faith except by preserving its blindness and by timorously guarding it from coming into contact with reason. This is an unfortunate but unavoidable consequence of the inner dichotomy of faith itself. For whenever the teaching of faith deviates even a little from its basic purity, the deviation, growing little by little, cannot help coming into conflict with faith. The lack of wholeness and inner unity in faith compels one to seek unity in abstract thinking. Human reason, having received equal rights with Divine Revelation, first serves as the ground of religion, and then replaces it.

When I speak of the division within faith and of the abstract-rational basis of religion, I do not refer only to the Protestant confessions, where the authority of tradition is replaced by the authority of individual understanding. We see, in Latinism no less than in Protestantism, abstract reason at the very foundation of religious doctrine, in spite of the fact that, in its struggle with Protestantism, Latinism denied rationalism solely on the basis of tradition. For it was only in its opposition to Protestantism that Latinism placed church tradition above human reason. On matters of faith in relation to the Universal Church, however, Rome prefers abstract syllogism over sacred tradition, which is the repository of the common consciousness of the whole Christian world and holds the Universal Church together in a living, indissoluble unity. This preference for syllogism over tradition was actually the only condition for the separate and independent rise of Rome. For how else could the Roman Church have become divorced from the Universal Church? It defected from it only because it wished to introduce new dogmas into the faith, dogmas unknown to Church tradition and born of the arbitrary deductions of the logic of Western peoples. This is the root of that initial division in the very basic principle of Western religious doctrine, from which developed first Scholastic philosophy within faith, then the Reformation in faith, and, finally, philosophy outside of faith. The Scholastics were the first rationalists; their progeny are called Hegelians.

The orientations of Western philosophies, however, differed according to the various religious confessions from which they arose; for every particular confession inevitably assumes a special attitude of reason toward faith. This special attitude of reason toward faith determines the particular character of the thought that derives from it.

The Roman Church separated from the Universal Church as a consequence of a deduction of formal-logical reason that sought a superficial connection of concepts and derived from it its conclusions about their essence. It was only such superficial reason, only this placing of syllogisms above the living consciousness of all Christendom, that could wrest Rome from the Church. Having deprived itself of the support of universal tradition and the shared, unanimous sympathy of the whole Church, the Roman Church was compelled to seek support in some sort of theological system. But since human reason, particularly the rationalistic type, may comprehend the Divine variously, according to the personal conceptions of each individual, and since the contradictions in theological arguments could no longer be resolved through the inner concord of the whole Church—visible and invisible, the Church of all ages and all peoples—the unanimity of thought of the Western Christians had to be safeguarded by the external authority of the hierarchy.

External authority, independently of any inner authority, thus became the ultimate basis of faith. Consequently, the relationship between faith and reason assumed such a character that reason had to submit *blindly* to a religious doctrine affirmed by the external authority of the visible Church. I say "blindly," because no inner cause could be sought for a given theological opinion when the truth or the falsity of opinion was determined by the arbitrary opinion of the hierarchy. Hence we had Scholasticism with all of its rationalistic refinements, which sought endlessly to reconcile the demands of reason with the affirmations of the hierarchy and in so doing constantly drifted away from the demands of reason into a countless multitude of heretical systems and interpretations.

Meanwhile, leaving the supreme decision concerning divine truths to the reason of the hierarchy—which acted without reference to tradition and the fullness of the Church—the Roman Church had to recognize its hierarchy as the source of all truth and to subject to the verdict of the same hierarchical opinion the whole body of human thought, the whole development of the mind in learning and social life. For everything is concerned to a greater or lesser extent with questions of divine truth; and, if the reason of the hierarchy once transgressed the limits of Divine Revelation, it had no reason to stop its movement. The example of Galileo is no exception; it expresses the constant law of the general relationship of the Western Church to human thought. Therefore, the Reformation was necessary if reason was to be rescued from complete blindness or complete absence of faith, and it had to grow out of the same principle from which the Roman Church derived its right to its separate distinctiveness and universal interference. The only difference was this: the right of judgment over Divine Revelation preserved in the tradition was transferred from the reason of a temporary hierarchy to the reason of all contemporary Christianity. Instead of a single external authority equally binding upon all, the personal conviction of each individual became the basis of faith.

This constituted the other extreme of the same deviation from the truth. The boundaries between natural human reason and Divine Revelation were violated equally by the Roman Church and by the Protestant confessions, but in a different manner. This is why their respective attitudes toward culture were different. In the first case the basis of faith was tradition, subjected to the sole judgment of the hierarchy; it thus bridled the general development of reason with its own arbitrary opinions and endeavored to channel all thinking into a single arbitrary form. In the second case, all that was left of the tradition was the letter of the Scriptures, whose meaning depended on each individual's personal understanding.

These two attitudes were bound to give rise to two entirely opposite intellectual orientations. Under the influence of Latinism the mind had willy-nilly to reduce all its knowledge to one system. The main truth was given, the way it was interpreted had been determined, and many features of its relationship to reason were indicated; it remained only to bring the whole system of thought into agreement with the given concepts and remove from reason everything that might contradict them. In contrast, Protestantism, in addition to the letter of the Scriptures, had only the personal opinions of the reformers for the guidance of the mind, opinions that were irreconcilable in their most essential principles. For the basic relationship between humankind and God—the relationship of free will to grace and predestination, and other, similar rational attitudes of faith—were understood by them in an entirely different way from the very beginning. That is why human reason had to seek a common basis of truth outside the traditions of faith—within the individual's own thinking. It was therefore necessary that a rational philosophy should come into existence, not to develop existing truth further, not to become imbued with it, nor to rise to its level, but above all to discover it. Besides, not having a single and firm foundation for truth in faith, could people fail to appeal to thought abstracted from faith? The very love of divine truth compelled them to seek a rational philosophy. If rational philosophy, developing outside Divine Revelation, enticed people into unbelief, the initial blame for this misfortune lies, of course, not with Protestantism but with Rome, which, having the truth and comprising a living part of the living Church, consciously and deliberately broke away from it.

Concerned more with superficial unity and outward dominion over minds than with inner truth, Rome preserved the monopoly of interpretation for its hierarchy; nor could it act otherwise if it did not wish to break up into a multitude of contradictory opinions. The people were not supposed to think, to understand the Liturgy, nor even to read the Divine Scripture. They could only listen without understanding and obey without questioning. They were considered an unconscious mass upon which rested the edifice of the Church—a mass that must remain unconscious in order that the Church might remain standing. For this reason almost all independent thought originating sincerely and naturally within the Roman Church of necessity turned into opposition to the Church, which rejected and persecuted almost all outstanding thinkers. Every stirring of the mind not in accord with its arbitrary concepts was heresy, for its concepts, stamped with the authority of the hierarchy, officially penetrated all the spheres of reason and life.

In contrast, the Reformation was instrumental in the development of the intellectual culture of the peoples that it rescued from the intellectual oppression of Rome, the most intolerable of all oppressions. This constitutes the chief merit of the Reformation: it restored to human beings their dignity and also won for them the right to be reasoning beings. Just the same, there was no power in this reason that could continue to sustain it above the natural commonplace level. Torn from sympathetic relations with the one true Church, screened off from such relations by Rome, the Protestant peoples saw nothing divine around them except the letter of the Scripture and their inner conviction. And, in their joy over their liberation from intellectual bondage, they overlooked the truth in the deified letter of the Scripture—that God not only brought to earth a teaching but also established a Church, to which He promised uninterrupted existence to the end of time; and that He established His teaching within His Church, not outside it.

Protestants saw nothing except falsehood and delusion between their own time and the early centuries of Christianity. They thought that, in spite of the promises of the Savior, the gates of hell had prevailed over the Church [Matt. 16:18], that the Divine Church had been dying before they came along, and that it was left to them to resurrect it upon the foundation of the Holy Scripture. The Holy Scripture, however, receiving no unanimous interpretation, acquired different meaning according to the individual's personal views. Consequently, and in order to satisfy every individual consciousness, it was necessary to find a common basis of truth not only in human reason as such, but necessarily in that part of reason available to *every* individual. This is why the philosophy inspired by Protestantism had to limit itself mainly to the sphere of logical reason, of which every person was equally capable regardless of any individual inner capacity and makeup. The coordination of all cognitive powers into a single force, the inner wholeness of the mind essential for the comprehension of the integral truth—this could not be within everyone's reach. Only reason—relative, negative, logical reason—could be considered a general authority; it alone could demand from every particular individual the absolute acceptance of its deductions.

This is why we observe that rational philosophy developed almost exclusively in Protestant countries. After all, what is termed French philosophy is, strictly speaking, English philosophy transferred to France at a time when faith was on the decline. Although Descartes was French, and although in the middle of the seventeenth century almost all thinking people in France adhered to his system, even at the beginning of the eighteenth century it had spontaneously lost its place in the common conviction of the people, so little did it conform to the particular nature of the people's thought. The change that Malebranche wished to make in it had even less stability.[2] Meanwhile, for German thought, Descartes became the fountainhead of all philosophy.

France might have produced its own philosophy—a positive philosophy—if Bossuet's Gallicism had not merely been a diplomatic formality, but had developed more fully, more consciously, and with greater inner freedom, and had freed French civilization from Rome's intellectual oppression before it lost faith. The elements of this potential French philosophy were contained in what there was in common between the convictions of the Port-Royal school and the special opinions of Fénelon.[3] For besides dissimilarities to the official concepts of Rome, a feature common to both was that they strove to develop the inner life in its depth and sought the living bond between faith and reason beyond the sphere of external concatenation of concepts. Port-Royal and Fénelon received this orientation from the same source, from the part of Christian philosophy that they found in the ancient Church Fathers and that Rome's teaching could not encompass.

Pascal's thoughts could have been a fruitful embryo for this philosophy new to the West. His unfinished work [the *Pensées*] not only

---

2. Nicolas de Malebranche (1638–1715), French metaphysician, principal follower of Descartes. — ED.

3. Jacques Bénigne Bossuet (1627–1704), French orator, writer, theologian, and public figure. François de Salignac de la Mothe Fénelon (1651–1715), French prelate and writer, argued for a liberalized education for women (1687); he wrote a defense of the Semiquietism and mystical doctrine of Mme. Guyon (1697); his publication of *Télémaque* (1699), considered to be a satire on the king and his policies, caused him to fall into disgrace. Port-Royal was an abbey in Paris where several important philosophers (most notably Pascal) stayed, brought together by the attraction of Jansenism with its emphasis on predestination, a denial of free will, and the belief that human nature is incapable of goodness. — ED.

revealed new grounds for the understanding of the moral order of the world, for a recognition of the vital relationship between Divine Providence and human freedom, but also contained profound hints of a new way of thinking, differing equally from those of Roman Scholasticism and rational philosophy. If the sparks of his ideas had united in the common consciousness with those that warmed Fénelon's soul when, in defense of Guyon, he collected the Holy Fathers' teachings on the inner life, then from the combined flame there would surely have issued a new, original philosophy that might have saved France from unbelief and its consequences. Of course, such a philosophy would not have been the pure truth, since it still would have remained outside the Church. But it would have come closer to it than any rational speculation. However, the machinations of the Jesuits destroyed Port-Royal and its group of solitary thinkers. With them also perished the nascent, life-giving orientation of their thought. The cold, solemn logic of Bossuet failed to grasp what was vibrant and warm in Fénelon's deviation from the official thought of Rome, and with self-satisfaction he invoked papal authority to compel Fénelon to renounce his cherished convictions out of respect for papal infallibility. In this manner, France's indigenous philosophy died in embryo, and French civilization, which demanded some sort of intellectual relaxation, had to submit to Voltaire's raucous laughter and to the laws of an alien philosophy—all the more hostile to French religious convictions for having nothing in common with them. In England, Locke's system could still be somewhat reconciled with faith, alongside which it developed. In France, however, it assumed a destructive character, and passing from Condillac to Helvetius it destroyed the last vestiges of faith by its dissemination.[4]

Thus among those nations whose intellectual life was subject to the Roman Church an indigenous philosophy was impossible. At the same time, however, the growth of civilization demanded thinking capable of recognizing and comprehending it. Between the thriving science of the world and the formal faith of Rome lay a chasm that the thinking Catholic had to cross with a leap of desperation. Human reason could not always manage this leap, nor was it always in accor-

---

4. Étienne Bonnot, Abbé de Condillac (1714–1780) and Claude-Adrien Helvetius (1715–1771), both French empiricist philosophers. — ED.

dance with the conscience of the sincere Christian. Hence rational philosophy, born in Protestant countries, spread to Catholic lands as well, permeating all European civilization with one common character and replacing the former unanimity of faith of the Western nations with the unanimity of abstract reason.

But human thought did not arrive at its final conclusion all of a sudden. Only gradually did it cast aside all incidental data, finding them insufficiently reliable for the basic affirmation of the original truth. At the beginning its activity split in two directions. Among the Romance nations, which by their historical character strove to combine inner self-consciousness with external life, arose an empirical or sensuous philosophy, starting with separate observations and moving on to general conclusions, deducing all the laws of being and thinking from the order of external nature. Among nations of Germanic origin, which as a result of their historical distinctiveness bore within themselves a constant sense of the separation between external and inner life, there arose the desire to deduce laws for external being from the very laws of reason. Finally, both philosophies merged into one intellectual view based on the identity of reason and being, and out of this identity they developed that form of thought that encompassed all other philosophies as separate rungs of an unfinished ladder leading to the same goal.

But, arising from the totality of Western European civilization and accommodating the general result of its intellectual life, contemporary philosophy, like all contemporary European civilization, in its last flowering has been completely severed from its root. Its conclusions have nothing in common with its past, toward which it maintains an attitude not of a culminating, but of a destructive force. Entirely independent of its past, it appears now as a distinctively new principle and is giving birth to a new epoch in the intellectual and social life of the West. It is still very difficult to determine the true nature of its effect upon European civilization, for its characteristic influence is just beginning to be discerned; its ultimate fruits are concealed in the future.

Moreover, this new system has dominated earlier European philosophical convictions for too brief a period to give us the right to think that its fundamental assumptions and its dialectical thought-process are the exclusive property of our time. In the general life of humanity, contemporary philosophy is not as new as is customarily assumed. It is new in modern history, but for human reason in general it is familiar, and hence the future consequences of its supremacy over people's minds have already been more or less indicated. For the same spirit of thought dominated the educated world several centuries before the birth of Christ. Aristotle's basic views (not those attributed to him by his medieval interpreters, but those that emerge from his works) are completely identical to Hegel's views. And the manner of dialectical thinking ordinarily deemed the exclusive characteristic and particular discovery of Hegel was, even in the days before Aristotle, the unmistakable attribute of the Eleatic school. This is true to the extent that, when we read Plato's *Parmenides*, it seems that, in the words of Heraclitus's disciple we hear the Berlin professor himself arguing that dialectics is the chief function and real task of philosophy. He sees in it a miraculous force that transforms every determinate thought into its antithesis and from this produces a new definition. He makes abstract notions about being, non-being, and becoming the foundation of the thinking process that embraces all being and knowledge. This is why the difference between the new philosopher and the ancient philosophers consists not in the basic point of view attained by reason, nor in the special manner of thought invented by him, but entirely in the consummate fullness of his systematic development and in the wealth of intellectual acquisitions that human curiosity has managed to amass for humankind in the course of its two-thousand-year search. Reason now stands on the same rung, not higher, and perceives the same ultimate truth, and no further. Only the contours of the horizon have been marked more clearly.

The Western mind seems to have a special kinship with Aristotle. Appreciation for his thought goes back to the very beginning of Western European civilization. The Scholastics, however, utilized his system merely as the foundation for a new truth, not derived directly from it but taken by them from tradition. When, with the renaissance of learning, Aristotle's unlimited authority fell, it seemed that all appreciation of him would be lost forever. Europe celebrated its liberation from him with some delight, as a great and redeeming event for the human mind. Hegel traveled a different road, which stood outside Aristotle's system, but came all the same to a meeting point with him, both in his final conclusion and regarding the basic relationship of the mind to truth. He constructed another system, but as Aristotle himself would have constructed it if Aristotle were resurrected in our time and if, without changing the level on which human reason stood in his day, he simply related the problems of contemporary civilization to his point of view. Hegel's pupils, substituting their own terminology for that of Aristotle, recognize in his system a faithful though incomplete reflection of the system of their teacher. The voice of the modern world echoed the world of the past.

Ancient Greek philosophy originated not directly from Greek religious beliefs, but under their influence and parallel to them; it sprang up from their inner discord. The inner discord of faith eventually led of necessity to abstract reasoning. Abstract reasoning and the tangible and active diversity of the contradictory teachings of faith, standing in essential opposition to each other, could be reconciled in the mind of the Greek only in the contemplation of the beautiful and perhaps also in the hidden meaning of the mysteries. That is why the sense of the beautiful in the Greek stands between the tangibility of Greek mythology and the abstract reasoning of Greek philosophy. To the Greek the beautiful was the focus of all intellectual life. The unfolding of the meaning of the beautiful, one might say, comprises the whole essence of Greek civilization, both inner and outer. But the limits of its development were contained in the very nature of the beautiful: the growth of one of its elements entailed the destruction of the other. To the extent that reasoning developed, mythological faith weakened, and Greek beauty faded along with it. For the beautiful, like the true, disappears in abstraction when it does not rest on the essential. Rising on the ruins of beliefs, philosophy undermined them and thereby destroyed the creative wellspring for the development of Greek civilization. Philosophy, initially the expression of Greek civilization, became at the stage of its full development the contradiction of the old Greek civilization, and although it still bore the outward signs of mythology, it actually had its own independent distinctiveness. It was born in and it grew out of Greek concepts, but in its maturity it became the legacy of all humanity as the separate fruit of reason, rounded and ripened, and eventually torn from its natural root.

It may be said that the dominion of pagan beliefs over human culture came to an end with the final development of Greek civilization, not because there were no more believing pagans, but because the leading thought of civilization now stood outside the pagan faith, transforming mythology into allegory. Only immature and, therefore, impotent thought could remain pagan; but as it developed it fell under the sway of philosophy.

Thus, in this negative manner, Greek philosophy appears to have been useful in the history of humanity by educating the mind, liberating it from the false teachings of paganism, and through rational guidance, leading it to that neutral condition in which it became capable of accepting a higher truth. Philosophy prepared the field for the Christian seed.

But between the time of Aristotle and the general submission of world culture to Christian doctrine, many centuries elapsed, in the course of which many different and conflicting philosophical systems nourished, consoled, and disturbed human reason. Few of these systems, however, were characterized by extremes; in general, culture grew out of what was shared by the extremes, out of the middle ground. Between the virtuous pride of the Stoics and the sensual philosophy of the Epicureans, between the alluring heights of the soaring mental constructs of the Neoplatonic school and the unfeeling, implacable, all-uprooting plow of skepticism stood Aristotle's philosophy, to which the human mind constantly returned from extreme deviations, and which cast the logical net of its indifferent system into the one-sided extremes of thought that had diverged from it. That is why it may be said that, whereas in the ancient pre-Christian world there were several different philosophers of various, mutually contradictory sects, the vast majority of thinking humanity and all of culture's moral and intellectual power belonged to Aristotle. Precisely what influence did Aristotle's philosophy have on culture and on the moral dignity of humankind? The solution of this problem is important, and not only for the history of the world of the past.

It would seem that the clearest and briefest answer to this question lies perhaps in the moral and intellectual tenor of the centuries when this philosophy was dominant. The Roman citizen of the time of the emperors bore the living stamp of the principles of Aristotelian philosophy. For the ultimate meaning of any philosophy lies not in individual logical or metaphysical truths, but in the relationship in which it places humanity with respect to the ultimate truth that is sought—in the inner imperative that dominates the mind imbued with the philosophy. In the final stage of its development, every philosophy produces a twofold result, or, more correctly, two aspects of the final result: the total product of consciousness and the preponderant imperative arising from this product. The ultimate truth that sustains the mind points to the treasure that people will seek in learning and in life. At the end of a philosophical system, between its primordial truth and its cherished goal, lies not thought possessing a specific formula, but only the spirit of the thought, so to speak, its inner power, its innermost music that accompanies all the stirrings of the soul of those convinced by it. This inner spirit, this living force, is characteristic not only of supreme, well-rounded, and consummate philosophical systems. A philosophical system belongs in the academic domain, but its power, its ultimate imperative, concerns the life and culture of all humanity.

One must admit, however, that Aristotle's philosophy, when not serving to support an alien system but acting independently, had a very lamentable influence on human culture, an influence that was in direct contrast to the influence it exerted on its first student, the great conqueror of the Orient [Alexander the Great]. The striving for something better within the bounds of the commonplace, for the prudent (in the ordinary sense of the term), and for the possible as determined by external reality, were the final conclusions of the kind of rationality suggested by Aristotle's system. There was only one student who did not find these teachings to his liking; all the others found them perfectly congenial. It seems that the more Alexander listened to them, the more energetically he developed his own original, antithetical ideas—as if to defy his teacher's counsel. It may even be that without the stimulus of prudent mediocrity all the extremism of his imprudent genius would not have developed in him. But the rest of humanity submitted to the influence of rationalistic philosophy all the more willingly since, in the absence of supreme convictions, the tendency toward the mundane and the prudently commonplace automatically become the predominant characteristic of the moral world.

Aristotle's system broke the wholeness of human intellectual self-consciousness and transferred the root of people's inner convictions from the moral and aesthetic sphere into the abstract consciousness of deliberative reason. The means with which it sought to know the truth were limited to the logical activity of the mind and to the detached contemplation of the external world. External existence and the expressible verbal aspect of thought constituted the only data from which it derived whatever could be derived by the logical concatenation of concepts, and one must admit that it derived from them all that could be derived in this manner at that time. In Aristotle's view, reality was the complete embodiment of supreme reason. All the disharmonies in the physical and moral world were simply imaginary, and not only were lost in the total harmony, but in fact provided essential tones for its eternally unchanging fullness. In his opinion the world never had been and never would be better. It had always been sufficiently beautiful, for it had no beginning and would have no end. It would remain eternally whole and unchanged in its totality, while constantly changing and experiencing destruction in its parts. But he conceived this integral and satisfying world in the cold system of abstract unity. He saw the highest good in thought that comprehends this unity through the diversity of individual phenomena accompanied by an external life of contentment and tranquillity—that is, physical and intellectual comfort.

He said that only when human beings are liberated from worldly needs can they begin to love wisdom (whereas the Stoics held that only wisdom can free people from worldly wants and burdens). In Aristotle's opinion, virtue does not demand the higher realm of being but consists in finding the golden mean between evil extremes. Virtue derives from two sources: from the abstract deductions of the mind, which, being abstract, lend no strength to the spirit and have no essential compulsory force, and from habit, which in part is the product of the abstract desire to reconcile will and the dictates of reason and in part arises from the accidental nature of external circumstances.

It is obvious that this pattern of thought could produce very intelligent spectators among the varied phenomena of humanity, but only extremely insignificant people of action. And in fact Aristotle's philosophy had a destructive effect on human moral worth. By undermining all convictions that existed above the level of rationalistic logic, it destroyed all motivations capable of elevating people above their personal interests. The spirit of ethics declined. The mainsprings of inner originality weakened. People became the obedient tools of surrounding circumstances, a deliberating but unwilling result of external forces—intelligent matter obedient to the power of mundane motives: personal advantage and fear. The few examples of

Stoic virtue are rare exceptions—striking contrasts to the general frame of mind—that confirm rather than deny the notion of the general absence of inner independence. For Stoicism could arise only as an intense contrast, a depressing protest, a desperate consolation for the few in the face of the knavery of the many.

Nevertheless, even those thinkers who did not follow Aristotle exclusively, and who only studied his system, unconsciously introduced the results of his teaching into their understanding of other philosophers. Cicero, in the struggle between the ruin of his fatherland and his own personal security, thus sought justification for his pusillanimity in Plato. He saw in Plato, however, only the meaning that was in accord with Aristotle. That is why he consoled himself with the thought that Plato did not counsel useless resistance to force and intervention in the affairs of a senile nation. Moral insignificance was generally stamped on everyone; and if in the time of the Caesars, with the complete decline of inner human dignity, external civilization had been even more highly developed, if there had existed railroads and electric telegraphs and artillery and all the other discoveries that now subject the world to the authority of heartless calculation, it is difficult to say what would have become of poor humanity.

Such was the influence of ancient philosophy, primarily Aristotelian philosophy, on human culture. There was no salvation for human beings on earth. God alone could save them.

Christianity, however—which altered the spirit of the ancient world and resurrected the lost dignity of human nature—did not reject ancient philosophy unconditionally. For the harm and falsehood of philosophy lay not in the development of the mind it produced, but in its final conclusions, which depended on the fact that it considered itself the highest and only truth, conclusions that were eliminated as soon as the intellect recognized a superior truth. Philosophy then took a subordinate position, appearing as relative truth and serving as a means confirming the supreme principle in the realm of a different civilization.

Although engaged in a life-and-death struggle with the falsehood of pagan mythology, Christianity did not destroy pagan philosophy; rather, Christianity transformed it by accepting it in accordance with its own superior philosophy. The brightest lights of the Church (Justin, Clement, Origen, insofar as he was Orthodox, Athanasius, Basil, Gregory, and most of the great Holy Fathers upon whose work, so to speak, the Christian teaching became established amid a pagan civilization) not only were thoroughly versed in ancient philosophy, but also utilized it for the rational construction of the first Christian philosophy, which combined the development of learning and reason into one all-embracing vision of faith. The true aspect of pagan philosophy, when pervaded with the Christian spirit, served as the intermediary between faith and external human culture. And not only at the time when Christianity was still combating paganism, but in the entire subsequent existence of Byzantium, we see that a profound study of the Greek philosophers was the common legacy of almost all teachers of the Church. After all, Plato and Aristotle would only be of use to Christian culture as great researchers of reason; they could not endanger it as long as Christian truth occupied the summit of human civilization. For it should not be forgotten that, in its struggle with paganism, Christianity did not concede reason to it, but, permeating paganism, placed in its own service the whole intellectual activity of the world, past and present, to the extent that the world was known.

If there was danger anywhere that a Christian people might deviate from the true teaching, that danger lay primarily in ignorance. The growth of rational knowledge, of course, does not offer salvation, but it protects from false knowledge. It is true that where the mind and the heart have once been permeated by divine truth, there the degree of learning becomes a side issue. It is also true that consciousness of the Divine is equally compatible with all stages of reason's development. But in order that divine truth might permeate, animate, and guide human intellectual life, it must subordinate external reason to itself and dominate it, not remain outside its sphere of action. Divine truth must stand above other truths in the general consciousness as the sovereign principle pervading all culture. For each separate individual, Divine truth must be supported by the unanimity of cultivated society. Ignorance, on the other hand, keeps minds from vital intellectual communion through which truth is sustained, advanced, and cultivated among people and nations. Ignorant reason, even when accompanied by the most righteous convictions of the heart, gives birth to unreasoning zeal, from which in turn springs the deviation of the reason and the heart from true convictions.

Such was the case of the West just before its defection. The ignorance of the peoples exposed their intellectual life to the irresistible influence of the lingering traces of paganism, which communicated to their thought the rationalistic nature of Rome's superficially logical abstraction; this deviation of reason in turn compelled them to seek the superficial unity of the Church in place of spiritual unity. Ignorance also enticed them into excessive zeal against the Arians so that, not being satisfied with the rejection of the heresy, they created a new dogma concerning the Godhead in direct opposition to the Arians, under the influence of this same superficially logical thought—a dogma they regarded as true only because it was the direct opposite of one form of heresy, forgetting that the direct opposite of an error is generally not the truth, but only the other extreme of the same error.[5]

Thus, as a result of the Western peoples' ignorance, their very striving for church unity tore them from it, and their very striving for Orthodoxy tore them away from Orthodoxy.

Of course, it was not ignorance *alone* that tore the West away from the Church. Ignorance is only a misfortune. Humanity could not be separated from the saving truth without moral guilt. But the possibility and the basis of this guilt lay in ignorance; without it even the popes' love of power could not have succeeded. Only through the combined action of papal love of power and the ignorance of the people could the illegitimate addition to the Creed come to pass; this was the initial triumph of rationalism over faith, the illegitimate recognition of the supremacy of the popes, and the permanent obstacle to the return of the West to the Church. But, having once broken away, the Roman confession descended, as though sliding down the smooth slope of a mountain, to all those deviations that alienated it further and further from the truth and produced all the destructive features of Western culture with all its consequences for itself and for us. I say "for us," for the fate of all humanity is in a state of living and sympathetic reciprocity, not always noticeable, but real just the same. The defection of Rome deprived the West of the purity of the Christian teaching and at the same time halted the development of

---

5. The Arians were those who adopted the teachings of Arius (A.D. 250–336), the Greek ecclesiastic in Alexandria who promoted the Neoplatonic doctrine that God is alone, unknowable, and separate from every created being, that Christ is a created being and not God in the fullest sense but a secondary deity, and that in the Incarnation, the Logos assumed a body but not a human soul; he was declared a heretic at the Council of Nicaea (325). — ED.

social civilization in the East. What should have been accomplished through the combined efforts of East and West was now beyond the power of the East alone, which was thus condemned only to preserve divine truth in its purity and holiness, without being able to embody it in the external civilization of the nations.

Who knows? Perhaps this external impotence of the East was destined to continue until another nation might grow and mature in place of declining Rome, a nation illumined by true Christianity at the very time the West was breaking away from the East. Perhaps this nation was destined to arrive at intellectual maturity exactly at the time when Western civilization by virtue of its own development would destroy the power of its heterodoxy and would pass from false Christian convictions to indifferent philosophical convictions, returning the world to the era of pre-Christian thought. For a Christian heterodoxy is less capable of receiving the truth than the absence of any Christian convictions. The latter case would present at least the external possibility of true Christianity gaining supremacy over human culture.

There is no doubt that all actions and endeavors of private individuals and nations are subject to the unseen, barely audible, and often completely imperceptible current of the general moral order of things, which sweeps before it all general and particular activity. But this general order of things consists of the sum of individual wills. There are moments, there are situations, when the state of things is, so to speak, in the balance, and a single movement of the will can determine its direction.

The West faced such a situation at the time of its defection. For although popular ignorance weighed heavily upon the actions of the popes, there is no doubt that the firm and decisive will of one of them at that time might yet have prevailed against the error of the people and might have preserved the truth in the Western Church. There was such a fateful moment, when the Lord seemed to place the fate of the whole world in the hands of one person. Had he been firm in the truth, the world would have been spared centuries of errors and misfortunes. The various peoples would have developed in the sympathetic communion of faith and reason, jointly destroying pagan remnants in the human mind and in the life of society. The East would have given to the West the light and strength of intellectual culture; the West would have shared with the East the development of public life; everywhere culture would have been established upon the firm rock of Divine Revelation. The best spiritual forces would not have been wasted in useless upheavals, demolishing the old evil of false construction with the new evil of destruction. The best bloom of the nations would not have perished from the deadly incursions of alien barbarians or from the lingering oppression of internal pagan violence, which continued to triumph over the civilization of the Christian peoples. Social life, developing harmoniously, would not have destroyed earlier acquisitions with every new success and would not have sought the ark of salvation in the mundane calculations of industry or in the supra-celestial construction of utopias. Universal civilization does not rest on a dream or on an opinion, but on truth itself, which supports it harmoniously and steadfastly. All this depended on one moment and was perhaps in the power of one man. But that man did not stand firm, and Western civilization, deprived of sympathy for the Universal Church, was directed toward earthly goals. The Eastern Church, incapacitated by the violence of still predominant paganism and deprived of the aid of its Western brethren, took refuge in the monastery.

It appears, in fact, that there was yet another moment, in the sixteenth century, when the Western world could have returned. The eyes of many Europeans were opened by the writings of the Holy Fathers that were brought from Greece after its fall. They were shown the difference between the Christian teaching and that of Rome. At the same time the abuses of the Roman Church reached such tremendous proportions that the people became clearly convinced that the Church needed to be reformed; but no one had yet been able to decide how to accomplish such reform.

"I am now studying the papal decrees," Luther wrote to Melanchthon; "I find so many contradictions and so much falsehood that it is beyond my power to believe that they were inspired by the Holy Spirit Himself and that we were to base our faith upon them. After this I shall take up the study of the Ecumenical Councils and see whether the teaching of the Church should not be affirmed upon them in conjunction with the Holy Scripture (certainly bypassing the papal decrees)."[6]

---

6. Philipp Melanchthon (1497–1560), German Humanist and religious reformer. The parenthetical phrase is Luther's as given by Kireevsky. — ED.

If Luther had only remembered at the time that fully half of the world calling itself Christian recognized only seven, not sixteen, Ecumenical Councils, and that half of the Christian world was innocent of the Western Church's abuses that agitated his soul with righteous indignation, then perhaps instead of composing a new confession according to his personal notions, he might have turned directly to the Universal Church. He might still have done this, because the convictions of the Germanic nations had not yet led them to a final decision, except to their hatred of the pope and the desire to escape the arbitrary rule of Rome. All the nations that he roused would have followed him, and the West again could have been united with the Church, especially since the remnants of the Hussite movement were one of the most important causes of Luther's success; and it is well known that the Hussite movement was imbued with recollections and echoes of the Orthodox Church.[7] Luther, however, refused to remember the Orthodox Church, and he compared not only the seven Councils, but all those that the Romans call "Ecumenical." As a result of this comparison he wrote to Melanchthon, "I have been studying the definitions of the Councils. They also contradict each other like the papal decrees. It is obvious we have no choice but to take as the basis of faith the Holy Scripture alone."

Thus the Reformation was accomplished; its fate was decided by a misunderstanding—whether deliberate or unwitting, God alone knows. In the seventeenth century the Protestants addressed to the Eastern patriarchs an inquiry about the faith, but it was too late. Protestant opinions had already formed and were aflame with all the heat of new convictions and new, untested hopes.

In mentioning these relations between the beliefs of an entire people and the accidental nature of the moral arbitrariness of private individuals, we are not deviating from our subject. On the contrary, we

---

7. It is noteworthy that the Moravian Brethren, whose doctrine has been changed for the most part under the influence of the Protestant faiths, continue to confess to the present time, and alone in the entire Western world, the dogma of the Holy Trinity in accordance with the teaching of the Orthodox Church. But they themselves do not realize the full importance of this distinction, and the general character of Western civilization is as yet unable to encompass such a realization. [The Hussites and Morvian Brethren were proto-Reformation movements in the Czech lands that began in the early fifteenth century. — ED.]

would get a false impression of the development of human thought if we should separate it from the influence of moral and historical chance. There is nothing easier than to represent every fact of reality as an inevitable result of the supreme laws of rational necessity, but nothing would so distort the actual understanding of history as these imaginary laws of rational necessity, which are actually only laws of rational possibility. Everything must have its own measure and occupy its proper place. Of course, every moment in the history of humanity is the direct consequence of the preceding moment and in turn gives birth to the moment that follows. But one of the elemental forces of these moments is human free will. Not to recognize this is deliberately to delude oneself and substitute the external symmetry of concepts for the actual consciousness of the living truth.

From these two moments in the life of Western Europe—when it could have reunited with the Orthodox Church but did not merely because of the accidental action of human will—we see that the civilization of Western Europe, though completely different from Orthodox civilization, is still not quite as far from it as it may appear at first glance. In the very essence of Western civilization lies the necessity of separate periods of development, between which it is free from preceding influences and is therefore capable of choosing its direction.

If, however, at the beginning of the Reformation two solutions were possible, after its full development there was no longer any way out except the one actually taken. Constructing the edifice of faith on the personal convictions of the people is the same as building a tower according to the notions of each worker. All that believing Protestants had in common were certain distinctive beliefs held by their first leaders, the letter of the Holy Scripture, and natural reason, upon which the doctrine of faith was to be erected. At the present time one would hardly find many Lutheran pastors who would agree on everything in the Augsburg confession; but when they assume their appointment, all promise to accept it as the basis of their religious doctrine. In the meantime, natural reason, upon which the Church was to be affirmed, outgrew the faith of the people. Philosophical concepts increasingly replaced, and are still replacing, religious concepts. Passing first through a period of doubting unbelief, then through a period of fanatical unbelief, human thought finally went over to indifferent unbelief and together with it to the consciousness of an inner barrenness and the search for a living conviction, something that would bind person to person—not by means of cold agreement on abstract convictions, not through the superficial connection of external advantage, but through the inner sympathy of an integral being pervaded by one love, one reason, and one aspiration.

But where can the West find such living convictions? To return to what it formerly believed is impossible. Forced conversions, artificial faith—these are like the attempts of some theater-lovers to convince themselves that the sets are reality itself.

Having broken the wholeness of the spirit into fragments, and having left the higher consciousness of truth to detached logical thinking, in the depth of their self-consciousness, people were torn from all connections to reality, and they themselves appeared on earth as abstract beings, like spectators in a theater, capable of sympathy, love, and aspiration for all things on the sole condition that the physical personality not suffer and not be disturbed. For the only thing that their logical abstractness did not allow them to repudiate was physical being.

Consequently, not only was faith lost in the West, but also poetry, which in the absence of living convictions became transformed into a barren amusement; and the more exclusively poetry sought imagined pleasure alone, the more tedious it became.

Only one serious thing was left to human beings: industry, since the reality of being survived for them only as the physical person. Industry rules the world without faith or poetry. In our time it unifies and divides people. It determines one's fatherland; it delineates social estates; it lies at the foundation of state structures; it moves nations; it declares war, makes peace, changes mores, lends direction to learning and determines the character of civilization. People bow down before it and erect temples to it. It is the real deity in which people sincerely believe and to which they submit. Unselfish activity has become inconceivable. Industry has acquired the same significance in the contemporary world as chivalry in the time of Cervantes.

Incidentally, we have not yet witnessed everything. This might be only the beginning of the unlimited domination of industry and of the ultimate phase of philosophy. Proceeding hand in hand, they have yet to run the full cycle of the new development of European life. It is hard to see what European civilization may come to if some sort of inner change does not occur among the European peoples. It is obvious that this possible transformation could consist only of a transformation in basic convictions or, in other words, in a change in the spirit and orientation of philosophy, for this transformation now constitutes the entire focus of human self-consciousness.

But, as we have seen, the character of the dominant philosophy depends on the character of the dominant faith. Philosophy may not derive directly from faith; it may even be in contradiction to faith; but it is still born of the peculiar orientation given to reason by the peculiar character of faith. The same sense that enabled humankind to understand the Divine also helps humans to understand truth in general.

Under the influence of the Roman confession this sense found expression in logical rationality, which, however, acted only sporadically, lacking the ability to gather itself into a separate whole, for the fullness of its activity was destroyed by the intervention of external authority.

Under the influence of the Protestant confessions this rationality reached complete development in its separation and, conceiving itself as something supreme in the fullness of its development, called itself "reason" [*die Vernunft*], in contrast to its former fragmented activity, to which it reserved the term "rationalistic understanding" [*der Verstand*].

But for us, who were brought up outside the Roman and Protestant spheres of influence, neither manner of thinking can be completely satisfactory. Although we submit to Western civilization—for we do not yet have our own—we can submit to it only as long as we are not conscious of its one-sidedness.

In the Orthodox Church the relationship between reason and faith is completely different from their relationship in the Roman Church and in the Protestant confessions. The difference is partly that in the Orthodox Church Divine Revelation and human thought are not confused. The boundaries between the Divine and the human are transgressed neither by science nor by Church doctrine. However much believing thought might strive to reconcile reason and faith, it would never mistake any dogma of Revelation for a simple conclusion of reason, and it would never endow a conclusion of reason with the authority of revealed dogma. The boundaries stand firm and inviolable. No patriarch, no assembly of bishops, no scholar's profound consideration, no authority, no impulse of so-called public opinion at whatever time could add a new dogma or alter a former one, or ascribe to its interpretation the authority of Divine Revelation—passing off in this manner an explanation from human reason for the sacred teaching of the Church, or projecting the authority of eternal and steadfast truths of Revelation into the realm of learning subject to development, changeability, errors, and the individual conscience of each person. Every extension of Church teaching beyond the limits of Church tradition leaves the realm of Church authority and, as a private opinion, is more or less respectable, but now subject to the verdict of reason. If a new opinion is not recognized by former ages, no matter to whom it might belong, even if it be the opinion of an entire nation or of the greater part of all the Christians at a given time, it would exclude itself from the Church if it wished to pass for a Church dogma. For the Orthodox Church does not limit its self-consciousness to any particular epoch, however much this epoch might consider itself more rational than any former. The sum total of all Christians of all ages, past and present, comprises one indivisible, eternal, living assembly of the faithful, held together just as much by the unity of consciousness as through the communion of prayer.

This inviolability of the bounds of Divine Revelation is an assurance of the purity and firmness of faith in the Orthodox Church. It guards its teaching from the incorrect reinterpretations of natural reason on the one hand, and, on the other, guards reason against the illegitimate intervention of Church authority. So that for the Orthodox Christian it will forever remain equally incomprehensible how it was possible to burn Galileo for opinions that differed from the convictions of the Church hierarchy,[8] and how it was possible to reject the credibility of an apostolic epistle on the ground that the truths that it expressed were not in accord with the notions of some person or some epoch.

But the more clearly and firmly the bounds of Divine Revelation are defined, the more imperative it is for believing thought to reconcile the concept of reason and the teaching of faith. For truth is one, and striving for the consciousness of this unity is the constant law and the basic stimulus of rational activity.

---

8. It seems that Kireevsky is confusing Galileo with Giordano Bruno. — ED.

Believing reason, as it becomes freer and more sincere in its natural activities, aspires more fully and more correctly toward divine truth. For the Orthodox thinking person, the teaching of the Church is not an empty mirror that reflects the features of each personality. It is not a Procrustean bed that deforms living personalities according to one, arbitrary yardstick. It is rather the highest ideal toward which believing reason can aspire, the ultimate limit to the highest kind of thought, the guiding star that burns on high and, being reflected in the heart, lights up for reason the path to truth.

But, to reconcile faith and reason, an Orthodox thinking person must do more than construct rational concepts according to the tenets of faith, selecting the appropriate, excluding the offensive, and thus cleansing reason of everything that contradicts faith. If Orthodox thinking consisted of such a negative approach to faith, the results would have been the same as in the West. Concepts irreconcilable with faith and derived from the same source and in the same manner as those compatible with it would have an equal right to recognition. Thus the same painful dichotomy would occur in the very basis of self-consciousness and would sooner or later unavoidably draw thought away from faith.

But this is precisely the main distinction of Orthodox thinking, that it seeks not to arrange separate concepts according to the demands of faith, but rather to elevate reason itself above its usual level, thus striving to raise the very source of reason, the very manner of thinking, to the level of sympathetic agreement with faith.

The first condition for the elevation of reason is that one should strive to gather into a single indivisible whole all one's individual powers, which in the ordinary human condition remain in a state of dispersion and conflict; that one's abstract logical capacity should not be considered the only organ for comprehending truth; that one should not consider the voice of enraptured feeling, uncoordinated with other forces of the spirit, a faultless guide to truth; that one should not consider the promptings of an isolated aesthetic sense, independent of other concepts, as the true guide to the comprehension of the supreme organization of the universe; that one should not even consider the dominant love of one's heart, separate from the other demands of the spirit, as an infallible guide to attaining the highest good; but that one should constantly seek in the depth of one's soul that inner root of understanding where all the separate forces merge into one living and integral vision of the mind.

And, for comprehending truth in this concentration of all spiritual forces, reason should not subject the thoughts present before it to a sequence of individual judgments by each of its separate faculties, attempting to coordinate all their verdicts into a common meaning. But in integral thinking, with every movement of the soul, all the soul's strings should be audible in full accord, blending into a single harmonious sound.

The very manner of human thought is constantly elevated by the inner consciousness that, in the depth of the soul, there is a shared living center of all the separate forces of reason, which is hidden from the usual state of the human spirit, but accessible to the person who seeks it, and which alone is worthy of attaining the highest truth. While humbling one's rationalistic conceit, this consciousness does not constrain the freedom of the natural laws of reason. On the contrary, it strengthens one's independence and, at the same time, willingly subordinates it to faith. One then views all thinking emanating from a higher source of understanding as incomplete and therefore erroneous knowledge. Such knowledge cannot serve as an expression of the highest truth, though it might be useful in its subordinate position and at times might even be a necessary step for knowledge that is on an even lower level.

This is why the free development of the natural laws of reason cannot be harmful to the faith of those whose thought is Orthodox. Orthodox believers might become infected by unbelief, though only through a deficiency of external indigenous culture. They could not arrive at unbelief through the natural development of reason, as thinking people of other confessions have done. For Orthodox believers, basic notions about faith and reason guard against this misfortune. To them, faith is not a blind notion that is in the state of *faith* simply because it has remained undeveloped by natural reason, nor is it a notion that should be *elevated* by reason to the level of *knowledge* by breaking it down into its component parts to demonstrate that nothing is contained there that could not be found in the consciousness of natural reason without the help of Divine Revelation. Neither is faith merely an external authority before which reason must be struck blind. It is, rather, an external *and* an inner authority at the same time—higher reason that grants life to the mind. The development of natural reason serves faith only as a series of steps, and, by transcending the usual state of the mind, faith informs reason that it has departed from its original natural wholeness, and by this communication instructs it to return to the level of higher activity. For Orthodox believers know that the wholeness of truth requires wholeness of reason, and they are constantly preoccupied with the quest for such wholeness.

Given such a conviction, the entire chain of the basic principles of natural reason that can serve as points of departure for all possible systems of thought is below the reason of the believer, just as in external nature the whole chain of organic entities is below human beings, who are capable of an inner consciousness of God and prayer at all levels of development.

Standing on this highest level of thought, Orthodox believers can easily and harmlessly comprehend all systems of thought that derive from the lower levels of reason; they can see the limitations and relative truth of those systems. For the lower form of thought, however, the higher form is incomprehensible and appears nonsensical. Such is the general law of the human mind.

This independence of the basic thought of Orthodox believers from lower systems that might come into contact with their minds is not the exclusive possession of learned theologians, but is contained in the very air of Orthodoxy, so to speak. No matter how undeveloped the faculties of the believer's understanding are, all Orthodox believers are conscious in the depths of their souls that divine truth cannot be encompassed by considerations of ordinary reason, and that it demands a higher, spiritual vision acquired not through external erudition but through inner wholeness of being. That is why they seek true thought about God where they think they can find a pure, integral life that assures them of the wholeness of reason, and not where academic learning alone is exalted. That is why it is very rare for Orthodox believers to lose their faith solely because of logical arguments capable of changing their abstract notions. For the most part, Orthodox believers are enticed by unbelief, but not convinced by it. They lose faith not because of intellectual difficulties, but because of the temptations of life, and they import rationalistic considerations only in an attempt to justify to themselves the apostasy of their own hearts. Later on, their unbelief becomes fortified by some sort of rational system that replaces their former faith. Thus it becomes difficult for them to return to faith without first clearing the way for their reason. But as long as they believe with their hearts, logical argumentation is harmless for them. There is for them no thought separated from the memory of the inner wholeness of the mind, of that concentration of self-consciousness that is the true locus of supreme truth, and where not abstract reason alone, but the sum total of human intellectual and emotional forces places a single stamp of credibility on the thought that is present to it—just as on Mount Athos each monastery bears only a part of the seal that, when all its parts are put together at the general council of monastic superiors, constitutes the one legal seal of Athos.

Consequently, two activities are always combined in the thinking of Orthodox believers. Following the development of their own understanding, they follow at the same time the very manner of their thinking, constantly striving to elevate reason to a level where it can be in sympathy with faith. Inner consciousness—or sometimes only a vague awareness of this desired, ultimate limit of the mind—is present in every exertion of their reason, in every breath of thought, so to speak. And if the development of an original civilization in the world of Orthodox believers ever becomes possible, it is obvious that this feature of Orthodox thought deriving from the special relationship of reason to faith must determine its predominant orientation. Only such thought could eventually liberate the intellectual life of the Orthodox world from the distorting influences of alien culture and from the stifling oppression of ignorance, both of which are equally odious to Orthodox culture. For the development of thought, which endows all intellectual life with a particular meaning—or, more precisely, the development of philosophy—is determined by the union of the two opposite ends of human thought: the end where thought is wedded to the highest questions of faith and the end where it touches upon the development of learning and external civilization.

Philosophy is not one of the sciences, and it is not faith. It is both the sum and the common foundation of all sciences and the conductor of thought between the sciences and faith.

Where there is faith but no development of rational learning, philosophy cannot exist.

Where learning and civilization have developed but there is no faith, or where faith has disappeared, there philosophical convictions replace convictions of faith and, appearing in the form of prejudice, give direction to the thought and life of a nation. Not all who share philosophical convictions have studied the systems from which they derive, but all accept the final conclusions of these systems on the basis of their faith in the convictions of others. Resting on these intellectual prejudices, on the one hand, and stimulated by the problems of contemporary civilization, on the other, human reason engenders new philosophical systems corresponding to the mutual relationship between established prejudices and contemporary learning.

But one of two things must happen where the faith of a nation shares a common meaning and orientation, and where the civilization borrowed from another nation has a different meaning and orientation: the external civilization will force faith out, giving rise to corresponding philosophical convictions; or else faith, overcoming that external civilization in the thinking consciousness of the nation, will produce its own philosophy out of its very contact with that civilization, giving a different meaning to the external civilization and imbuing it with a different dominant principle. This occurred when Christianity appeared in the midst of pagan civilization. Not just learning, but pagan philosophy itself was transformed into an instrument of Christian culture and incorporated into the body of Christian philosophy as a subordinate principle.

As long as external culture continued to live in the East, Orthodox Christian philosophy flourished. Orthodox Christian philosophy was extinguished, however, when freedom died in Greece and its civilization was destroyed. Traces, however, have been preserved in the Writings of the Holy Fathers of the Orthodox Church, like living sparks ready to flare up at the first contact with believing thought and again to light up the guiding beacon for reason in its search for truth.

Yet, it is impossible to restore the philosophy of the Holy Fathers as it was in their time. Having grown out of the relationship of faith to the civilization of their day, it had to correspond to the problems of its own time and to the civilization where it developed. The development of new aspects of systematic and social learning also demands a corresponding new development of philosophy. But the truths expressed in the speculative Writings of the Holy Fathers could serve the development of philosophy as a life-bearing embryo and a bright guiding light.

To counterpoise these precious and life-giving truths to the contemporary state of philosophy; to become imbued with their meaning as much as possible; to consider in relation to them all questions of contemporary learning, all logical truths acquired by science, all the fruits of the millennial experience that reason has acquired in its diverse activities; and to derive general conclusions from all these considerations corresponding to the present demands of culture—these are tasks whose accomplishment could change the whole orientation of the culture of a people where the beliefs of the Orthodox faith are in disagreement with a borrowed civilization.

The satisfactory solution of this great problem demands the concerted action of like-minded people. A philosophy that does not wish to remain just a book on a bookshelf, one that is instead to become living conviction, must also develop from the living interaction of convictions that, in various ways but unanimously, strive for a shared goal. For everything essential in the human soul can be developed only socially. Personal convictions must enter into a real, and not merely hypothetical, encounter with the problems of surrounding civilization. For thoughts that illuminate the mind and warm the heart can be kindled only out of real relationships to something essential.

Even so, in order that we may understand the relationship that may exist between the philosophy of the ancient Church Fathers and contemporary civilization, it is not enough to apply the requirements of our time to this philosophy. It is necessary to keep constantly in mind the connection of this philosophy with the civilization of its day in order to be able to distinguish what is essential in it from what is only transient and relative. At that time the level of learning and the character of its development were not the same as they are today, and the things that agitated and disturbed the human heart were not the same as those that agitate and disturb it today.

The ancient world found itself in irreconcilable conflict with Christianity, not only when Christianity was struggling with polytheism, but even when the state called itself Christian. The world and the Church were two opposite extremes that in essence were mutually exclusive, although outwardly they tolerated each other. Paganism was not destroyed with the coming of monotheism. It flourished in the structure of the state; in the laws; in the selfish, callous, coercive, and cunning Roman government, among officials insolently venal and openly deceitful; in the law courts, which were manifestly corrupt and capable of disguising flagrant injustice as formal legality; in the mores of the people, immersed in venality and luxury; in the Roman customs and entertainments—in a word, in the totality of the social relations of the Empire. Constantine the Great proclaimed the government to be Christian, but he did not manage to reform it in the Christian spirit. Although physical martyrdom ceased, moral martyrdom remained. The legal and public recognition of Christian truth was a great achievement, but the embodiment of this truth in the structure of the state required time. If Constantine's heirs had been pervaded by the same sincere respect for the Church, Byzantium might perhaps have become Christian. Instead, its rulers were for the most part heretics or apostates who oppressed the Church under the guise of protection, using it only as an instrument of their own power.

Meanwhile, the very composition of the Roman Empire was such that it was hardly possible for its governing authority to renounce its pagan character. Roman power was based on abstract statehood. There was no nation of which the central government could be the expression, and sympathetic relations with which could have established a better life for the state. The Roman government constituted an external and coercive link between many different nationalities who were alien to one another in language and mores and whose interests conflicted. The strength of the government rested upon the equilibrium of national animosities. This coercive knot held people together, but could not unite them. Any public and local spirit, which is the food and sustenance of public morality, was repugnant to the government. The nations had their native lands, but the concept of fatherland had disappeared and could not have been restored except through an inner unanimity of thought.

Only the Christian Church remained as the inner, living bond among the people. Only love for their heavenly fatherland united them. Only the unanimity of thought in faith led them to a living mutual sympathy. Only a unity of inner convictions firmly established in their minds could have led them in time to a better life on earth. That is why the longing for unanimity of thought and spirit in the Church constituted the full expression of their love of God, love of humanity, love of fatherland, and love of truth. The citizens of Rome and the sons and daughters of the Church had nothing in common. Only one possibility for social action remained open to Christians, and that consisted in complete and unconditional protest against the world. Byzantine Christians could preserve their inner convictions only by

sacrificing their public life, which they achieved by accepting martyrdom and by fleeing into the desert, by shutting themselves up in
monasteries. The desert and the monastery were, one could say, almost the sole arena for the Christian moral and intellectual development of humanity. For Christianity, rather than avoiding intellectual
development, incorporated it into itself.

As a result of this state of affairs, problems concerning contemporary civilization could not attain a social character; hence philosophy
had to limit itself to the development of the inner contemplative life.
Similarly, it could not embrace an interest in history, which rests upon
an interest in social matters. Moral issues affected philosophy only to
the extent to which they were related to the solitary, inner life. Philosophy was almost oblivious of external human life and the laws of development of family, civic, public, and state relations. Although the
general principles of these relations are found in philosophy's general
concepts of humanity, they did not lead to systematic conclusions.
Perhaps general moral concepts were the more purely and profoundly
revealed in the isolated intellectual life of the monasteries, the less interference there was by transitory, worldly influences in monastic life.
But their inner purity and depth did not display the fullness of external development that another epoch and another state of civilization
would have demanded of them.

The inner, contemplative life of those times, however, and the
problems of the socio-philosophic civilization of our day, reveal a
common element: human reason. The nature of reason, considered
from the eminence of a focused thought about God, and verified by
the highest development of inner, spiritual contemplation, appears in
a guise entirely different from that of a reason that limits itself to the
development of external everyday life. Of course, its general laws are
the same. But when reason attains to its highest level of development
it displays new aspects and new forces of its nature, which also shed
new light on its general laws.

The concept of reason that has been elaborated in recent philosophy, and whose expression is to be found in the system of Schelling
and Hegel, would not unconditionally contradict the concept of reason that we find in the speculative works of the Holy Fathers if only it
did not pass itself off as the highest instrument of cognition and if, as
a result of this pretension to the highest power of cognition, it did not

limit truth to that aspect of cognition that is accessible only to this abstractly rational manner of thinking.

All false deductions of rational thought result only from its pretension to the highest, complete knowledge of the truth. If rational thought recognized its limitations and saw itself as one of the instruments for the cognition of truth—not as the only one—it would also present its deductions as provisional and referent solely to its limited point of view. Rational thought would then anticipate other, supreme, and more truthful deductions from another, supreme, and more truthful way of thinking. Rational thought is accepted in this sense by thinking Christians who, by rejecting its ultimate results, can with greater benefit to their mental development examine its relative truth and accept as the lawful achievement of reason everything that is true and enlightening in the development of its speculations, however one-sided.

If, however, philosophical reason realized its limitations, it would, by developing even within these limitations, adopt another orientation capable of leading it to the supreme fullness of knowledge. But such an awareness of its limitations would mark a death sentence for its absolute authority. That is why it has always feared this realization, the more so as it has always been close to it. It constantly altered its forms in order to avoid it. No sooner would its inadequacy be understood than it would evade this misunderstanding by appearing in another guise, leaving its earlier form in the hands of its adversaries, like an empty skin it has shed.

Thus, in order to avoid charges of inadequacy, it passed from formal-logical proofs to empirical observations on the one hand, and to the inner consciousness of truth on the other, calling its earlier manner of thought *rationalistic*, and its new—*rational*. But having also discovered the inadequacy of the new form in the course of its development, philosophical reason referred to it too as *rationalistic* and proceeded to *pure reason*. When Jacobi excoriated the narrowness of the theory of pure reason, as expressed in the systems of Kant and Fichte, he learned to his surprise, at the end of his lengthy polemics extending over many years, that everything he had said about *reason* should be applied to the *rationalistic understanding*.[9] The theory of

---

9. Friedrich Heinrich Jacobi (1743–1819), German philosopher and writer, developed his philosophy of immediately conveyed truths, or "philosophy of feeling" (*Gefühlsphilosophie*) in response to the rationalism of Spinoza and Kant. — ED.

Kant and Fichte proved to be rationalistic. The development of reason was to begin with the system of Schelling and Hegel. In 1802, pointing to Schelling's system, Hegel wrote, "Only now could the philosophy of *reason* in the strict sense begin, for the cycle of rationalistic development came to an end with Fichte's system."

Thus, reason, as understood by the most recent philosophy, should not be confused with the logical understanding, which consists of the formal concatenation of concepts and is impelled by syllogistic deductions and proofs. According to the laws of intellectual necessity, reason in its latest aspect derives its knowledge not from abstract notions, but from the very root of self-consciousness, where being and thought are united in one absolute identity. Its thinking process consists not of logical development set in motion by abstract conclusions, but of dialectical development deriving from the very essence of the object. The object of thought, present to the mind's eye, transforms itself from one species to another, from one concept to another, constantly acquiring a more nearly complete meaning. And as the mind concentrates on the object of its thought, it discovers in it an inner contradiction destroying its former concept of it. This contradictory, negative concept confronting the mind also reveals its insolvency and discovers in itself the necessity for a positive foundation latent within it, which now appears as the union of the positive and negative categories into a single *complex* (the concrete).

This new concept, however, in turn scarcely appears to the mind as the final result of consciousness, when in its very pretension to ultimate independence it reveals its inadequacy and displays its negative side. This negative side once again brings out its positive, which is again subjected to the same transformational process until finally the whole cycle of the dialectical development of thought is completed, progressing from the initial principle of consciousness toward a general and pure abstraction of thought, which constitutes at the same time general essentiality. Then, by the same dialectical process, consciousness is given full content by the entire development of being and thought, which are understood as an identical phenomenon of realized rationality and self-conscious essentiality.

But, having pronounced its final word, philosophical reason at the same time furnished the mind with an opportunity to realize its limitations. The same dialectical process that had served reason in the construction of its philosophy was subjected to the same disintegrative assumptions, whereupon it showed itself to rational consciousness as solely the negative aspect of knowledge, comprising only potential truth, not actual truth, and standing in need of another form of thinking—which would be the positively known, not the hypothetically known, and which would be just as superior to logical self-development as a real event is superior to the merely potential.

This consciousness of the limitations and the unsatisfactory character of the latest expression of philosophical thought now constitutes the highest stage of the intellectual development of the West. This is not the opinion of dilettantes in philosophy, not the outcries of people attacking philosophy from some tangential motivation; it is not even the judgment of people like Krause and Baader.[10] They, with their penetrating philosophical thought, did much to help in the development of recent philosophy; but their protest against its absolute truthfulness was unable to change the direction of philosophical development, because they did not command enough authority over people's minds. They acted powerfully in another field, which lies unseen between science and life, but none of them founded a special school of philosophy.[11] The one-sidedness and unsatisfactory nature of rational thinking and most recent philosophy (as the fullest manifestation of rational thinking) were recognized and expressed with obvious and irrefutable clarity by the same great thinker [Schelling] who was the first

---

10. Karl Christian Friedrich Krause (1781–1832), German philosopher who advocated human unity, universal development, and panentheism (the "all-in-God" philosophy); the German philosopher and theologian Franz Xavier von Baader (1765–1841) detested Hume's empiricism and Kant's rationalism. He called for a return to the mystical tradition of Boehme, Eckhart, et al. He sought a theistic philosophy reconciling nature and spirit, science and religion, the individual and society. — ED.

11. Chalybäus cannot be included in the category of philosophers opposed to the latest orientation of philosophy. For although his principles are basically somewhat at variance with Hegel's view of the general laws of reason, these differences do not remove him from the sphere of rational, abstract thinking. Görres, who was one of the most celebrated followers of Schelling, and who went over from philosophy to faith, also could not exert any influence on the general development of the mind, because his transition was accomplished not as a result of the correct development of consciousness, but as a result of his personal peculiarity and of extraneous influences. [Heinrich Moritz Chalybäus (1796–1862), academic philosopher; Johann Joseph von Görres (1776–1848), supporter of the French Revolution who became an ultramontane advocate of the papacy. — ED.]

to create the latest philosophy and to elevate, according to Hegel's admission, rational thought from formal rationality to essential reason.

For the latest German philosophy can be attributed to Schelling as much as to Hegel. It was begun by Schelling and was confirmed in its new foundation and developed in many of its separate elements by him, and together with Hegel he can be credited with introducing it into the general consciousness of Germany. Hegel, who was long reckoned a pupil and follower of Schelling, is responsible for the more detailed development of recent philosophy that embraces all branches of science and represents the consummate roundedness of a methodically constructed system. Schelling was able to recognize clearly the limitations of this philosophy because it was his own thought.[12]

Schelling's authority and, even more, the obvious justice of his views with respect to the limitations of rational thinking, visibly shook Germany's absolute confidence in the conclusions of the latest philosophy and were one of the factors that accounted for the growing indifference to philosophy. Of course, there are still Hegelians, and they will continue to exist for a long time, for the whole character of contemporary civilization is in tune with their orientation. A new orientation is possible, however, when thought at the very peak of its development has acknowledged its inadequacy. The majority, which comprises the crowd, may for a long time continue to hold obsolete views, but the conviction of the crowd cannot restore to them the former spark of confidence. The celebrated Erdmann calls himself the "last Mohican" among Hegel's pupils. New celebrities in the field of philosophy are no longer to be seen, and they are hardly possible any longer.[13]

---

12. In his history of philosophy, Hegel indicates several differences between his system and Schelling's, but these differences belong to that period of Schelling's philosophy when his thought had already begun to take a different direction—which, incidentally, Hegel himself mentions. The only difference between Schelling's first system and Hegel's system is to be found in the method by which the basic thought is expounded. The inner contradiction of thought that Schelling presents in the combined manifestation of the two polarities and of their identity appears in Hegel in the consecutive movement of consciousness from one definition of thought to its antithesis. With respect to *intellectual contemplation*, of which Schelling spoke and which was not encompassed by Hegel's system, it may be said that it had no essential significance in Schelling's first system either. Schelling mentions it, but he does not develop it. This was only a harbinger of the future direction of his thought.

13. Johann Erdmann (1805–1892), prominent "right-wing" Hegelian. — ED.

But Schelling's last system could not yet have a real influence on people's minds, because it combines in itself two antithetical aspects, one of which is almost certainly true, while the other is almost certainly false. The first, the negative, shows the inadequacy of rational thought; the second, the positive, presents the structure of a new system. But these two aspects lack essential cohesion; they may be separated from each other, and perforce will be separated. Then the negative influence of Schelling's thought will be incomparably stronger. Once he was convinced of the limitation of autonomous thought, and of the necessity of Divine Revelation preserved in tradition, and simultaneously of the necessity of living faith as supreme reason and the essential element of cognition, Schelling did not convert to Christianity, but came to it naturally through the profound and correct development of his rational self-consciousness. For the possibility of human reason being conscious of its basic relationship to God is implanted in the very core of human reason, and in its very nature. Human thought may hover in abstract oblivion of its basic relationships only if it has broken away from this vital profundity or if it has failed to reach it. By virtue of his innate genius and the extraordinary development of his profound philosophical thought, Schelling is one of those beings who are born not once in centuries but once in millennia.

In his search for Divine Revelation, however, where could he find its pure expression corresponding to his rational need for faith? A Protestant from birth, Schelling was, nevertheless, sufficiently sincere and conscientious in his inner convictions that he could not fail to see the inadequacies of Protestantism, which rejected the tradition preserved in the Roman Church. He often expressed this view, with the result that for a long time there were rumors in Germany that he had gone over to the Roman Church. But he also saw clearly in the Roman Church the confusion of true and untrue tradition, of the Divine and the human.

A heavy lot belongs to those who languish in the grip of an inner thirst for divine truth and cannot find the pure religion capable of satisfying this all-pervasive need. They have only one alternative: to seek out and obtain by their own powers from the confused Christian tradition whatever corresponds to their inner notion of Christian truth. A lamentable task—to compose one's own faith!

Here Schelling was guided not by speculative considerations alone, whose inadequacy he so clearly realized. In addition to studying the Holy Scriptures, he sought support for his thought in all of humanity's actual consciousness of God, inasmuch as it preserved the tradition of the primordial Divine Revelation to humanity. In the mythology of ancient peoples can be found traces of a Revelation that, although distorted, had not been lost. The fundamental relationship of early humanity to God appeared in every nation in a peculiar, circumscribed form, as humanity became divided into different groups according to the branching out of the various nations. This peculiar form of God-consciousness determined the very character of a nation. But inside all these more or less distorting limitations there remained the unchanging, permanent features of the general essential nature of Revelation. The agreement between these general inner and basic principles of each mythology and the basic principles of Christian tradition expressed for Schelling the pure truth of Divine Revelation.

Such a historical view of human beliefs could be an extremely rich source from which Christian thought might draw if its preliminary stages rested on a firm foundation. But the vagueness of the preliminary conviction and of the inner meaning of mythology, subject to the more or less arbitrary interpretation of the investigator, were the reasons why Schelling's Christian philosophy was neither Christian nor philosophy. It differed from Christianity in its most fundamental dogmas, and from philosophy by the very manner of cognition.

Moreover, while asserting actual truth based not on abstract speculation but on thought imbued with faith, Schelling ignored that special form of the inner activity of reason that constitutes the essential attribute of believing thought. For the form of rational activity changes in accordance with the level to which reason ascends. Although reason is one and its nature is one, its forms of action are different, just as its deductions are different, depending on the level on which it finds itself and on the force that impels it and guides it. For this impelling and animating force derives not from thought confronting reason, but proceeds from the very inner condition of reason and moves toward thought, where this force finds its rest and through which it is communicated to other rational individuals.

This inner nature of reason usually escapes the attention of Western thinkers, who are accustomed to abstract, logical thinking where all knowledge depends on the formal development of the object of thought and where the whole meaning is absorbed by the expressible aspect of thought. They therefore ignore the inner power of the mind that, in the objects of a living knowledge that transcends the formal nature of logical concatenations, accomplishes the movement of thought and constantly accompanies it. This inner power is suspended, so to speak, above the expression of thought and communicates to it meaning incompatible with external definition and results independent of external form. Hence Schelling sought the expression of theological dogmas in the writings of the Holy Fathers without appreciating their speculative concepts of reason and the laws of higher cognition. Hence the positive side of his system, lacking the inner character of believing thought, found little sympathy in Germany and finds even less in Russia. Russia might be enticed by the logical systems of alien philosophies that are still new for her, but with respect to believing philosophy she is stricter than other European countries, having lofty examples of religious thought in the ancient Holy Fathers and in the great spiritual writings of all times, not excluding the present. On the other hand, the negative aspect of Schelling's system, embracing the inadequacy of rational thought, could scarcely be so impartially appraised in Germany, which is accustomed to its abstract and logical thought pattern, as it has been in Russia. There, after an initial youthful enthusiasm for an alien system, Russians can return more easily to essential reason, particularly when this essential reason is consonant with their historical uniqueness.

For this reason I believe that German philosophy, in combination with the development it has received in Schelling's final system, could serve us as the most convenient point of departure on our way from borrowed systems to an independent philosophy that will correspond to the basic principles of ancient Russian civilization and be capable of subordinating the divided civilization of the West to the integral consciousness of believing reason.

III

FRAGMENTS
Ivan Kireevsky

EDITOR'S INTRODUCTION

Kireevsky's "Fragments" were first published a year after his death by Aleksei Khomiakov (*Russkaia Beseda* n. 5 1857). Elsewhere, Khomiakov wrote that "they were to comprise part of an article, which in its turn was to serve as the continuation of the already published article 'On the Possibility and Necessity of New Principles in Philosophy.'"[1] Beyond this, little is known about the circumstances of their composition or the state in which Khomiakov found them, so it is difficult to judge the extent to which they can be considered a finished work.

The "Fragments" are Kireevsky's most definitely religious work, pointing the way to a new kind of religious thought that was to crown his critique of European culture and philosophy. Kireevsky's positive ideal is clearly based on his personal experience of Orthodox monasticism, on the moral wisdom that is attained through the inner transformation of the whole human being through spiritual labors. The "Fragments" allow one only to guess how Kireevsky would conceptualize this process of growth into integral being. The preeminent organ of knowledge is the heart, and the superior method of knowledge is faith.

Most important, perhaps, is the way that Kireevsky appears to incorporate the idea of sobornost. Although Kireevsky still stresses the underlying unity of knowledge, his formulations now seem to indicate that he conceives of this unity only *in* and *through* the Church, understood as the Body of Christ. Tradition is vital not only because it is a component of wholeness, but also because it provides a living connection with God Incarnate. Wholeness cannot be *composed* of its various elements; it must be *revealed* in the life of the Church. Kireevsky's "Fragments" have been translated by Robert Bird from the first volume of the 1911 edition of his *Works*.

---

1. A. S. Khomiakov, *Polnoe sobranie sochinenii* (Moscow, 1900): III 269.

Fragments

Old Russian, Orthodox Christian civilization, which lay at the foundation of all social and private life in Russia, was the basis of the specifically Russian mindset that strove toward an inner wholeness of thinking and created the special character of native Russian mores, instilled with a constant memory of the relation of all temporal things to the eternal and of all human things to the Divine. This civilization, traces of which are still preserved among the people, was arrested in its development before it could bring forth lasting fruit in life or even manifest its blossoming in reason. On the surface of Russian life there reigns a borrowed civilization, which grew up from a different root. The contradiction of the main, conflicting principles of the two civilizations is the primary, if not the only reason for all evils and insufficiencies that can be noticed in the Russian land. Both civilizations might be reconciled in a kind of thinking whose foundation would contain the very root of old Russian civilization, and whose development would consist of the recognition of all Western civilization and the subordination of its conclusions to the prevailing spirit of Orthodox Christian philosophy. Such a reconciling thinking would be the beginning of new intellectual life in Russia, and—who knows?—perhaps would find echoes in the West among sincere thinkers who seek truth without prejudice.

Whose fault was it that old Russian culture was unable to develop and dominate over the culture of the West? Was it the fault of external historical circumstances, or the fault of the internal weakening of the Russian's spiritual life? We are not concerned here with a solution to this problem. We shall only observe that the character of a culture that strives toward inner, spiritual wholeness differs from a logical culture, a sensual-empirical culture, or in general one based on the development of the disintegrated powers of reason by the fact that the latter has no essential relation to moral mood. Therefore, a culture based on disintegrated reason is neither elevated nor lowered by the inner height or lowness of people. On the contrary, having once been attained, such culture remains the eternal property of human beings, regardless of the mood of their spirit. Spiritual culture, on the other hand, is living knowledge: it is attained in proportion to human inner striving for moral elevation and wholeness, and it disappears together with this striving, leaving in the mind only its external form. One can extinguish it within oneself by not sustaining constantly the flame from which it was ignited.

Consequently, it seems impossible not to suppose that, although strong exterior causes apparently prevented the development of a distinctive Russian civilization, the Russian was not free from guilt for its decline. The striving for external formality that we observe in Russian schismatics gives one occasion to think that a certain weakening occurred in the original tendency of Russian civilization long before the Petrine revolution. When we remember that at the end of the fifteenth and the beginning of the sixteenth centuries there were strong parties among the representatives of the Russian civilization of that time that had begun to confuse what was Christian with what was Byzantine, and that they wanted to determine the social life of Russia, which was then still searching for balance in imitation of Byzantium, we realize that the decline of Russian civilization began at this very time and, perhaps, in this very striving. For it is the case that, as soon as Byzantine laws began to interfere in the matter of Russian social life, and models began to be taken for Russia's future from the past order of the Eastern Roman Empire, the fate of native Russian civilization was decided in this very intellectual movement. By submitting the development of society to a foreign form, Russians deprived themselves of the possibility of vital and regular growth within their indigenous culture, and although they preserved the holy truth pure and undistorted, they constrained free mental development within it. Thus, at first Russians exposed themselves to ignorance and then, as a consequence of ignorance, submitted themselves to the insurmountable influence of foreign civilization.

Although foreign culture belongs almost exclusively to the upper, so-called *educated* class of the Russian people, and whereas the primordial culture of Russia is preserved in its arrested development in the mores, customs, and inner mindset of the so-called common people, the conflict of these two types of culture is accompanied by equally harmful consequences for both classes. Neither here nor there is there anything whole or homogeneous. In Russia, foreign civilization cannot provide even the fruits that it brings to other countries, because it does not find a root in the Russian earth; nor can the native civilization preserve its significance, because all of external life is filled with another meaning. This conflict is even more harmful morally than intellectually, and the majority of the Russian's bad habits, which are attributed to various incidental reasons, occur only due to this main discord in Russian life.

The very way external foreign civilization spreads among the Russian people determines the character of its moral influence. For this spread is accomplished, as I already mentioned, not on the strength of inner conviction, but on the strength of external temptation or external necessity. Russian people see something holy in the customs and mores of their ancestors; in the customs and mores of the adventitious civilization they see only something tempting or advantageous, or simply violently irrational. Therefore they usually submit to civilization in spite of their conscience, as an evil that they could not find the strength to withstand. In accepting foreign mores or customs, they do not change their ways of thinking, but instead betray them. First they are carried away or submit, and only then do they form a mindset according to their own way of life. In order to become civilized, therefore, they must first become more or less apostates in relation to their own inner convictions. Even without first-hand experience it is easy to guess the consequences of such a principle of civilization for the moral character of the people. True, until now, thank God, the Russian people has not lost its pure faith and many valuable qualities that are born of this faith; but, unfortunately, one cannot deny that it has already lost one of the obligatory bases of social morality: respect for the sanctity of truth.

Here we have touched upon a topic that none of those who have any love for their fatherland can speak of with equanimity. For if there is any evil in Russia, if there is any disorder in her social relations, if there are any reasons at all for Russians to suffer, all such evils are rooted primarily in disrespect for the sanctity of truth.

Yes, lying is, unfortunately, easy for Russians. They consider lying a sin that is generally accepted, inevitable, and almost not shameful—some external sin that arises from the necessity of external relations, which they view as a kind of irrational force. They thus readily give their lives without hesitation for their convictions and suffer all deprivation in order not to dirty their conscience, while at the same time lying to gain a penny or for a glass of wine; they lie for fear, for advantage, and without advantage. This is the surprising way that their conceptions have been formed over the last century and a half. They do not value their spoken word at all. Their word is not they themselves, but their object, which they own by the right of Roman property—that is, they can use it and abuse it and answer to no one. Russians do not even value their oath. Peddlers of buns on the square of every city who go to every market ten times a day swear they did not see a fight that took place before their very eyes. Every time land is sold and every time it is taken possession of, all the surrounding neighbors gather to swear without knowing about what and not even showing any interest in learning about what. And this absence of truth in a people whom ancient travelers praised for a love of truth, who so valued their oath that, even when in the right, they were prepared to drop a lawsuit rather than give an oath.

At the same time, deprived of truthfulness in speech, how can people hope to see the establishment of truth in their social relationships? Until they cultivate within themselves an absolute respect for the truthfulness of speech, what external supervision can protect such a society from abuses that can be seen, appraised, and corrected only by that society itself?

But, thank God, this absence of truth has not yet penetrated to the very depth of the Russian's soul; there are still areas of life where the sanctity of truth and faithfulness to one's word have remained holy for Russians. This part of the Russian's heart, which is still free from infection, affirms the possibility of Russia's future rebirth. There are revealed to thought many paths by which the Russian might be reborn into the previous harmoniousness of life. All of them probably lead to the desired goal, for the achievement of this goal is still possible while the strength of the Russian spirit is not yet spent, while faith is not yet extinguished, and while the seal of the previous wholeness of being still lies on the dominant condition of the Russian's spirit.

One thing, however, is certain and beyond doubt: the harm that foreign civilization creates in the intellectual and moral development of the Russian people cannot be eliminated by a forced removal of this civilization or of its source—European learning. In the first place, such a removal is impossible. No quarantines can stop thought, and they can bestow it only with strength and the attraction of a secret.

Second, even if it were possible to stop the entry of new ideas, it would nevertheless be harmful for Russian civilization, since in Russia so many conceptions are circulating that have come from the West that new ones could only weaken the harm of the earlier ones—decomposing them and clarifying them, reducing them to their abstract foundation, with which they must stand or fall. For today the entire development of the European mind, as it achieves self-consciousness, is being reduced to its final principle, which acknowledges its own inadequacy.

At the same time, earlier concepts of the West could be more harmful in Russia for having lost the opposition inherent in their own development, remaining unfinished and unacknowledged, but requiring only application and incarnation. If Russia had not discovered Schelling and Hegel, how would Voltaire's and the Encyclopedists' reign over Russian culture have been destroyed? In the end, however, even if it were possible to completely expel Western civilization from Russia, short-term ignorance would expose it again to the very strong influence of foreign culture. Russia would return to the epoch of Petrine reform, when all that is Western was introduced and considered good for Russia simply because it was not Russian, for it brought civilization. And what would come of this? All the fruits of Russia's apprenticeship of one and a half centuries would be destroyed in order for her to begin again the very same course of study.

One of the most direct paths toward eliminating the harm caused by foreign civilization—which stands in contradiction to the spirit of Christian culture—would be to subordinate the entire meaning of Western civilization to the dominance of Orthodox Christian conviction by developing laws of indigenous thinking. We have seen that the Orthodox Church understands Christian philosophy differently than does the Roman Church or Protestant confessions. The quandaries that Christian thinking encountered in the West cannot be attributed to Orthodox thinking. No special genius is needed to develop such indigenous, Orthodox thinking. On the contrary, genius, which necessarily presupposes originality, could even harm the fullness of truth. The development of this thinking should be the common task of all believing and thinking people—all those acquainted with the writings of the Holy Fathers and with Western culture. The potential for this is ready: on the one hand, there is Western thinking, which on the strength of its own development has reached a consciousness of its unsoundness and requires a new principle not yet known to it. On the other hand, there is the profound, loving, and pure philosophy of the Holy Fathers, which represents the embryo of this superior philosophical principle. Its simple development, in accordance with the modern state of learning and in concert with the requirements and issues of modern reason, would itself comprise, without any clever discoveries, that new science of thinking that would destroy the unhealthy contradiction between mind and faith, between inner convictions and external life.

But the philosophy of the Holy Fathers is merely the embryo of this future philosophy, which is needed by the whole of contemporary Russian civilization. It is a living, clear embryo, but one that has yet to be developed and does not yet comprise the very science of philosophy. For philosophy is not the main conviction, but a mental development of the relationship between this main conviction and modern civilization. Only out of such a development can philosophy attain the strength to communicate its direction to all other sciences, being their first foundation and their final result. To think that we already have a philosophy ready, contained in the Holy Fathers, would be extremely erroneous. Our philosophy must yet be created, and created, as I said, not by a single individual; it should grow in common view through the sympathetic cooperation of a unanimity in thought.

Perhaps it is for this very reason that benevolent Providence allowed the Russian people to pass through ignorance to submission to foreign civilization, so that in the struggle with foreign forces Orthodox culture could master, in the end, the entire intellectual development of the contemporary world (which it inherited from humanity's entire previous intellectual life), and so that, enriched with worldly wisdom, Christian truth could that much more fully and triumphantly display its dominance over the relative truths of human reason. For, despite the apparent predominance of foreign civilization, despite the harm it has caused to the people's moral character—having shaken the sense of justice in one class and the sense of both justice and divine truth in another—despite all the evil caused by it, Russia still has indubitable pledges of rebirth into her previous Orthodox wholeness. Those pledges are the living faith of the people in the Holy Orthodox Church, their memory of their previous history, and the clearly surviving traces of the previous inner wholeness of their existence, which have been preserved in the customary and natural mood of their spirit—in this still-sounding echo of their previous life, nurtured within a homogeneous social composition that was permeated with the Orthodox teaching of the Church.

Thus, analyzing with care and objectivity the relation of Western philosophy to Russian culture, one can say without self-delusion, that the time for a full and general revolution in Russian thought seems to be near. Consider how the insufficiency of Western philosophy requires a new principle, which Russian thought fails to find in the entire body of Western culture; how this higher principle of knowledge is preserved within the Orthodox Church; how vivifying the development of thought in accordance with this higher principle could be for reason and science; how the very wealth of modern external knowledge could serve as a stimulus for this development and as its support in human reason; how unconstraining it would be for all that is true in the natural achievements of human reason—how vivifying for all that requires life; how satisfactorily it could answer all the questions of mind and heart that demand but do not find solution. When we consider all of this, we have no doubt that it will develop soon; but we are surprised that this new self-consciousness of the mind, so urgently required by the entire sum of our intellectual and moral culture, has not yet developed.

The possibility of this kind of knowledge is so close to the mind of any educated, believing person that it seems that a single accidental spark of thought would be enough to ignite the flame of an inextinguishable striving toward this new and vivifying thinking, which is to bring faith and reason into harmony, fill the emptiness that divides the two worlds requiring union, affirm spiritual truth in the human mind by its clear dominion over natural truth, and elevate natural truth by correcting its correlation to spiritual truth, tying together at last both truths into one living thought. For truth is one, as the human mind is one, created to strive toward the One God.

* * *

Believing philosophy will accept the guidance of the Holy Fathers as the first grounds for its self-comprehension, all the more as this guidance cannot be surmised by abstract thinking. For the truths expressed by the Holy Fathers were achieved by them from immediate, inner experience and are communicated to us not as a logical conclusion, which is also possible for our own reason, but rather as the testimony of eyewitnesses concerning a country they have been to.

If believing philosophy fails to find in the writings of the Holy Fathers ready answers to all questions of the mind, then, basing itself on the truths expressed by them and on its own supreme conviction, it will search in the sum of these two indications for a direct path to the comprehension of other objects of knowledge. And in any case the method of thinking in the believer's mind will be distinguished from reason that searches for conviction or relies on abstract conviction. Apart from the firmness of fundamental truth, this unique feature will be comprised of the data that reason receives from the holy thinkers, who were educated by superior vision, and of the striving toward inner wholeness that does not allow the mind to take dead truth for living truth, and finally of that extreme conscientiousness with which sincere faith distinguishes eternal and divine truth from the truth that may be [achieved] by the opinion of a person, a nation, or an epoch.

* * *

The task: To work out a social self-consciousness.

True convictions are beneficent and strong only in their sum.

Beneficent forces do not grow in solitude. The rye will be strangled among weeds.

* * *

The unity of the knowledge of God has disintegrated into various attractions to particular benefits and into conflicting features of particular truths.

* * *

A word should be not a box in which an idea is enclosed, but a conductor that communicates it to others; not a cellar where the treasures of mind and knowledge are collected, but a door through which they are carried out. And the strange law of these treasures: the more that are carried outside, the more remain in store. The giving hand is never impoverished. [Prov. 28:27]

* * *

A word, as the transparent body of spirit, should correspond to all its movements. Therefore it should ceaselessly change its color in accordance with the ceaselessly changing linkage and resolution of thoughts. In its iridescent sense every breath of mind should palpitate and be answered. It should breathe with the freedom of inner life. Therefore a word that is ossified in scholastic formulas cannot express the spirit, as a corpse does not express life. However, even if it changes in its connotations, a word should not be altered in its inner composition.

* * *

The essential is generally inaccessible for abstract thinking alone. Only essentiality can touch the essential. Abstract thinking deals only with the limits and relations of concepts. The laws of reason and matter, which comprise the content of abstract thinking, by themselves do not have essentiality, but are only a sum of relations. For only a reasoning and free personality is what is essential in the world. It alone has a distinctive significance. Everything else has only a relative significance. But for rationalistic thinking the living personality dissolves into abstract laws of self-development, or it is a product of incidental principles, and in both cases it loses its actual meaning.

* * *

Therefore abstract thinking, touching on objects of faith, from the outside may be very similar to the teaching of faith; but in essence it has a completely distinct significance for the very reason that it lacks the meaning of essentiality, which arises from the inner development of the sense of an integral personality.

In a great number of systems of rationalistic philosophy we see that dogmas concerning the unity of the Godhead, His omnipotence, His divine wisdom, His spirituality and omnipresence, even His trinitarian nature—are possible and accessible to a non-believing mind. The non-believing mind may even allow and explain all the miracles accepted by faith, reducing them to some special formula. But none of this has religious significance, simply because rationalistic thinking is incapable of a consciousness of the living personality of the Godhead and this personality's living relationship with the human personality.

* * *

Consciousness of the relationship between the living Divine personality and the human personality serves as a foundation for faith—or, more correctly, faith *is* that very consciousness, more or less clear and unmediated. Faith does not comprise purely human knowledge, does not comprise a special concept in the mind or heart, does not fit into any one epistemological capability, does not apply to logical reason, or heartfelt feeling, or the call of conscience. Rather, faith embraces the entire wholeness of the human being and appears only in minutes of this wholeness and in proportion to its fullness. Therefore, believing thought is best characterized by its attempt to gather all the separate parts of the soul into one force, to search out that inner heart of being where reason and will, feeling and conscience, the beautiful and the true, the wonderful and the desired, the just and the merciful, and all the capacity of mind converge into one living unity, and in this way the essential human personality is restored in its primordial indivisibility.

It is not the form of the thought that presents itself to the mind that produces in it this concentration of forces; but mental wholeness gives rise to the meaning that grants the real comprehension of a thought.

* * *

This striving for intellectual wholeness as a necessary condition for comprehending higher truth was always an inalienable property of Christian philosophy. From the times of the Apostles until our own, it has comprised its exclusive feature. But ever since the Western Church fell away it has remained primarily in the Orthodox Church. Although other Christian confessions do not reject its legitimacy, they do not consider it a necessary condition for the comprehension of divine truth. According to the opinion of Roman theologians and philosophers, it seems it was enough that the authority of divine truths be recognized once in order that the further comprehension and development of these truths be completed by abstract and logical thinking.

Perhaps it was due to a special partiality for Aristotle that their theological writings bear the character of logical exposition. The very path of thinking was completed by an external linkage of concepts. They sought to make logical justification into a dogma of faith. This logical exposition also presented moral demands based on the abstract, rationalistic comprehension of dogmas, just like an abstract conclusion. A strange birth of the living from the dead! A formidable demand of strength in the name of a thought that itself is powerless!

* * *

Separated from other cognitive capacities, logical thinking comprises the natural character of a mind that has fallen away from its wholeness. The entire order of things that occurs as a result of this divided state of human beings itself leads their thinking to this logical separation. Faith is superior to natural reason precisely because the latter has sunk deeper than its original natural level. It is for this reason also that it is not necessary for it to rise to the original unity in order to be penetrated by faith.

* * *

Theological studies are neither possible nor necessary for everyone; the study of philosophy is not accessible to everyone. Constant and special exercise in that inner attention that cleanses and gathers the mind toward its higher unity is also not possible for everyone. It is possible and necessary, however, for everyone to bind the direction of their life with their fundamental conviction of faith, to harmonize with it their main occupation and every particular matter, in order that every action might be an expression of the one striving, that every thought might seek a single foundation, every step lead to a single goal. Without this, human life will not have any meaning, the mind will be a counting machine, the heart a collection of soulless strings through which whistles an inadvertent wind; no action will have a moral character, and there will be no human beings, properly speaking. For human beings are their faith.

* * *

There is no consciousness so undeveloped that it would lack the strength to be penetrated by the main conviction of Christian faith. For there is no mind so dull that it could fail to understand its own insignificance and the need for higher revelation; there is no heart so limited that it could not understand the possibility of a different love, higher than the love earthly objects arouse in it; there is no conscience that could not feel the invisible existence of a higher moral order; there is no will so undeveloped that it could not bring itself to a full self-sacrifice for the supreme love of its heart. From such forces, faith is composed. Faith is a living need for redemption and an unconditional gratitude for redemption. This is its entire essence. From here all the subsequent development of a believing mind and life receives its light and meaning.

* * *

Each Christian is in spiritual communion with the fullness of the entire Church.

All Christians know that, throughout the world, the same battle is being fought that is being fought within their own inner consciousness—the battle between light and darkness, between the striving for the higher harmony and wholeness of being and the languishing in natural discord and disunity; between the freedom of human will, which creates the spiritual personality, and servitude to external attractions, which turns a person into a weapon of other forces; between magnanimous self-sacrifice and fearful selfishness—in other words, between the task of redemption and freedom, on the one hand, and the violent power of the natural, discordant order of things, on the other.

No matter how little this consciousness is developed, Christians know that in the inner disorder of the soul they act not alone and for themselves only; they know that they perform the common task of the entire Church and of the entire human race, for which the redemption was completed and of which they are only a part. Only together with the entire Church and in living communion with her can Christians be saved.

* * *

Each moral victory hidden within a single Christian soul is a spiritual victory for the entire Christian world. Each spiritual force created within a single person invisibly attracts the forces of the moral world to itself and emboldens them. For, as in the physical world, celestial bodies gravitate toward each other without any material mediation, so in the spiritual world each spiritual personality, even without visible action, simply because it abides on a moral height, lifts and attracts to itself all that is similar in human hearts. But in the physical world, each being lives and is supported only by the destruction of others; in the spiritual world the creation of each personality creates all, and each breathes the life of all.

* * *

At all times there have been and are people penetrated by the higher light and force of faith. From them, as light beams from stars, the true teaching of faith spreads over the entire Christian world. In the history of the Church one can often see the visible paths of this light. One sees it penetrating from places illuminated by the higher teaching into countries where it has been eclipsed by human will; one sees how this light was extinguished in places that were the most illuminated by it; and one sees how it is again lit, having been brought from other countries that earlier lay in darkness. For the grace of truth never diminishes in the kingdom of God.

The history of Mt. Athos.

* * *

The spiritual Hierarchy. Jacob's Ladder. Living truths—not those that comprise the dead capital of the human mind, not those that lie on the surface of the mind and may be attained only by external teaching, but those that light the soul, can burn and go out, give life to life, are preserved in a mystery of the heart and, by their nature, cannot be clear and common to all. Expressed in words, these living truths remain unnoticed; expressed in deeds, they remain incomprehensible to those who have not experienced their immediate touch. For this very reason, the writings of the Holy Fathers are especially valuable for all Christians. The Holy Fathers speak of a country they have been to.

* * *

The relation of faith to reason—or which degree of knowledge does faith comprise?

Various relationships between inner self-consciousness and knowledge of God.

* * *

The consciousness of the all-penetrating connectedness and unity of the universe precedes the conception of the single cause of being and arouses a rational consciousness of the unity of the Creator.

The immeasurability, harmony, and divine wisdom of the cosmos bring reason to a consciousness of the omnipotence and divine wisdom of the Creator.

But the unity, omnipotence, divine wisdom, and all other concepts of the Divine nature of the first cause, which reason can only surmise from contemplation of the external cosmos, do not yet impart to the latter the consciousness of that living and personal self-essence of the Creator that lends essentiality to our intellectual relations to Him, transferring the very inner movement of our thoughts and feelings toward Him from the sphere of speculative abstraction into the sphere of living, responsible activity.

* * *

This consciousness, which completely changes the character of our idea of God, and which we cannot surmise directly from the mere contemplation of the external cosmos, arises in our soul only when to the contemplation of the external world is joined independent and unwavering contemplation of the inner and moral world, which reveals to the mind's eye an aspect of superior vitality in the most superior conceptions of reason.

* * *

Faith is not trust of another's assurance, but an actual event of inner life, through which people enter into essential communion with divine things (with the higher world, with heaven, with the Godhead).

* * *

The primary cause of human delusion is in not knowing what we love and what we want.

* * *

The need for happiness, love, harmony, truth, sympathy, emotion, activity, oblivion, and self-comprehension—all these legitimate and essential needs of the human heart arise from a single root of life, to which few succeed in raising their self-consciousness.

Justice and righteousness are rarer than love, for they are more difficult, require more sacrifice, and give less pleasure.

* * *

We readily double our sacrifices to lessen our obligations. How often we meet magnanimous and, at the same time, unjust people— beneficent and ungrateful, generous and miserly, squandering money on what should not be bought and miserly with regard to what they are obliged to give; dedicated by caprice, hard with those who deserve their dedication, hateful, perhaps, within the circle that Providence placed them, but worthy of love and wonder as soon as they leave it; they seek occasions for philanthropy and flee whole series of obligations, imagining that they can pay for a violation of the most essential, most immediate obligations with arbitrary and often useless sacrifice. Not labors, nor sacrifices, nor dangers, but the correctness of order is unpleasant to such people. It is easier for them to be sublime than honest. But I cannot say that it is easier for them to be merciful than just, for the mercy of the unjust is not mercy.

* * *

All is connected in good and evil. The good is one, just as the truth is one. Justice is to mercy as the trunk of a tree to its crown.

* * *

Thinking that is separated from the heart's strivings is the same sort of entertainment for the soul as unconscious merriment. The more profound such thinking is, the more important it seems, the more flighty it essentially makes us. Therefore, serious and strenuous study of the sciences can also be considered a kind of entertainment and mental distraction for leaving one's self. Such false seriousness and false utility chases away the true. Social pleasure does not act so successfully nor so quickly.

* * *

The feeling of the restoration (healing) of our inner unity and harmony.

* * *

To believe is to receive from the heart the same evidence that God Himself gave His Son.

* * *

Faith is the gaze of the heart toward God.

* * *

Justice, morality, the spirit of the people, human dignity, and the sanctity of lawfulness can all be felt only along with an awareness of the eternal religious relations of humanity.

* * *

The world of free will has its truth in the world of eternal morality.

IV

ON THE "FRAGMENTS" DISCOVERED AMONG I. V. KIREEVSKY'S PAPERS

Aleksei Khomiakov

EDITOR'S INTRODUCTION

Khomiakov added this long postscript to his publication of Kireevsky's "Fragments" in the fifth issue of *Russian Colloquium* (*Russkaia Beseda*) for 1857. It is Khomiakov's first systematic exposition of his philosophical views, which would evolve in a significant, yet consistent fashion over the following years until his own death in 1860. Since Khomiakov's other essays on philosophy are available in English, this essay has been deemed a sufficient sample of Khomiakov's thoughts on the subject.[1]

Khomiakov's philosophy consists of two parts: incisive criticism of German Idealism and an attempt to bridge the gap between subject and object that was bequeathed to the nineteenth century by Kant. Khomiakov always considered Hegel to be the main point of departure for Russian philosophy, unlike Kireevsky, who believed that Schelling had overcome Hegelian one-sidedness. Already in 1849 Khomiakov believed he had found Hegel's Achilles' heel in that the concept of negation that lies at the basis of Hegelian dialectic introduces an inadmissible relation into Hegel's deduction of the absolute. Khomiakov took this blunder to prove that it is impossible to account for relative concepts without first positing a substratum of being independent of thought; the Left-Hegelians, whom

---

1. For abridged translations of the later essays, both written as letters to Yury Samarin, readers are referred to *Russian Philosophy. Volume I: The Beginnings of Russian Philosophy*; *The Slavophiles*; *The Westernizers*, ed. James M. Edie, James P. Scanlan, and Mary-Barbara Zeldin, with the collaboration of George L. Kline (Chicago: Quadrangle Books, 1965), pp. 221–269.

Khomiakov derides, as much as admit this by positing the primacy of matter.

On the positive side, Khomiakov returns more or less to the Kantian scheme of transcendental subject and unknowable object. He shows the insufficiency of a strictly cognitive resolution of this dilemma, such as Schelling had presented in his philosophy of identity. The one-sidedness of rationalistic knowledge can be overcome only by its integration with the intellectual principle of life, the will, which effects a communication of an object's essence through its energies. The resulting picture of a force field of homogeneous energies is both a reinterpretation of Kireevsky's philosophy of integral being and a philosophical basis for sobornost.

Khomiakov's essay has been translated from the 1900 edition of his works (vol. 1) by Robert Bird.

On the "Fragments" Discovered among I. V. Kireevsky's Papers

It would be useless to embark here upon a detailed analysis of the fragments printed above. It is probable that few readers have read them without profound sympathy, even if they do not share the mind-set that is expressed in them. But I find it not without use to add to these fragments several words concerning the particular topic that was to be addressed by the unfinished article.

It is difficult to follow the philosophical thread that was to tie together the individual ideas, which were drafted in the form of individual notations or meditations. But all of these latter express the same thing—the need for spiritual wholeness in order to achieve full understanding, and a recognition of the relation of faith to reason, which is not alien to faith but an inferior element, or rather an element that finds its full existence only in faith. This last feature belongs only to a strictly consistent teaching, such as is possible only in the Church, for which Ivan Kireevsky was an eloquent spokesman. I shall attempt, as far as I am able, to clarify this teaching itself and its relationship with other, long-known and recognized, schools of thought.

The profound respect with which Kireevsky spoke of former great figures of science, and the reasonableness of his view of them, both prove how highly he valued their labors and how profoundly he had studied them. In truth, there are two dangers that await those who decide to lead human thought by a new path without gaining full acquaintance with the old paths it has already passed; either they will search out what has long since been explained, or they will labor over a system that has already been tested and found to be untenable. Only a clear knowledge of previous philosophical schools grants the right to proclaim them erroneous or unfinished and to try to create a new, more complete and harmonious teaching. The labor of past generations is not to be rejected, but to be absorbed and re-formed into the new labor of the contemporary generation and into the future labor of generations to follow.

Aristotle, the rightful master of the ancient philosophical world and the idol of the medieval philosophical world, was deposed by a revolt of great and free thinkers; but only the idol was deposed, not the king of ancient philosophy, whose name the idol bore; Aristotelian criticism and method triumphed when pseudo-Aristotelianism fell. The merits of the Stagirite did not die and could not die, for they contained elements of immortality.[2] Upon the ruins of his fallen authority there arose a multitude of teachings under the banners of empiricism, sensualism, idealism, or mysticism. There appeared many names worthy of the grateful memory of thinking humanity (such as Descartes or the incomparably versatile genius of Leibniz). But whether due to insufficient capacity, depth, or logical rigor, all these doctrines, all these schools found a real, if unconscious, temporary resolution in Hume's witty skepticism, which was, however, petty and arid. Kireevsky already explained why the human mind wandered for so long over false paths and why these paths were chosen: he showed the dependence of philosophical thought on religious belief, and the influence of Latinism and Protestantism on the entire intellectual development of Western Europe.

Hume's skepticism (and especially his attack on the generally accepted connection between cause and effect) provoked Kant. This radiant and rigorously logical mind delivered the fatal blow to Pyrrhonism [skepticism]. "The laws of reason are not subject to doubt for they are precisely reason itself, the very *I* of the human being; and human beings cannot doubt their *I*, for the simple reason that they cannot experience such doubt. There is no region to which they might transfer themselves in order to affirm their doubt, and there is no instrument or process by which they might experience such doubt. The word *Pyrrhonist* is an [empty] sound, not a meaning." Thus might one express the rigorous and simple position that Kant derived in formulas, which are as unattractive in their expression as they are insuperable in their consistency. They express his profoundly reasoning nature. Kant's position became the cornerstone of all modern philosophy and, I dare to add, all future philosophy.

I do not recall who made the very witty and quite profound comment that ancient philosophy said: "I feel, therefore I am" (*sentio, ergo sum*); modern philosophy, freed from scholastic Aristotelianism, said: "I think, therefore I am" (*cogito, ergo sum*); and Kantian philosophy

---

2. *Stagirite* refers to Aristotle, who was born in Stagira in Macedonia. — TRANS.

says: "I am, therefore I am" (*sum, ergo sum*). There is a lot of truth to this. The fullness of being human was tied to people's doubtless confidence in themselves. Rationalistic forms of thought, however, were present at the birth of the great new German school; they were expressed in the peculiarities of its founder, and they were bound to develop further due to one-sided religious beliefs. Thus it occurred. Kant himself, without comprehending the full import of the conclusion he achieved, was preeminently a rationalist in his subsequent theories, and he founded his entire system (to the extent that it remained true to itself) on logical thinking only. Reading him, you feel that he could hardly have ended up on a different path. In the very first steps of his teaching there is a hidden "therefore," which ties the immediate being of people to a being newly acquired through the labor of thought. Logical formulas, when admitted to this higher region of self-consciousness, were bound to develop into rationalism.

Fiery Fichte followed the same path but in an even more decisive manner, recognizing *that which is* for human beings only in their personal understanding within the dichotomy of the *thinking I* and the *thought I*, *I* and *not-I* (or subject and object). The same path was followed by the greatest genius of all the representatives of this movement, the sort of genius that is born but once in millennia, according to the late Ivan Kireevsky: Schelling. He supplemented Fichte's teaching by reconciling the conflict between the thinking and the thought (or the negation *I—not-I, subject—object*) with the very act of consciousness (subject-objectivization); with this thesis he completed the magnificent development of the self-sufficient spirit in its logical definition.[3]

This path was rational, purely rationalistic, but rationalism here struck its limit. Even if Schelling really found initial, unmanifested being identical to non-being, he did not draw from this thesis a scientific formula such as might have served as the logical beginning of further development. In fact, this visibly abstract being possessed for him all

---

3. I think that it would be more correct to call this moment not subject-objectivization (*Subject-objectivirung*), but object-subjectivization (*Object-subjectivirung*), for in the law of consciousness the thinking principle (το πρῶτον), when it receives the return reflection of the object, really turns into the subject through self-recognition.

the character and rights of *that which is*, for it crossed over into object and into the entire world of phenomena and consciousnesses by some inner, unconscious, arbitrary force. Did Schelling have enough perspicacity to realize that it was impossible to go any further in this direction? Or was his strength insufficient even to try to continue it? Or, finally, did his rich soul sense, even in a vague way, the poverty of rationalism; in any case Schelling halted. His further activity, still brilliant in the variety, profundity, and wit of individual thoughts and considerations, still useful in its scientific resistance to resurgent Hegelianism, belongs neither to the history of the school nor to the history of pure philosophy. A series of brilliant errors, mingled with high truths that remained unconnected by any rational thread, glimmers of poetic surmises lost in the fog of arbitrary gnosticism: this is Schelling's final epoch, about which Kireevsky spoke in his final article with such warm love and such doleful sympathy.

Schelling's great disciple Hegel attempted to complete what had stalled his teacher's genius. *That which is* had to be completely discarded. Concept itself, in its fullest abstractness, was to resurrect everything from its own depths. Rationalism, or the logical understanding, was to find its final crown and divine blessing in the new creation of the entire world. This was the enormous task that the German mind set itself in Hegel, and one can only admire the boldness with which he undertook its resolution. He first takes the simplest knowledge from the realm of everyday life and submits it to the judgment of the logical understanding or, more precisely, of rationalistic dialectic. From one definition, which always turns out to be incomplete and unsatisfactory, he ascends to another and higher definition, on which is then pronounced the same verdict, and so on and so on, higher and higher, from crudely tangible earth to the refined and invisible ether of thought, and finally up to objectless knowledge, to utter emptiness, for which only one name is possible—*being*. Hegelianism will pass just like any error, and even now it is more alive in everyday life than in philosophy. Hegel's phenomenology, however, will remain an immortal monument to mercilessly rigorous and consistent dialectic, about which thinkers who have been fortified and improved by him will never speak without reverence. It is amazing only that, to this day, no one has noticed that this immortal creation is a decisive condemnation of all rationalism and proves its inevitable end.

Hegel, however, saw this end only as the beginning of creative reconstitution. The intellectual process already completed in the phenomenology deprived being of any definition and any content. Such being does not differ from non-being in any way, and finds, in its very identity with non-being, the strength for new forward motion—or, if one may say so, for unraveling from inside. In this action it crosses a series of degrees of fulfillment, which are hardly expressible in translation (for they are connected to the very essence of the German language), and it finally reaches its supreme fulfillment in spirit. Hegel's logic can be called the *inspiriting of abstract being (Einvergeistigung des Seyns)*. This would be its fullest definition, apparently never formulated before. Never have human beings posed for themselves such a terrible task, such a daring undertaking—eternal, self-resurrecting creation from the depths of the abstract concept, devoid of any inner essence: the self-sufficient transition from bare potentiality into all the multiform and rational essentiality of the world. The fiction of mythology and the petty negation of Mephistopheles disappear before this actual Titanism of the human rationalistic understanding. Hegel was called "*der letzte Heros des deutschen Geistes*" (the last hero of German thought); he should rather be called *der letzte Titan des Verstandes* (the last Titan of the rationalistic understanding). But he himself hardly comprehended his significance. A well-meaning fanatic of the rationalistic understanding—which he mistook for reason—he believed in the legitimacy and, so to speak, sanctity of his labor; and when, at the end of his career, he said in heavy contemplation, "there is something missing in my philosophy" (*es fehlt doch etwas an meiner Philosophie*), his words expressed a doleful feeling of weakness, unperturbed by any admixture of moral self-condemnation. His purely rationalistic nature, formed by the general intellectual labor of Germany and German Protestantism, was completely honest unto itself.

It stands to reason that the impossible remains impossible. From the very first step in this contrasting of being and nothing, in this *plus-minus*, in this polarity or, at the very least, nominal dichotomy, there is already a category introduced from outside, introduced by thought—therefore, by what already is. Hegel himself vaguely sensed this and, in passing, even admitted it (I believe it was at the beginning of the section about the essential—*Wesen*). Hegel's entire enterprise fell at its genesis. The same kind of leaps were repeated in the development of the system, in the transition to the essential, in crossing from the law of illusion (*der Schein*) to the phenomenon (*die Erscheinung*), in the transition from freedom (*Freiheit*) to will (*Wille*), and so on. But the great thinker never attained to a clear awareness of his mistake. For him the formula always conditioned the phenomenon.[4]

The rationalistic understanding again beat against its own limits. The dogmatic significance of Hegel's logic was a fruitless phenomenon, but it was decisive in a negative sense, for it destroyed the faith in rationalism by its very untenability. I believe, however, that it might yet bring forth positive fruits. One only has to analyze it as the study of the categories through which *essential* spirit aspires to its own self-consciousness in the phenomenon, casting aside several inconsistencies that flow from the initial false formula, and the reader's mind would be enriched by many profound and rational conclusions. People who have already rejected Hegel's authority will feel that they can calmly admit their agreement with him in the clear moments of his powerful thought. But this itself condemns Hegel's task and all self-reliant rationalism of the school he completed and destroyed.

The cycle of German philosophy was completed. Hegelianism, the final conclusion of German philosophy, was rejected and condemned by all who remained at all faithful to its method of dialectic. Hegelianism is in the past for philosophical science; but it continues to exist for historical science as an aspiration that has not yet been outgrown. Any philosophy is capable of turning into something similar to faith or, more precisely, into a prejudice accepted blindly by people

---

4. I first expressed this conclusion some time ago, in a still unpublished article. Hegel's explanation of the reason for the earth's elliptical and self-rotational motion can serve as a quite clear example of his error: he finds the reason for this motion in the existence of the very formula of this motion. Such confusion in the clearest minds, such laxity in the most rigorous minds, should not surprise those who are familiar with the philosophical sciences. Does not the famous definition of time and space, created by Leibniz and perfected by Kant ("space is the order of coexisting phenomena, while time is the order of consecutive phenomena"), already contain time itself, hidden in the words: "coexisting and consecutive"? And how is this different from the famous question: *Quare facit opium dormire?* ["Why does opium make one sleep? (Because that is the nature of opium.)]. Perhaps, one could express it more rigorously: space is the order of equal self-placement; time is the order of causality, transferred into the world of phenomena.

who have never belabored their minds with philosophical constructs. This observation of Ivan Kireevsky relates preeminently to Hegelianism due to the extreme decisiveness of its tenets, which are distinguished by a certain special character of self-confident power, and due to "the particular sympathy of modern civilization for its orientation" (Kireevsky's words). As a matter of fact, apart from moral sympathy, all falsely oriented minds that believe in the vital strength of a formula, regardless of its essence, display sympathy with Hegelianism. There is a hidden, unconscious Hegelian, so to speak, in those French who declare, in their self-satisfied way, that they have no need of Germanic mists—that they need life" as though by speaking such a demand they would create life within themselves. There is such a "Hegelian" in the political ideologist who believes that free forms will evoke a free spirit; in the benevolent, fanatical socialist who thinks that the banner of fraternity will foster a fraternal heart in the human breast; in the natural scientist rejoicing at a cell, who hopes to observe, in its particular law of combining material atoms, some independent, almost arbitrary tendency to develop into any kind of organism, even of a spiritual kind; in the political leader who believes that institutions, deprived of any historical life, will receive new development in history; in the friend of enlightenment who is convinced that you can educate the nation by sticking the outer forms of culture on it; and, finally, in the historical critic who, without finding any understandable formula in the past, denies in a good-natured way that the past had any life whatsoever. But all this will pass. This is the tail, so to speak, and not the head—or, more precisely, this is the unconscious rot of a system in society, not its conscious life in learning. The German school has ended.

Much in the contradiction between the law and real phenomena could have brought the German school to reason even before it achieved its final and revelatory development. But the German mind was too enamored with its rationalistic thinking to sense the error, which had not yet been exposed. When the disintegration of the laws of reason and a profound investigation of its effects revealed to Kant's disciples a truth that had been partially guessed by antiquity, that the spirit passes from its primordial and undeveloped subjectivity (using this school's own language) to the stages of object and consciousness, they should have encountered the following conclusion, which follows from the Kantians' own tenets: either the reflection of reason in the object and consciousness is meaningless, or the reflection of the universal spirit in its object and self-consciousness fully corresponds to it. Thus, for the spirit there is not, nor can there be, any temporary achievements with respect to itself; only full and perfect self-possession exists. Process and development appear only as the qualities of the individual spirit or a partial appearance of the spirit, such as the human being. Indeed, at no instant of their existence do human beings appear as that which *is*, but only as that which *strives* to be. It is this striving that comprises the inner human life; any halt in human striving is inner death. But all of these phenomena of the individual are utterly foreign to the universal.

Another sphere gave rise to exactly the same kind of conclusion—one that goes even farther beyond the narrow limits of rationalism. This sphere makes the weakness of the German school especially apparent, but it was incapable of attracting that school's attention. I mean [the sphere of] moral development. Kant posited as a moral law the perfectly true tenet: "You must, because you are able" (*Du sollst, weil du kannst*). Hegel posited a new tenet, also correctly: "You must, because you are unable" (*Du sollst, weil du kannst nicht*). Again [we find] the same contradiction between the law of the general and that of the individual, which can be explained only by the qualities of the human being as an individual phenomenon and, consequently, as a phenomenon that fails to find fullness for itself in anything. Fullness and perfection are the law; but for human beings, only striving without achievement is possible. In striving to leave human boundaries (for the law of the spirit, or universal fullness, is inherent within human beings), one encounters other individual phenomena similar to oneself and, by means of them, complements one's own limitedness. But such complementation is impossible as long as those others remain external with respect to oneself. They must be assimilated, but not by transferring them into oneself (which is also impossible, since we have dominion only over ourselves); but one passes over into them through the moral force of sincere love.

Therefore any sincere, self-forgetting love is an acquisition; and the broader its sphere and the fuller it carries us beyond our limits, the richer we will become within ourselves. In sacrifice, or self-oblivion, we find a surplus of expanding life, and in this surplus we become radiant, triumphant, and jubilant. Whenever we halt in our striving, whenever we lose what we have acquired (despite the law inherent within us), we are impoverished, squeezed more and more within our narrow bounds, as if into a coffin that we find repellent and hateful, but that we are unable to leave, because we do not want to. Is this not what we were taught from above to call eternal death?

Such are some of the conclusions that the German school could have derived naturally from the opposition of the universal spirit and individual spiritual phenomena; but it passed them by unnoticed, engulfed in its boundless predilection for rationalistic thought. And this is one of the reasons why it has given so few good fruits, and why it has even had such a harmful influence in the moral sphere.

Where then is the sphere where it has been truly fruitful, and what is the measure of its merits? This is the real question. And now, when rationalistic philosophy has come to a halt, having exposed itself, when faith in it has disappeared, is it really possible that another, higher philosophy, a truly rational philosophy might arise? This new question flows from the first one.

The very fall of the German school is its greatest triumph. It has fallen not due to the exhaustion of its own representatives, who remained powerful to the end; not from the weakening of interest in society, which has followed it with constant and almost superstitious attention; and not from its disintegration into small shards engendered by the shakiness and obscurity of the tenets derived by its main teachers. Likewise, it was not forced out by a new doctrine that arose in strength. No. Of all philosophical schools it alone has completed its path in full, rigorous to its final conclusion. It halted and fell only when it came up against the impossible, against the task of restoring or, more precisely, of reconstituting that which is out of an abstract law. It has earned irrevocable and immortal glory in the history of philosophy. It has completed and demarcated the cycle of abstract, purely rationalistic thinking. It has defined its laws with rigor and clarity for all of humanity and all times. There is no thinker who could speak about it with anything but reverent gratitude, and we should consider fortunate those who tempered their dialectical abilities in the frigid but mighty streams of the Kantian doctrine.

This school has completed its path, it has crossed into the realm of the past, and any attempt to continue its existence would be fruitless and irrational. This is the reason why Hegel's disciples, who once idolized his conclusions superstitiously while betraying his method, whose rigor would have exposed their internal contradictions, have already received in Germany the derisive nickname "Hegelings" (baby Hegels), and why with respect to their mentor they have become almost the same as the scholastics were with respect to Aristotle. This is no longer a school.

But what was the basis of the school's one-sidedness and, consequently, limited nature? The answer has already been given. It was that the philosophy of the rationalistic understanding considered itself the philosophy of reason; Ivan Kireevsky expressed this conclusion in an even clearer fashion when he said that it only had access to the truth of the possible, but not the truth of the actual, in other words, to the law, and not the world within which the law is made manifest.

The dialectic of knowledge fully corresponds to the logic of the object of knowledge; they are identical, but at the same time there is a great difference between them. First, passing one and the same line, they pass it in opposite directions.[5] Second, knowledge itself, or abstract, rationalistic knowledge, has access only to the law of an object, but not its reality. Knowledge, when opposed to the object of knowledge, places it in a negative relation to itself. But any negation, in the philosophical sense, posits the negated only as a possibility, not as what really is, reserving reality for itself.[6] It is a translation of the real into the realm of the possible, into a law. In German rationalistic philosophy, knowledge claims reality for itself, and the world appears to it only as possibility, as an abstract law.

This is true not only for the knowledge of the outer world—no, it is just as true for the inner world, for the spirit that knows itself. In the spirit, self-knowledge appears in the realm of the positive, whereas the spirit itself and all of its other forces appear in negation. The path of development is distorted, for in reality the logical object of knowledge precedes knowledge (but not the capacity for knowledge, it stands to reason); and the restoration of the law of reality is absolutely impossible, for such a restoration would also have to be

---

5. Dialectically: I perceive an object, and therefore it exists. Logically: the object exists, and therefore I perceive it.
6. The word *negation* I take in the sense of opposing *I* and *not-I*.

derived dialectically—that is, by an act of thought that necessarily negates any reality apart from its own.[7] We might say that we have outgrown German philosophy for we have understood its one-sidedness, not with the vague comprehension of an unsatisfied spirit, but with the clear consciousness of reason. The dialectical development of the Kantian school does not fully reflect the known (the object), for it reflects it without its reality. It is not only not the philosophy of universal reason, but it is not even the philosophy of manifest (objectivized) reason. It must be acknowledged to be the science of the dialectical understanding (analytical reason), and in this sense it is a great and immortal monument to human genius.[8]

Thus, the object of knowledge is not fully reflected in the sphere that is studied by philosophy, or in rationalistic knowledge, for [there] it is reflected without its reality, as something abstract. But is the object of knowledge itself, in its full reality, an image of the spirit as it passes to self-consciousness? This is certainly the case if one understands the law of spiritual development correctly; for what would the spirit know if it did not know itself at the stage of being an object for its own thought? If the spirit only partially passes into the image it is no longer itself, and it projects something other than itself, and it knows something other than itself. Consequently, according to the law the object of knowledge in its fullness is a full image of the spirit. But this is not the case in human reality. We have seen that the perceived spirit does not fully pass over into abstract knowledge (as daily experience actually convinces any attentive observer); we feel

---

7. On this topic, and on the perversion of the development of concepts (especially in Hegel's interpretation of history), I have spoken in two, as yet unpublished, articles.

8. In this respect, it is most similar to algebra and pure mathematics in general, in which the law of quantity excludes any material reality; for in any application of arithmetic, even the most elementary, one of the factors is taken for the pure manifestation of the quantitative law (a rouble is not multiplied by yards, or vice versa, but by a quantity). Indeed, we might note the same thing in any definition as a result of its negative character. We understand that no particular law can manifest itself outside of *that which is*, or what is given (e.g., a circle outside of size), but some believe that the entire complex of particular laws, the law in its common features, can manifest itself out of itself. They do not understand that there also remains a relation between the law and its manifestation. They are conditioned by *that which is*, out of which arises given reality, which carries with it its own law.

that we ourselves do not fully pass to the stage of being known (the object). This is clear to anyone, and is clearer still to an artist.

But, if we eliminate any surmises that are susceptible to a more or less rational doubt, we shall settle only on the energy of the spirit or reason: will. It is impossible to deny that will is the inalienable property of reason. Anyone who has grasped the idea of energy as a universal, as *all-energy*, will understand the logical certainty of will. But we must add that Hegel clearly derived it in the section on self-negating negation (*Negation der Negation*). True, he derived it as *freedom*, and consequently only as potential, for such is the manner and sphere of his thought; but *freedom in the positive manifestation of energy is will*.

Now the question arises: Does will—the inherent energy of reason—ever cross over to the stage of the object of knowledge (or object)? Never. Whenever a thought enters the world of phenomena, it simultaneously enters the realm of necessity and ceases to display any features of will. Will itself does not pass into a perceived image. Indeed, let people pose themselves even the simplest of tasks, even to move the body slightly, to turn one's head to the right or left, to raise or lower one's arm. Until people perform such a task, they feel free; they feel that the will is able to decide whether one should perform this movement and in which direction. As soon as the movement is accomplished, however, where are the traces of will? How can rationalistic knowledge find the presence of will? One stands perplexed with the unsolved question; was the choice not a matter of necessity? For human beings, will belongs to the *pre-objective* sphere.

Meanwhile, philosophy has thus far known only the reflection of the object in rationalistic knowledge, and if it was unable to grasp (as we have said) the very reality of the object, which does not cross over into this knowledge, all the more was it unable to gain access to the sphere of forces that do not pass into the objective image. Therefore, will was also beyond its grasp. Consequently, you do not find any trace of will in German philosophy. Keep in mind that I speak of such traces as they are justified by the logic of philosophy, and not of such illegitimate word-mongering by which a notion is sometimes forced into the correct development of a theory, even though it does not follow from it and is even completely foreign to it, but only because it is inevitably evoked by the requirements of reason and by one's intellectual conscience.[9]

Meanwhile, apart from its importance and, more precisely, its supremacy in the realm of moral concepts, will in fact occupies a place equal to the rationalistic understanding in the definition of all our concepts. It is unnecessary to prove the well-known truth that people have access only to changes in their self-consciousness; that they are able to encompass things external to them only to the degree that they accept those things into the jurisdiction of thought (for sensation itself is only the *consciousness of impressions*); and, finally, that people see the entire world as the same kind of object, the same kind of object of knowledge, as are the manifestations of a person's inner essence, or *I*. This is where Germany stopped: one object, one object of knowledge.

Nevertheless, no matter how vivid the imagination that presents the object and the sensations caused by it, the surprised professor will not harness an imagined horse to an imagined carriage, and will not attempt to drink an imagined beer from an imagined mug. But if a man is ill, and if echoes of the outer world have already received independence from that man himself—as they do not when he is healthy—then one might find him moving his arms as he harnesses the phantom of a horse to the phantom of a cart, and as he greedily draws to his mouth an imagined vessel. In its healthy state, the will differentiates between phantom objects and the outer world; the absence of will or the sick man's consciousness destroys the borders for the understanding, and it merges images of the inner and images of the outer into a single, chaotic formlessness.

An external object is disobedient to the will, whereas an inner object is engendered by it, or governed by it, as long as that object is not a captive echo of the external world. The will places its stamp on the object, and if this stamp is absent, the object of thought becomes a phantom, a phantasm, or what we call illusion par excellence. Every object—any object of knowledge (as an object of knowledge)— enters the human *I* in an identical way; beyond that, however, their relationship to personal understanding differs. The will determines

---

9. Thus is Hegel's substitution of *will* for *freedom*, supported by several preliminary sophisms.

some phenomena as *I and from myself*, whereas it determines others as *I but not from myself*, thus exposing the difference in first principles that give rise to the existence or change of the very objects of knowledge. The will therefore accompanies every concept, and thus does the will expose the first principle that precedes the phenomenon; thus the will, and it alone, limits the actual bounds of the personality. It is true that, although the will's existence as an energy is not subject to any doubt, its existence as a free energy (in the person) is not so obvious. Many are prepared to see it as the simple relation of the individual center to the forces of the universal periphery, which affects the individual in an unnoticeable fashion. This doubt, just like reason's doubting of its own existence (which Kant destroyed), does not exist in fact, only in words. Reason is really unable to doubt itself due to the entire realm of rational actions, to which such doubt itself belongs; and this is precisely why reason is unable to doubt the will, for the entire realm of moral consciousness, which is conditioned by the consciousness of free will, *could not exist for reason* without this consciousness, *even as a phantom, or phantasm, or category*. This doubt, whether imagined or verbally articulated, can be explained, in the first place, because free will, as a pre-objective energy of thought, can never pass into an object perceived by dialectical understanding; second, because human free will is incomplete and imperfect, like reason itself; and the individual phenomenon (the human being) strives only to exert will, just as it strives to exert reason; for the individual phenomenon itself is only striving, not being in the sense of *that which is*.

Rationalistic knowledge does not encompass the reality of that which is known; the object of knowledge does not contain its first principle in the fullness of its energy, and therefore can all the less communicate it to knowledge even in the abstract. Meanwhile we speak about one and the same reality, about one and the same unmanifested forces, and consequently we know them. What kind of knowledge is this that is not the knowledge of the rationalistic understanding? It cannot have self-sufficient existence removed from the reality of what is known, but by the same coin it is filled with this reality and understands the very connection of this reality to the reality of the as yet unmanifested first principle. Such knowledge beats with all the pulses of life; it receives from life all of its variety and fills life with its meaning. It does not endeavor to prove itself and its laws; it does not doubt itself and is incapable of doubting itself. In the unmanifested such knowledge feels the possibility of manifestation, and in the manifested it recognizes the faithfulness and legitimacy of the manifestation with respect to its first principle. It does not pilfer the realm of the rationalistic understanding, but equips the rationalistic understanding with all the necessary information for its independent action; and it is mutually enriched by all of the wealth of the rationalistic understanding. Finally, it is living knowledge to the highest degree, and it is incomparable in the highest degree.

This is still not universal reason, for reason in its universality also embraces the entire realm of the rationalistic understanding; this is what German philosophy sometimes presents under the extremely indeterminate expression "unmediated knowledge" (*das unmittelbare Wissen*). This might be called inner knowledge, but what, due to the preeminent character of its entire realm, should be called faith. Reason lives by the perception of the phenomenon in faith and, detaching itself, acts upon itself in the rationalistic understanding. Reason reflects the life of the object of knowledge in the life of faith, and it reflects the logic of its laws in the dialectic of the rationalistic understanding.[10]

A certain man who was born blind acquires knowledge, and among the sciences he encounters optics. He studies it and grasps its laws, wittily characterizing some of its phenomena (comparing, for example, bright crimson to the sound of a horn). Perhaps he even enriches it with several new conclusions. A groundkeeper, however, sees this learned blind man. Which of them knows light better? The scientist knows the laws of light, but those laws might be similar to the laws of other forces. Perhaps there is even a force subordinate to the most characteristic law—that of interferences. But who knows anything even similar to light itself? The seeing groundkeeper knows it, but the learned blind man lacks even the faintest concept of it; whatever he knows about its laws was learned on the basis of information supplied

---

10. One might propose, as one of the many reasons why the word *faith* never occupied any place in German philosophies, the weakness of the word *glauben*. It is something intermediate between "I believe" and "I imagine." Words have a boundless effect on thought. This is one manifestation of the intellectual guardianship that a nation exercises over human beings.

by those who see. What we see in comparing these two individuals occurs also within each person through the comparison of unmediated knowledge, which is from faith, and mediated knowledge, which is from the rationalistic understanding. This unmediated, living, and absolute knowledge, or faith, is the reason's ability to see, as it were.

Our unforgettable Kireevsky indicated the historical causes for the realm of the rationalistic understanding becoming the object of exclusive study in recent philosophy. Kireevsky stated that this realm, in all its utter abstractness, is equally accessible to each individual personality, regardless of its inner height and organization. It stands to reason that he did not intend to affirm that rationalistic capabilities are equally developed in all people. He knew that one mind moves just as easily and freely in the most convoluted and complex web of dialectical constructs as in a simple, everyday conversation, whereas another can hardly crawl up a ladder of simple syllogisms by the sweat of its brow. But he was correct to recognize that rationalistic truth is equally accessible and equally obligatory for all, for accessibility does not refer to the ease, but the possibility of its achievement. Thus the laws of morality, beauty, and living consciousness, in their endless variety, are largely inaccessible to many, and in their wholeness are, of course, inaccessible to anyone. The laws of pure mathematics, however, are accessible and incontrovertible for all (however bitter their study might be in some cases); and all the formulas of dialectical reason in this respect are similar to pure mathematics. "The coordination of all cognitive powers into a single force, the inner wholeness of the mind essential for the comprehension of the integral truth—this could not be within everyone's reach" (Kireevsky's words [see page 240]). Individual capacities for reason differ from one another not in their capacity for speculation, but in their ability to see.

The category of logical relations—the realm of the rationalistic understanding—is extremely poor and monotonous. The phenomena of spiritual and intellectual life are infinite in variety, and (like the organs of sense perception in the physical world), in order to correctly and fully perform their functions, they must be congenial with the general laws of nature, not only in form and geometric outline, but also in their entire chemical composition and dynamic structure. They differ in various people according to their relative perfection. Thus in the intellectual and spiritual world, in order to understand truth, the rationalistic understanding itself must be congenial with all the laws of the spiritual world, not only with respect to its logical organization, but also with respect to all its inner vital forces and abilities. Therefore the degrees of understanding are infinite. On the other hand, however, the task of communicating its acquisitions to others is also extremely difficult for higher reason, because (in Kireevsky's words) "standing on this highest level of thought, Orthodox believers can easily and harmlessly comprehend all systems of thought that derive from the lower levels of reason; they can see the limitations and relative truth of those systems. For the lower form of thought, however, the higher form is incomprehensible and appears nonsensical. Such is the general law of the human mind" [see page 261].

In everyday life, experience convinces a nearsighted person and justifies the farsighted, whom the nearsighted one would otherwise have considered a liar. It is not this way in intellectual life, especially at its highest stages of development, where experience is utterly or almost impossible. If such an experience even appears, it usually happens that those who are self-satisfied and nearsighted manage to pass away, together with their entire generation, before the historical development of humanity is able to justify their farsighted contemporary.

Thus, in order to grasp the rational wholeness of that which is, in order to understand its true and living reality, in order to feel the pre-objective movement of omnipresent thought, and, finally, in order to perceive all that, when accepted, is defined by consciousness of the will as *I but not from myself*, one needs reason, congenial with all the laws of all that is in reason, not only with respect to dialectical understanding but also with respect to all living and moral forces of the spirit. What we have just shown with an example taken from the material world is true just as rigorously and certainly for the world of spiritual phenomena, and a person is able in this very way to understand all the laws of any moral stimulus (for example, love), without grasping in the slightest the reality itself of this stimulus and remaining a blind optician of the rational-spiritual world.

Therefore, all of the most profound truths of thought, the whole higher truth of the striving of will, are accessible only to reason, which is inwardly organized in full moral congeniality to omnipresent reason. The invisible mysteries of the things of God and humanity are revealed only to reason. This fullest development of inner knowledge and rational vision has been called faith par excellence, and it has been defined with amazing rigor by the greatest of the divinely illumined thinkers of the Church. They simultaneously recognized that this supreme development is still not the final development of universal reason (which, due to worldly imperfection, is impossible), but only a reflected vision of it, as if in a mirror. And we shall preserve this name for the superior degree that has been named as such, and we shall leave the name of inner knowledge, perhaps *living knowledge*, for the lower degrees. We shall remember, however, that the entire ladder receives its characterization from its highest degree—faith. And we shall remember that faith does not pilfer the realm of the rationalistic understanding but instead preserves the freedom of the rationalistic understanding with its own independence, while at the same time enriching the analysis of the rationalistic understanding with the infinite wealth of data acquired with its clairvoyance.[11]

Having shown that only inner, moral agreement with universal laws can broaden the realm of knowledge and elevate thought to its maximum height, we must now study these same laws in order to bring the mood of our own spirit into agreement with them. The way [to do this] has been revealed to us of old; it is the living way that itself leads humanity forward to its highest goal. The law of love appears to the undistorted soul as the first, highest, and most perfect of the universal laws of willing reason or reasoning will (for such is the definition of the spirit itself). Therefore, agreement with it is the preeminent means of fortifying and broadening our intellectual sight, and the stubborn disharmony of our intellectual powers must be submitted to it and organized according to its structure. Only when we accomplish this labor will we be able to hope for a fuller development of reason. Of course, this view makes the philosophical sciences seem less defined and accessible than the previous conception of them. On the other hand, they actually become more varied, richer, and more fruitful; for according to Kireevsky's definition, "philosophy is nothing but the transitional movement of human reason from the realm of faith to the multifarious applications of everyday thought."

---

11. This distinction between inner, or living, knowledge and, so to speak, external, or formal, knowledge is clearly demarcated in some works of Orthodox literature.

We have affirmed that love is the first and highest of the moral world's laws, in accordance to which our reason must be structured in order to achieve knowledge. Love is preeminently necessary for rational development. This tenet itself is rich with consequences. Love is not an indifferent striving: it demands, finds, and creates response and communion, and in response and communion it grows, becoming stronger and more perfected. Thus, the communion of love is not only useful, but fully necessary in order to grasp truth; the comprehension of truth is founded upon love and is impossible without it. Truth, inaccessible to any individual method of thought, is accessible only to the sum of methods of thoughts tied by love. This trait sharply distinguishes Orthodox teaching from all others: from Latinism, which rests on external authority; and from Protestantism, which liberates the personality for freedom in the deserts of rationalistic abstraction. What has been affirmed concerning higher truth relates also to philosophy. Philosophy, which seems the achievement of the few, is actually the creation and heritage of all.

Thus we see that, by means of rigorous conclusions, philosophical thought returns to the unshakable truths of faith, and that the Church's reason is the supreme possibility for human reason without restraining the latter's own particular development. This justifies Kireevsky's comment that "true convictions are beneficent and strong only in their sum and in the development of social self-consciousness" [see page 283]. Thus, finally, the philosophical sciences, understood in their entire living capacity, necessarily find their point of departure in faith and return to it, and also give freedom to the understanding, strength to inner knowledge, and fullness to life.

* * *

My intention was to clarify the teaching to which the late Ivan Kireevsky belonged; as far as I was able, I have fulfilled it. I am happy if I have acquainted the reader with ideas that hitherto had been unexpressed, and if I was able to be just to the memory of our unforgettable thinker, who was stopped by death at the midpoint of his eloquent teachings.

PART THREE

Twentieth-Century Responses to Khomiakov

Pavel Florensky

Nikolai Berdiaev

I

EXTRACTS FROM THE WRITINGS OF
Pavel Florensky & Nikolai Berdiaev

EDITOR'S INTRODUCTION

Slavophile thought in general, and Khomiakov's thought in particular, had a vast influence on the Russian religious renaissance of the latter part of the nineteenth and early part of the twentieth centuries. In fact, modern Russian religious thought, in its ontological "face," can be seen as originating in the thought of Khomiakov and Kireevsky. Among the major figures influenced by the Slavophiles are Fyodor Dostoevsky, Pavel Florensky, Sergius Bulgakov, Nikolai Berdiaev, and Lev Karsavin.

In this section, we present brief extracts from Pavel Florensky's essay "Around Khomiakov" and longer extracts from Nikolai Berdiaev's book on Khomiakov. These extracts exemplify how two major Russian religious thinkers of the early twentieth century responded to Khomiakov's ideas.

Florensky (1882–1937) is becoming recognized as the greatest Russian thinker of the twentieth century and one of the greatest of any age, land, or culture. An incredible polymath whose range encompassed mathematics, philosophy, theological aesthetics, linguistics, and electrical engineering, he made his most indelible mark as a Russian Orthodox theologian (in such works as *The Pillar and Ground of the Truth* from 1914) and as an invigorator of contemporary Eastern Orthodoxy. Florensky's essay has the reputation of being perhaps the most critical appraisal of Khomiakov's thought in the Russian philosophical literature: perhaps the greatest Orthodox theologian of the twentieth century harshly criticizes the greatest Orthodox theologian of the nineteenth century. It is in this essay that Florensky accuses Khomiakov of "Protestantism."

"Around Khomiakov" (*Okolo Khomiakova*) was first published as a brochure in 1916. It is composed mainly of a highly critical review of V. Z. Zavitnevich's two-volume biography of Khomiakov: *Aleksei Stepanovich Khomiakov* (2 vols., Kiev: 1902, 1913).

* * *

A major representative of the Russian Silver Age, Nikolai Berdiaev (1874–1948) is perhaps Russia's greatest existentialist philosopher and one of the greatest European philosophers of personalism. His development of the philosophy of freedom may be unparalleled in the twentieth century.

This section will present substantial extracts from three chapters of Berdiaev's book: *Aleksei Stepanovich Khomiakov*, Moscow, 1912. As one would expect, Berdiaev highlights the importance of freedom in Khomiakov's theology. His assessment of Khomiakov is generally positive, but he points out what he considers a fundamental defect of Khomiakov's thought: the absence of a cosmological element. Lacking this element, Khomiakov is deprived of the apocalyptic yearnings that Berdiaev sees as the essence of the "new religious consciousness" (See footnote on page 334).

These excerpts by Florensky and Berdiaev were translated for this volume by Boris Jakim.

1.

From "Around Khomiakov"

PAVEL FLORENSKY

Even in his own lifetime Khomiakov was recognized by friends and foes alike to be the head of that orientation of Russian thought that received the scarcely appropriate, grotesque moniker *Slavophilism*. Both the government and the intelligentsia saw Khomiakov as the source or at least the center of a new idea. Both the praises and the censures of theological circles were directed not at this Slavophile or that Slavophile but almost exclusively at him. It seems that three-quarters of all questions regarding the Slavophiles or Slavophilism boils down to the question of Khomiakov, and the Slavophile group as a whole is usually conceived of as "Khomiakov and the others." Is that fair? We answer *yes* even without deciding beforehand the question whether Khomiakov is superior to the other Slavophiles in talent, intelligence, learning, and conviction. Khomiakov was and remains the ideological center and leader of Slavophile thought not only or rather not so much in himself as in the position he occupies. For he is the preeminent investigator of that sacred center from which the thoughts of the Slavophiles emanated and to which they returned—that is, Orthodoxy, or, more precisely, the Church. He looked into himself more penetratingly and consistently than the others. He spoke more insistently than any of the others about the decisive turning point that threatens the people's worldview—a turning point that depends on an incorrect relationship with the Church—and about the historic collapse that will result from this. Slavophilism is a worldview that, in its intent, is linked directly to the Church; and Khomiakov is the center of the Slavophile group, leading Slavophile thought by virtue of the fact that, according to its general meaning and according to the direct acknowledgment of the Slavophiles, especially the elder ones, the Church—with which in essence he concerned himself inwardly his entire life—is the center of creaturely being.

Khomiakov's entire being is constituted by reflection on the Church, and it is therefore understandable that the attitude toward the Church of those who judged Khomiakov turned out to be, in one way or another, decisive also in their assessment of Khomiakov. I say "in one way or another" because, in some appraisals of Khomiakov, one can hear statements diametrically opposed to this. On the one hand, for those who love the Church but who do not see her in Khomiakov or, rather, perceive in him a replacement of the Truth of the Church by something else, something homemade, as well as for those who do not love the Church at all and do not feel her reality—Khomiakov's doctrine is an indeterminate and obscure doctrine of something dreamy and illusory. It is a system concerning an empty place, and therefore it is sophistry, virtuoso but empty wordplay, brilliant idiosyncrasy. In thus attacking Khomiakov, representatives of the Church sometimes join with ardent Westernizers.[1] On the other hand, for people who in some sense took into account the reality of that Church about which Khomiakov spoke and who acknowledged that he was speaking about the authentic Church and not of some impotent void, a void invented according to the model of the abstract absolutes of German idealism, and who therefore were afraid of the excess (in their opinion) reality of this Church and looked askance at the very possibility of the Church standing where She, by her very meaning and right, should stand. To those who saw in the Church an obstacle on the road to a semi-ecclesial and extra-ecclesial order of society—whether statism or socialism—Khomiakov's power seemed harmful. Neither extreme statists nor revolutionary and socialist activists liked Khomiakov's doctrine. Both sensed in him if not a future victor then at least a real opponent. Both converged in considering him a dangerous foe.

Aside from these enemies of his who rejected Khomiakov for one reason or another, there remained, finally, a group of people whose attitude toward Khomiakov was unconditionally positive. In Khomiakov's doctrine they saw the pledge of a better future for Russia, the first sprout of a national self-consciousness, the beginnings of a new, truly Orthodox theology, and so on—in a word, they saw in it the dawn of a new culture through which the Slavic world will shine for humanity.

At the present time there is hardly any need to demonstrate the significance of Khomiakov the thinker and the nobility of his person. No one doubts his talents and intellect, nor the purity of his person and

---

1. See footnote on page 337. — TRANS.

the selflessness of his intentions. There is also no doubt that Khomiakov's ever-increasing fame is, in recent times, ready to burst into an intense flame, in connection both with the current aversion to Western culture and with the Slavophilism that has raised its head. But to give the subjective loftiness of his person and the elastic freshness of his thought their due is not yet to go very far in objectively assessing his inner life and the system of his thought. Moreover, an objective assessment of his worldview and of his personal attitudes should give a firmer basis for reviewing and perhaps reevaluating his subjective life. Who knows? Perhaps, in the dispassionate light of an objective *ecclesial* assessment, dubious spots will appear on the snow-white garment of his religio-philosophical convictions. Or, perhaps, on the contrary, Khomiakov's system will turn out to be even more impeccable than it is usually thought. But in any case we must be ready to accept that what captivates us in Khomiakov *may* turn out to be not as captivating and not as *right* in all senses of this word as almost everyone accepts without discussion.

"Ye shall know them by their fruits" (Matt. 7:16). Until recently, however, Khomiakov's doctrine consisted only of sprouts. Nevertheless, at the present time this doctrine is maturing and seems ready to bear fruit. Are these good fruits? The fact of the matter is that these fruits are dualistic in nature. We see that, in its most talented representatives, Russian theological thought, in one way or another, accepted Khomiakov's doctrine that all that is fresh in theology is a refraction, in one way or another, of Khomiakovian ideas.... But his ideas have also been accepted by thinkers who are quite distant from the true Church—even Leo Tolstoy's non-Orthodox teaching can, in its own way, lay claim to Khomiakov's heritage. Moreover, Khomiakov's ideas have turned out to be convenient for polemicizing with Catholicism....

There is a danger, however, in such polemic; by getting rid of the chaff of Catholicism, does not this polemic also risk tearing the wheat of Orthodoxy out of the soil? For example, by getting rid of the apparent chaff of authority in the Church, which supposedly does not exist in Orthodoxy, does one not risk getting rid of the principle of fear, the principle of power, and the obligatory nature of the canonical order? At the present time—which in general has such a great tendency to negate norms and even to struggle against all norms—does not this dissolution of canons in an abyss of altruism represent a very serious danger? As dangerous aspects of Khomiakovism one must also cite Khomiakov's critique of the Catholic doctrine of the sacraments and the Protestant doctrine of the Divine inspiration of the Bible. Containing *some sort* of truth, this critique inevitably leads to a clearly nonchurchly pragmatism or modernism, which destroys the very essence of the doctrine of the sacraments, leaving only an external, intrinsically *not* valuable shell of this doctrine.

Even Khomiakov's main idea in his anti-Catholic polemic—the reproach that Catholicism has destroyed unity by proclaiming new dogmas, the reproach that it has usurped the rights of the universal Church—replaces the inner core of church unity with its external forms. It is marked by the sin that Khomiakov attributes to the Western world: legalism. In other words, Khomiakov and Khomiakovism, which were problematic for his contemporaries, have not only not stopped being problematic for us but are even manifesting a new series of problems that require investigation. The chief problem, chief not only from our standpoint but also from the standpoint of Khomiakov himself and his worldview, a problem inevitably sprouting from the very ground of his doctrine, is the question of the ecclesiality of Khomiakov himself. But now, with the open appearance of pragmatism, modernism, and their offshoots, this question has not only not been clarified but has even become confused to the extreme. Who is Khomiakov? "A teacher of the Church," to refer to Samarin's expression, which has become a cliche? [see page 183] Or the progenitor of a refined Russian socialism, as his contemporaries characterized him? Did he found a new school of theology, one that finally was truly Orthodox, and not Catholic and not Protestant? Or was his doctrine a refined rationalism, a "Hegelianism," as his opponents somewhat naively called it, a system of extremely flexible and therefore extremely corrosive formulas, eating away at the foundations of the Church?

Furthermore, in the domain of the state, was he a faithful servant of autocracy, this foundation of the Russian government? Did he desire to strengthen and elevate the imperial throne or, on the contrary, should we see in Khomiakov the creator of the most popular and therefore the most dangerous form of egalitarianism? I repeat: who was Khomiakov? A defender of the roots of old Russia or an uprooter of her primordial foundations in the name of a dreamy vision of a projected Russia of the future? Did he humbly accept the sacredness of the Russian people, wishing to cleanse it of the accidental dirt lying on its surface, or, a proud reformer, did he try to prescribe for Russia something he (or the Moscow circle of Slavophiles) concocted? For to prescribe, on the basis of *one's own* authority, even with the purest of intentions, what the Church should be, is not to recognize the Church, but only to recognize oneself....

Thus, who was Khomiakov? This question is not a formal one. Khomiakov makes himself vulnerable to a dualistic interpretation.... By no means do I have the right to assert that these questions [concerning the interpretation of Khomiakov] must be decided in a way unfavorable for Khomiakov. But they *must* be posed, especially in our time. These questions touch upon not only the fundamental problem of Khomiakov but also upon many currents of Russian life today. I think it can be asserted with certitude that the most essential needs of our time, of the Church, of government, of society, are connected with the question of Khomiakov....

Does not Khomiakov, a waterfall of ideas and themes, provoke many acute and troubling doubts?

The chief of these is, of course, the attribution of Protestantism to Khomiakov. For Khomiakov, the essence of Protestantism consists *only* in protest against Romanism, but with the fundamental premises and characteristic modes of thought of the latter preserved. But is that really the case? The development of Protestantism and its derivatives *after* Khomiakov has undeniably shown that Protestantism, as the chief expression of the culture of recent times, is based on humanism, the elevation of humanity, the divinization of humanity. To use a term borrowed from philosophy, Protestantism is based on *immanentism*, meaning humanity's intention to create all reality out of itself, outside of and apart from God, that is, out of nothing, and, first and foremost, sacred reality; to create this reality in all senses, beginning with the formation of concepts and ending with spiritual reality.

Meanwhile, the essence of Orthodoxy is *ontologism*—the "reception of reality from God" as given, not as created by humanity. The essence of Orthodoxy is humility and gratitude. But what do we see in Khomiakov?... Inquiring more attentively into Khomiakov's theories, we, to our sorrowful surprise, see the same spirit of immanentism that constitutes the essence of Protestantism, although in an immeasurably improved form—chiefly through the introduction of the idea of sobornost (though it should be noted that the idea of the sobornost of consciousness is not completely foreign to Western philosophy, for instance, to Kant, not to mention Schelling of the final period, Feuerbach, Comte, and so on).

Of course, Khomiakov had received an Orthodox education and was knowledgeable about the sources of doctrine and Church history, and this made him cautious in those places where one would expect to find an expression of divergences between Khomiakov's thought and the Church's understanding. And an extraordinarily powerful dialectic—the well-known "Khomiakovian" dialectic—imparted to his argumentation a flexibility and persuasiveness that could blunt even the most dubious and dangerous propositions. But despite Khomiakov's caution and his sincere desire not to conflict with Church doctrine, do not the very foundations of his opinions seem suspicious for an Orthodox believer when they are examined attentively? Whereas, for a man of the Church, the Church expresses the Truth—for "that is the Holy Spirit's desire," and her task is to *discover* the Truth abiding in God that is independent of her—Khomiakov's theory of the Church leaves the impression that the decrees of the whole Church are true because they are the decrees of the *whole* Church. This word *whole* suggests that the decrees of the Church are not a discovery of the Truth but an *invention* of the Truth, as if the Truth were immanent to human reason, even if the latter is taken in its sobornost, and not transcendent to human reason and revealed to the latter from its transcendence. I have used the word *impression*. Yes, impression, for this sort of aim could not have distinctly arisen in Khomiakov's consciousness, and even less could he have expressed it. Khomiakov's thought tends to evade ontological determinacy, glistening before us in its play of mother-of-pearl. But this play of surface tones, brilliant but not substantial, and therefore changing their contours at the slightest turn of the head, does not yield a stable content of thought and leaves alarm and doubt in one's heart. Immanentism—that is the flavor of Khomiakov's theories....

To be sure, here in Khomiakov we are dealing only with *shadings* of thought. But is it far from these shadings to the Catholic "fabrication of dogmas?" Meanwhile, Khomiakov's polemic against Romanism is connected precisely with these shadings. Khomiakov is made indignant not by the falsity of decrees of Western councils but by the fact that they represent violations of *unity*. And the fault of the Catholics appears to consist not in the fact that they profess false dogma but in the fact that they are *not together* with the East. Here, the significance of human agreement or disagreement is exaggerated, and the dignity and value of the Truth are diminished. To be sure, Khomiakov speaks of God's grace and, in an imprecise turn of phrase, even almost identifies God's grace with the Church, but nowhere from the general *meaning* of his system is it seen that God's grace has, for Khomiakov, an essential, living, and not only a decorative significance, for *consensus omnium in amore* [the consensus of all in love] is sufficient for Khomiakov's Church, and, in itself, this *consensus* gives knowledge of the Truth. But does not Romanism also refer to God's grace, as does Protestantism?

Thus, Rome's fault consists in stealing a right that does not belong to it, but that belongs to the *whole* Church. Here, Khomiakov himself, under the guise of a temporary concession to the terminology of his opponents, manifests the immanent-earthly character of his theology, for he himself bases his argument on legal concepts. But even apart from this self-contradiction, the replacement of purely legal concepts by sociological concepts, on which Khomiakov's whole construction is based, by no means proves the ecclesiality of his doctrine, but only proves that he wishes to expel law and compulsion, the element of the Roman nations, and replace them by social relation and kinship, the element of the Slavonic nations....

The free self-assertion of humanity—being that is immanent to humanity, manifested in the organization of love—is more valuable to Khomiakov than anything else. Indeed, he is a "great altruist," as Professor Zavitnevich calls him.[2] But great altruism in itself by no means resembles the Church, for the Church has its foundation in something that is *outside* humanity; but for altruism, as well for all humanism, the firmest foundation is the inner, immanent powers of humanity. The proposition we have expressed here about Khomiakov may appear unexpected, but if it is accepted, it will throw an unexpected light upon Khomiakov's struggle against the ontological element in religion.

---

2. Florensky's essay mainly comprises a review of V. Z. Zavitnevich's book on Khomiakov. See the Editor's Introduction to this section for bibliographic information.—TRANS.

2.

From Aleksei Stepanovich Khomiakov

NIKOLAI BERDIAEV

*From Chapter III: Khomiakov as Theologian.
Doctrine of the Church.*

Khomiakov is, first and foremost, a remarkable theologian, the first free Russian theologian. In Eastern Orthodox theology he occupies one of the first places after the ancient teachers of the Church. Yury Samarin, his faithful disciple, writes in his introduction to Khomiakov's theological works:

> In past times, those who performed for the Orthodox world the kind of service that Khomiakov performed, those who, by a logical clarification of one or another side of Church teaching, could win for the Church a decisive victory over come error or other—were called teachers of the Church. [see page 182]

In what does Samarin see the source of the power of Khomiakov's theology?

> Khomiakov represented an original manifestation of *total freedom in religious consciousness*, one nearly unprecedented in our land [page 165]. Khomiakov *lived in the Church* [page 161].
> Not only did Khomiakov *value* faith, but he was deeply certain that it was *stable, unshakable*. Thus, he did not fear for it, and because he did not fear, he always looked at all things with eyes wide open. He closed his eyes to nothing; he did not try to evade anything; he never tried to deceive himself, to lie to himself. Completely free, that is, completely truthful in his convictions, he demanded the same freedom, the same right to be truthful for others. [page 165]

He valued faith as the *truth*, and not as satisfaction for himself, apart from and irrespective of its truthfulness. [page 166]

I *acknowledge, submit, subordinate* myself; hence, I do not *believe*. The Church offers faith alone, evokes faith alone in the human soul, and does not settle for less. In other words, the Church receives only *free* individuals into her bosom. Anyone who brings her a slave's acknowledgment without believing in her is not within the Church, is not of the Church. [page 169]

... The Church is not a doctrine, not a system, and not an institution. The Church is a living organism, an organism of truth and love, or more precisely: *truth and love* as an organism. [page 171]

In Samarin's opinion

Khomiakov was the first to look at Romanism and Protestantism *from inside the Church*, and therefore *from above*. Therefore, he was able to *define* them. [page 173]

Samarin's words are perhaps too enthusiastic, but there is much truth in them. Khomiakov's great significance consists in the fact that he was a *free* Orthodox, felt himself free in the Church and freely defended the Church. There is no scholasticism in him, no selfish class interest as regards the Church. There is not a trace of the seminarian spirit in his theology, nothing official. It is as if with Khomiakov a stream of fresh air entered Orthodox religious thought. Khomiakov was the first lay religious thinker in Orthodoxy; he opened a path for free religious philosophy through the litter of scholastic theology. He was the first to overcome scholastic theology. With his own example he showed that the gift of teaching does not belong solely to the priesthood, that it belongs to each member of the Church....

Russian scholastic theology was not Orthodox in the real sense of this word; it did not express the religious experience of the Orthodox East as a special path; it was not experiential, not living. This theology servilely followed foreign models and deviated either toward Catholicism or toward Protestantism. Khomiakov was the first *Orthodox* theologian to be an independent thinker, to have an independent attitude toward Western thought. Khomiakov's theology expressed the experience of the Russian people, the living experience of the Orthodox East, not scholastic formalism, always moribund. Khomiakov was more Orthodox in theology than many of our bishops and professors of religious academies; he was more Russian.... He is the founder of Russian theology....

Khomiakov's theological activity, his militant defense of the Orthodox Church seemed suspicious. His freedom was not understood. Khomiakov wrote to Ivan Aksakov: "In many cases I permit myself not to agree with the *so-called* opinion of the Church."[1] The "so-called opinion of the Church" seemed un-churchly to him; he saw in it only the private theological opinion of certain hierarchs. Official churchmen could not tolerate such love of freedom. The attitude of professors of religious academies, official and professional theologians, toward Khomiakov's theology was very negative. They considered it an incursion into a domain they had monopolized. How could a private person, an officer and landowner, a mere writer teach about the Church! Maybe his ideas were Orthodox, but the whole endeavor was a brazen one. Nevertheless, Khomiakov began a new era in the history of the Russian theological consciousness and, in the end, had an influence also on the official theology....

Khomiakov will be eternally remembered, first and foremost, for his statement of the problem of the Church and for his attempt to reveal the essence of the Church. Khomiakov approached the essence of the Church from within, not from outside. First of all he did not believe that it is possible to formulate a concept of the Church. The essence of the Church is inexpressible; like all living organisms, she cannot be encompassed by any formula, is not subject to any formal definitions. The Church is, first of all, a living organism, a unity of love, ineffable freedom, the truth of the faith not subject to rationalization. From the outside the Church is not knowable or definable; she is known only by those who are within her, by those who are her living members. The sin of scholastic theology was that it attempted to formulate rationalistically the essence of the Church; that is, it attempted to transform the Church from a mystery known only to believers into something subject to the knowledge of objective reason.

---

1. Khomiakov's *Works* (*Sochineniia*), vol. 8, p. 189.

Khomiakov was an implacable enemy of that intellectualism in theology against which Le Roy and other Catholic modernists are rebelling at the present time.[2] This intellectualism has always been more alien to the spirit of Orthodoxy than to the spirit of Catholicism. Vladimir Solovyov had a much greater proclivity toward intellectual scholasticism than Khomiakov. Khomiakov in his relation to the Church and the dogmas was more of a voluntarist than an intellectualist; he had a tendency toward what the Catholic modernists call moral dogmatism. For him the sole source of religious knowledge and the sole guarantee of religious truth was love. And he ascribed significance to the dogmatic differences between Catholicism and Protestantism only insofar as love was violated in them. The affirmation of love as a category of knowledge constitutes the soul of Khomiakov's theology. First and foremost, he asserted the living organism of the Church against all moribund mechanicity, against all rationalization of the Church. Contemporary Catholic modernists, as well as Protestant modernists, who often struggle helplessly against ecclesiastic-dogmatic rationalism and intellectualism, have much to learn from Khomiakov. In him, the intellectualism and rationalism of theological scholasticism are overcome not through personal effort but by the truth of the Orthodox Church. They are overcome ecclesially.

Khomiakov was, first and foremost, a man of the Church, and he taught ecclesially about the Church. Modernists too often see the Church as opposing freedom, and desire to rectify the deficiencies of the Church through free effort. Khomiakov, on the other hand, always believed that freedom is found only within the Church, that the Church is in fact freedom, and therefore, for him, free theology was ecclesial theology. Freedom was actualized for him in sobornost, not in individualism. Khomiakov felt himself free only in the Church, not outside the Church.... Any attempt to seek freedom outside the Church, freedom from the Church, to see the source of freedom not in the sobornost of the Church but in solitary individuality would have seemed insane.

---

2. Edouard Le Roy (1870–1954), French philosopher of science, ethics, and religion. His pragmatic view of discursive religious truth was supported by the Catholic modernists. He held that the validity of dogmas cannot be proved, nor do they profess to be provable; rather they depend upon a rigid and externally imposed authority. — TRANS.

If Khomiakov brilliantly succeeded in revealing the organic essence of the Church, this was only because he was nourished by the experience of Eastern Orthodoxy, which contained no intellectualism, no external despotism. This could not be the work of an individual thinker. Even the prejudiced Solovyov admits the enormous significance of Khomiakov in stating the problem of the Church. Solovyov is forced to admit that, prior to the Slavophiles, there was virtually no organic, inner understanding of the Church in the history of Christian thought....

It is difficult to find a freer sense of the Church. Nothing coerces Khomiakov. In his relation to the Church there is nothing from outside; all is from within. For him, life in the Church is life in freedom. Indeed, the Church is unity in love and freedom. The Church is not an institution and not an authority. The Church has nothing juridical, no rationalization. For Khomiakov, wherever one finds genuine love in Christ, freedom in Christ, unity in Christ, there one finds the Church. No formal characteristics define the essence of the Church. Even the universal Councils are genuinely universal and therefore authoritative only because they are freely and lovingly sanctioned by the people of the Church. Free sobornost in love—that is where one finds the true organism of the Church. This is a very bold conception of the Church, which must frighten official theologians. This conception may be alien to theological scholasticism, but it is close to the spirit of sacred tradition and the Holy Scripture. Khomiakov ascribes special significance to sacred tradition, since he sees the spirit of sobornost in it. For him the Holy Scripture is only an inner fact of the life of the Church, that is, it is grasped through sacred tradition....

Khomiakov's definitions and formulas are truly universal. Every free child of the Church will be compelled to agree with his doctrine of the Church; only slaves will rise against it. But Khomiakov spoiled his work to some extent with an obvious prejudice. His teaching of the Church took on a polemical form; he defended Orthodoxy by attacking the Western communions. And the result was that, for him, the entire holiness of the universal Church of Christ—freedom, love, organicity, unity—was contained only in Eastern Orthodoxy, whereas none of this was contained in Catholicism, which exhibited only human errors and sins. A deficiency of love for the Western Christian world is Khomiakov's undeniable sin. He kept pretending that Eastern Orthodoxy in general and the Russian Church in particular have not committed any historical errors or human sins. Before the face of the ignoble West all is well in the Russian and Greek Church. All is divine in this Church, and the human is subordinate to the divine. Lack of love for Catholicism marked Khomiakov and all the other Slavophiles, and led them to assert the superiority of Protestantism over Catholicism. This attitude toward Catholicism constituted the fundamental error of the Slavophiles.

Least of all am I inclined to deny the mystical superiority of Orthodoxy, which immaculately preserves Christ's truth. But Catholicism too contains the mystical essence of the Church, unity in love and freedom. Genuine sacraments are performed in the Catholic Church too; the apostolic succession is not interrupted; sacred tradition is preserved; mystical communion between the living and the dead exists. One must distinguish the Christian Catholic world from papism with its errors, from the sins of the hierarchy. Catholicism's errors are relative errors, not absolute ones. Khomiakov greatly exaggerated when he accused Catholicism and the whole of Western religious thought of rationalism. He himself was not completely free of rationalism. At times one perceives a Protestant-like moralistic tendency in Khomiakov, a tendency that mars his Orthodox theologizing. Khomiakov did not know, did not understand, and did not value Western mysticism, whether Catholic or free. He always had in mind official Catholic theology and had little feeling for the mystical life of Catholicism, for the mysticism of the Catholic saints, for Catholic religious experience.

After all, it is impossible to understand Orthodoxy from the official theology; rather it is necessary to gain an insight into the intimate religious life of the people, into Eastern asceticism, the mysticism of the Orthodox saints. The same thing must be said about Catholicism. It is not exhausted by scholastic theology and papism. Catholicism has its own profound and mysterious life, its mystical trepidation, its holiness. Khomiakov did not wish to see any of this. He identified Catholicism exclusively with the textbooks of dogmatic theology and canon law, with papal politics, with the morality of the Jesuits. This essential error of Khomiakov and the other Slavophiles is connected with the fact that their religious consciousness did not penetrate down to the primordial mystical foundations. Khomiakov virtually ignored religious mysticism; he said practically nothing about Catholic and Protestant mysticism; he didn't know Jacob Boehme. It is a fatal error to equate the whole of Catholicism with rationalism and juridical formalism, denying all mysticism in the West....

The sobornost of the Church, the fundamental idea of Slavophilism, in which the Slavophiles saw the essence of Orthodoxy, does not have formal and rational features. Sobornost has nothing juridical, nothing reminiscent of state power, nothing external and coercive. Although Khomiakov did not like to use the word *mystical*, the sobornost of the Church *is* mystical.... Sobornost is a living organism; the people of the Church live in it. The authority of the ecumenical Councils too is not external, not formal, not rationally expressible, not translatable into juridical language. The ecumenical Councils have authority only because truth for the living *sobornyi* organism of the Church was revealed in them. The Church is not authority. The Church is the Christian's life in Christ, in the body of Christ, free life, full of grace....

The significance of Slavophile theology in Russian religious thought is enormous. One needs to remember the mustiness of the theological atmosphere into which the religious thought of the Slavophiles entered like a jet of fresh air, a living, not a scholastic thought. The Slavophiles brought religious themes into Russian philosophy and Russian literature. They introduced theology into Russian culture as a theme of Russian life. For the Slavophiles, Orthodox theology was not Byzantine rhetoric but the work of life. In official theology, even the moral side of Orthodoxy had preeminently a rhetorical significance, but in the religious thought of the Slavophiles this side came to life. The Slavophiles were, to use a contemporary expression, pragmatists in theology. In a certain sense, their religious philosophy was a philosophy of action; it was directed against intellectualism in theology.

In many ways, contemporary Catholic modernism approaches Khomiakov's conception of the Church. What Le Roy calls "moral" dogmatism, contrasting it with "intellectualistic" dogmatism, is, in essence, the same thing that Khomiakov asserted. And for Khomiakov the dogmas have, first and foremost, a living, moral significance, a pragmatic significance, not an intellectual, theoretical one. Khomiakov sees the sources of dogmatic knowledge in the mutual love of Christians, that is, he has an active, pragmatic understanding of these sources. Khomiakov also gives an active, pragmatic interpretation to the dogmatic schism between East and West. He sees the source of this schism in the deficiency of the West's love for the East, in a moral defect, a defect of life. Christian dogmas are revealed in the life of the Church, in religious experience. Khomiakov is as much a foe of scholastic, intellectualistic theology as the contemporary modernists....

We shall see that Khomiakov's philosophy was a philosophy of action, but more religious and therefore more profound than the contemporary philosophy of action. We can say with a sense of satisfaction that the most recent forms of theologizing and philosophizing in the West are moving toward what our Slavophiles have long been asserting and developing. And the first among the Slavophiles was Khomiakov, the head of the Slavophile philosophy of the Church.... Khomiakov's fundamental idea, which he shared with all the Slavophiles, was that the source of all theologizing and all philosophizing should be the integral life of the spirit, organic life, and that everything must be subordinated to the religious center of life. This idea is the source of Slavophile philosophy and of all Russian philosophy. The West is taking different roads to this very same idea. The integral life of the spirit is given only in religious life, only in the life of the Church. With faith in the true life of the Church are connected all of Russia's hopes for the realization of a higher form of culture than in the West and for the fulfillment of its mission.

However great Khomiakov's theological achievements might be, no matter how dear he is to us, his religious consciousness was limited, confined, incomplete. There is little of the prophetic spirit in him. Khomiakov denied the dogmatic development of the Church, did not see a Divine-human process in the Church. Orthodoxy for him was finished, "perfect"; God's revelation has achieved fullness in it. Khomiakov did not await a new revelation in Christianity and did not admit the possibility of such a revelation. For him the Orthodox Church was, first and foremost, the preservation of what was holy. The prophetic and creative side was disclosed to him little. There is no place for the eschatological problem, the problem of the end, in Khomiakov's theology; there is not a half-word about it in the whole of his religious philosophy. Khomiakov did not associate his Russian messianism with the apocalypse. There is also no apocalypse in his philosophy of history. Apocalyptic forebodings, apocalyptic terror, the apocalyptic tragic sense are alien to Khomiakov.

I have already said that this distinguishes that entire generation, all of Slavophilism. These people had not yet entered the cosmic atmosphere of the apocalypse, the new religious epoch. The Slavophiles were innovators, almost revolutionaries, in theology; their love of freedom was astonishing. That was the free disclosure of Christ's truth. But they still belonged to the old religious consciousness. The new religious consciousness that is dawning in the new cosmic epoch is not changing the unshakable holiness of the Orthodox Church, but it recognizes not only priesthood but also prophecy.[3] It is full of presentiments of the culminating revelation of the Holy Trinity, a revelation full of the tragic sense of the end of history. For the new religious consciousness the Church is a Divine-human process, a process that cannot yet be finished, that will attain fullness only at the end of history. The denial of the possibility of a new Christian revelation is the limit that confines Khomiakov and, after him, the whole of Slavophilism. This confining limit is the source of the degeneration of Slavophilism, of its uncreative fate. Priesthood is unshakable. But where is the kingdom and where is prophecy? A further sign of the incompleteness of Khomiakov's religious consciousness is the fact that he has virtually no religious cosmology.

Out of fear of the magic strain in Catholicism, Khomiakov falls at times into Protestant moralism. For him, sacraments have rather a spiritual-moral meaning than a cosmic one. Khomiakov's religious consciousness preeminently discloses those aspects of sacraments that are connected with spiritual rebirth, while aspects that are connected with cosmic transfiguration are virtually hidden for him. Khomiakov does not have a presentiment that the mystery of God's creation is revealed in the revelation of the cosmic nature of the sacraments. This is alien to his consciousness. In the sacraments one is given not only the spiritual and moral rebirth of the human soul but also a prefiguring of the transfiguration of creation, a new cosmos, where eating will be the Eucharist, union will be marriage, and the awesome aqueous element will become baptism. Sacraments are a

---

3. The "new religious consciousness," a worldview that appeared in Russia at the beginning of the 20th century, was, to some extent, opposed to historical Christianity. It yearned for new revelations, attempted to create a religiously based social utopia, but, at the same time, was full of eschatological expectations. — TRANS.

prefiguring of a new life in a new cosmos. The whole fullness of life must become a sacrament, must become full of grace, and all activity must become a divine act. That sacraments are a path to cosmic transfiguration, to the transfiguration of the whole flesh of the world—this cannot be found in Khomiakov. He was even afraid of underscoring the objective-cosmic nature of sacraments, since he was afraid of that tendency toward pagan magic of which he accused Catholicism. But too great a protest against Catholicism easily leads to Protestantism. It seemed more Orthodox to him, more certain to underscore the subjective-spiritual side of the sacraments. In this was perhaps expressed Khomiakov's insufficient sensitivity to the mystical side of Christianity.

Cosmic mystery does not occupy the center of Khomiakov's conception of Christianity. Khomiakov's religious philosophy has virtually no religious cosmology. How alien Boehme's cosmic mysticism would have appeared to him! Khomiakov has little feeling for the world soul, for the eternal feminine, for all that was so close to Vladimir Solovyov. He finds no room for Sophia, the Wisdom of God. Khomiakov's religiosity was one-sided, exclusively masculine. He is all in Logos. He thought and taught in Logos, not in the world soul. And the trepidation and alarm of the world soul was not transmitted to him. The limitations of his exclusively male consciousness hid from him that apocalyptic terror that is filling the world soul in the new cosmic epoch and that apocalyptic newness that is being born in the consciousness of the new epoch. Mystical sensitivity was totally absent in Khomiakov. He was too stubbornly a male and too stubbornly a "lord of the manor." He did not wish to surrender to any presentiments; it was not sweet for him to submerge himself in the abysses of the world soul. He knew the world soul only from the side of hunting and agriculture. He knew only the earth that produces bread and the woman who gives birth to children. Another earth, another femininity, he did not know and did not wish to know. The mysticism of sex was alien and unnecessary to him. For him, it is the sacrament of the old marriage on the old earth that is being celebrated. He does not yearn for a new marriage on a new earth.

Khomiakov's religious consciousness does not aspire to the Coming City, and his religious philosophy has no place for theocracy. Orthodoxy never confused the Church with the City. This constitutes the gigantic difference between Orthodoxy and Catholicism, which identified the Church with the City of God, with the kingdom of Christ on earth. For the Catholic consciousness the City of God is already realized in the life of the Church, and therefore the consciousness that aspires to the Coming City, the apocalyptic consciousness, does not easily sprout from Catholic soil. The Orthodox do not feel they belong to the realized City, and therefore it is easier for the apocalyptic seeking of the Coming City to sprout from Orthodox soil. Orthodoxy is more John's Christianity; Catholicism is more Peter's. But in historical Orthodoxy there is no chiliasm, no apocalypse. There is holiness and priesthood, but no prophecy and kingdom. Khomiakov confesses historical Orthodoxy as the religion of the priesthood, without prophecies of the City. And he knows only one City—holy Russia. For him this City is sanctified by Orthodoxy, and he wants to know only about the historical Russian theocratic kingdom....

Khomiakov gives a national-historical, rather than mystical, grounding to the idea of holy Russia. He sees the temptation of the confusion of the Church with the City, with the kingdom. For him Orthodoxy was without governmental power, did not aspire to a kingdom in the world. In this he saw all the greatness of Orthodoxy. Khomiakov justly criticized Catholicism but he unjustly denied in Christianity all movement toward the City. Here is the limit to his ancient Orthodox consciousness. For him the Russian kingdom was an Orthodox kingdom, for it was the kingdom of the Orthodox Russian nation. This kingdom is sanctified through the national spirit. But there was no holy flesh, no holy body in this kingdom. There was no mystical City. The Slavophiles cleansed Orthodoxy of all filth. They were the ideal apex of the Orthodox consciousness and cleared the path to a new religious consciousness. The new religious consciousness begins when one becomes conscious of Christ's Church as the cosmic kingdom. The holiness of Orthodoxy must become the dynamic force of history. By Orthodoxy the Slavophiles desired to sanction for always the powerless, passive, nonvolitional character of the Russian nation. The Church is freedom, the Church is love, but the Church is not power. And the Russian nation does not desire power. It desires only freedom and love. The Russian nation does not desire a kingdom; it desires only the Church. The prophecy that the Church will become the City was concealed from the Slavophile consciousness.

From Chapter IV: Khomiakov as Philosopher.
Epistemology and Metaphysics.

Khomiakov and Ivan Kireevsky are the founders of Slavophile philosophy, which can be called the national Russian philosophy, reflecting the whole distinctiveness of our national thought. Their sudden deaths prevented the two Slavophile thinkers from developing their philosophy. The founders of Slavophilism did not leave us large philosophical treatises, did not create systems. Their philosophy was fragmentary; it reaches us in the form of several articles full of profound intuitions. Kireevsky had barely started grounding and developing Slavophile philosophy when he died from cholera. The same fate awaited Khomiakov when he wished to continue Kireevsky's work. There was something providential in this. Perhaps *such* a philosophy should not be a system. Slavophile philosophy constitutes the end of abstract philosophy, and therefore cannot be a system of abstract philosophy. Slavophile philosophy is the philosophy of the integral life of the spirit, not of the abstract reason, not of intellect separated from this integral life. The idea of integral knowledge based on the organic fullness of life is the seminal idea of Slavophile and Russian philosophy.

Following Khomiakov and Kireevsky, our indigenous creative philosophical thought has always set for itself the task of disclosing not abstract, intellectual truth but truth as the way and the life. This peculiar character of Russian philosophy was also expressed in the opposing camp, even in our positivism, which always strove to unite truth with justice. Russians do not allow that truth can be revealed purely intellectually, rationalistically; they do not allow that truth is only a judgment. And it appears that no epistemology, no methodology has the power to shake the prerational conviction of Russians that the apprehension of being is given only to the integral life of the spirit, only to the fullness of life. Even our quasi-Westernizing[4] and quasi-positivistic philosophy aspired to this synthetic religious integrity,

---

4. The "Westernizers" (Russ. *zapadniki*), proponents of a worldview in mid-nineteenth-century Russia traditionally opposed to that of the Slavophiles, were members of the liberal (and even socialist) westward-looking intelligentsia. They believed that backward Russia had to adopt European culture as quickly as possible. Important representatives of this "Westernizing" outlook (Russ. *zapadnichestvo*) were Herzen, Belinsky, and Turgenev. — TRANS.

although it was powerless to express this Russian thirst. Our creative philosophical thought, having Slavophile roots, consciously set for itself the task of asserting an organically integral religious philosophy against all rationalistic fragmentedness.... The first Slavophiles were convinced that Russia had remained faithful to the integral truth of the Christian Church and was therefore free of the rationalistic fragmentedness of spirit. Russian philosophy must be a continuation of patristic philosophy. The first intuitions of this philosophy were born in Kireevsky's soul. Khomiakov was its strongest dialectician....

The whole distinctiveness of Khomiakov's epistemology lies in the fact that he asserts a *sobornyi*, or ecclesial, epistemology. Being can be known only by the *sobornyi*, ecclesial consciousness. Individual consciousness is incapable of knowing truth. The self-assertion of the individual consciousness is always at the same time the fragmentation of the integral life of the spirit, the separation of the subject from the object. The integral spirit, which alone can acquire higher Reason, is always connected with sobornost.

> The most profound truths of thought, the whole higher truth of the will's striving are accessible only to a reason inwardly organized in full moral harmony with the all-existent reason, and the invisible mysteries of Divine and human things are revealed only to a reason thus organized. (Khomiakov's *Works*, vol. I, p. 282)

The source of true philosophy can be found only in religious life, since *sobornyi* consciousness is achieved only in religious life. In religious fragmentation the spirit breaks apart, and individual *ratio* is triumphant rather than *sobornyi* reason. Khomiakov sees the source and criterion of knowledge in the love, in the ecclesial communion of Christians. This is a very profound and daring thought. In the chapter on Khomiakov as a theologian we saw how for him communion in love is the source of religious knowledge. He develops the same idea in his philosophy. He writes:

> Of the universal laws of the willing reason or the reasoning will, the first, supreme, most perfect law is, for the undistorted soul, the law of love. Consequently, accord with this law

can preeminently strengthen and expand our mental vision, and to this law we must subjugate and with it we must harmonize the stubborn discord of our intellectual powers. Only by performing this feat can we hope for the most complete development of reason. (ibid., p. 283)

And further:

Communion in love is not only useful but wholly necessary for the attainment of truth, and the attainment of truth is based on this communion and is impossible without it. Inaccessible to individual thought, truth is accessible only to the combination of thoughts linked by love. This feature sharply distinguishes Orthodox teaching from all other teachings: from Latinism, which depends on external authority; and from Protestantism, which emancipates the individual into the desert of rational abstraction. (ibid.)

One must insist on the fact that sobornost, communion in love, was, for Khomiakov, not a philosophical idea, taken from Western thought, but a religious fact, taken from the living experience of the Eastern Church. Only remembering this can one understand Slavophile philosophy. Sobornost has nothing in common with "consciousness in general," with the "supra-individual subject," and other suchlike abstractions invented by philosophers secluded in their studies. Sobornost is taken from being, from life, not from one's head, not from books. *Sobornyi* communion in love is the ontological presupposition of Khomiakov's epistemology. His whole epistemology is based on this fact of being, and not on a doctrine of being. The touching of being, the intuition of being are possible only in the integral life of the spirit, in *sobornyi* communion. And this leads to faith being revealed in the basis of knowledge.

Faith is prior to, more primordial than knowledge. In the primordial, nonrationalized consciousness, reality is apprehended by faith. Khomiakov's philosophy leads to the identity of knowledge and faith. Khomiakov writes:

I have called *faith* that capacity of reason that apprehends actual (real) data, conveyed by faith to the analysis and consciousness of the rational understanding.Only in this domain do data still bear the fullness of their character and the features of their origin. *In this domain, which precedes logical consciousness and is filled with a vital consciousness that does not need proofs and arguments, human beings are conscious of what belongs to their mental world and what belongs to the external world* [Berdiaev's italics]. Here on the whetstone of will there is revealed to human beings what is produced by their creative (subjective) activity in their objective world and what is independent of this activity. Time and space, or rather phenomena in these two categories, are perceived here as independent of this subjectivity or at least as dependent on it only to a very small extent. (ibid., p. 327)

Reason lives by the perception of phenomena in faith. (ibid., p. 279)

The fullness of human reason or spirit is conscious of all the phenomena of the objective world as its *own*, but as originating either from it itself or not from it. In both cases it receives them immediately, i.e., by faith. (Ibid., p. 328)

The difference between what is real and what is illusory and also between what is subjective and what is objective is established only by an act of faith, which precedes logical consciousness. Being is perceived by faith; it is given prior to the rationalistic fragmentation of the integral life of the spirit. The triumph of the rationalistic consciousness leads to an obliteration of the distinction between what is real and what is unreal. Therefore, illusionism and meonism are victorious in contemporary philosophy.[5] Only faith that precedes all rationalization provides the identity of the subject and the object and allows being to be known. "Complete understanding," says Khomiakov, "is the transformation of what is understood into a fact of our own life."[6] Nearly the same thing, but in different words, was expressed by Franz Baader when he said that to know the truth is to be truthful.[7] Only in faith does a person become true, does he transform what is understood into a fact of his own life. And faith is, first and

---

5. *Meonism* (from the Greek *me on*, "nothing") refers to a nihilistic philosophy that was fashionable at the turn of the century. — TRANS.

6. Khomiakov's *Works*, vol. 1, p. 330.

7. See footnote on page 269 in this volume. — TRANS.

foremost, a function of the will as the nucleus of our integral spiritual being. The doctrine of the will, of the willing reason and rational will, is the center of Khomiakov's epistemology and metaphysics.... Khomiakov takes as his point of departure the integral spirit, in which will and reason are not sundered....

The identity of thought and being is given in the willing reason, in rational thought. Will occupies the central place in Khomiakov's epistemology, but his epistemology is ontological in character. For Khomiakov, will is not a psychological concept. His metaphysics and epistemology cannot be interpreted as psychologism. Psychologism is always a product of the isolated, individual soul. Sobornost is opposed to all psychologism. Khomiakov's philosophy can be called concrete spiritualism, precisely concrete, not abstract. His spiritualism is not traditionally dualistic. The idea of the freely creative spirit is the fundamental idea of all Russian philosophy....

Khomiakov, along with Kireevsky, can be recognized as the founder of an indigenous tradition in Russian philosophy. Russian philosophy has preeminently an ontological character. Epistemology always occupies only a subordinate place in it and logical problems are not specially worked out. *Concrete being*—that is the goal of Slavophile and Russian philosophy. But can a national philosophy exist? Should a philosophy not strive to be true rather than national? Of course, philosophy should strive for the truth; its essence is love of wisdom. But the wisdom disclosed in humanity must have flesh and blood. In the great work of the disclosure of the truth, always one, there can be various missions and callings. Each epoch calls on various nations to disclose different aspects of the truth. This is related with the will of a given nation, with the fundamental aspiration of its spirit. The will of the Russian nation—the wholeness of its spirit—is directed toward disclosing the mystery of being; it sets the ontological tasks for Russian thought. The religious nature of the Russian nation presents the Russian consciousness with the task of creating a synthetic religious philosophy, of reconciling knowledge and faith. This is the direction given to our creative powers by our religious nature. The ontological and religious aspiration of Russian philosophy is not to subordinate the truth to nationality but, through our nationality, to disclose the ontological and religious side of the truth.

Khomiakov prefigured the path of creative Russian philosophy; he laid the foundation of the tradition. But Khomiakov's epistemology and metaphysics were as undeveloped as Kireevsky's and remained fragmentary. The cosmological side of metaphysics is not developed in Khomiakov. He has almost no cosmology; he has no philosophy of nature, because cosmology was virtually absent in his religious consciousness. He has no doctrine of the world soul. This absence of cosmology is the main shortcoming of Slavophile philosophy. Consequently, Slavophilism was inferior—not superior—to Schelling, who emphasized the problems of the philosophy of nature and cosmology. Khomiakov was not able to link the great idea of sobornost with the doctrine of the world soul. His religio-philosophical consciousness was too much repelled by the undying truth of paganism, the truth about the earth. *She*, mother-earth, the eternal feminine, is virtually absent in Khomiakov's philosophical as well as religious consciousness. But only with *her* is the cosmological aspect of religious philosophy connected. Indeed, Christian cosmology is the doctrine of the world soul, of the eternal feminine, of mother-earth, this bridge connecting Christianity with paganism. In paganism, one was given the feminine-earthy foundation of the Church—*she* with whom Logos was united. The absence of cosmology in Khomiakov's consciousness led to a spiritualistic tendency; in Khomiakov, psychology predominates over cosmology. In its further development in the person of Vladimir Solovyov, Russian philosophy—religious in spirit—posed the cosmological problem, the doctrine of the world soul. And that was a great step forward.

Although Slavophile philosophy was fragmentary in character, and although neither Khomiakov nor any other Slavophile wrote any large philosophical treatises, this philosophy produced ripe fruits in the history of Russian thought. A Russian philosophical tradition was formed; an indigenous philosophical school became possible. Directly continuing the Slavophile tradition in philosophy were the greatest of all Russian philosophers, Solovyov, and then Prince S. Trubetskoi.[8] Solovyov's two main philosophical treatises (*Critique of Abstract Principles* and *The Philosophical Principles of Integral Knowledge*) are permeated with a Slavophile spirit. Solovyov derived

---

8. Sergei Trubetskoi (1862–1905) was a follower of Vladimir Solovyov; he combined a profound mystical sense with a rigorous critical idealism. — TRANS.

both the idea of the critique of abstract principles and the idea of the affirmation of integral knowledge from Khomiakov, though Solovyov did not sufficiently acknowledge this. Khomiakov was the first to attempt to overcome all abstract rationalism and all abstraction through the philosophy of integral knowledge, of knowledge of the integral spirit. Khomiakov affirmed integral, organic reason. Solovyov synthesized Khomiakov's fragmentary thoughts into a system. But Solovyov's method of philosophizing was strongly marked by Hegelianism. Perhaps that was why Solovyov was able with relative ease to give Slavophile philosophy the form of a system. Khomiakov was freer of Hegelianism.

I do not wish to say, however, that Solovyov's philosophy was a mere repetition of Slavophile ideas. Solovyov had a great creative mind, and he creatively transformed all influences. And a critique of abstract principles was not realized by Khomiakov but only sketched out. Solovyov brilliantly executed this critique. Solovyov had a philosophical range and a universal breadth that Khomiakov did not have. Solovyov was our only creator of a universal philosophical system on the model of the great systems of the West, chiefly Germany. That was his contribution to Russian culture. Khomiakov left us only philosophical fragments, whereas Solovyov left us philosophical treatises. But Solovyov too, as a Russian, felt the swirl of the spirit of life around him and therefore could not exclusively surrender himself to the philosophical investigations of the scholar's study.

One must underscore a nuance that distinguishes Solovyov from Khomiakov. Khomiakov's spirit of philosophizing tends to be voluntaristic and pragmatic while Solovyov's tends to be intellectualistic and logistic. And in this, Khomiakov is closer to us than Solovyov. After Solovyov, the Slavophile tradition in philosophy was continued by Prince S. Trubetskoi, whose remarkable work *On the Nature of Consciousness* is permeated with a Slavophile spirit and develops the Slavophile idea of sobornost in its epistemological aspect. The whole of creative Russian philosophy struggles against individualism, against the fallen reason, and for the sobornost of consciousness, for the acquisition of Logos. In Russia, philosophy as an abstract principle is overcome, and thereby a way is given out of the dead end where contemporary European civilization finds itself. A possibility is provided for overcoming the crisis of philosophy.

Russians are called to create a religious philosophy, a philosophy of the integral spirit. This is affirmed by our whole national character, by the fundamental and primordial aspiration of our will. Will poses tasks for thought, and for our thought our will is always posing the task of capturing, in an integral way, the meaning of being and life. Our creative thought is not directed at the solution of special problems of epistemology and logic. Our more native and necessary task is to solve the problems of religious ontology, the philosophy of history, ethics. This is a fact that must be taken into account. Khomiakov can be recognized as the founder of Russian philosophy for the simple reason that he penetrated into the most intimate interests of Russian thought, philosophized about what was tormenting the Russian spirit. In Russia, philosophy begins from a different end than in Germany. And this, first of all, is a distinction according to life, not according to logic; it reflects different world-feelings. Russia cannot renounce its world-feeling but instead seeks the source of its philosophy in it. We begin our philosophy with life and philosophize for life; in this sense we are innate pragmatists before all "pragmatism." But our pragmatism is not relative and skeptical, since it is connected with religious experience, in which absolute life is given.

Even the areligious, atheistic Russian intelligentsia, which confessed various forms of distorted positivism, unconsciously aspired to the philosophy of the integral spirit and was hostile to the Slavophile philosophy only because of its fatal apostasy. But it is particularly important to define the connection between Russian philosophy and Russian literature. The Russian national spirit found its perfect expression in the art of the great Russian writers. Our literature is the most metaphysical and most religious literature in the world. In order to feel what philosophy can and should be in Russia, it is sufficient to remember Dostoevsky. Likewise, from Richard Wagner, one can guess the spirit of German philosophy. Russian philosophy treasures its connection with Russian literature. And this connection, which always bears witness to its organic connection to the soul and body of Russia, cannot be broken by any epistemology, logic, and methodology. Abstract logic is powerless to defeat the spirit of life, which has its own organic logic.

Khomiakov inquired of the spirit of life, inquired of it before anything else, and that is his whole significance. The point of departure of Khomiakov's philosophy, which is the point of departure of all Russian philosophy, does not require or admit an "epistemological" grounding in the sense of Kantian critical philosophy. From the outset this philosophy does not recognize the primacy of such epistemology; this philosophy is ontological in its origin; it begins with life, with being, with the given; it does not give freedom to the apostatic rationalistic understanding and its pretensions. Epistemologism[9] is the philosophy of the abstract, rationalistic understanding, whereas ontologism is the philosophy of the integral reason.[10] The integral reason grasps not abstract categories but concrete realities. Therefore, the dispute of the critical epistemologists against Slavophile philosophy appears to them to be a logical, scientific, cultural dispute, whereas the adherents of Slavophile philosophy understand that this dispute is one of will and life, a religious argument. The path of Slavophile, or Russian, philosophy presupposes election, Eros, the energizing of the whole spiritual being. In this sense, this path is akin to the best philosophical traditions of Greece, the traditions of the philosophy of Eros....

Sub specie aeternitatis there is something abiding and unchanging in Khomiakov's philosophy. The idea of the philosophy of the integral spirit is given to us for all time as something we must work out. And the self-degeneration of the abstract rationalistic understanding, the fallen reason, is revealed to us for all time. The fallen reason must rise, must regain its lost integrity and organicity. Only then will a philosophy of being become possible, and only a philosophy of being is an essential philosophy. But I have already pointed out that cosmology and the philosophy of nature are virtually absent in Khomiakov's philosophy. A philosophy that is faithful to the testament of the Slavophile spirit must first of all develop a cosmology. This was done in part by Solovyov; but the method he used was overly dialectical. The fact that the philosophy of nature theme did not become the fundamental one for Khomiakov confirms once again that Slavophile

9. The term *epistemologism* (Russ. *gnoseologizm*) refers to the view that the problem of the "theory of knowledge" (how we can know anything) must be solved before a metaphysics can be attempted. — TRANS.

10. The crucial terms *razum* and *rassudok* are rendered here as "reason" and "rationalistic understanding," respectively. See the discussion of these terms in the General Introduction to the present volume. — TRANS.

philosophy was not Schellingianism on Russian soil, but an original and indigenous phenomenon. This is a phenomenon that is kindred in spirit to Franz Baader, but also completely independent of him, since it was nourished not by the mysticism of Jacob Boehme, whom Khomiakov, by his own admission, did not know at all, but by the mysticism of Eastern Christianity.

I emphasize once again that, in its spirit, Khomiakov's philosophy is an ecclesial philosophy and cannot be understood otherwise. This philosophy is faithful to the truth of the Church, is nourished by the mystical perception of concrete realities, possesses not an abstract but an organic reason. Only faithfulness to the fundamental tradition of the philosophy of Khomiakov and Kireevsky, only the awareness of one's fatherland will lead to the philosophical rebirth of Russia. Creative culture is impossible without tradition, without succession, without one's distinctive character. Only by its national culture does each people serve the world culture, does it do the universal work in its national flesh and blood. Khomiakov had a profound understanding of this and indicated to the Russian consciousness the path on which it could serve the work of universal rebirth. We must of course always learn philosophy from Europe. We must, like Kireevsky, love Western culture, but we must also, finally, repay our debt to Western thought, to which we are obligated for much. We are now entering an epoch when Russian philosophy can and must lead Western philosophy out of its dead end, rescue it from meonism and illusionism.

From Chapter VIII: Khomiakov's Significance. The Fate of Slavophilism.

The fate of Slavophilism is a sad one. To this day the Slavophiles have not received a just assessment. The Slavophile doctrine has been mocked by foes and betrayed by so-called friends and followers. The most important phenomenon in the history of our self-consciousness was either ignored or interpreted incorrectly. Slavophilism is a complex phenomenon, combining heterogeneous elements, sometimes very contradictory. Despite the external harmoniousness and organicity of the Slavophile doctrine, it was from the very beginning pregnant with various possibilities. Various paths emanated from it: the path of freedom and the path of compulsion; the path of evolution and the path of reaction; the path of mystical hopes and the path of positivistic-naturalistic pretensions. Slavophilism included both Russian Christianity and Russian paganism, both Christian messianism and pagan nationalism, both the theocratic-anarchic rejection of all state power and the absolutization of the historically relative forms of state power, both the freedom from all external forms and enslavement by the class system. All these contradictions were fatally manifested in the further destiny of Slavophilism. Slavophilism began to degenerate into various elements; different paths began to emanate from it....

The Slavophiles did not express all the traits of the Russian and Slavic character. For example, Russian and Slavic revolt and rebelliousness—very profound religious, national traits—are virtually absent in Slavophilism. But revolt and rebelliousness are not less characteristic of Russians than humility and subservience. Russians do not have their city; they seek the Coming City; the nature of the Russian nation is characterized by an everlasting pilgrimage. Gogol, Dostoevsky, Solovyov, and Tolstoy are pilgrims. The type of the pilgrim is the beloved type of the Russian people. The search for the City is powerfully expressed in the figure of the pilgrim. In the Slavophiles, the spirit of Russian rootedness predominated over the spirit of Russian pilgrimage. Pilgrims walk upon the earth, but the element of air is more powerful in them than the element of earth. Khomiakov was not a pilgrim.

Of the Slavophile generation of the 1830s and 1840s, only Gogol had an agitated, searching spirit close to the spirit of our time. Of course, the Slavophiles, too, thirsted for Christ's truth about the earth, for Christ's City; but for the triumph of this truth they demanded not so much pilgrimage and airy flight as rootedness in the earth. The great truth of the Russians, however, is that they cannot be reconciled with this earthly city, with the city organized by the prince of this world, that they are seeking the Heavenly Jerusalem, descending upon the earth. This radically distinguishes Russians from people of the West, who have arranged their lives beautifully and are content, who have their city. The Catholic West believes that it has its city. This City is the Church: in the hierarchical structure of the Church, with the pope at the top, the city of God is realized, Christ's thousand-year kingdom has arrived. The atheistic West believes that the City is being realized in the bourgeois state or will be realized in the socialist state. Orthodox Russia did not think that the Church is already the City; the Orthodox consciousness distinguishes the Church from the City. And for Khomiakov the Church was never the City. In the Orthodox Church there is neither true nor false chiliasm. And chiliastic seeking remains. In Slavophilism the chiliastic yearning was weakened not by a false doctrine of the Church but by a false doctrine of nationality, in which Christianity was mixed with paganism. In the best of the new Russian art one senses a Slavic spirit of alarm, revolt, and pilgrimage. According to this art one can judge how much has changed since the time of Slavophilism.

In summing up, we must say that Slavophilism is both degenerating and evolving, and that this dualism of its fate is connected with the differentiation of the various elements of Slavophilism. The pagan-nationalistic elements, the elements of settled life, the selfish class elements, the positivist-statist elements are degenerating and decaying. But one also sees the creative evolution of the truth of Slavophilism, that is, of the elements that are authentically ecclesial, Christian-mystical, national-messianic. There is an undying truth in the ecclesial and national consciousness of the Slavophiles; this truth can be silenced neither by reactionary-pagan nationalism nor by atheistic internationalism. But our social feeling-capacities and social consciousness are so dirtied and contaminated that they cannot orient themselves in the fate of Slavophilism, at first glance unclear and tangled. We do not have an authentic national intelligentsia—a popular reason in which the fate of Russia would reach the level of conscious understanding.

The consciousness of the Westernizers fails to confront the riddle of Russia; it is a riddle of the Slavophile consciousness. The Slavophiles, not the Westernizers, wrestled with the riddle of what the Creator has in store for Russia and what path He has prepared for her. Chaadaev wrestled with this riddle early on—Chaadaev the "Westernizer," foe and friend of the Slavophiles.[11]

---

11. Peter Chaadaev (1794–1856) can be called the first Russian philosopher. In his first major philosophical work, he accused Russia of egoism, and he claimed that she had contributed nothing to history. Later he adopted a more sympathetic view of Russia, Russian thought, and Russian Orthodoxy. His outlook is thus between that of West and East, and he can be viewed as laying the foundation for the thought of both the Slavophiles and the Westernizers. — TRANS.

But Chaadaev's Westernizing had nothing in common with mainstream Westernizing. Our Westernizing was always deeply provincial; in it there was always so much imitation of the fashions of the capitals. Also, our Westernizing was that of immature youth; one sensed that its thought was sophomoric. The Westernizers never had true universalism; one would be more likely to find true universalism in the Slavophiles or in Chaadaev. And it is easy to understand why. Authentic universalism belongs only to the religious consciousness. In the majority of cases, the Russian Westernizing consciousness is areligious and antireligious, atheistic and materialistic. This exposes the youthful provincialism of Russian Westernizing, since the consciousness of the Western nations is by no means necessarily atheistic; it also contains religious consciousness and religious truth. The great Western culture is nevertheless, first and foremost, a universal culture. The land of holy wonders has great graves that the generation of Russian Westernizers does not venerate.[12] It has not only the graves of Marx and Spencer, but also those of Dante and Jacob Boehme. In order to venerate the graves of Dante and Boehme, however, one needs to be more mature and universal than our Westernizers. In venerating the great graves of the West we wish to be greater Westernizers than all our Westernizers; we wish to be more cultured and more universal than our Westernizers. But this means that we do not wish to be Westernizers, because in Europe there are no Westernizers; Westernizing is a provincial phenomenon.

Russia, the East and the West—that is the universal theme that our generation and the next generations are destined to develop. In this theme, indicated to us by the Slavophiles, all strands converge. Russia stands at the center of two currents of world history: Eastern and Western. Only Russia can resolve the question of the East for European culture. But two Easts exist: the Christian East and the non-Christian East. Russia herself is the Christian East-West, and her truth is, first and foremost, the Orthodox truth. But elements of the non-Christian East have entered into the flesh and blood of Russia, into her way of life, and have poisoned her. Russia can fulfill her universal

---

12. "Land of holy wonders" is a phrase from a famous poem of Khomiakov's. This phrase is often cited to indicate Khomiakov's great respect for European culture. See the General Introduction to the present volume, p. 14. — TRANS.

Christian mission only by overcoming in herself the extreme, non-Christian East, only by cleansing herself of it, that is, by becoming conscious of herself as the definitively Christian East-West, and not the anti-Christian East.... Russia is great and is called to a mission only insofar as she guards the Christian truth. If Russia has a world mission, this mission is the unification of the East and the West into one Christian humanity.

If a great and indigenous culture is possible in Russia, this can be only a religiously synthetic culture, not one that is differentiated analytically. And everything that was great in Russia's spiritual life possessed such a religiously synthetic character. The religiously synthetic spirit has left its mark on Russian literature, on Russian philosophy, and on the Russian search for integral truth in all things and everywhere. Our national spirit rejects politics as an abstract, self-sufficient principle. And, in general, we dislike abstract, self-sufficient principles. Slavophiles guessed this direction of our national spirit, thereby performing the feat of national self-consciousness.

A Slavophile Bibliography

Anthologies of Russian Thought

A Documentary History of Russian Thought: From the Enlightenment to Marxism. Trans. and ed. by W. J. Leatherbarrow and D. C. Offord. Ann Arbor, Mich.: Ardis, 1987.

The Mind of Modern Russia: Historical and Political Thought of Russia's Great Age. Ed. Hans Kohn. New Brunswick, NJ: Rutgers University Press, 1955; Harper Torchbook edition: New York: Harper & Row, 1962.

Russian Intellectual History: an Anthology. Ed. Marc Raeff. Introduction by Isaiah Berlin. New York, Chicago, Burlingame: Harcourt, Brace and World, Inc., 1966.

Russian Philosophy. Volume I: The Beginnings of Russian Philosophy. The Slavophiles. The Westernizers. Ed. James M. Edie, James P. Scanlan, and Mary-Barbara Zeldin. With the collaboration of George L. Kline. Chicago: Quadrangle Books, Inc., 1965, 1969. (Knoxville, Tenn.: University of Tennessee Press, 1976, 1984, 1987).

Ultimate Questions: An Anthology of Modern Russian Religious Thought. Ed. and with an introduction by Alexander Schmemann. Crestwood, NY: St. Vladimir's Seminary Press, 1965, 1977.

Works by A. S. Khomiakov
(Khomyakov, Khomiakoff, Chamecoff)

Polnoe sobranie sochinenii. 3rd ed. 8 vols. Moscow: I. N. Kushnerov, 1900–1911.

Sochineniia. 2 vols. Ed. V. A. Koshelev. Moscow: Medium, 1994.

L'Eglise Latine et la Protestantisme au point de vue de l'Eglise d'Orient. Recueil d'articles sur des questions religieuses, écrits à différentes époques et à diverses occasions. Lausanne et Vevey, 1872.

Birkbeck, W. J. *Russia and the English Church During the Last Fifty Years: Correspondence between William Palmer and M. Khomiakoff, 1844–1854.* London: Rivington, Percival & Co., 1895.

"The Church is One." Pp. 192–222 in Birkbeck, *Russia and the English Church* (reprinted separately: London: SPCK, 1948; New York: n.p., 1953).

"Russia and War. [Letter to a Foreign Friend on the Eve of the Crimean War.]" Pp. 108–112 in *The Mind of Modern Russia*

"[On Catholicism.]" Pp. 88–89 in *A Documentary History.*

"On Humboldt." Trans. Valentine Snow. Pp. 209–230 in *Russian Intellectual History.*

"On Recent Developments in Philosophy: Letter to Y. F. Samarin." Trans. Vladimir D. Pastuhov and Mary-Barbara Zeldin. Pp. 221–269 in *Russian Philosophy I.*

"[On the Church.]" Pp. 90–91 in *A Documentary History.*

"On the Western Confessions of Faith." Trans. Ashleigh E. Moorhouse. Pp. 31–69 in *Ultimate Questions.*

"To the Serbians. A Message from Moscow." Trans. Peter K. Christoff. Pp. 247–268 in *An Introduction to Nineteenth-Century Russian Slavophilism: A Study in Ideas. Vol. I* (See below).

Works by I. V. Kireevsky (Kireyevsky, Kireevskii)

Polnoe sobranie sochinenii. 2 vols. Ed. M. O. Gershenzon. Moscow: Put', 1911.

"A Reply to A. S. Khomyakov." Pp. 79–87 in *A Documentary History.*

"On the Nature of European Culture and Its Relation to the Culture of Russia. Letter to Count E. E. Komarovsky." Trans. Valentine Snow. Pp. 175–208 in *Russian Intellectual History.*

"On the Necessity and Possibility of New Principles in Philosophy." Trans. Peter K. Christoff. Pp. 171–213 in *Russian Philosophy* I.

Works by Ivan Aksakov

Sochineniia. 7 vols. Moscow, 1886–1887.

"Address to the St. Petersburg Benevolent Slav Society after the Assassination of Alexander II." Pp. 354–362 in: Olga Novikova. *Skobeleff and the Slavonic Cause.* London: Longmans, Green & Co., 1883. Reprinted as "Russia and Autocracy." Pp. 112–115 in *The Mind of Modern Russia*; pp. 378–382 in *Readings in Russian Civilization.*

"[Various political writings]." Pp. 24–35, 53–60, 98–106 in Olga Novikova, *Russia and England from 1876–1886. A Protest and an Appeal.* London: Longmans, Green & Co., 1880.

Works by Konstantin Aksakov

Polnoe sobranie sochinenii. 3 vols. Moscow, 1861–1880.

"Memorandum to Alexander II on the Internal State of Russia." Pp. 95–107 in *A Documentary History.*

"On the Internal State of Russia." Trans. Valentine Snow. Pp. 231–251 in *Russian Intellectual History.*

Works by Yury Samarin

Sochineniia. 12 vols. (11 published). Moscow: Izd. D. Samarina, 1877–1911.

Secondary Literature in English on the Slavophiles

Arsenev, N. "Alexey Khomyakov, 1804–1860." *St. Vladimir's Seminary Quarterly* vol. 5 (1960), pp. 3–10.

Berdyaev, Nikolai. *The Russian Idea.* Trans. R. M. French. Revised, with an introduction by Christopher Bamford. Hudson, NY: Lindisfarne Press, 1992.

Bolshakoff, S. *The Doctrine of the Unity of the Church in the Works of Khomyakov and Moehler.* London: SPCK, 1946.

Christoff, Peter K. *An Introduction to Nineteenth-Century Russian Slavophilism. A Study in Ideas. Vol. I: A. S. Xomjakov.* The Hague, Paris: Mouton, 1961.

———. *An Introduction to Nineteenth-Century Russian Slavophilism: A Study in Ideas. Vol. II: I. V. Kireevskij.* The Hague, Paris: Mouton, 1972.

———. *K. S. Aksakov: A Study in Ideas.* Vol. III of *An Introduction to Nineteenth-Century Russian Slavophilism.* Princeton, NJ: Princeton University Press, 1982.

———. *Iu. F. Samarin.* Vol. IV of *An Introduction to Nineteenth-Century Russian Slavophilism.* Boulder, Colo.: Westview Press, 1991.

Gleason, Abbot. *European and Muscovite: Ivan Kireevsky and the Origins of Slavophilism.* Cambridge, Mass: Harvard University Press, 1972.

Gratieux, Albert. *A. S. Khomiakov and the Slavophile Movement.* Trans. from the French by Elizabeth Meyendorff. 2 vols. Belmont, Mass.: 1982.

Lukashevich, S. *Ivan Aksakov, 1823–1886: A Study in Russian Thought and Politics.* Cambridge, Mass.: Harvard University Press, 1965.

O'Leary, P. P. *The Triune Church: A Study in the Ecclesiology of A. S. Khomiakov.* Freiburg: Universitätsverlag Freiburg Schweiz, 1982.

Riasanovsky, Nicholas V. "Khomiakov on Sobornost." *Continuity and Change in Russian and Soviet Thought.* Ed. E. J. Simmons. Cambridge, Mass.: Harvard University Press, 1955.

Riasanovsky, Nicholas V. *Russia and the West in the Teaching of the Slavophiles: A Study of Romantic Ideology.* Cambridge, Mass.: Harvard University Press, 1952.

Walicki, Andrzej. *The Slavophile Controversy: History of Conservative Utopia in Nineteenth-Century Russian Thought.* Oxford: Clarendon Press, 1975.

Zenkovsky, V. V. *A History of Russian Philosophy.* 2 vols. Trans. George L. Kline. New York, London: Columbia University Press, 1953.

Zernov, Nicolas. *Three Russian Prophets: Khomyakov, Dostoyevsky, Solovyov.* London: SCM Press, 1944.

INDEX

About the Translators

BORIS JAKIM is one of the foremost translators of Russian religious thought into English. He has translated works by S. L. Frank, Vladimir Solovyov, Pavel Florensky, and Sergius Bulgakov. Lindisfarne Books has published his translations of Bulgakov's *The Holy Grail and the Eucharist*; Solovyov's *The Crisis of Western Philosophy*; and his new edition of Solovyov's seminal work, *Lectures on Divine Humanity.*

ROBERT BIRD received his Ph.D. in Slavic languages and literatures from Yale University and is currently Assistant Professor of Russian at Dickinson College. He has published numerous studies and translations of Russian philosophy and modernist literature. A volume of his translations of selected essays by the Russian poet and thinker Viacheslav Ivanov is forthcoming from Northwestern University Press.

LIBRARY OF RUSSIAN PHILOSOPHY

Though it only began to flourish in the nineteenth century, Russian philosophy has deep roots going back to the acceptance of Christianity by the Russian people in 988 and the subsequent translation into church Slavonic of the Greek Fathers. By the fourteenth century, religious writings, such as those of Dionysius the Areopagite and Maximus the Confessor, were available in monasteries. Until the seventeenth century, then, except for some heterodox Jewish and Roman Catholic tendencies, Russian thinking tended to continue the ascetical, theological, and philosophical tradition of Byzantium, but with a Russian emphasis on the world's unity, wholeness, and transfiguration. It was as if a seed were germinating in darkness, for the centuries of Tartar domination and the isolationism of the Moscow state kept Russian thought apart from the onward movement of Western European thinking.

With Peter the Great (1672–1725), in Pushkin's phrase, a window was cut into Europe. This opened the way to Voltairian freethinking, while the striving to find ever greater depths in religious life continued. Freemasonry established itself in Russia, inaugurating a spiritual stream outside the church. Masons sought a deepening of the inner life, together with ideals of moral development and active love of one's neighbor. They drew on wisdom where they found it and were ecumenical in their sources. Thomas à Kempis's *Imitation of Christ* was translated, as were works by Saint-Martin ("The Unknown Philosopher"), Jacob Böhme, and the pietist Johann Arndt. Russian thinkers, too, became known by name: among others, Grigory Skovoroda (1722–1794), whose biblical interpretation drew upon Neoplatonism, Philo, and the German mystics; N. I. Novikov (1744–1818), who edited Masonic periodicals and organized libraries; the German I. G. Schwarz (1751–1784), a Rosicrucian follower of Jacob Böhme; and A. N. Radishchev (1749–1802), author of *On Man and His Immortality*.

There followed a period of enthusiasm for German idealism and, with the reaction to this by the Slavophiles Ivan Kireevksy and Aleksei Khomiakov, independent philosophical thought in Russia was born. An important and still continuing tradition of creative thinking was initiated, giving rise to a whole galaxy of nineteenth- and twentieth-century philosophers, including Pavel Yurkevitch, Nikolai Fedorov, Vladimir Solovyov, Leo Shestov, the Princes S. and E. Trubetskoi, Pavel Florensky, Sergius Bulgakov, Nikolai Berdiaev, Dmitri Merezhkovsky, Vassili Rozanov, Semon Frank, the personalists, the intuitionists, and many others.

Beginning in the 1840s, a vital tradition of philosophy entered the world stage, a tradition filled with as yet unthought possibilities and implications not only for Russia herself but for the new multicultural, global reality humanity as a whole is now entering.

Characteristic features of this tradition are: *epistemological realism*; *integral knowledge* (knowledge as an organic, all-embracing unity that includes sensuous, intellectual, and mystical intuition); the celebration of *integral personality* (*tselnaya lichnost*), which is at once mystical, rational, and sensuous; and an emphasis upon the *resurrection* or *transformability* of the flesh. In a word, Russian philosophers sought a theory of the world as a whole, including its transformation.

Russian philosophy is simultaneously religious and psychological, ontological and cosmological. Filled with remarkably imaginative thinking about our global future, it joins speculative metaphysics, depth psychology, ethics, aesthetics, mysticism, and science with a profound appreciation of the world's movement toward a greater state. It is *bolshaya*, big, as philosophy should be. It is broad and individualistic, bearing within it many different perspectives—religious, metaphysical, erotic, social, and apocalyptic. Above all, it is universal. The principle of *sobornost* or all-togetherness (human catholicity) is of paramount importance in it. And it is future oriented, expressing a philosophy of history passing into *metahistory*, the life-of-the-world-to-come in the Kingdom of God.

At present, in both Russia and the West, there is a revival of interest in Russian philosophy, partly in response to the reductionisms implicit in materialism, atheism, analytic philosophy, deconstructionism, and so forth. On May 14, 1988, *Pravda* announced that it would publish the works of Solovyov, Trubetskoi, Semon Frank, Shestov, Florensky, Lossky, Bulgakov, Berdiaev, Alexsandr Bogdanov, Rozanov, and Fedorov. According to the announcement, thirty-five to forty volumes were to be published. This is now taking place.

The Esalen–Lindisfarne Library of Russian Philosophy parallels this Russian effort. Since 1980 the Esalen Russian-American Exchange Center has worked to develop innovative approaches to Russian-American cooperation, sponsoring nongovernmental dialogue and citizen exchange as a complement to governmental diplomacy. As part of its program, seminars are conducted on economic, political, moral, and religious philosophy. The Exchange Center aims to stimulate philosophic renewal in both the East and West. The Esalen-Lindisfarne Library of Russian Philosophy continues this process, expanding it to a broader American audience.

It is our feeling that these Russian thinkers—and those who even now are following in their footsteps—are world thinkers. Publishing them will not only contribute to our understanding of the Russian people, but will also make a lasting contribution to the multicultural philosophical synthesis required by humanity around the globe as we enter the twenty-first century.